Praise for *Conditic*

"How does a lie get created and sold as truth?" In *Condition Critical* Alice Rothchild grabs for the truth behind the lies, writing with extraordinary moral clarity and a sharp eye for the injustices, absurdities, and cruel historical ironies that define Palestinian life on both sides of the Green Line. From the tortured alleys of Jerusalem's Old City and the "unrecognized" Bedouin communities of the Negev to the cities, villages, and refugee camps of the West Bank, Rothchild provides an impassioned and informative tour of the "rabbit hole" of Israel's occupation.

—**Ben Ehrenreich**, Author, *The Way to the Spring:*
Life and Death in Palestine

"Never—I repeat, *never*—have I encountered such a wondrous amalgam of innumerable personal stories, a wealth of information and data, systematic historic explanation, and perfectly articulated ethical-political thought. Alice Rothchild is one of those Jews who is in a 'special kind of exile,' criticizing Israel from a singular, insider, activist place. The three visits to Israel that she chronicles, ranging from June 2013 to March 2015, provide the narrative context for a literary trip that engages facts and ideology, individuals and organizations, towns, villages, cities, and refugee camps, the sweep of history and the present, current critical condition. And what about the future? Rothchild hints that we do not have the 'privilege of despair.' Still, read the book... and weep!"

—**Anat Biletzki**, Albert Schweitzer Professor of Philosophy,
Quinnipiac University, and Professor of Philosophy,
Tel Aviv University. Chair of the Board (2001–2006) of B'Tselem,
The Israeli Information Center for Human Rights
in the Occupied Territories

"Prepare to enter the world of contemporary Israel/Palestine through the unsparing eyes of an informed and passionate observer—a respected US physician struggling to understand the lived realities of Jews and Palestinians caught up in a trap unlike any other on earth. In serial chronicles, Alice Rothchild shares with the reader her deep knowledge about people on both sides of the divide who persist in different realms of oppression and oppressed. Israelis endure the status quo as they see it; Palestinians suffer from intricately encroaching strictures on their lives and dreams. This book represents years of dedicated time and love, bearing witness to what is still a most important place to us all."

—**Jennifer Leaning**, Director, François-Xavier Bagnoud Center
for Health and Human Rights, Harvard University

Just World Books
Timely Books for Changing Times

Just World Books exists to expand the discourse in the United States and worldwide on issues of vital international concern. We are committed to building a more just, equitable, and peaceable world. We uphold the equality of all human persons. We aim for our books to contribute to increasing understanding across national, religious, ethnic, and racial lines; to share more broadly the reflections, analyses, and policy prescriptions of pathbreaking activists for peace; and to help to prevent war.

To learn about our existing and upcoming titles or to buy our books, visit our website:

www.JustWorldBooks.com

Also, follow us on Facebook and Twitter!

Our recent titles include:

- *The Gaza Kitchen: A Palestinian Culinary Journey*, by Laila El-Haddad and Maggie Schmitt
- *Lens on Syria: A Photographic Tour of its Ancient and Modern Culture*, by Daniel Demeter
- *Never Can I Write of Damascus: When Syria Became Our Home*, by Theresa Kubasak and Gabe Huck
- *America's Continuing Misadventures in the Middle East*, by Chas W. Freeman, Jr.
- *Arabia Incognita: Dispatches from Yemen and the Gulf*, edited by Sheila Carapico
- *War Is a Lie*, by David Swanson
- *The General's Son: Journey of an Israeli in Palestine*, by Miko Peled
- *The People Make the Peace: Lessons from the Vietnam Antiwar Movement*, edited by Karín Aguilar-San Juan and Frank Joyce
- *Baddawi*, by Leila Abdelrazaq

CONDITION CRITICAL

LIFE AND DEATH
IN ISRAEL/PALESTINE

Other works by Alice Rothchild:

Broken Promises, Broken Dreams: Stories of Jewish and Palestinian Trauma and Resilience, 2nd edition, 2010

On the Brink: Israel and Palestine on the Eve of the 2014 Gaza Invasion, 2014

CONDITION CRITICAL
LIFE AND DEATH
IN ISRAEL/PALESTINE

ALICE ROTHCHILD

Just World Books
Charlottesville, Virginia

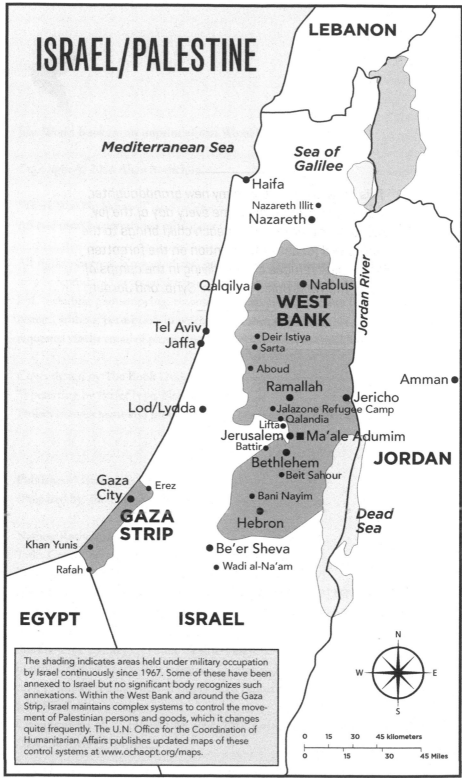

ISRAEL/PALESTINE

LEBANON

Mediterranean Sea

Sea of Galilee

● Haifa

Nazareth Illit ●
Nazareth ●

Jordan River

Qalqilya ● ● Nablus

WEST BANK

Tel Aviv ●
Jaffa ●

● Deir Istiya
● Sarta

● Aboud

Amman ●

Ramallah ●

Lod/Lydda ● ● Jericho

● Jalazone Refugee Camp
● Qalandia
Lifta ●

Jerusalem ● ■ Ma'ale Adumim
Battir ●

JORDAN

Bethlehem ●
● Beit Sahour

Gaza City ● Erez

GAZA STRIP

● Bani Nayim

Hebron ●

Dead Sea

Khan Yunis ●

Rafah ●

● Be'er Sheva
● Wadi al-Na'am

EGYPT

ISRAEL

N
W — E
S

The shading indicates areas held under military occupation by Israel continuously since 1967. Some of these have been annexed to Israel but no significant body recognizes such annexations. Within the West Bank and around the Gaza Strip, Israel maintains complex systems to control the movement of Palestinian persons and goods, which it changes quite frequently. The U.N. Office for the Coordination of Humanitarian Affairs publishes updated maps of these control systems at www.ochaopt.org/maps.

| 0 | 15 | 30 | 45 kilometers |
| 0 | 15 | 30 | 45 Miles |

Cartography by Marc Whitaker and © 2016 Just World publishing, LLC

Contents

Preface

In October 2014, I heard Indiana University's religious studies professor Shaul Magid describe those Jews who engage in critical activism on Israel/Palestine as entering a "special kind of exile." These words resonated deeply for me. I had spent my early years in a very familiar American Jewish place, with immigrant Orthodox roots and a Hebrew school upbringing. But then, I encountered the activism of the 1960s; I started to learn about Israel's increasingly belligerent occupation of the West Bank, Gaza, and East Jerusalem and its multiple, hard-to-defend wars, and I developed a growing awareness of "cross-sectional" issues around racism, police brutality, militarism, and US foreign policy. I found I had to re-examine the meaning of my own Jewishness in light of the uncomfortable consequences of Zionism, and I started to grapple with my own personal responsibility as a Jew and a US citizen in a world rife with contradiction, fear, and conflict.[1]

I discovered that within the United States, there were wide chasms between the dominant national mythos regarding the founding of the State of Israel and its struggle for survival, and the experience of Palestinians who lived the other side of that struggle. I found that we do not yet have a common language, even the words for "the region" are contradictory: Palestine; Israel; Judea and Samaria; Greater Israel; '48 Israel and the Occupied Palestinian Territories; liberated, disputed, or administered territories; the Zionist entity; the Promised Land. I realized that there is a multi-billion dollar industry developed by US and Israeli governmental agencies, public relations firms, and think tanks to shape the "Israel brand." Their framing influences the words and concepts we use and the way our mainstream media understands and covers the news.

As I searched for an honest conceptual language, the chasms between the different framings of "the conflict" became glaringly obvious: Is this a clash of civilizations, another example from a several-thousand-year history of Jewish persecution and determined survival, this time rising out of the ashes of the Holocaust? Is this a struggle for a haven for Jews everywhere? Or, is the current occupation (as opposed to liberation) begun in 1967 actually a continuation of more than one hundred years of colonization of Palestine, of treating Jews as more deserving, more human than Palestinians, and of Palestinians periodically (like many indigenous peoples) fighting back? More importantly, does a national settler movement triggered by European anti-Semitism, that is grounded in the privileging of Jews and the belittling, dehumanization, or hatred of Arabs, inexorably lead to where we are today?

My first step was to understand the realities on the ground and—largely to compensate for the limits of my own education and the inadequacies of our media—to focus on the voices and experiences of dissident Israelis and Palestinians in Israel/Palestine (for want of a better topographic term). Thus began my complicated, difficult journey. In 2003, I began co-organizing annual delegations to the region, mostly with American Jews for a Just Peace (AJJP) and Jewish Voice for Peace. We focused on health and human rights concerns, interviewing and working with individuals and organizations throughout Israel/Palestine. In 2012, I joined a delegation organized by the Dorothy Cotton Institute and Interfaith Peace-Builders that explored the Palestinian nonviolent resistance movements and their Israeli allies, examining the parallels with the US civil rights movement. I was in Israel and the West Bank in June 2014 and bore witness to much of the tense buildup to the attack on Gaza that Israel launched the following month; and in March 2015, I had the privilege of providing health care and documenting facts on the ground in postwar Gaza with Washington Physicians for Social Responsibility.

I was always eager to share what I learned through this work with as broad a public as possible. In the early years, I recorded my experiences in a nightly audio diary: transcriptions of those "notes from the scene" led to a first book, *Broken Promises, Broken Dreams: Stories of Jewish and Palestinian Trauma and Resilience*. In 2010, I began seriously blogging, both for my own sanity and also to share what I was seeing and hearing with anyone willing to listen.[2] The daily ritual of crossing lines, observing, listening, meticulously documenting the realities on the ground, absorbing the physical and emotional trauma and the pain all around me, and later (cathartically) pushing SEND, allowed me to start each day with fresh eyes and an open heart.

This book is a result of those efforts and a tribute to the power of bearing witness and reporting in real time. It aims to describe to you, the reader, the daily experiences of people in this region, unfiltered by newspaper editors, advertisers, or the Israeli messaging industry. The book's title, *Condition Critical: Life and Death in Israel/Palestine*, clearly references my work and my professional culture as a physician. In medicine, a patient's condition refers to an overall assessment of her health, or lack thereof, and the chances for her survival. By reporting from the ground the minutiae of daily life, I am not only checking the wellbeing of Israelis and Palestinians, with a focus on mental and physical health, but also sharing intimate stories that are a metaphor for greater truths about the region's general condition.

This process can be challenging on many levels. For starters, we can only know history if we have unhindered access to the contradictory stories of, and evidence from, the past. Scholars and activists have referred to the Israeli-driven process of deliberately erasing the traces of Palestine's past as "memoricide"[3] or "sociocide."[4] Every nation builds its own founding mythology and national belief system, which are built as much on suppressing or "forgetting" key parts of the historical record as on remembering others. With Israel, this policy of "forgetting" occurs within the context of its nation building and territorial expansion, racist attitudes toward the "other," and justifications for military and state behaviors within a certain framing (built on narratives related to Biblical promises, the Nazi Holocaust, the permanent victimization of the Jews, terrorism, and so on.) The deliberate, state-sponsored erasure of Palestinian voices and evidence of the Palestinians' centuries-old presence in the region thus constitute a form of historical genocide, of attempting to destroy the memory of a people's history and thus the people themselves.

To confront this reality as a Jewish person is extremely painful and entails a mix of ethical and psychological dilemmas. In our minds, we are the good people; we are the victims of anti-Semitism; we do not commit massacres or steal land. At the same time, our victimhood gives us permission to do whatever is necessary to feel safe. Understanding that a consequence of the founding of the State of Israel was the destruction of an indigenous people (composed of Muslims, Christians, and Jews) who had lived there for centuries and who objected to being colonized requires acknowledging a buried history in which we are deeply complicit. Even more challenging, acknowledging responsibility ultimately leads to the need for apology and compensation. Most people are aware that in the course of the founding of the State of Israel, 700,000 Jewish refugees arrived from Europe and Arabic-speaking countries. What is often overlooked is the 500-plus Palestinian villages destroyed and the 750,000 people dispossessed before and during what is known alternately as the Israeli War of Independence or the Palestinian Nakba. A second major and mostly forgotten Palestinian expulsion occurred at the time of the 1967 War.

The 1967 Israeli conquest of East Jerusalem, the West Bank, and Gaza affected these three areas in different ways. Turning to Jerusalem, I find that many visitors to the city are awed by its beauty and religious power, but they are also unaware of a largely invisible world weighted down by thousands of years of conflicting narratives, religious claims, and a multilayered history. Overlying this is the ongoing fifty-year colonization of East Jerusalem, which is the focus of Palestinian economic and political power and the presumed capital of the increasingly ephemeral Palestinian state. Understanding this historical tension is critical. In 1947, under the United Nations Partition Plan, Jerusalem was designated as an international city under UN protection.[5] During the 1948–49 Arab-Israeli War, Jewish forces seized West Jerusalem and Jordan captured East Jerusalem, which included the Old City and multiple religious sites. In the 1967 Six-Day War, Israeli forces seized East Jerusalem and within days annexed it and surrounding West Bank areas as part of an expanded municipality, declaring Jerusalem as the "eternal, undivided capital of Israel."[6]

The reality, often hidden from the public, is that since 1967 there has been a continuous Judaization of East Jerusalem, along with the bureaucratic and active dispossession of Palestinians, one by one, and the transfer of territories—internationally recognized as occupied areas—to Jewish settlement. Through listening and researching, I felt the impact of these policies and their consequences for dispossessed Palestinians; and I detected the underlying racism, overt violence, and overwhelming Jewish privilege that make this all possible.

The West Bank was once a part of Mandate Palestine, the British-controlled territory between the Jordan River and the Mediterranean Sea that was carved out of the Ottoman Empire after World War I. The 1949 Armistice Agreement gave a seal of approval to the continuation of Jordan's control of this area, which continued until it was occupied by Israeli troops in the 1967 War and brought under Israeli military rule. The West Bank and Gaza represent 22 percent of historic Palestine and are recognized by international law as occupied territory, though successive Israeli governments have claimed that this area, which they call "Judea and Samaria," consists of "liberated," "disputed," or "administered" territories, much or all of which was promised by God to the Jewish people and is in any case necessary for the "security of Israel." The Oslo Accords in 1993 divided the West Bank into Area A (about 15 percent of the total land, consisting of Palestinian cities and under Palestinian Authority control), Area B (about 25 percent of the land, containing Palestinian villages that are under Palestinian civil control but joint Palestinian-Israeli security control), and Area C (60 percent of the land, under Israeli control of both civil and security affairs, and the location of most of the Jewish settlements built since 1967). In actuality, the Israeli Defense Forces (IDF) reserve the ultimate right to control everything throughout Areas A, B, and C.

When Israelis hear I am heading into the West Bank, I have been asked, "Do you travel with an armed guard? Is it dangerous?" and I want to reply, "It is only dangerous if you arrive fully armed with intentions to take the land, steal the water, and imprison the local population. Unarmed, I feel very welcomed." At the moment one crosses the mythical Green Line, the Armistice line from 1949, the impact of the steadily expanding Jewish settlements, the hundreds of kilometers of so-called "bypass roads"[7] that slice through the countryside, the five hundred or so checkpoints that control the movements of Palestinians (but not Jews), and the ongoing brutality of the military occupation becomes breathtakingly clear.[8]

At the same time, mention the word "Gaza" and most people think militant suicide bombers, Qassam rockets, conservative Islamic women covered in hijabs and abayas, and young men, faces obscured by balaclavas, hurling instruments of destruction and chanting slogans calling for the end of Israel. But Gaza's reality is far more complex and nuanced than that media-fueled caricature, which is often devoid of any historical or human context. The Gaza Strip, once a part of Mandate Palestine, was under Egypt's control after the 1949 Armistice. Then in the 1967 war, Gaza, like the West Bank, was occupied by Israeli troops and placed under military rule. In 2005, Israel unilaterally removed its Jewish settlements and troops from the interior of Gaza. But it retained strict control over all of Gaza's borders and much of its economy, crippling any possibility of economic development. In 2006, the Palestinians of the occupied territories held a legislative election under strict Israeli-international control, whose conduct was recognized everywhere as free and fair. The Islamic Resistance Movement, Hamas, won the election. In response, Israel and the United States imposed a crushing international blockade on Gaza and started planning a coup against Hamas's leadership, which was located in Gaza. In June 2007, the attempted coup failed and Hamas took control of the whole Gaza Strip, inflicting an ignominious rout on the coup plotters. Since then, the IDF has massively attacked Gaza three times—2008, 2012, and 2014—and has repeatedly undertaken smaller military actions while enforcing a very severe siege by land, sea, and air.

What is lost in this description of Gaza are the voices and lives of physicians, mental health clinicians, UN and human rights workers, teachers, students, youth groups, artists, and ordinary people who have survived multiple devastating wars and Israeli incursions that have destroyed their homes, hospitals, schools, and water and electricity infrastructure.[9] Everyone has not only lost the physical and emotional stability of their lives and that fundamental sense of personal safety that is part of normal existence, but they have often lost multiple family members as well. When I traveled to Gaza I bore witness to 1.8 million traumatized and extraordinary survivors; I also came to love and respect the immense warmth, humor, and energy of the people in this forgotten and demonized place.

I invite you to join me bearing witness on the frontlines, traveling to East Jerusalem, the West Bank, and Gaza (all occupied according to international law), and investigating the conditions in Israel that do not usually make the prestigious pages of the *New York Times*. I focus on particular issues that are not only the consequences of the occupations that started in 1967, but also the consequences of building a state that privileges its Jewish citizens over its indigenous Palestinian citizens. This state now controls a population half of whose members are not Jewish but Palestinian, living under second-class citizenship or military rule. Utilizing my background as an obstetrician-gynecologist, I also examine the implications of the occupation on medical care and health care delivery systems, and the ability of ordinary citizens to access basic care and wellness.

Clearly, my understanding of Israel is very different than when I started. While I do appreciate the tremendous accomplishments of the state (with massive US support), I am mostly concerned with the contradictions that poison these accomplishments: the ongoing occupation of East Jerusalem and the West Bank, the siege of Gaza, the second-class citizenship of Palestinians with Israeli citizenship, and the still-unresolved issue of the Palestinian refugees of 1948 and 1967. I have a much deeper understanding of the consequences of the war of 1948 and Zionism as a political movement, the realities for Palestinians, and the results of establishing a state where Jews are advantaged over everyone else and where there has been a steady expansion of borders and increasing militarization of Israeli society. I worry about the cost of all of this to Palestinians worldwide as well as to Jewish Israelis (who are increasingly turning to the right and becoming more racist and militaristic), and the price for Jews in the Diaspora and the impact of all of this on the tinderbox that is the Middle East.[10] I hope to challenge you with this information and to inspire you to learn more and become an activist in the struggle for justice. Complicity through either ignorance or silence is a dangerous position in this complicated world.

October 2, 2016

Judaization and the Master Plan

June 15–20, 2013

This chapter and the next cover the delegation we took to Israel/Palestine in June 2013. This was the ninth such delegation I had been part of, aiming to explore, experience, and document the "facts on the ground." On these delegations I draw deeply on my skills as a physician: suspending my preconceptions, observing empathically, building toward a new understanding and activism grounded in justice and the possibility of hope and unexpected alliances. I bear witness to trends that have become increasingly obvious since 2004 when I first started documenting realities beyond the dominant mythos of a "heroic, democratic, and principled Israel."

On this delegation, I was struck by the increasing ghettoization of the ethnic-Palestinian communities in Israel and the occupied territories; the active policies to "Judaize" Palestinian communities in Israel and the West Bank, and particularly in East Jerusalem; and the brave and the persistent civil society activism within Palestinian society. In the visits to Jerusalem, the mixed cities of Jaffa and Haifa, the Palestinian city of Nazareth, and its (Jewish) big sister Nazareth Illit, that are chronicled here, I everywhere saw the consequences of the deeply engrained Israeli policies that advantage Jews greatly over their Palestinian neighbors. I saw, too, the harms inflicted by a Jewish right wing that, with the support and often the encouragement of the military, had grown increasingly violent and unchallenged.

1

When we ventured beyond the "Tel Aviv bubble," the contradictions within Israeli society and the implications for those living under occupation revealed an extremely troubling form of institutionalized discrimination. We found that in Israel, Jewish "nationality" had long trumped citizenship when it came to rights, resources, and privilege; and religious claims and the more fanatical Jewish elements of society were increasingly being used to seize and control more and more of East Jerusalem and the West Bank in a planned and systemized fashion. These facts should give everyone pause.

I found my years of studying the largely invisible details of life in Israel/Palestine very informative. Back in 2010, Ala Jaradat, the program manager of Addameer, a Palestinian human rights organization focused on prisoners and legal aid, had helpfully unraveled the complex civil and human rights issues that faced Palestinians, particularly those who protested the conditions of the Israeli occupation and military rule. I learned that since 1967, the Israeli military had used a broad range of military orders to control the population; these ranged from what road a Palestinian could use to whether he could dig a well for water. There was a stunning list of potential security offenses, from reading the poetry of Mahmoud Darwish, the Palestinian poet who gave voice to the anguish of dispossession and exile, to wearing political symbols, including that of the beloved cartoon character Handala. Jaradat explained that it was illegal to protest the seizing of your own land. Throwing stones at the separation wall was considered destruction of state property; throwing stones at a soldier, attempted murder; and assisting an injured person at a demonstration—including a medical worker—assisting a terrorist. These military orders gave the IDF broad control over the lives of people and organizations, and the IDF used these powers in an often unpredictable and arbitrary manner.

In 2011, we met with Professor Yehouda Shenhav of Tel Aviv University, who challenged many of our assumptions about peacemaking. He explained that the Green Line, used as a starting point for numerous "peace plans" working toward a two-state solution, had already been largely erased by Jewish settlements; yet leftist political approaches to solving the Israeli-Palestinian struggle still clung to the relevance of this now-vanished boundary. He argued that the concept of a Jewish state was problematic as long as the existence of that state was a recipe for the future transfer of Palestinians. He judged the racist, fascist tendencies of the current era to be a continuation of what had happened in 1948, noting that the Jewish state established that year was based on ethnic cleansing, the destruction of villages, massacres, and the dispossession of hundreds of thousands of indigenous Palestinians. He asked, "How does a Jewish racial state cope with non-Jews? There is no difference between Meretz and Avigdor Lieberman except in degree of sincerity. When threatened, all Jews become Lieberman." Meretz is a left-leaning party that supports a two-state solution, opposing the occupation and supporting human rights and social and environmental justice, all within an explicitly Zionist context. Avigdor Lieberman is the Russian-born founder of the Yisrael Beiteinu (Israel Is Our Home) party, the current defense minister, and former foreign minister who lives in a West Bank settlement and openly supports the transfer and ethnic cleansing of Palestinians, loyalty oaths for citizens, and other anti-democratic, hard-right policies.[1]

During that same 2011 delegation, I was challenged by an alternative tour of Jerusalem, in the course of which our guide discussed the endemic discrimination against Mizrahi Jews. Mizrachis arrived in Israel starting in the 1950s, coming from countries like Yemen, Iraq, and Iran. Upon arrival, many were sprayed with DDT and were then lodged in crude tents before being settled in the tough buffer zones at the edge of the Jewish state. Our guide also reviewed the spasm of discrimination against Sudanese and Eritreans who had fled oppressive regimes, walked across the Sinai, and entered Israel across the poorly guarded Egyptian border. About a month earlier, there had been race riots in south Tel Aviv, where shop windows, cars, houses, and even a kindergarten were smashed. I heard talk of a Jewish *Kristallnacht*, with in this case poor Mizrahi Jews, from the bottom of the Jewish economic ladder, turning their rage and racism on the newly arrived African refugees.

That same guide took us to the separation wall—1 meter below ground, 8 meters above. The wall thrust deep into the occupied West Bank, snaking around so it was designed to be 702 kilometers long, twice the length of the Green Line. Construction had begun in 2002 and now the wall was 62 percent completed. Most Israelis claimed that the wall had protected them against suicide bombing attacks, but that claim ignored the facts that most bombings stopped in 2004 when many Palestinian factions abandoned the tactic, that the wall still had many gaps, and some 140,000 Palestinians still crossed illegally from the West Bank every year, mostly looking for work. Those contradictions cried out for our attention.

In recent years, the level of racism and fear in Israel has exploded, and the occupation has become more constrictive and institutionalized. At the same time, Palestinian resistance, from children's theater in refugee camps to the focus on international law along with human and indigenous rights, has been growing. In June 2013, our delegation started its tour in the Old City, examining the day-to-day experience of Palestinians with Israeli IDs who live in a state that does not want them. We ended the tour in a refugee camp in the West Bank where generations of displaced Palestinians struggle with the long aftermath of the dispossession they and their families suffered in 1948.

Through the Looking Glass
June 15, 2013

We begin in the Old City of Jerusalem, in the Al Quds Community Action Center established in 2000 to serve the needs of the Palestinian Jerusalemite community. Hamad Shihabi is an attorney who works on the crucial legal issues that face East Jerusalemites, Palestinians who since 1967 have had the unfortunate dilemma of possessing an Israeli residency ID but no citizenship. They are faced with a myriad of challenges, including home demolitions, barriers to family reunification, lack of adequate national insurance, taxes without acceptable local services, and, given the ancient, conflicted history of the place, face-offs with the malignant Department of Antiquities. Their precious IDs can be easily revoked by Israeli authorities: in 2008, more than 4,000 East Jerusalemites, out of a population of 250,000, lost their IDs. At that point they became stateless and began a byzantine and circuitous legal struggle to nowhere.

Under a gracefully arched ceiling, the heat permeating the thick walls, Hamad takes us through the labyrinthine Alice-in-Wonderland kind of world that is East Jerusalem, where there is a kind of endemic insanity reminiscent of something only the Queen of Hearts and the White Rabbit might find reasonable. For instance, if an East Jerusalemite (this only applies to Palestinians) takes another nationality, she loses her ID. Or, if someone builds without a permit (which is virtually impossible for a Palestinian to get), he loses his ID and is fined. The fines are based on each meter of non-permitted building done—600 shekels ($180) per meter—which accumulate on a daily basis, and they are only getting harsher. There are legal ways to request extensions but little possibility of ever obtaining one. Hamad talks about families that "self demolish" (they literally destroy their own homes) to avoid the increasing fines. He explains that there are extensive zoning and permitting rules, but they aren't applied universally, as only Jewish families ever get permits to build in the Muslim Quarter. Palestinian lands are unregistered in East Jerusalem according to the Israeli Land Authority, so there are always conflicts about the evidence for ownership. In 2011, Israeli authorities revoked the IDs of all Hamas members in parliament and reserve the right to revoke IDs whenever it is "reasonable."

Hamad's personal story is equally disturbing: his father, who is originally from East Jerusalem, has a West Bank ID; their family lands were lost in 1948 and 1967. His mother has an East Jerusalem ID, but their home, which was once in Jerusalem, is now "outside" of the city, so they rent in Beit Hanina, which is "in" the city. Because they have different IDs and haven't been permitted to complete the process of family reunification, his father has to travel separately and go through different checkpoints than the rest of the family. I listen to all of this in my post-travel exhaustion and think once again I have arrived in a land of official insanity! Then I remember the Jewish state's overarching goal: to force Palestinians, one way or the other, to leave their historic and ancestral homes.

We make our way through the winding streets of the Old City, up and down stairs, through dark, dusty stone tunnels and glorious snatches of sun to the Shehaba clan's quarters. One hundred people from 22 families live in 120 rooms, curling around dark stairways, opening into bright courtyards. I see kids tumbling and playing, a kitchen tucked behind a door, a glimpse of a living room. Their papers date back to four hundred years of documented ownership as a *waqf*, a form of Islamic trusteeship designed to protect the family from dispossession.

In the 1960s a group of ultra-Orthodox Jews claimed that the entry to the Shehaba family quarters was a "religious site" and began praying and performing Bar Mitzvot while purposefully blocking the entry to the Shehaba homes. Both the numbers of ultra-Orthodox and the aggression they displayed increased, and then came the demands to knock down walls, to make male and female prayer areas, and to build tunnels connecting to the tunnels under the Al Aqsa Mosque. The local residents complained and the authorities put up police barricades along their entry to separate them from the *meshugas*. They also installed a security camera that I suspect is there to improve surveillance of the Shehaba folks and their comings and goings. The nearby sign says in English and Hebrew "Small Wailing Wall," but in Arabic it says "Shehaba Quarters."

We wend our way up the ancient stones, and in classic Palestinian fashion, we are shortly sitting in another Shehaba home where our host was born and raised. We are soon sipping sweet juice and enjoying his curly haired two-year-old daughter. The only sign of tension in this frequently threatened home is his constant smoking. He studied antiquities in Italy and now works at the Khalidi Library, founded in 1725, but his true passion is restoring old documents. He shows us an elegant book of Islamic laws he restored, the pages dating back 420 years. The crowded living room is filled with stuffed chairs, an oriental rug, plastic white lilies, paintings of Al Aqsa Mosque. We hear a *muezzin* calling in the background. This antiquities expert is dignified and calm in this sea of disordered behavior. As we leave him, he is graciously smiling and says repeatedly: "You are most welcome."

As if this is some kind of bad movie, by the time we get to the bottom of the stairs at the entry to the family quarters, a large crowd of ultra-Orthodox Jews have gathered to pray, loudly and boisterously in their self-assured religiosity. They are guarded by a cluster of soldiers with large automatic weapons and a clear intent to use them if needed.

Dropped down the rabbit hole again.

The Prisons Within

June 16, 2013

Randa Wahbe from Addameer Prisoner Support and Human Rights[2] has a cheerful, youthful enthusiasm that contrasts with the grim experiences of Palestinians within the Israeli court and prison systems. Established in 1992 and today boasting seven lawyers and a dedicated staff, Addameer is a Ramallah-based human rights organization supporting prisoners and working to end torture and human rights violations through monitoring and solidarity campaigns.

I have always been struck by the number of doctors, teachers, ambulance drivers, students, farmers, activists, and so on, who report having been detained in Israeli prisons at some point in their lives, and I have read Physicians for Human Rights–Israel's studies of torture within these jails, but Randa has the numbers behind this troubling story.

There are currently 5,000 Palestinians in prison. Since 1967, 800,000 Palestinians have been arrested, which translates to 20 percent of the total Palestinian population and 40 percent of the male population imprisoned or detained at some point in their lives. The key issues include torture during interrogation and raids, administrative detention, child imprisonment, the use of prolonged isolation, medical negligence, arrests of human rights activists, and hunger strikes and their health implications. As of May 2013, there are 4,979 Palestinian prisoners in Israeli jails, including 16 women, half of them mothers; 139 of the prisoners are under the age of 18. The number of administrative detainees, 158, is actually low, but these folks can be held indefinitely with no charges, no trials, and secret files. In 2013, there has been an uptick in imprisoned journalists, with thirteen currently detained, half between January and May.[3]

There are four interrogation centers, three detention centers (including Ofer, just outside Ramallah), and seventeen prisons, mostly inside Israel. This is actually against international law, as Palestinian families cannot access these prisons because they are unable to obtain permits. It is an injustice that further isolates and demoralizes the prisoners.

Many arrests occur at home in the middle of the night with a massive military presence, military jeeps surrounding the home, soldiers breaking down the door, sleepy family members corralled, photographed, and interrogated one at a time, including small children. The prisoner is taken, blindfolded, shackled, and put into a military jeep that will either go to a settlement or interrogation center. The interrogation can last for ninety days and is renewable; the prisoners can be denied a lawyer for sixty days, which is another renewable restriction.

Prisoners regularly report physical and psychological torture during interrogation—twenty-hour sessions, isolation cells two by four meters in size with a hole in the floor for bathroom needs. Prisoners may be tied up in stress positions for hours during interrogation, experience physical abuse, sleep and sensory deprivation, and threats of sexual violence, directly against children and indirectly against their family members. As expected, forced confessions are common, and seventy-three prisoners have died in custody since 1967, allegedly due to torture. In February 2013, at the age of thirty, Arafat Jaradat died during his first (and last) arrest. He had been accused of throwing stones. While in custody he requested a medical exam due to severe back pain and was rewarded with an extension of his interrogation. The autopsy revealed he had severe bruising and fractured ribs, but no action was taken against his torturers.[4] Even more frightening, Randa reports that when he was originally arrested, the security forces told him to say good-bye to his wife and children since he would never see them again.

In the Palestinian prisoner experience, interrogation is followed by the farce of military court proceedings, where innumerable international laws are violated. Randa describes temporary buildings, intrusive searches for all attending the trial, inadequately trained military judges, and a court inundated with soldiers. The proceedings are conducted in Hebrew; the translators are deplorable, misinterpreting and injecting their own opinions; the shackled prisoner has often not met his attorney before; and the average hearing lasts three minutes. Needless to say, almost everyone is convicted.

So for what crimes are Palestinians languishing in jail? There are 2,000 military orders in the West Bank, but number 1651 is the most common and includes participation in demonstrations, destruction of public order, raising the Palestinian flag in Jerusalem, and belonging to an illegal party. The military frequently goes after political activists who are convicted of writing slogans on walls or throwing stones; that offense warrants ten years' imprisonment for a stone thrown at a nonmoving object, and twenty years for one thrown at a moving object.

Ninety percent of children who are arrested are accused of throwing stones; 60 percent are arrested between midnight and 5:00 a.m., ripped from their beds at night in front of terrified and powerless parents; and until recently, children 16 and older were tried as adults. Palestinian childhood appears to be an ephemeral and brief experience thanks to occupation. There are seven hundred child detainees per year, more than eight thousand since 2000.[5] Randa describes a number of tragic cases of young children detained, strip-searched, mentally and physically tortured; for instance, they will have their braces ripped off one tooth at a time, interrogated, and pushed to be government collaborators in order to protect their families. Families are also forced to pay huge court fees. These traumatic experiences in children have major long-term implications. Some children stop speaking, refuse to attend school or leave home, and suffer from bed-wetting, a loss of interest in life, and fear of participating in any future political activities.

With the females in detention, there have been several births, the women shackled during delivery, the children removed after the age of two, and no extra food provided after childbirth. The women report sexual harassment and repeated strip searches.

Media and human rights organizations have reported on the recent hunger strikes, protesting issues such as repeated strip searches, extended administrative detention, extreme overcrowding, lack of hygiene, and inadequate medical care. There are often eight prisoners per cell, and they are given three hours in the open yard per day. All of these basic requirements are treated as privileges that can easily be revoked. Because of the increasing privatization of the prisons, prisoners now have to pay for the food and personal items from the canteen, cleaning products, and clothes, and the money to cover these provisions, raised by often poor families, is split between the private company, Dudush, and the Israeli Ministry of Prisoner Affairs.

Prisoners are economically exploited and can sometimes exchange a month from their sentence for two thousand shekels. And then there are repeated examples of medical negligence: fifty-two prisoners have died from deliberate negligence, such as denial of cancer treatment, and less egregious issues such as malnutrition, deliberate errors in the clinics such as pulling the incorrect tooth, lack of treatment for chronic disease, and lack of adequate treatment of injuries that become even more serious medical problems.[6] Apparently, the "health care" is often provided by soldiers in white coats with some first aid training. A recent hunger striker developed hepatitis when non-sterile instruments overtly contaminated with blood were used for a tooth extraction. I wonder where are the doctors, the psychologists, the professionals who above all are trained to do no harm? Where is the out-cry from the Israeli Medical Association? When is blindness and ignorance acknowledged as symptoms of racism and growing fascism within a country that claims to operate according to democratic principles?

Randa explains that Addameer clearly "does not have a whole lot of wins in military court," but they continue to provide free legal aid, work in the Jerusalem high court to reveal these gross injustices built into the sys-tem, provide advocacy work, and put pressure on international governments. Ninety-five percent of their work is with political prisoners; consequently, given the repressive political climate, their office has been repeatedly raided, computers and records removed by Israeli soldiers. They have also attracted the ire of the Palestinian Authority, which increasingly collaborates with the Israeli military court system. Addameer works closely with the United Nations and with the Israeli advocacy organization Adalah, and has begun contacts with prisoner support groups in the United States, drawing obvious parallels.

We ask Randa if there are any signs of hope, and she tells us of a new campaign[7] against the British/Danish security company G4S, which owns child detention centers in the United States, provides security in Israeli pris-ons, runs immigration detention centers in the United Kingdom, and pro-vides security for the Hajj in Saudi Arabia.

It seems that once again, we are all in this together, one way or another. It also seems that in Israel/Palestine, military might tramples the rights of the powerless, the youth, the activists, the Arabs, the very human people engaged in a struggle for survival that is easily visible if you choose to see it.

Divide and Conquer

June 16, 2013

The posters in the offices of the Stop the Wall campaign grab our attention immediately: in one, three hulking men hack the concrete barrier with pick axes; in another, a cartoon elderly woman lifts a tiny boy off the main gun of a menacing Israeli tank; in a third, the words "To exist is to resist" float above walls crisscrossing between crowded Palestinian houses, a helicopter hovering above; in a fourth, a disembodied head, mouth screaming, emerges from the wall with a fist in chains.[8]

Jamal Juma begins his PowerPoint presentation, and we are immediately washed by a torrent of bad news. In 2002, the northwestern city of Qalqilya became the first city to be completely encircled by the separation wall. It took one year to build, imprisoning forty-one thousand people and separating them from thirty-two surrounding villages, their agricultural lands, and groundwater sources. Once a commercial hub for both Israelis along the border and local Palestinians, Qalqilya in less than six months suffered the closure of six hundred stores and loss of four thousand inhabitants who left in desperation. In the first winter, the city was severely flooded by mountain water that flowed in but had no place to drain. Jamal explains ironically that this is the future for the West Bank.

By 2005, it became clear that the Israelis planned three main encircled areas—northern, central, and southern—using a combination of walls and the strategic insertion of Jewish settlements. Jamal reviews the long history of Palestinian struggle against a variety of colonial projects dating back to the 1900s and the emergence of Palestinian nationalism. Things took a major downturn with the signing of the Oslo Accords in 1993.

Jamal informs us that in the early 1990s, with the US-led invasion of Iraq and subsequent decrease in the power of one of Israel's main enemies, the country turned its attention to its internal affairs. In 1992, the government gathered scientists and thinkers to create a twenty-year strategy for the future of Israel, in case of war and in case of peace, in cooperation with more than thirty international research institutions. By 1997, the eighteen-volume master plan was completed, nine thousand pages devoted to Jerusalem alone. The current state of the occupied territories is the direct result of those plans.

Then, in 2000, the Herzliya Conference launched a study to plan four major projects that have also had a direct impact on the appalling fate of the Palestinians:

1. For Palestinians with Israeli citizenship in the Galilee, a program of development aimed at Judaization of the area.
2. For Palestinians in the Negev, a similar development/Judaization program.
3. For Greater Jewish Jerusalem, settlement expansion into the West Bank and depopulation of Palestinians.
4. For Palestinians in the West Bank and Gaza, increasing disengagement.

The plan is geared toward controlling Palestinian demographics and increasing the Jewish presence. In the Galilee, following the findings of major studies that figured out how to move Jews from the coast to the mountains, the government invested in high-tech industrial zones with housing, schools, and economic opportunity. In the Negev, one hundred thousand Bedouins were collected and brought to five reservations—the word in Hebrew for this process translates to "concentrating them." This threatened to destroy the Bedouins' lives and culture, and they responded by settling to protect their ancestral lands, creating a host of unrecognized villages without any services, in abject poverty and constantly under threat of repeated demolitions.

In Jerusalem, a combination of Judaization and ethnic cleansing seeks to decrease the Palestinian population from the current 35 percent to 12 percent. With almost scientific precision, Jamal describes how that will happen.

1. The first step is to expand the boundaries: frame Greater Jerusalem to include the Jewish settlement blocks and surround it all with 181 kilometers of wall snaking deep into the West Bank. Thus, the Adumin Bloc would add thirty-three thousand Jewish settlers; the Etzion Bloc, forty-three thousand; and the Givon Bloc, another twelve thousand. Throw in the controversial E1 area to complete the ring, and then ghettoize the local Palestinians. Twenty-two villages, with 225,300 people once

part of Jerusalem, would then be located outside of the Holy City.

2. The second step focuses inside Jerusalem, in the Old City. Start in 1967 by destroying the historic neighborhood along the Wailing Wall. Then allot millions of shekels to Judaize the Old City, moving in Jewish families house by house. There are now ninety Israeli outposts inside the Old City, with plans to displace all fifty thousand residents of Silwan, now officially the City of David, and fully Judaize the Holy Basin, creating a de-Arabized area all the way to the Mount of Olives, where four thousand people who are already settled await their happy co-religionists. Top this off with a highly political and heavily criticized archeological excavation in the City of David, designed to prove Jewish exclusivity to a city that has been occupied innumerable times over thousands of years (by the Canaanites, Egyptians, Israelites, Philistines, Assyrians, Babylonians, Greeks, Romans, Arab Caliphate, Crusaders, and Ottomans, to name a few), displacing 1,500 Palestinians to make space for the parking lot for tourist buses. Continue in a similar process in the neighborhoods of Shu'afat and Sheikh Jarrah, and link them all together with a light rail that ends at the Damascus gate, thus gradually eliminating all Palestinian identity in the area.

Jamal highlights the multiple well-funded new projects entailed in the development plan: museums, hotels, tunnels under the ancient walls, car parks, tourist overviews, and sixty-three new synagogues, including one to be built next to the wall of the Old City. The synagogue will be taller than the Al Aqsa Mosque—in my view, the architectural equivalent of giving everyone the finger.

At this point we are all sunk in a strange combination of depression, horror, shame, and outrage. I can only wonder if there is any historical memory left among the power brokers in Jerusalem, descendants from the ghettos of Europe and the survivors of the racist, ethnic cleansing of the Holocaust.

Jamal continues undaunted. He focuses on the growth of Jewish settlers in the West Bank, up to 650,000 since it all began in 1967. He talks about the geopolitical impact of the wall, the fourteen thousand kilometers of apartheid roads with forty-eight bridges and tunnels to keep Palestinians and Jewish settlers from actually seeing each other, the increasingly privatized checkpoints—now called terminals—and the industrial zones. I will explain the zones, since that was news to me. Apparently, after having to traverse multiple roads to avoid the bypass highways, and being forced to wait since early morning to stuff through humiliating turnstiles at checkpoints, Palestinian workers now are "blessed" with a new dubious employment opportunity: industrial zones. Israel, in conjunction with the World Bank, is working on ninety-two zones along the borders created by the wall, which Jamal refers to as "do-it-yourself apartheid." There are currently industrial zones in twelve of the largest Jewish settlements, where thirty thousand Palestinians work under oppressive conditions with no labor protections for fifty to seventy shekels per day. Joint industrial zones are planned with the help of Germany and Japan, to name a few internationals that have taken a concern for the local economy and what is now called "immigrant capital." The Israelis are busy attracting international investment from Jenin to Jericho; fifty-eight companies have invested in the settlements. Jamal reminds us that the barbed wire that runs along this barrier is made in South Africa.

To give this a sense of reality, we are soon bouncing along in yellow taxis heading for the town of Qalandia, a village totally encircled by wall, separated from the nearby refugee camp of the same name, crowded up against the industrial zone for the Jewish settlement of Atarot. Between us and the nearby town of Al Ram are two more walls. All of this was once part of Jerusalem but now exists in a kind of no-man's-land, unclaimed, ungoverned; no taxes are collected but neither is the sewage. Drug gangs terrorize people at night. Jamal moved to this area from Beit Hanina in East Jerusalem after his imprisonment (he was accused of organizing demonstrations) because he could no longer tolerate the military vehicle sitting outside his house and frightening his children.

From there we go to the once vibrant Bir Nabala. Since 2006, it has been a ghost town, completely emptied by the economic impact of the wall, houses locked and deserted, stores shuttered, homes demolished, raw sewage running near the wall where pigeons roost in once elegant homes, and a few souls hang on with a couple of goats and a horse. At night this street becomes dangerous and infested by gangs of drug dealers. I sense not only the overall cantonization of the West Bank, but also these micro-isolations—village by village, family by family, son by son—the silent expulsion, the ongoing invisible Nakba.

Back in the taxi, the undulating voice of Mohammed Assaf sings on the radio. He is one of the three contestants left on *Arab Idol*, a spinoff of

American Idol, where he is competing with an Egyptian and a Syrian. He sings a beguiling song about a magic kaffiyeh. I am told that everyone in the West Bank is rooting for him.

The Occupation Lives at Home

June 17, 2013

Sami Abu Shehadeh, Tel Aviv-Jaffa municipal council member and semi-permanent graduate student in modern history at Tel Aviv University, notes with a mixture of bluntness tinged with irony, "Our state is killing our people since its establishment as part of daily life, and it didn't stop in '48."

Sami explains that until the Second Intifada, the one million Palestinians with Israeli citizenship were largely invisible, despite constituting 20 percent of the population and living under military occupation until 1966. Only 9 percent of such Palestinians currently live in mixed cities. In Jaffa, as in Lod and Haifa, Arabs and Jews demographically live together, but not in actuality, and there is minimal public conversation about the racism fundamental to this reality.

Jaffa, a southern suburb of Tel Aviv, joined the city in 1950 to form a combined municipality, but the city is one of the oldest in the world, dating back some six thousand years. Two hundred years ago, the city was transformed by the Jaffa orange. Through the export economy fueled by that crop, Jaffa became one of the largest Arab cities in the world with a population in the vicinity of 120,000, including thousands of unregistered Arab workers from all over the world. The southern neighborhood of Ajami was developed in the 1800s and was once a center of economic, cultural, and intellectual activity. Tel Aviv was founded in the early 1900s by several Jewish families as a northern Hebrew neighborhood of Jaffa, and it exploded in population over the decades. The story of Jaffa and Tel Aviv is a microcosm of the story of the Nakba.

Jaffa was occupied in 1948 and many terrorized inhabitants fled, leaving a few thousand "present absentees" herded into the fenced-in ghetto of Ajami. The street names were all changed to the names of Jewish leaders and Jewish religious references. The wealthy Palestinian homes were seized as absentee property, although the owners were often living a few blocks away; some Arab homes were subdivided to absorb Jewish refugees from Romania or Bulgaria, leaving the original Palestinian family in one room with a bathroom and kitchen to share with Jewish immigrants.

As we walk with Sami through the old stone streets, passing massive gentrification projects, with gorgeous purple bougainvillea cascading over walls, I am struck by the rows of bike rentals and the big recycling bins; having arrived from East Jerusalem, I am amazed to see what a funded and functional local government can actually accomplish. We stop by an old pharmacy dating back to 1924. The pharmacist's grandfather graduated with a degree in pharmacy from a university in Istanbul and came to Jaffa in 1919; he joined the Ottoman army. His father graduated in pharmacy from Beirut, and now the son, Yusif, is carrying on the family tradition.

We turn on to Sha'rev Nik Anur Street, formerly Talamas Street, and stand in front of a graceful villa, once the Talamas home, belonging to a wealthy Christian Palestinian family active in the orange trade. Oranges were the most important commodity in the Palestinian economy. In the 1930s, five million boxes of oranges were shipped per year, with over four hundred million oranges picked, sent to warehouses for individual wrapping in silk paper, and then sent to the port to waiting ships. Because there was not enough local labor, starting in the late 1800s, thousands of workers from Egypt, Morocco, Algeria, and all over the Arab world were brought in. After the Nakba, Palestinian workers were dispersed throughout the Arab world and this elegant old mansion was turned into eight apartments. "A travesty," comments Sami.

We continue wandering toward the majestic Mediterranean Sea. Sami explains that there are seventeen neighborhoods in Tel Aviv-Jaffa (called Yafo by Israelis), and Ajami is the "weakest." We snap photos of magnificent mansions, old wealthy Palestinian homes facing the sea, now gentrified and selling for many millions as the locals are priced out of existence with nowhere to go. This is clearly expulsion via the free market. One of the "For Sale" signs on a gorgeous seaside apartment is being sold by a company appropriately misnamed "Home Land."

Sami reviews the attack on Jaffa in 1948, the lack of any Arab army defenses, the violent siege and expulsion, and the clear Zionist intent to create a Jewish state without any of the bothersome indigenous inhabitants. Jaffa went from 120,000 people to 3,900, with the remainder killed or scattered all over the Arab world. For those who remained, the trauma is unimaginable. Children and parents were separated, lost, injured; mothers gave birth in the midst of the fighting; friends disappeared. The remaining Arabs were rounded up and fenced into the neighborhood of Ajami, which European Jews, fresh from their own catastrophe, aptly named "the ghetto." Those who fled beyond the state borders were now declared "enemies." The survivors were not allowed to ask what happened to their lost relations. To ask, "Where is my mother?" was futile because she was now part of an enemy state, if she was alive at all. The loss and physical and emotional trauma were profound. The normal trappings of a happy, functioning society—weddings, court systems, dressmakers, carpentry shops, hospitals—all disappeared in the war and its aftermath. Sami exclaims ironically, "Now we are a minority in our homeland and the Israelis are immigrating to us."

For Sami, the second Nakba was the seizing of all Palestinian property, libraries, possessions—"the biggest armed robbery in the twentieth century." Under the Absentee Law, all Palestinian property was counted as "neglected property" if the owner was not present in the home from which he had just been expelled and tossed into Ajami ten minutes away. Even more painful for the Jaffa Palestinians was seeing their homes, their furniture, their gardens occupied by newly arrived Jewish immigrants. Poverty-stricken locals would go back to the now-Jewish homes and beg for a blanket or some personal item. Wealthy factory owners became impoverished workers in their own factories. Wealthy businessmen like the Hassouneh family, major orange exporters, became workers in their former orchards. The psychological humiliation was as great as the physical loss.[9]

The third Nakba, states Sami, is coexistence. He asks us to imagine the Arab family sharing their home with the new immigrants who periodically leave to join the Israeli military for a mission in Gaza where that Arab family's relatives now live. "Maybe they will kill my brother?" the family wonders. And then the soldier returns and shares the bathroom and the kitchen. In the wake of this additional psychological catastrophe, many men became dysfunctional, drug addicts, or alcoholics—their habits probably supplied by Israeli soldiers and Bedouins—while the women coped as women will do. In the course of three terrible years, Ajami was transformed into a small, poor, criminal neighborhood.

From the 1960s to 1980s, Ajami was slated for destruction—three thousand apartments were razed to make way for hotels and a park that engineers planned along the water. The garbage from the demolished homes was thrown along the beach, creating a huge mountain of toxic materials. Ultimately, the plans were scrapped because the chemicals kept exploding and the area was unsafe for construction. It is now a lovely park with bright new playgrounds and palm trees hiding this dark, secret past.

Similar to West Bank Palestinians, folks in Jaffa were unable to obtain building permits. Naturally, because families were growing and needed to expand their community, renovations occurred. Now, however, the State is claiming that not only were fines due forty years ago for the original transgression, but that they had accrued interest, with the penalties rising to millions of shekels. Thus four hundred Arab families, who are, by the way, citizens of Israel, are under demolition orders due to the crime of renovation and expansion. Sami describes a host of other Kafkaesque situations focusing on state ownership and inheritance laws for Palestinian citizens.

Since the 1990s, gentrification and neoliberal market policies have dominated the scene. Since the welfare state cannot "fix" these problems, let the free market take over, so goes the logic. The wealthy move in and the locals cannot afford to stay, then schools close, local markets close. "We are a beautiful cemetery of thousands of houses," explains Sami. While 5 to 10 percent of local Palestinians are doing well, 50 percent are on welfare.

The latest threat is the plan to build national religious Jewish settlements in the Arab neighborhoods to "strengthen" the Zionist ideology of lax secular Jews and to change the demographics of those communities. Thus the ultra-Orthodox want to "settle in the heart" (i.e., within the Green Line, in Israel proper), and if any settlers are removed from the West Bank, these right-wingers will "burn the State from within." Interestingly, the Yossi Beilin left agrees that demographics are a problem but disagrees with this solution (Beilin was active in the Labor and Meretz parties and worked on a number of peace proposals, including the Oslo and Geneva Accords), while the Avigdor Lieberman right is ready to transfer Palestinians without any further charades. Regarding this position, Sami muses: "So my beautiful eight year-old and five-year-old are demographic bombs," while large Jewish families are "blessed by children." He describes a recent tortured political fight between settlers on the one side and Palestinian activists and businessmen on the other. The fight went to the High Court and involved illegal dealings by the Israeli Land Authority and court decisions wreaking of racism and cowardliness. Mixed cities are now considered the "greatest danger to Zionism," and people talk openly of their preference for "clean" kindergartens, "clean" schools, "clean" neighborhoods.

As Sami reflects, "We are trying to survive; we lost in 1948 and we have nowhere to go." The housing issue is critical, but all the city planning is done by Jews, for Jews, with no concern for the social impact on the local community. The problem is, he points out, "most of the wars, we are here and they are there. Our wars ended but we are here and they are here and this is the cultural reality." Sami wonders what kind of multicultural reality is possible in this racist environment. What are the rights of the Jews in this situation? What kind of society do we want to create? He suggests that a mixed educational system instead of the current arrangement, fragmented into Arab (i.e., poorly funded and inadequate), secular Jewish, and Orthodox systems might be a start. He notes that 20 to 25 percent of Arabs already send their children to secular Jewish schools to get a better education. But then what kind of history would be taught in a mixed school? Do you tell Jewish children that their grandfathers ethnically cleansed a whole city? These are not popular questions, but that has never stopped Sami from asking them.

Haifa: Love and Sex in the Age of Apartheid

June 18, 2013

We arrive in the stunningly beautiful port city of Haifa, a muggy heat descending over steep hills winding to the port. We see towering cranes like gigantic blue flamingos perched along the shore, the over-the-top Baha'i Temple and Gardens shimmering up the terraced mountain at the edge of the German Colony area where we are staying. Our first stop today is with a group of dynamic women from Muntada: The Arab Forum for Sexuality, Education and Health, and Aswat, a gay women's empowerment group.[10]

Safa Tamish is the intense and lively director of Muntada, a community-based feminist group founded in 2000 that is devoted to working on sexuality and sexual rights for Palestinians in Israel. This started as a project within an Israeli family-planning organization, but became independent due to the complex intersections of sexuality, national identity, cultural sensitivity, occupation, and the consequent spoken and unspoken dynamics of power.

I suspect that most readers share the Western view of Palestinian/Arab culture: that it is repressive and patriarchal, women are characteristically dominated by their fathers and husbands, and sexual issues, let alone queer issues, are off the agenda. We learn quickly from the women that the culture is far from monolithic and that there is a tremendous amount of nuance and complexity that needs to be understood. Safa has a huge dose of chutzpah and creative energy. She describes going into different settings, often starting her efforts with student councils, working on projects based on listening and respect for the local community, learning from each other. Once there is obvious mutual respect, then much is possible.

Working in a conservative Bedouin community, she understood the challenges that every mother faces when she has to explain the basics to her child and answer the typical questions about sex, birth, etc. Using nonthreatening interactive training, with techniques such as role-playing, she never encountered opposition, despite working in villages that were traditional and patriarchal. She believes in community empowerment, done respectfully and quietly. In the course of her work with girls in tenth to twelfth grade, she found that almost 90 percent of the tenth-grade girls were engaged, and by twelfth grade, many were married. But after completing Safa's program, none of the girls married while they were attending school.

By 2006, as the projects and political pressure grew, Muntada was able to become an independent Arab association. Safa found that Zionist funders had no interest in Arab-led projects, and Arab funders had no interest in working with Israelis. Additionally, the organization's original name was associated with family planning and by implication, control of the supposed population crisis created by Palestinians. Due to all the talk about the "demographic threat" from "procreating Palestinians," the name became political poison. Women needing contraception could also readily obtain them through the Israeli national health service and did not need a separate agency.

As an independent organization with twenty-eight volunteers, Muntada also wants to work with and serve the needs of Palestinians in the West Bank and Arab world as well as in Israel with a focus on sexuality and reproductive health. Their initial funding came in 2007 from the Global Fund for Women, and later from other internationals, the European Union, Oxfam, local ministries for social welfare, and the Ministry of Education. They are concentrating on community interventions and empowerment, professional training, and the development of educational guides and social media grounded in a human rights framework.

They are now developing culturally sensitive school programs, having abandoned the Western models, which are sometimes useful but culturally tone deaf. So how does this work in the real world? Safa told us that it is often tough. Men are often gender-insensitive; they need to be challenged without being imposed upon. The tolerance of the women gets tested, which then challenges the men.

Last year, there was a two-day training on sexuality in Nablus in the West Bank. All the men sat on one side, all the women on the other; two women were completely covered and two men were *sheikhs* with long beards. They stated that Sharia law had all the answers and felt that this project was being funded by the West, with a Western agenda. Safa thanked them for their comments and began the program unintimidated. The next day they were role-playing and she asked the *sheikh* to explain to his daughter, "What is masturbation?" When he refused, she explained, "But she is your daughter. Do you want her to learn this from the internet?" He replied, "No," blushed, and then finally did the role-play. Others in the program reported that this experience has created dramatic changes in the school and the *sheikh* is now recommending the program to everyone!

She tells us another story, her face lively and expressive. The group wanted to teach a lesson about puberty to seventh graders. First they got the permission of the principal, then invested in training the teachers and obtaining credits from the Ministry of Education. After the training, they evaluated the program and found that little had changed. So they developed a questionnaire for the students, asking them what topics were of interest and who and what were their resources. The sixth and seventh graders asked questions about oral sex, anal sex, contraception, and pornography! The next step was to develop a letter for parents explaining the need for a revised program. When the outraged parents objected to the program's sexually explicit content, Safa presented them with the results of the children's questionnaire.

When she asked the teachers to identify the most useful outcome of this work, one reported that she had been teaching the poetry of love in an intellectual way, but now she began talking more comfortably. During these discussions she discovered that one of her fifteen-year-old girls was involved in a "casual marriage," an arrangement with an older man, and many girls were having sex with taxi drivers. The teacher was really able to talk about love and relationships and felt she had reclaimed her educational role as a teacher in this course. She also reported that she was now hugging her husband in front of her children and that the family was much less cold and more physically intimate.

Last year, Muntada created a youth program for sixteen- to nineteen-year-olds that treats sexual rights as human rights. The students made films on topics that included premarital sex, and wanted to have a big public ceremony marking the films' releases. Safa admits she was terrified at the community response, but the films opened in the cinema in Nazareth in front of more than two thousand people. The audience responded positively, and one parent told her, "I am so proud you." Their website is growing and includes professionals such as sex therapists and gynecologists answering questions, and Arabic translations of scientific articles. It received 370,000 hits last year, the majority of which were from Saudi Arabia.

Safa has started similar work in the West Bank, where Muntada has just graduated their third class from its program, despite the cultural and social challenges. She finds that West Bankers were once open-minded but have become increasingly conservative. The youth have lost their ability to dream; not only are they physically occupied, but their minds are occupied as well. There is a sense of internalized defeat. Safa does not believe in partial liberation. She sees personal and national liberation as equally necessary. She notes that, during the Arab Spring, the young people who demonstrated in Ramallah also demanded personal and national liberation. Sexual liberation, she explains, is intimately tied to fighting checkpoints, apartheid laws, and repressive family reunification prohibitions.

"Sexual liberation is part of our national liberation. It has to be in parallel. My struggle is to contribute to the building of the civil society in Palestine, and part of that building is working on sexual rights."[11]

Things are even more challenging for the Lesbian/Gay/Bisexual/Transgender community. A woman I will call Suhair (she asked that I use a pseudonym as she is not fully "out" to her own family and work colleagues) explains that her group, Aswat (which means "Voices" in Arabic), is a feminist social change organization of gay Palestinian women that is also part of the overall political struggle. The group was started in 2003 by eight women, all activists in Israeli LGBTQ and other progressive organizations, to create safe and empowering spaces to engage in the personal, social, and political struggles the women faced as "a national indigenous minority living inside Israel; as women in a patriarchal society; and as LBTQI [lesbian, bisexual, transgender, questioning, queer, and intersex] women in a wider hetro-normative culture."[12] At first they had been welcomed in Israeli organizations but had to keep their national identity closeted. They found that the vast majority of LGBTQ groups do not support Palestinian rights and actively promote "pink-washing," the use of gay-tolerant tourism, gay pride events, sexy ads in US magazines, etc., to portray Israeli culture as superior to Palestinian culture, and in a way that ignored the conflicts around homosexuality within Israeli society. The women did not feel they could prioritize their rights, so they created a discourse that combines resistance to all oppression, including occupation and homophobia. At the same time, while Palestinian queer women are not unique in the challenges they face, they cannot begin to think of sexual freedom without the right to be free from occupation.

Suhair shares her own personal story as a teenager, when she was questioning her sexuality, without any venues, Arabic sources, supports—whether in school, at home, or with friends. She discovered a phone support group in Tel Aviv called White Line, but their only suggestion was to get out of Haifa and come to Tel Aviv. She finished high school, got into Tel Aviv University, and had "the best time in my life" out of the closet, but still felt she was the only lesbian Palestinian in the world. She had many Jewish friends, but then something weird happened. When she was invited to parties, friends told her she didn't look Palestinian and suggested she change her name to "sound Israeli." (She is "Israeli," just not the right kind of Israeli.) She tried to be cool, but was choking inside. Her friends reassured her they just wanted her to have a good time, no hassles. One day, she packed up her stuff and went home to her more conservative family and culture. "Gay haven Tel Aviv is not a gay haven for Palestinians," she explains. "The soldier at checkpoint does not care if I am gay or straight."

Suhair notes that Palestinian society has been living at the margins of marginality for decades, and she feels that acutely as a high school teacher. The total investment in education for Palestinian students is one-third that of their Jewish counterparts, from ages three to eighteen. The budgetary discrimination affects the level of kids' exposure to sexual education, the availability of manuals, directories, and websites written in Arabic, and the number of opportunities available to the educators and the educated. The lack of support within the educational system for LGBTQ Palestinians is further complicated by a segregated school system and a generally conservative society that does not easily tolerate nontraditional relationships.

A woman I will call Layla (also not fully "out"), another member of Aswat, agrees that Palestinian society is far from monolithic, but that it is difficult to be a lesbian in a Palestinian organization, or a Palestinian in a Jewish Israeli gay organization. She had always felt a need to hide one of her identities until she found Aswat. She tells me about the complexities of the Palestinian community, the wounds of homophobia and realities of occupation that are embedded in her mind, the lack of modern writings on homosexuality, the fact that sexual freedom is only possible with economic freedom. She works with women to write and publish their personal stories, to join with intellectuals and other feminist organizations like Muntada to support each other in solidarity and sisterhood. There are also joint efforts being carried out through the Boycott, Divestment, and Sanctions campaign, Palestinian Queers for BDS, alQaws, and the promotion of the rights of queer Palestinians by the BDS movement.

As the three women talk, we learn that among Palestinians, their language is being transformed into a shallow mix of Arabic, Hebrew, and English that they see as the consequence of settler colonialism and occupation. In this form of Arabic, most women have no name for their genitals, that vague "down there" place that is unnamed, untouchable. "Everything starts with words," Safa exclaims. "In Arabic literature there are 990 names for the genitals, each animal has a different name for its genitals. Poets in the ninth century wrote about homosexuality and bisexuality and it was acceptable."

They also reflect on issues related to men who are part of their work. In a male-dominated society, to believe in your partner's rights requires a willingness to give up some of your own privilege; not all men are ready to do that. But male privilege for Palestinians is extremely complex, for they too lack privilege; they suffer from economic discrimination and humiliation, much like marginalized men of color in the United States. Thus the conversation quickly comes to encompass issues that include gender, race, and class. This provocative discussion ends with a comment from one of our Black women delegates about the need to build a more just society: "But it is not your responsibility to build that in a dominant culture. It is my burden as a Black woman to educate my oppressors, but white men need to hold white men accountable." In Israel/Palestine, where Palestinian men are far from the dominant culture, the rude reality of second-class citizenship and occupation makes that struggle incredibly more difficult.

The Logic of Israeli Citizenship and Nationality: Down the Rabbit Hole Again

June 19, 2013

The Al Mutran Guesthouse in Nazareth is a charming old Arabic home transformed into a simple but elegant guesthouse with open patios, pink geraniums, and embroidered wall hangings. We are here to talk with journalist and author Jonathan Cook, who arrives filled with energy and a wealth of knowledge about history and politics. Originally from the United Kingdom and now an Israeli citizen, he is married to a spunky Palestinian woman with Israeli citizenship. (When she hears someone describe her Israeli identity, she firmly stresses, "No, I am '48 Palestinian.") He explains that he works as a journalist so his children who are Israeli Arabs will not have to live as second-class citizens.

Jonathan notes that discrimination inside Israel is not informal; it's systematic and institutionalized with practical implications that are obvious today. This is dramatically evident in Nazareth, a unique Palestinian city, the only one inside of Israel that is not "mixed." As we have learned, Acre (Akko), Haifa, Jaffa, and Lod (Lyd or Lydda)[13] are Jewish cities with Palestinian ghettos. They also have Palestinian citizens who are primarily not native to the city—i.e., many in Lod are Bedouins brought in to build Tel Aviv after the '48 expulsion.

As we settle in, sipping tiny cups of sweet, bitter coffee, Jonathan starts by reviewing the history of the area. In 1948, Nazareth was the only Palestinian city with the potential to become the Palestinian capital inside of Israel, and thus it represented a huge threat to the Jewish establishment. After the war, approximately two hundred Palestinian villages remained, but Nazareth was the only city standing. The villages survived sometimes because they were Christian, and Israeli leaders were concerned about their international reputations, and some had work relationships with the local *kibbutzim* and *moshavim*.

The 1965 Planning and Building Law identified 124 Palestinian communities, leaving 80 unrecognized villages where all housing was declared illegal and no services, electricity, or roads were provided. These harsh conditions were the reality for 10 percent of Palestinians with Israeli citizenship. Jonathan notes that Nazareth is different and enjoys privileges that the state has been unable to eradicate, largely due to the important Christian churches. There are three hospitals founded by religious orders, so there are qualified medical personnel and a supportive middle class. There are a dozen high-quality private schools also founded by religious orders, so Arabic children can be well educated and then they become the doctors and the lawyers that maintain the middle class. The segregated public Arab schools in Israel are so underfunded that the average Jewish student receives four to twelve times more funding. The state controls the curriculum, which is so narrowly Zionist that there is no chance for a foundation in Palestinian identity, culture, history, international literature, or ancient Islamic poetry. The children in Nazareth are spared that intellectual and emotional death.

Jonathan discusses a host of other laws that mirror the Israeli behavior that later occurred in the occupied territories after '67. In Nazareth, Israeli citizens lived under a military government for eighteen years, they needed permits to travel, and there was a network of collaborators that provided the eyes and ears of the Shin Bet, the Israeli General Security Services. Once a person became a collaborator, often out of fear, then the family and children became involved as well. With the Fallow Lands Law, if land is not attended for three years, the state seizes the land; thus Palestinians were also incentivized to become collaborators to protect their own lands. In the public schools, both teachers and students were informers, producing "a reign of terror" in the classroom.

Jonathan had a friend teaching English in a nearby village; one pupil asked, "What is the PLO [Palestine Liberation Organization]?" This was a dangerous question, so she answered in a neutral manner. The next morning, she received a call from the Shin Bet, who had evidence of the interaction, and she lost her job. This also can happen if someone goes to a demonstration or a march. This degradation of self-esteem and respect erodes any sense of pride in the education system. The head teacher may be the biggest collaborator in the school. Since the majority of Christian and Muslim children attend the dozen private schools in Nazareth, they are spared this humiliation and leave with a solid education.

It is also intriguing that Nazareth should be a major tourist city (remember the Angel Gabriel and the Immaculate Conception?), with graceful churches and a charming Old City. But any significant benefits for the Palestinians were thwarted through the mechanics of Israeli tourism (read: Jewish tourism). The authorities created tourism zones and nearby Tiberias became an approved enterprise Zone A, with big tax breaks for building fancy hotels, which were then not built in Nazareth where the real tourist attractions are actually located. This also means that the profits, even those from Christian tourism, go mainly to the Jewish tourism industry, so people stop at the local *kibbutz*, swing through the Basilica of the Annunciation, and then spend their tourist shekels in Tiberias.

This arrangement only changed in the 1990s when the Pope decided to visit; Nazareth was spiffed up, but not without producing resentments and conflicts between Christians and Muslims manipulated by the Israeli government, the Pope, George Bush, and Ariel Sharon. Then the Intifada broke out and the once-aspirational Renaissance Hotel was converted into a prison. This was also a useful temporary prison for the foreign workers imported during the Intifada to replace the banned Palestinians. These folks married Israelis, and when they got deported, they needed a temporary place to stay as well. Only recently has there been a rejuvenation of tourism in the Old City, for visitors and the growing middle class, but it continues to be fraught with legal barriers. The old *souk* is mostly filled with cheap products from China and Taiwan, and it is still recovering from being shut down for three years for renovation. A temporary market was set up in adjacent Nazareth Illit and is now a permanent and competitive fixture for that town.

For me, the most eye-opening part of Jonathan's comments revolve around the issues of citizenship. The Law of Return states than any Jew from Brooklyn to Mumbai can become an Israeli citizen because they are Jewish. Jonathan became a naturalized citizen because he wanted protection from expulsion or deportation, and he did not want to wait for the impending loyalty oath requirement. His wife, Sally, is an Israeli citizen because she is a Palestinian whose family stayed within the '48 borders, and in 1952 the citizenship law declared such people citizens. When they got married, it took Jonathan eight years and a host of legal threats to obtain citizenship.

In Israel, there is a difference between citizenship and nationality. Everybody here is a citizen, but there are 137 (!) nationalities per the classifications of the interior ministry. The courts refuse to recognize an Israeli nationality, but there is a Jewish nationality. Why is this? If there were an Israeli nationality, then this would be a state of citizens who are all recognized equally, and Jewish exceptionalism would disappear. By maintaining the different nationalities along with citizenship, Jews can continue to have rights that are not granted to other citizens. To add to the craziness, Israeli nationality is listed on Israeli passports, but that is only for the benefit of the border guards. The blue Israeli ID card is also secretly coded: if you are Jewish, your birth date is written using the Hebrew calendar; if you follow Jesus or Mohammed, the date is in the Gregorian calendar.

So by the state's standards, who exactly is a Jew? Under the Law of Return, a person is recognized as a Jew if one grandparent is Jewish. Jonathan notes that perversely, this is the same criterion the Nazis used. But Jewishness, as defined by the Orthodox rabbis, requires the presence of a Jewish mother. Because this contradiction existed, many "Jews" arrived claiming to be Jewish, but then were not recognized by the rabbis who control Israeli Personal Law. This led to an explosive crisis in the 1990s, when one million Russians arrived on Israeli shores. Perhaps the husband was Jewish à la the "Jewish mother" definition, but his Christian wife and four children were not. Suddenly the state was faced with a family of one new Jew and four non-Jews. This caused major social problems, which continue today; it is currently estimated that more than 350,000 "Jews" from the Soviet Union are actually not really Jewish—they are called "grey Jews."

Who is a Jew is critical because, for example, the non-Jewish (or sort of Jewish) children cannot marry as Jews in Israel, owing to the rule that all Jewish marriages are *only* done by Orthodox rabbis and the fact that civil marriage is not an option. (Consequently, some people have settled for having a quick wedding in Cyprus.) So there was a big fight regarding those who weren't definitively Jewish and what nationality to put on their Israeli ID cards. The court decided that a row of asterisks was a good solution. Consequently, when the Ethiopian Jews who were "rescued" and airlifted "home" were not considered Jewish enough by the Israeli rabbinate, they had to (re)convert to Judaism. This is a challenging process that includes sending one's children to religious schools, where they will study Torah but skip science, literature, multiculturalism, evolution, and other twenty-first-century topics.

Jonathan reminds us that this is really different than, let's say, Britain, which is a Christian state but also a state of citizens with equal rights under the law. In Israel, there is no symbolism to the "Jewish" in Jewish state. In the 1990s, post-Oslo, the popular solutions to this dilemma were all about separation, and the logical outcome was the building of the wall and an ever more constrictive permitting system that made it increasingly difficult to marry across the Green Line. Palestinians have struggled to obtain citizenship when marrying partners in Israel and have faced a judicial maze, endless delays, and changing laws that ultimately have functionally outlawed marriage between lovely Israeli Juliets and their West Bank Romeos on the grounds of "security," a reason in Israel second only to God, and to stop the right of return "through the back door." This has to be understood through the mindset of the ever-present threat to the "Jewishness" of the Jewish state and the perception that Palestinians are not just fellow human beings trying to follow their hearts and minds, but actually conniving Trojan horses, ready to set off the demographic time bomb. So remember that "Jewish" has been designated a nationality to make sure that state resources stay in the hands of the Jewish population, and the system is designed in mind-boggling detail to keep it that way.

We set off for a tour of Nazareth and Nazareth Illit. Walking briskly alongside Jonathan's wiry frame, we learn more about the fifty-seven laws that overtly discriminate against Palestinians. He reminds us that nationality always trumps citizenship, and the discrimination against non-Jews is so entrenched that it is invisible to most of the folks who love Israel as a symbol of Jewish redemption and justice.

He cites a host of examples:

1. Immigration: Jews can come anytime; Palestinians are totally unwelcome in an endless variety of ways.

2. Water: Water is a core right, but its allocation and cost are related to the nationality of the recipient. Palestinians in Area C are not entitled to water because they are not citizens of Israel, while Moishe, watering his lawn in the settlement next door, gets lots of water because he is a citizen. Palestinians in general pay much more for water. Water is subsidized by the state if it is used for agricultural or farming practices as in *kibbutizim* or *moshavim*, which by definition are only for Jews. At some point that changed, I think in response to Land Day, the commemoration of March 30, 1976, when thousands of Palestinians with Israeli citizenship protested the expropriation of their land in the Galilee; six were killed and thousands injured and jailed. Since then, Palestinians have been allowed to keep some of their farmland but not allocated any agricultural water, so they are forced to grow olive trees, which are highly drought-resistant. If they do not farm for three years, then the land is officially "fallow" and seized by the state.

3. Land: 93 percent of the land in Israel is nationalized for Jewish use only and controlled by the Israel Land Authority (which oversees 80 percent) and the Jewish National Fund (13 percent). If a Jew "buys" land, it is actually a ninety-nine-year lease that can be passed on to future generations. The family is the "guardian" of the Jewish land. Palestinians can't do this, obviously.

Jonathan argues that in Israel, nationality is really what the rest of us think of as citizenship, and citizenship is really more like residency. Nationality is the only thing that really counts, and Jews from Beijing to Buenos Aires are all potential members of this nation-state. Everyone else is treated more like (temporary) residents who just happen to be passing through and hopefully will leave real soon.

There was a recent report on higher education that found fourteen obstacles designed to prevent Palestinians from reaching that educational level. Jonathan talks about the current state of political parties, and comments that there is basically a Revisionist, Jabotinsky/Netanyahu type of politics that operates in a more colonial mode, with plans to beat the Palestinians into submission and then give them minimum rights. He feels that the Labor Party and its allies are actually more racist. They openly admit Palestinians will never settle for this life of discrimination; they want equality, so they must be separated and walled in. This brings us to the next phase of our day with Jonathan, a fascinating tour of Nazareth Illit, whose name means "upper" (i.e., up the hill) and "morally superior," which can be further translated as "Jewish only."

The Law of Unintended Consequences
June 19, 2013

Dripping with sweat from the penetrating sun, we board our bus with Jonathan Cook and begin the winding uphill drive to Nazareth Illit. We are greeted by enormous Israeli flags flapping listlessly in the inadequate breeze, as a brilliant view of the region opens before us. The Plaza Hotel, built to draw tourists and their shekels away from Nazareth, dominates part of the landscape. We stop at a lookout and can see Nazareth crowding up the opposite mountain slope and the valley below.

Jonathan begins his overview: Nazareth Illit was built as a development town, but today the old housing is "grotty" and a bit dilapidated. We can clearly see the modern "ring road" that separates Nazareth Illit from the dangerous Arabs below. The Judaization of this area is now shrewdly called "the development of the Galilee." The Ministry of Development sends 99.8 percent of its shekels to the Jewish community.

Per the usual patterns, the land was taken for "national purposes," and in 1956, with the Supreme Court's backing of this plan, rows of chunky concrete houses were built. Military documents clearly show that the goal of building this city was to swallow up the graceful and historic city of Nazareth and make Nazareth Illit the center of activity, turning Nazareth into a ghetto much like Lod. But Nazareth had capacities that gave it unusual resilience. Currently, Nazareth has a population of eighty thousand and remains a cultural center, while Nazareth Illit functions more like a settlement, with a population of fifty thousand.

Nonetheless, the same old strategy—break up, dominate, and fragment the Palestinian communities—is active in this region as well, so in spite of Nazareth's strength and resilience, the presence of Nazareth Illit has made it impossible for the surrounding Palestinian villages to join together to form a more powerful political force. The Israelis also moved the district court and administrative services from Nazareth up the hill, thus redirecting funds to the Jewish side of town. A bypass road was built to separate the two communities, after which the aforementioned "ring road" around the governmental buildings was also built, the land on which it runs later "annexed" to Nazareth Illit. In addition, the army maintains a large base in Nazareth (its land also annexed to Nazareth Illit), which Jonathan states is illegal, and there are other surveillance towers and, of course, the police headquarters.

In keeping with these obviously racist plans, Nazareth Illit was given resources to develop a major industrial center, including the well-known Elite chocolate factory (in 2004 the company joined Strauss-Elite and is now just Strauss) and other industries located near the Zipporia area, that land also annexed to Nazareth Illit. The annexing of land for large industrial companies, which are often heavily subsidized by the state and owned by Jewish corporations, contributes to the ongoing dispossession and impoverishment of Palestinians.

The 1965 Planning and Building Law, still binding today, forbids new Palestinian construction in Israel, despite the fact that since the law was passed, the Palestinian population has grown five to six times in size. In fact, a "blue line" was drawn around every city in Israel outlining the limits of future development in such a way that the line around Palestinian villages/cities hugged its demarcated boundaries while the Jewish communities were given generous space to grow. Furthermore, because Palestinians in Nazareth are only allowed to build up to four stories, they have nowhere to expand and thus are forced to illegally build beyond the "blue line." As a consequence of the constant surveillance described above and the vigilance of the Jewish "lookout" communities built in the Galilee that monitor Palestinian construction, forty thousand homes in the area live under demolition orders (remember, these are Israeli citizens). In order not to attract an international outcry, only about five hundred demolitions (which constitutes five hundred traumatized dispossessed families suffering a type of posttraumatic stress disorder that we can't imagine) occur per year, but the threat is always there. The remaining homes pay an annual penalty, amounting to an extra tax that only postpones the demolition.

The problem with the Israeli plan is that Nazareth Illit, as Jonathan admits, is not that nice a place to live. The mayor, Shimon Gapso, has called Nazareth "a nest of terror," so that might not be a selling point for the new neighbors. Starting in the late 1950s and increasing with Soviet immigration in the early 1990s, new immigrants were sent to Nazareth Illit, arriving at the Morganthau Reabsorption Center, and then were moved into permanent housing. But now that there are no new immigrants and the old ones are more economically stable and ready to leave, who will buy their houses in such an undesirable place? For the past ten years, middle-class Palestinians in Nazareth desperate for housing have been purchasing these houses, so today between one-fifth and one-quarter of the population in Nazareth Illit is Palestinian! This is possible because this city is not a cooperative town, which means there is no admissions committee to turn the new neighbors down on the grounds of being "socially unacceptable." There was no competition from Jewish families, and even though no one wanted to sell to Palestinians, in a free market system, money ultimately talks.

The mayor, at this point in a frustrated rage, hung along the road enormous Israeli flags serving as giant "Keep Out" signs. *Haaretz* also reported that he sought the advice of a rabbi from Hebron to develop a strategy to stop these trends. First, the rabbi of Nazareth Illit set up a yeshiva for the national religious camp, so there are now fifty armed, religious fundamentalist Jewish men living in Nazareth Illit. Then the mayor began building a new neighborhood with schools and synagogues and call centers for women to work in, specifically the ultra-Orthodox Haredim, who shun modern, secular culture, often support their husbands who study Torah, and typically have eight to ten children; as a result of this plan, the population is expected to jump by thirty thousand. All of these folks tend to be very aggressive, and there are now reports of shops destroyed and vicious assaults on Palestinians, including beatings and acid-throwing attacks. I might add that these crazies are also endangering secular Jews, who also resent being stoned. Thus the mayor has effectively stopped Palestinian migration into his city. But at this point, who will buy a once Jewish, now Palestinian home? What will happen to them? Secular Jews do not want to live here, and the ultra-Orthodox will not live in integrated neighborhoods. So much for the myth of the liberal Israeli democracy.

We Are the Stones

June 19, 2013

Jonathan Cook is not yet done. We are on an unconventional tour of Nazareth and we soon find ourselves listening to Abu Arab, a dignified seventy-eight-year-old man who is part of the Saffuriya Center for Cultural

Heritage. Standing in a large room in an otherwise nondescript apartment building, we see rows of relics, clay pots of all sizes, cooking and farming implements, faded dresses.

In 1948, Saffuriya was a thriving village of 7,000 people, two schools, three mosques, one church, olive presses, around 120,000 dunams[14] of agricultural land, generous amounts of water, and a vigorous community of people with prolific crops and animals. On the sixteenth night of Ramadan, the Zionist forces attacked, and 80 percent of the village fled in a haze of terror and bullets. The next day the surrounding villages were occupied. Abu Arab's family fled and kept walking until they reached Lebanon; picture the frightened children, the hunger, the thirst, the blistered feet, the total loss and fear.

The eight hundred people who remained were counted and received Israeli ID cards. They were told to collect all their remaining furniture and possessions and load them into trucks that drove away with their belongings. After eight months they were instructed to gather and were given twenty-four hours to leave or be killed. Those who refused to leave were forcibly evacuated by Jewish soldiers. The group took their case to the Israeli Supreme Court, claiming citizenship rights related to their possession of Israeli ID cards. They had IDs denoting place of birth (Saffuriya), place of residence (Saffuriya), occupation (farmer). Over the course of five months, eighty villagers were killed, shot while collecting food for their families. The court canceled the hearing, relying only on the testimony of the Israeli military, and the town was declared a closed military zone for the next eighteen years. Some ten Jewish settlements and moshavim were built on the bulldozed site.

At this point in Abu Arab's story, our translator, Hind, is having increasing difficulties; the tears are starting to flow, and as I look into the faces of our delegates, those who have come from Palestine are quietly weeping as well. We are all feeling a tremendous sadness as Abu Arab's words sink in. He keeps placing his hands over his heart, and I wonder if that is where he stores his all-too-painful memories.

His family stayed in a Lebanese village, and after three months, his sister Hazal became ill and died. The whole family was traumatized and his mother stopped functioning, spending her days at her daughter's grave. After ten months, his father talked with his three sons and said they have to leave for Beirut or Palestine, or their mother will go crazy. They chose Palestine.

They walked toward the border for two nights and one day, reaching an Israeli village where they stayed for six months until they could get Israeli ID cards. I can hear the outrage in Abu Arab's voice when he comments on

Theodore Herzl's famous quote, "A land without a people . . ." We are here bearing somber witness to that lie.

Like many Saffuriyans, Abu Arab's family moved to Nazareth. In 1978, there was an Israeli assault on one of the five cemeteries in Saffuriya, and many dunams were destroyed. After a long battle and negotiation, the town's members and descendants obtained the right to fence in and maintain their historic cemetery. After Oslo, Saffuriyans joined the Organization for Displaced Villages, following the path of many former inhabitants of destroyed villages. Today, they are demanding their right to return to their village and to live in their homes as citizens of the country.

Abu Arab's face is brown and wrinkled with a thick head of greying hair. A pack of cigarettes sits in the pocket of his neatly pressed white shirt. In a calm, determined voice he explains that real peace depends on the Zionist recognition of their crimes against Palestinians. The victims need to be compensated, and refugees inside and outside the country need to have their right of return respected and realized. Because recognition of the Nakba, compensation, and right of return have been eliminated from the international conversation, "the Zionist mentality has the seeds of its termination . . ." Peace will come, "if not for us, then our children or our grandchildren." He explains that he is against Zionists, not Jews, and that he remembers a time when Jews and Palestinians lived together peacefully. He admits that thirty Jewish families now live in the village. "They do not have to leave; we want to live with them."

For forty-five years, Abu Arab has had a small shop in old Nazareth, and thirty years ago he noticed that people were throwing away things that he felt ought to be saved. He started gathering artifacts and helped start this cultural heritage museum in which we stand so that his people will remember the villages they came from. He reminds us of the famous quote in reference to Palestinians: "The old will die and the young will forget." But he questions the truth of those words, assuring us that if Jews can remember something for two thousand years, surely Palestinians can remember for sixty-five. Abu Arab is strongly against violent resistance. "We are against war and the shedding of any blood." He warns that the Israeli dependence on power and war is not sustainable. "Many regimes have fallen . . . nothing remains in a valley except the stones. We are the stones."

Jonathan takes us past a *moshav* that is mostly Bulgarian and Romanian to the site of the old Saffuriya. One house remains in the distance, converted into a guesthouse, and there is a working orphanage. We see a forest planted by the Jewish National Fund, but the area is a fenced-off closed military zone. I feel like we are walking in a ghost town: piles of hewn stones, disappeared houses and schools, voluptuous, towering *saber* cactus, an old church without a roof, a buried reality for a people that refuses to forget.

Balata: The Occupation of Body and Mind
June 20, 2013

Visiting and staying overnight at the Balata Refugee Camp in the Yafa Cultural Center guesthouse is always a sobering reality check, and every year the camp feels more desperate. Mahmoud, the forty-seven-year-old head of the health unit at the camp, says nothing that changes my mind.

Balata is a mirror of all the other camps where generations of refugees have waited and fought and survived for decades. It was established in the early 1950s by the United Nations after the refugees, then estimated at 830,000, had lived without official support for two years all over the West Bank and surrounding Arab countries—in caves, in the mountains, churches, schools, and mosques.

We see a photo from 1953 capturing a clearly temporary arrangement: rows of tents with a stately camel standing in front. After five years, the UN Relief and Works Agency (UNRWA) started building small units, three by three meters for each family. Imagine a mother from a middle-class family from Jaffa, torn from all that she knows, trying to deal with her many, many children, a humiliated and unemployed husband, minimal resources, food handouts, poor sanitation, and a massive amount of trauma in the recent past. And then crowd everyone together in a totally inhumane situation. That is the history of Balata.

By the mid-1960s (this mother in our scenario now has been struggling for more than a decade), an infrastructure began to develop, a sewer system evolved, but horizontal expansion reached its limits and families started building vertically.

Mahmoud's grandfather was born in Haifa and came to the camp when his son was around ten years old. He had owned a successful restaurant and guesthouse, but fled when the bombing started, made an unsuccessful attempt to return for his belongings, then fled again with his family to Jenin, then Nablus, living in the mountains until he arrived at Balata. This proud, wealthy businessman lost everything and was now totally dependent on UNRWA.

Mahmoud's mother was born in August 1948. Her family, including Mahmoud's very pregnant grandmother, walked from the area near Lod to a cave in Rafidia, where she was born. After a year living in the cave, the family moved to Balata Refugee Camp, where his grandfather sold vegetables. Mahmoud's parents met in the camp and had seven children living in a sixty-square-meter house with family and grandparents. Because of the desperate living conditions, many of the refugees have left for Jordan, other cities in the Middle East, the Gulf, Europe, and the United States.

According to UN statistics, everyone in the camp is officially registered as a refugee and by the end of 2012, some twenty-nine thousand people were crowded together; each house is impossibly small, containing three to four generations, no privacy and no space. The houses are all attached to each other; Mahmoud comments, "Privacy is nonexistent, don't even know what it means, everybody is in everybody's business." Most houses are dark and humid, and there is mold and other health hazards. This creates much social stress, disputes, and psychological problems.

Not surprisingly, Balata became the political leader of refugee camps and has a long history of uprisings, demonstrations, and encounters with the Israeli Defense Forces. Reportedly, the First Intifada started here, and the first martyr was from Balata. During the Second Intifada, there were large numbers of militants and guns and a high level of violence within and against the camp, and almost every adult male resident of Balata has been in Israeli prisons.

The camp was largely a working-class area before 2000; 60 percent of the men worked in Israel. After 2000 and the start of the Second Intifada, the camp was totally shut down, surrounded by barbed wire, all entrances closed. Soldiers were everywhere and curfews, set for a period between one and one hundred days, were common. We became "a gated community," Mahmoud remarks ironically. In 2002, every three days the curfew was lifted for a few hours so that families could get food, the UN could bring in supplies, and the sick could get medical care. The children did not attend school and the educational system was destroyed. Workers were unemployed, snipers everywhere, and the foreboding construction of the separation wall began. Work and travel permits were virtually impossible. "We were guilty until proven innocent," says Mahmoud.

By 2006, things started to calm down, with the Palestinian Authority (PA) restoring some security, but it became clear they were protecting the Israeli settlers more than the local Palestinians. Settlements expanded, and the restrictions on the movement of Palestinians became tighter. The camp is clearly a pressure cooker waiting to explode; as the economic and living situations get worse and worse, there is more corruption, poverty, and unemployment. There is no functional economy, and the Israelis control the granting of official documents such as birth certificates, business licenses, and export licenses. While income has remained stable since 2004, prices have increased five to six times. In 2004, one kilo of bread cost one shekel; now it is four shekels. Businesses are shutting down.

More recently, laborers have been able to get work permits into Israel, but they represent only a meager fraction of all applications; never more than 10 percent requested are granted. Five to 10 percent of the workers still sneak into Israel illegally, a small segment compared to those employed by the PA, which hires 25 to 30 percent of Palestinian workers, and the private sector, which employs 10 to 15 percent. Unemployment in Balata, however, is currently 46 percent and higher for people under twenty-nine.

There are three UNRWA schools covering first to ninth grade, with a total enrollment of six thousand children ages six to fifteen. After ninth grade, students go outside the camp for public education. The classes are overcrowded, underfunded, and inadequate to meet the needs of the students. The enormous numbers of young people is a serious problem; there is no space in the camp, no playgrounds; they "can't breathe." The children born in the First Intifada were the fighters in the Second Intifada and have known no other life. They have witnessed or experienced more arrests, killings, bombings, suicide bombings, and social problems than we can possibly imagine.

Mahmoud then focuses on Palestinians in general in the West Bank. He notes that among the educated, unemployment is 56 percent. "I have 252,000 young people in Palestinian universities. When they graduate, how many will get a job?" They rarely can travel, and there is no functional economy. He talks about Area C, where the PA had plans to build a new city. There were blueprints, money was raised, engineers were ready, and on the day the project was due to start, the IDF declared the area a closed military zone. Mahmoud shares another frustrating fact: although the city of Jericho is in area A, it is surrounded by area C and a closed military zone. A large part of Jericho is very fertile with dates and palm trees. Two thousand Palestinian families lived there, but the Israelis seized their land, leaving 5 percent to the Palestinians. "What kind of businesses can you create here?" Mahmoud asked.

"In the past, the Gulf was our Mecca, but after the first Gulf War, they kicked us out of Kuwait," he continued. Cut off from that source of income and opportunity from "my Gulf brothers," as Mahmoud calls them, obtaining passports and traveling have become more challenging. So Palestinians feel increasingly cornered by Israelis and Arabs. "What will happen? They becoming suicidal, very violent." This is the first time I have heard of suicide in Palestinian society except for the rare suicide bomber, but now suicide is becoming more common.

Mahmoud runs a program providing psychosocial support; their biggest target is the youth, particularly in the boys' school, between fifth and ninth grade. I can hear the anger and frustration in his voice when he explains that the schools are awful and are beset by high levels of violence, low levels of education, and a 50 percent illiteracy rate. School means nothing; the students have nothing to look forward to, there are problems at home and in the street. There are increasing difficulties with all kinds of drug abuse and more children taking their own lives. He tells us a chilling story of a child who tried to enter an Israeli settlement, unarmed. "Why? Suicide is forbidden in Islam, but if killed, then becomes a martyr. If not killed, then he goes to prison, is fed, smoking, hanging with friends. This happens daily, because there is no solution, no future." Another chilling story: two nights ago, the Israelis arrested four young people; arrests like this happen twice a week. "But nobody is doing anything and nobody is even paying attention. Why are they getting arrested?" All four students were about to take their high-stakes high school diploma exam; their lives are now effectively destroyed.

Mahmoud's program is based in the school and provides psychosocial support and individual and family counseling. In each school there is one counselor for two thousand children. They provide lots of activities—music therapy, psychodrama, literacy. He finds the illiterate are the troublemakers, but "they are lost," often getting up early to work in the vegetable market to support their mothers before coming to an increasingly irrelevant school. Most violent kids are sons of martyrs; now these children beat their parents. They have experienced the humiliation of their parents at checkpoints and nighttime arrests where the whole family is terrorized and beaten, the father and mother shamed in front of their children. The Israeli forces have effectively attacked the psyches and sanity of Palestinian children, and destroyed the functions and authority of previously healthy families.

Mahmoud explains that in the past, they did not have those problems; respect for his parents was absolute. He got out of Balata through education, a degree from Birzeit University. "There is no other inheritance." He has three sisters and three brothers, all well-educated professionals: a nurse, a lawyer, a marketer, a hospital director, an adviser to PA prime minister Salam Fayyad on media, and one living in Rome, practicing alternative medicine. The next generation from Balata will not have the strengths that he and his siblings possess, or their options. "I will never live in Balata again, I will never raise my children in Balata. This is a very bad place; anyone would leave if given the opportunity. Sixty-five years is too long."

At this point we are leaving for a walking tour of the camp and I am feeling profoundly sad, and the trauma, rage, and despair makes me physically ill. The dirty streets, barefoot children, narrow stone paths, houses leaning over us, the look of hopelessness in many mothers, shopkeepers makes me put away my camera. The words "occupation tourism" invade my thoughts; I cannot look any more, but I cannot turn away. Perhaps all I can do is to share my outrage with you, and perhaps the next time someone says the question of refugees is "off the table," you can tell them about the resilient and tired men, women, and children of Balata Refugee Camp.

2

Fatal Embrace
June 20–25, 2013

I n the second half of our 2013 delegation, we made several visits to historic Palestinian villages and to Qalqilya, an important city in the West Bank that was coming into conflict with the Jewish settlements growing up all around it and suffering the settlers' theft of its land, water, and resources as well the devastation created by the separation wall. These visits provided a glimpse into what the lives of Palestinians had been like before 1948 (giving the lie to the "land devoid of people" mythology), and into what was lost when more than 550 Palestinian villages were destroyed that year.

We explored the history and disappearance of the ancient village of Lifta in 1948, the ongoing and steady disappearance of the Bedouins' lands inside Israel, and the Israeli government's crushing of internationally recognized indigenous rights in the Negev. We also explored the legacy of the nonviolent resistance movement that was born during the First Intifada in the town of Beit Sahour, near Bethlehem, and the work of Physicians for Human Rights–Israel (PHR-I) and Palestinian Medical Relief Society (PMRS) that takes clinicians from Israel and the West Bank to work in mobile clinics every Saturday, providing care to many communities living on the margins. I found the dedication of these people, Jewish and Palestinian, working together in solidarity, to be very inspiring.

I have often heard that an economic recovery, rather than a political one, is planned for the West Bank, both by the technocrats in Ramallah and the politicians in Jerusalem and Washington. As we traveled from village to village in 2013, hearing from the people trying to develop ecotourism, agriculture, or even a health care system, it became clear to me that under occupation, such projects were fatally constricted by checkpoints, permitting requirements, Israeli regulations, settlement growth, and settler attacks. It also became clear that the mechanics of occupation were largely not about Israeli security, but about seizing land and water and exploiting the poorly protected and poorly paid Palestinian workers in factories in West Bank industrial zones and in what Palestinians call "Israel '48," within the armistice line from the war of 1948.

I learned also that the healthcare system, which consisted of the Palestinian Authority's "Ministry of Health," PMRS, and other nongovernmental organizations, the UN's Relief and Works Agency, UNRWA, and the private sector, was deeply affected by the politics of occupation. The chaos in that system was not only a reflection of internal deficiencies and power dynamics, but also of the impossibility of developing a functioning medical system in an area struggling for funds, infrastructure, and supplies, in which the movement of personnel, medical supplies, and patients was all quite dependent on the support of the Ministry of Health and a host of foreign donors—and the cooperation of the Israeli government, which can [and does] close checkpoints or impose stiff tariffs, at will. In one telling episode, a colleague of mine was working at a PMRA pediatric clinic, checking for ear infections, sore throats, and diaper rashes. He asked for the heights and weights of his patients, a basic and critical pediatric measurement. He was told that heights and weights "were only done in the Ministry of Health clinics," a clear example of the dysfunctional fragmentation of medical care, to the grave detriment of the patients.

Another topic we explored during this part of our 2013 trip was the role that the Jewish National Fund [JNF], a "charitable organization," had played in the region over the decades. The JNF was founded in 1901 by a group including Theodore Herzl, one of the fathers of the modern Zionist movement. It acquired land in Palestine for exclusively Jewish use and was a critical force in the colonization of the area both before and after 1948. In 2015, its website boasted of "250,000,000 trees planted in what was once a desert,"[1] and described water summits, community-building projects, ecological development, and environmental innovation, especially in the Negev, as well as a commitment to citizens with disabilities and special needs. In all these pursuits, the website averred, the JNF was "dedicated to ensuring that no member of

Israeli society is left behind."[2] But we saw that behind the façade of all these laudable-sounding projects, the JNF was acting in close cooperation with the Israeli government and the Israeli Land Authority to occupy and develop land for Jewish use only. (Many social-justice activists called this process "green washing.") Because the JNF held, and still holds, 50 percent of the seats in the Israeli Land Administration Council, which controls 93 percent of state lands, and the JNF has bylaws that prohibit leasing land to non-Jews, it plays a crucial role in upholding these blatantly discriminatory policies.

Moreover, the JNF widely advertises the technical solutions it proposes for the Middle East region's chronic and severe problems of water scarcity and distribution, but it ignores the fact of Israel's total control over the distribution of the water resources of the occupied territories as well as Israel, and its meager and completely inequitable distribution of water to Palestinians. In 2014, as many as two hundred thousand Palestinians were not connected to running water, and the average Palestinian consumed seventy liters a day, far less than the World Health Organization's recommended *minimum* of one hundred liters.[3] Many experts have estimated that Gaza will have no drinkable water in 2016 due to the overuse of its only aquifer and Israel's bombing of its water and sewer facilities. And yet, the JNF continues to promote Israel as a high-tech nation dedicated to advanced water technology and conservation.[4]

When I was a child, I dropped many a quarter into the blue-and-white JNF *tzedakah* boxes (interestingly, they featured an aspirational map of "Israel" that extended from the Jordan River to the Mediterranean Sea); and I saved money to buy trees in Israel, to help "make the desert bloom." I was unaware that my trees were being planted on destroyed Palestinian villages in a campaign to systematically erase that history, and that this practice of erasure continues today with the aggressive displacement of Bedouin in the Negev and the planting there, by the JNF and other agencies, of the "Ambassador Forest." Additionally, few people are aware that for decades the JNF has, as Israeli-American sociology professor Jesse Benjamin reports, "employed its own paramilitary force, which in Orwellian fashion is named the Green Patrol, in order to uproot Palestinian trees, destroy Palestinian houses and crops, and confiscate livestock for resale to Jews. In one recent action in the Negev/Naqab Desert, the JNF teamed with military and police units, as well as Jewish highschoolers to destroy the historic Bedouin village of Al-Araqib to make way for planned Jewish settlements and suburbs."[5] Questionable behavior indeed, for a so-called apolitical "charitable organization" in a so-called democratic country.

—⋏⋏—

Deir Istiya: A Little Taste of Paradise

June 20, 2013

Amal, one of the Palestinian-American members of the delegation, has invited us to visit the village of Deir Istiya, where she was born in 1948. We drive through an unusually lush valley, olive and carob trees densely growing everywhere, and there is a joy in her voice, eyes glowing with a mix of pride and excitement. She explains that she and her peers are the sixth generation to be born in the village, and that two more have followed. She went to Cairo for university and now lives in St. Louis. Her father finished high school in Deir Istiya and ultimately became the mayor.

We are greeted by the current mayor of the town, Ayyub, who is Amal's cousin. Amal seems to be related to everyone we meet, either by blood or marriage. Ayyub is a warm and dignified man with laughing eyes, bushy eyebrows, and muscular arms. He explains that 4,000 people live here and 10,000 are out of the country (but obviously remain deeply attached to the land). The village school was first built in 1918, and the town prides itself on having a very educated population. Deir Istiya has a very unusual Old City dating back to Roman, Byzantine, and Mamluk times with multiple streets, rooms, and apartments all clustered together—clearly a wealthy and well-constructed town. In the 1990s, with the support of the UN Development Program, the US Agency for International Development, and a Palestinian ministry, a project to renovate the city was begun in the hopes of bringing in commerce and tourism.

There is a peachy golden shimmer to the old stones in the blazing Mediterranean sun, glorious views, winding streets, and ancient doorways, something close to a lush, magical paradise. Amal is beaming as she points out where various relatives lived, where she played as a child, where she is renovating her house in the newer district of town; everyone appears warm and happy to see her. Her uncle Ayyub gives us a detailed tour, explaining the holes in the walls for guarding the city, Roman-style archways, stone insets for oil lamps, geometric tiles, water wells, and the massive renovation projects for private homes as well as guesthouses and larger facilities. One building was owned by the ruling Qasim family, and they had very low doors constructed so that visitors would have to enter bowing down to them. I can feel his big dreams for his town's vibrant rebirth as a tourist center coming to life. His big dreams are looking for funding.

The village owns thirty-six thousand dunams of land and is the second-largest village in Palestine in terms of land. They are known for their extra virgin fair trade olive oil. But this is Palestine and there has to be a catch. Eighty-seven percent of the village land is in Area C, while the village itself is in Area B. We climb up uneven steps to a high roof, the thin graceful minaret in view; white stone houses of all shapes and sizes surround us; tall, dark blue cedars point to the sky. By standing in one spot and rotating around, I can see five Jewish settlements in the distance on the surrounding hilltops in Area C: Ariel, Emmanuel, Nofim, Revana, and Yaqir. The threat of further loss of land and constant settler harassment is palpable.

Ayyub excitedly reports that they are attacked by settlers daily. There are repeated assaults during the olive harvest: orchards have been confiscated or uprooted, farmers on donkeys have been hit by cars, run over, and shot, and harvested olives, wrapped in large bags, have been stolen. Once again, I am taken aback by the behavior of settlers, their aggressive, lawless arrogance, and immoral, racist behavior toward the people who have lived here for generations.

We drive out of the village and turn into a valley, a bumpy road surrounded by terraced olive groves. This is Wadi Qana, part of the food basket in the Salfit District. This is also where the Jewish settlements on the surrounding hills have dumped their raw sewage, contaminating the water and driving out the forty families who used to live here. A delicate hudhud bird with a bright orange body and zebra-like stripes on its back flits between the lemon and orange trees. Goats cluster on the rocky walls. Ayyub says there are thirteen natural springs in the area that have provided water for centuries, but the Israelis have dug deep into the reservoirs, lowering the water levels so that only three springs are functional. In 1987, houses in the orchards were demolished and trees uprooted. In 1993, the area was officially declared a nature preserve by the Israeli government. This means that the Palestinians cannot fix the road, which is crumbling as the valley floods with water during the winter. Many families have small houses tucked around the trees where they live during harvest time. Since 1967, no renovations have been permitted; Palestinians plant trees secretly, often on Jewish holidays, and court cases are threatening the farmers. Because of the decrease in available water, the farmers have been shifting from growing orange and lemon trees to olive trees. We pass a cave where some people live; others stay here by day and leave by night. We see the stream running down the valley, green with sewage. To add insult to injury, the Israelis have released pigs, probably wild boars, in the area and they are eating the small olive trees and vegetables.

We get to one of the springs contained by stone walls. Families sit in the shade, barbequing, and small children are laughing and playing in a clear stream that leaves the green, pooling water. I worry about the bacterial count in the water, but for a moment, life almost feels normal. On Jewish holidays, Palestinian volunteers come to maintain the area as best they can, and on the most recent Land Day in March, for the first time they held a public event with five hundred people who came to do clean up and enjoy cultural events. Ayyub smiles and says this is a free open space available to the local villagers, and he clearly appreciates its natural beauty, an incredible treasure under threat from the settlements and the egregious behavior of the settlers.

Battir: The Colonization of the Conifers
June 21, 2013

We are staying in Beit Sahour near Bethlehem, in a guesthouse that, dating back to 1948, was first a place for poor women to sew clothes; it then became a childcare center and is now a renovated guesthouse. Everyone is talking about *Arab Idol* and if Mohammed Assaf, the sweet-faced guy from Gaza, will win the music competition. A more serious topic of conversation is Rami Hamdallah (the prime minister replacement after the technocrat Salam Fayyad resigned), who himself quit after two weeks on the job. Fayrouz is crooning on the van radio. Another day in Palestine and we are off for a hike in Battir, southwest of Bethlehem.

Our guides, Hassan and Hamad, are movie-star handsome as far as I am concerned, and that is distracting enough for me. They explain that the town of Battir has natural water springs that were developed during Roman times into a complicated and clever irrigation system including aqueducts and carved tunnels for the surrounding farms and orchards. In 1950, the source spring was rehabilitated to provide fresh water for drinking, vegetable washing, and a Turkish bath for men. Ancient and modern systems were combined, water was divided equally between the farmers using an "eight-day week," as there were eight families. In the summer the water was divided according to the percentage of water volume available for each farmer, measured by a stick dipped into the collected water pool. Hassan explains that the Israeli-Palestinian struggle is largely about water; now the Palestinians are allowed to store 5 to 10 percent of their water, and the rest is collected by the Israeli companies and sold back to them at high prices.

There is a lot of inspiring history here, including in nearby Deir Yassin, four kilometers away, where many of the villagers fled in fear after the massacre in 1948. Approximately thirteen elders stayed in the village, "to live or die," and one man decided to resist. He collected clothes and house supplies and placed them in the houses so they would appear to be inhabited. He lit candles and oil lamps at night and asked people to collect wood. He made fires and built wooden symbols that looked like people and put sticks in their hands that appeared to be guns, silhouetted in front of the flames. The village fooled the Jewish forces for eight months.

Another critical piece of history is that there is a famous railroad track dating back to the Ottoman Empire that runs through the fields of Battir and once connected Turkey, Syria, Palestine, and Egypt. Part of the 1949 agreement with Jordan was that the village of Battir could keep ownership of the land on both sides of the railway tracks as long as the train was kept safe. But 1967 brought new rules, including a buffer zone of two hundred yards on each side of the tracks; since then, the only people allowed to cross have been the farmers. While there were incidents during the intifadas, no attacks have occurred since the 1990s. To complicate matters further, in 1993 after Oslo, 30 percent of Battir ended up in Area B and 70 percent in Area C, which means that the villagers are no longer permitted to store water or repair the irrigation systems (that have worked brilliantly for centuries) because those are mostly located in Area C.

We are traipsing up and down stone paths with the odd sound (for Palestine) of rushing water at our feet as we follow our guides, who seem part gazelle in terms of grace, speed, and agility. As we look into the valley, surveying the sweep of the train tracks, the lush plots of vegetables, and the crisscrossing of irrigation systems, Hassan tells us about another source of grave concern—the threat of the separation wall. The wall is to be built on the village side of the railroad tracks, assaulting an idyllic landscape and isolating the houses, land, and schools on the other side. Palestinians unsuccessfully submitted a proposal to have this area named a World Heritage Site and in a few weeks will have a hearing in the Israeli Supreme Court. Hassan notes that the village has honored the security agreements for 65 years, and there are already cameras on the hills watching every move, 24/7. We can see a white military vehicle perched opposite us on a nearby hill and more guard towers stationed up the hill in a Jewish National Fund forest. A train comes zooming by, but after Hassan notes that the Battir train station was demolished years ago, we suspect that no locals are aboard it. I stare intently at this magnificent valley with the sinking feeling that the next time I visit, there is a good chance that it will have been raped by the Israeli military machine and my heart will break, once again, for this land and its people.

Now that we are all exhausted, overwhelmed, and dripping with sweat, the hike begins! Hassan and Hamad are involved in a group developing eco-tourism. They have designed hiking trails that are respectful of the history, the farmers, and the environment, coursing through terraced olive groves, fruit trees, cool caves, Byzantine tombs, and soaring hills. Despite my creaky moving parts and pounding heart, I find the scenery awe-inspiring.

But the conflict is never far off. The JNF forests (which are not indigenous, grow quickly, are easily flammable, and change the soil pH so that local herbs and trees cannot survive, except for the hardy *saber* cactus) are doing battle. I call this the colonization of the conifers. Apparently, the wind carries the seeds in the pine cones, so the forest is spreading through the valley. The surrounding hills are all topped by creeping Jewish settlements and the associated bulldozers, walls, and barbed wire. Hassan and Hamad have placed hiking markers, like the blazes in United States national parks, but the settlers, who occasionally use these same paths, have scratched off the marks and covered them over with blue and white blazes (which are the respective international symbols for water and land), so now we have the battle of the blazes.

Hassan points to a huge tire perched in a bed of twigs near the path and admits this is "from us." With the collapse of civil infrastructure, garbage collection became and still is a huge problem in the West Bank, and a 17,000-cubic-meter dump site developed on the hill above us. This was a huge challenge, so a group of forty-five farmers and younger men cleaned it up, topped it with soil, plantings, and a supporting wall. This tire is an instructive reminder.

We stop to catch our breath at a future rest area that has a massive stone, which Hassan scales easily. There are a number of theories about this stone, but it probably fell from the surrounding cliffs and was used as a security lookout centuries ago. Nearby is a large unnatural pile of white stones. While building a bypass road above, the ever-environmentally-thoughtful Israelis had dynamited the area and these rocks came tumbling down, crushing trees in their path. A falcon soars gracefully in the blue sky, one of the few creatures around here that can move freely. I stumble across a young olive tree staked to a dead branch from a JNF pine tree; the cones are intermixed with the olive leaves. It's as if the trees are locked in a symbolic fatal embrace.

I am getting close to the end of my cardiovascular reserves, as Hassan walks briskly ahead, explaining that there are 258 houses in the fields that serve as watchtowers and places for farmers to stay during the harvest. As we head up the hill, the Jewish settlement of Har Gilo becomes clearer, built on the lands of Al Walajeh and Beit Jala. I can see a bulldozer busy at work. When we finally get to pavement (short of breath, flushed, and vaguely alive), I see a wooden sign with a red heart. It reads "Hosh Yasmin Organic Farm." Soon we are seated on the covered balcony, enjoying the sweet breeze, smell of thyme, good beer, gorgeous view, and some excellent food. Not your everyday hike.

Beit Sahour: A True Story of Bovine Resistance
June 21, 2013

Balding and neatly dressed, Iyad Rishmawi appears to be an older, respectable kind of gentleman, but the guy clearly has a sense of humor. He wants to talk about the First Intifada from the point of view of the people rather than the politicians, but first he wants to show us a short documentary film, *The Wanted Eighteen* (subsequently made into a full-length feature in 2015).

It seems that in 1987, the people of Beit Sahour, a town east of Bethlehem, wanted to protect eighteen cows so their children could have milk during the Intifada. They established a cow farm, represented in the film by cute cartoon cows with very human expressions. In the film, the old men and women of Beit Sahour recount the amazing story of those eighteen embattled cattle, declaring, "We can produce our own milk if we have cows."

When the first calf from this herd was born, people were thrilled and celebrated as if it were a firstborn child. By this point, the presence of nineteen cows had made the Israelis unhappy because they symbolized Palestine self-sufficiency and resistance. A large Israeli force took pictures of the cattle farm—including individual photos of each cow—threatened the men, and told them they had twenty-four hours to shut down the farm or the place would be demolished. The men were told, "Those cows are a serious threat to the national security of Israel!" So the people of Beit Sahour decided to hide their cows in different homes, basements, wherever it was possible, and people who knew nothing about cows took the animals and figured out how to take care of them. Israeli troops and helicopters were sent in looking for the cows, but they could not find them. It became patriotic to protect the cows from the Israeli Defense Forces, and the cows obviously agreed with that sentiment because they continued to produce milk. Bottles of milk were distributed secretly from house to house despite curfews and incursions, and the milk kept coming. The IDF searched for four years and never found the animals, and the people of Beit Sahour stood proud with a feeling of dignity and accomplishment. A true story of bovine resistance.

When we get over chuckling, Iyad makes some serious points. The First Intifada was a spontaneous, public mass movement of the entire community, a tipping point that started in 1948 and finally exploded in 1987. He reminds us that Ilan Pappé wrote that the Israeli generals in the 1950s called the War of Independence "the incomplete war," so the '67 War and the seizing of Gaza, the West Bank, the Golan Heights, and East Jerusalem had been on the to-do list for a long time. The Intifada was the answer to all those Palestinian memories and years of multiplied grievances.

"Why are they making hell for us, business, life, so many difficulties . . . driver's license, multiple permits, security clearances?" asks Iyad. The Israelis made selective use of Ottoman, British, Jordanian, and international laws, and if they needed a law that didn't yet exist, they issued a military order that became law.

At the end of the day, people were fed up and couldn't live under these conditions. He explains that he established the first pharmacy in Beit Sahour and it took ten years to get a phone line because the intelligence service would not give approval. All these measures were to complete the "incomplete war," and Palestinians responded with, "Enough is enough; no to occupation!" Iyad states that Palestinians must restore their pride; Israelis cannot make peace with slaves.

Beit Sahour was an important center for popular resistance. There was a unified leadership in the First Intifada, made up of all the factions of the Palestine Liberation Organization except religious movements. There were leaflets published weekly that explained the activities of the resistance, and Palestinians responded positively, forming active neighborhood committees. Despite the strong influence of the central leadership, there was a high level of democracy.

In 1988, there was a call to stop paying taxes to Israel, and 90 percent of the population responded, including Iyad. He was rounded up with three other pharmacists, arrested, and taken to military headquarters in Ramallah and then to military court for ten days. After his arrest, the tax revolt started, and he was arrested a few more times. In 1989, there was a major attack on Beit Sahour. Tax collectors and soldiers removed everything from people's homes. When they came for his pharmacy, there was nothing left to take, so they went to his house and took everything. They tried to extort a bribe from him that would get his possessions back, but he refused. He recalls a lady running after the soldiers, yelling that they forgot something. When they stopped, she threw a TV remote at them.

Iyad talks about how the IDF demanded to see IDs first, and if you did not follow subsequent orders, they would not return your ID. The people of Beit Sahour started bringing all their IDs and throwing them onto the table of the military governor. Iyad was there. He called friends in Jerusalem and in one hour, CNN, NBC, and other news networks piled into Beit Sahour. He was translating for reporters and by 4:00 p.m., thousands and thousands of people had gathered in front of massive piles of IDs. The military governor sent soldiers around 5:00 p.m., and the army surrounded the town and all the people crowding its streets. When the soldiers arrived, Iyad noted special squads, headed by a military deputy, who told the people to go home. But the people sat down, no stones were thrown, which left the deputy stuck over how to respond, so he ordered his soldiers to start beating people, using tear gas, and putting people in prison and administrative detention. Iyad smiles, "But they never figured out the leaders [of the protests]." Iyad's son adds this was a rare instance for Beit Sahour when Israelis were the ones reacting rather than Palestinians. At all levels of society there was a feeling of dignity. At school, the son boasted that his father was in prison, and his little sister tried to break curfew a few hours later. She wanted to go into the street, to get arrested to see her father.

Because the goal was to break the people's will, their pride and dignity were the biggest threats; even intelligent resistance was intolerable. During the Intifada, thousands were killed, many of them children. Iyad recalled that one child was shot for writing graffiti. Another innocent young man was caught by two soldiers who shot him point blank with rubber bullets and he died.

In 1988 the Palestinian Center for Rapprochement between Peoples was founded, and one of its first accomplishments was a meeting with thirty-five Israeli families and the establishment of a biweekly dialogue. "We celebrated breaking bread, not bones," remembers Iyad. "Accepting the other was part of us."

Iyad clearly mourns for those days: "That feeling is now gone. Today is totally different; we had hope and dignity then. We believed in what we were doing and we were right, behaving according to humanitarian law; we are here to exist and not meant to harm your existence. This was part of inner feeling. . . . Today we are not like that; internal unity within community is gone. We moved back to a tribal system of community, reactions for self-protection of each family."

When we ask him if he sees signs of hope, he thinks long and hard, but the inspiration in his voice is missing. Clearly the struggle has changed and the people have experienced several more decades of oppressive occupation with all of its negative consequences. I suspect that it is time for younger generations to bring their creativity and steadfastness to the forefront, and it is time to internationalize resistance as well. This time, in our global community, it is clear we are all responsible.

Symbolism Meets Solidarity

June 22, 2013

I have to interrupt this message with some delightful news: Last night around midnight, the streets all over Palestine erupted with joyous crowds, cars honking in a delirious cacophony. A young man from Gaza, Mohammed Assaf, was voted the winner of *Arab Idol*, and the UN Relief and Works Agency named him an ambassador of goodwill. A victory for Palestine and, I might add, a victory for the entertainment industry and adoring women everywhere.

Bright and early, three of us take a *service* (a large taxi, pronounced "sair veese") to Khalil (the Arabic name for Hebron), through open checkpoints and ominous but quiet guard towers. We meet up with Dr. Othman, a dentist, and Dr. Hassan Abu Amro, an optometrist trained in Saudi Arabia, in preparation for traveling to the village of Idha, eight kilometers from Hebron, just along the Green Line. We are traveling to the Saturday Mobile Clinic with PHR-I and PMRS.

Idha is surrounded by three Jewish settlements including Adora and Telem. As a consequence of the permits and checkpoints, travel in and out has become extremely difficult. The quantity and quality of water in Idha is problematic due to the large allotments going to the neighboring settlements, and the village is plagued by rats, which can be seen jumping among the vegetable stands. Poverty is on the increase, and the separation wall has wreaked havoc on the economy and people's personal lives for the past five to six years.

In desperation, the villagers started collecting garbage, metal, and car parts, including tires, which they burned to get the metal and sell it to the

Israelis. The burning garbage and tires created a massive toxic smog and predictable health problems. Combined with the polluted water, PMRS is seeing more cases of diarrhea, asthma, miscarriages, diabetes, hypertension, and smoking. PMRS and Red Crescent clinics, the private sector, and Ministry of Health hospitals cannot handle the community's medical needs. Hassan also notes that no one wants to talk about potential cancer risks, but the Dimona nuclear reactor is near Hebron. Israelis nearby receive some kind of prophylactic pills to reduce their risks, but nothing is offered to the local Palestinians.

More fragments of our conversation:

Yesterday, fifteen settlers with guns blocked a nearby road and threw stones at local Palestinians; during the attack lasting two hours, they were protected by the IDF. This also happened in Beit Ommar.

The IDF is becoming more aggressive and are training dogs to attack when they hear certain words like *Allahu Akbar.*

There is a proposed law in the Knesset (the Israeli parliament) to make it legal for settlers to fire on Palestinians (which of course they are already quite adept at doing), a sort of legal whitewashing in the vein of stand-your-ground law.

Both men are thoroughly disgusted with the Palestinian leadership and elite power holders. They are "thieves"; they have stolen international aid money and will steal more if Secretary of State John Kerry reinvigorates the (useless) negotiations and aid programs.

Nabil Shath, a Palestinian negotiator, recently explained to his Israeli associates that the Palestinian Authority is spending more money on Israeli security than on Palestinian health and security combined.

Hassan is warm, obviously intelligent, and insightful. He worked in Saudi Arabia for seventeen years and lived in a special compound so his wife and four children had more personal freedoms. They came back in 2000 because he felt there was going to be a Palestinian state and he wanted to serve his people, but now he worries "for my kids and their lives, their futures. What should I tell them? Sometimes I stand stunned. Am I going to create more hate? But still they can see what is on the ground." His twenty-three-year-old son, trained as an electrical engineer in Egypt and now unemployed, feels totally frustrated and wants to leave.

We drive into the village and see large bales of hay and huge mountains of charred metal fragments. For reasons that are not entirely clear to me, the mobile clinic is being "honored" by a large number of fully armed Palestine National Security forces who line the streets, direct the vehicles, and line up for photos with clinic staff. We crowd into a large room and on the stage there are municipal and PA dignitaries; Saleh, who directs the mobile clinic for PHR-I; and Alan, one of our doctors, sitting in front of a large photo of a smiling Arafat. We hear a history of the town and a thousand thank-yous in Arabic and Hebrew as a large crowd of patients gathers outside.

And then we start seeing patients. A local family doctor who will be my interpreter and will see the obstetric patients, a nurse from the United States, and I set up our "office" in a classroom. We have a real exam table along with an ancient ultrasound machine, and I have brought a flashlight, large bottle of Purell, various surgical instruments (to remove IUDs, sutures, etc.), and a measuring tape. I suddenly realize there are no drapes (not unusual) but, even more striking, no gloves, no speculums, and no basic lab work. A challenging moment for a gynecologist. (The gloves are finally located.)

And then the work begins, a veritable flood of women in hijabs, blue, black, plaid, sparkling decorations, and long *jilbabs*, buttoned up to the neck and long sleeves, one niqab totally covering a lovely woman's face. I try guessing ages and realize that everyone ages prematurely under the stress of poverty and occupation. The heat is oppressive, and we are dripping with sweat. I feel for the women who are covered. They are alone, or in twos and threes, some with small children, some argumentative, some focused, and everyone has an earnest story and a long list of medical issues that frequently include back pain, abdominal pain, vaginal discharge, symptoms of urinary tract infections, and hot flashes. There are questions about irregular bleeding, pain on intercourse, infertility. Everyone who is not trying to get pregnant has an IUD. I try to reach across the language and cultural barriers; instead of, "Are you sexually active?" I ask, "Are you married?" I already know that many women take hormones to delay menses when they travel to Mecca. I am listening carefully, empathically, woman to woman. There is no medical charting, no vital signs, no prevention, but soon we are in a rhythm of brief history-taking, strategic exams, lots of education and empathy, and then a wild search through the donated medications, or on-the-spot decision-making for referrals and testing that may or may not be possible given all the restrictions on movement. I am sure many symptoms are stress related and there is no simple treatment for that. My basic strategy is: Is this very serious? What is the most likely diagnosis given an utter lack of adequate information? What is the most we can do quickly here? The hardest part for me is the women with menopausal symptoms. I have always wondered how women covered in multiple layers deal with hot flashes, and it is a challenge to give culturally appropriate advice.

And of course we have lots of antibiotics and antifungals, and steroid ointment, but no free hormone therapy, and I have no idea what is available in local gynecology offices. There is a rich herbal tradition in Palestine, but that is way beyond my First World US experience.

Hours later, the clinic is over and the women who are still waiting are angry and disappointed, but turned away by PA soldiers with guns. I have seen twenty-four patients and the entire staff has seen over seven hundred. I feel a bit run over and my pregnant colleague is wilting. The organizers are pleased, and we are hosted by the village with chicken, rice, and Turkish coffee in the company of more officials and more men with guns.

The power of working in this Saturday clinic for me, year after year, is hard to explain. There is the potent symbolism of a Jewish-American doctor working in a mobile clinic in a neglected village in the West Bank and the solidarity I feel with the Israeli and Palestinian clinicians and the sea of patients we serve. There are women who actually receive appropriate care by my First World standards, and I find one woman with a breast mass and one with a pelvic mass who definitely need further care. But more importantly, the women understand that a doctor from some faraway place came to their forgotten village to provide care and see them as deserving human beings. They are not invisible. I am also working in solidarity with the Israelis (Jewish and Palestinian) and the West Bank clinicians who are swimming against the cultural and political tides of their own societies, and I want to stand with them as well. It is really the most concrete thing I can do.

We Shall Not Be Moved: Bedouins in the Negev

June 23, 2013

Today, as part of a tour with Thabet Abu Ras of Adalah: The Legal Center for Arab Minority Rights in Israel,[6] we take the long drive south to the Naqab to meet with Arab Bedouin communities in Israel facing displacement.

I am always learning from the landscape and I am familiar with the renaming of everything Palestinian that has been ongoing since 1948, but today I learn a new twist to this practice of linguistic erasure. Along the highway, we see signs in Hebrew, English, and Arabic. It turns out that the Arabic names are actually transliterated from the Hebrew, thus engineering a process to create a different word in Arabic, de-Arabizing the names of historic places. Thus "Jerusalem" in Hebrew is "Yerushalayim," and in Arabic a transliteration of "Yerushalayim," rather than "Al Quds," which is the centuries-old Arabic name for Jerusalem. If you think about this, the messaging is that not only are Palestinians invisible, but they are actually immigrants who were not really here before the State of Israel got around to naming everything.

We meet up with Thabet, a political geologist and director for the southern office of Adalah, waiting along the highway with two interns. The land is fairly flat, bone dry, and clearly desert. We turn off the modern highway to the unmarked, unrecognized village of Araqib, bumping over an unpaved road of rocks, packed sand, and deep potholes, past rows of recently planted Eucalyptus trees on one side and a cemetery and cluster of Bedouin tents and shanties on the other. We stop at a large, flat-topped tent made of wide sheets of plastic and wooden supporting planks, and sit down on the ground on the oblong created by long rugs and pillows. We are introduced to the *sheikh* and to Haia Noach, the executive director of the Negev Coexistence Forum for Civil Equality.[7] The *sheikh* is wearing a long black robe and Arab headdress, and when his cell phone rings, it is a familiar tango jingle.

As we are served bitter coffee prepared in a pit in the center of the floor, the *sheikh* explains to us in vivid detail the many "crimes against humanity" that have been committed against his village, which has been demolished fifty-two times and rebuilt fifty-two times. In 1999, the Israelis started crop dusting his fields with poisonous chemicals, and repeated the process five times. The chemicals affected the fields, animals died, and there was an increase in miscarriages. "Where was the UN protecting human rights?" he asks. We are invited to download a video of the village before and after the crop dusting from a computer that is plugged into an electrical socket tacked to a supporting beam. He suggests that it is the racism in the Israeli medical system that has hindered any research into this medical catastrophe.

On June 2, 2010, Israeli forces arrived, assisted by helicopters, dogs, and horses, and leveled the village. He calls this "a Nazi crime." His thick brown hands gesture as he speaks. He describes the demolition where houses were obliterated; food, milk, medicine were destroyed; and 4,500 fruit and olive trees and grape vines were uprooted. "We are people. We have zero unemployment. We live from the fields." He says it is amazing that the Israelis want to change them from independent farmers living in the desert to poverty-stricken factory workers controlled by Jewish bosses in reservation towns.

Another round of coffee and tea as the *sheikh* continues his account. Six months after the village was demolished, forty trucks arrived and removed all the rubble. The court ordered the Bedouins to move into their ancestral cemetery, the one we passed on arriving, currently the only secure place for the families to live, although they have no water or electricity. "The dead protects the living." The Israelis killed one hundred sheep and sixteen Arabian horses. The Bedouins were fined by the courts for the police costs the Israelis incurred during the attack. The Israelis also planted the Bedouin land with rows of water-hungry Eucalyptus trees that form the Ambassador Forest, and foreign ambassadors are encouraged to plant saplings here in the name of their countries. However, when the South African ambassador visited the *sheikh*, he condemned these policies and refused to plant a tree.

In a case of bitter irony, we watch a large water tanker pull up and start watering these fledgling trees, but there is no water for the people; in fact, Jews and Arabs are forbidden to provide water to the Bedouin. Another water tanker arrives.

The *sheikh* states he has documentation to prove the JNF is responsible for this tree planting on their historic lands. Having lost their lands, he asks, "Where do we live? How do we eat?" They also have no roads or schools. The children have to travel to the distant town of Rahat, "a failed refugee city," and the families continue to dig wells in search of water. He questions, "Would Israel do this to a Jewish citizen?" The answer is clearly no, and in fact, the government has provided full support to religious Jews who have been individually acquiring farms in the area.

To make matters worse, the Bedouins are labeled as criminals. "Israel treats us like we are a security threat like Iran," the *sheikh* says, adding that there are currently fifty-eight cases in the Israeli courts against him, all for the crime of being on his own land. He urges, "We want to live with Jews; the criminals are the government and the police." Many Israeli NGOs support the struggles of the Bedouin. For instance, Adalah petitioned the Israeli Supreme Court to stop the crop dusting (it's worth noting the material used was Roundup, made in the United States).

The *sheikh*'s son, Aziz, explains that the village of Araqib was first demolished in 1948, but the people stayed and asked for recognition. They were mostly ignored until 2010, when arrangements to totally demolish the village got serious. He describes the soldiers arriving at 4:00 a.m., demolishing sixty-five homes, leveling the village. Prior to that there were 573 villagers. "Before, we were employed, working, cultivating the land—wheat in the winter, olive oil, cheese, milk, all organic." Every family had small side jobs; he and his wife had four hundred chickens and sold eggs, bringing in six to seven hundred shekels per week. Now the Bedouins have been converted into slaves, working twelve-hour days, missing their wives and children. Aziz says that the Prawer Plan, which was designed to regulate the settlement of the Bedouins in the Negev and ignores concepts in international law such as transitional justice, semi-nomadic property rights, and native rights, "means to kill us. We shall not be moved. There is no option. If we leave, we will die." The police are threatening to destroy the cemetery that was built in 1914.

We are introduced to Haia Noach, who talks about advocacy and awareness campaigns. She has been arrested a number of times for protecting the Bedouin. She states most Israelis do not want to know about what is going on; they deny the occupation and the racism in their own society. The Prawer Plan represents a new frontier for a conflicted area, one centered on taking control of large tracts of land by planting trees through the JNF, creating industrial zones and army bases on expropriated land. The discussion of the morality of forestation projects is now at a standstill, as hundreds of thousands of trees have already been planted. There is even an evangelical group that is planting one million saplings with the JNF to hasten the apocalypse. She reminds us that that the indigenous population had no knowledge of the laws that allow for confiscation if land is not occupied for a certain period of time, that Bedouins often lack land titles, or only have traditional titles that are conveniently ignored, and that the courts are snarled with cases and counterclaims. She is hoping for a legal breakthrough as there is a growing awareness about the rights of indigenous peoples.

Wadi al-Na'am, the Largest Unrecognized Village in Israel
June 23, 2013

We are back on the highway with Thabet from Adalah, and I am puzzled why Israeli authorities are putting so much energy into displacing the Bedouins. He explains that the Naqab is half of Mandatory Palestine, 60 percent of Israeli territory, and contains 8 percent of the total Israeli population. Currently, one-third of the population of the Naqab is on 2 percent of the land, and if all the Bedouin land claims were honored, that amount would be approximately 3.5 percent of the Naqab, which is really not a big deal. What this devotion to a relatively tiny area means is that land is a matter of identity (the same love and passion for land is expressed in Hebrew as in Arabic songs), as well as a matter of colonization and de-Arabization. The process mirrors historical developments in the West Bank where much of area C encompassed the ancestral lands and villages of the Dirat tribe that existed long before 1948.

In 1948 some Bedouins were evicted from the Naqab, and in the 1950s the state gathered the Bedouin into the "Sayig," a designated area that was then declared a closed military zone. Later the Israeli state declared much of the area for agricultural purposes, which meant the Bedouin were not allowed to do any construction. In the 1960s, the state become more aggressive and gathered Bedouin into a number of townships, punishing those who refused by declaring their homes to be unrecognized villages. It should be remembered that the nearby Israeli city of Be'er Sheva was founded in 1900 with the purchase of two hundred dunams from the Hazazin Bedouin tribe, all very recent history.

We are about to visit Wadi al-Na'am, the largest unrecognized village in Israel, populated by some ten to fifteen thousand people, all under threat of displacement. The Israeli authorities have announced the closure of the schools starting August 23; in transferring the children, they will apply pressure on the parents to move. The students are on a general strike in response to the closure. We are meeting with the traditional leader of the local committee, an entity serving as the political organization of unrecognized villages.

Such villages are not on any maps—some existed before 1948, some are the result of previous dispossessions and now are under threat again. Thabet explains that since 1948, Israeli policy has included:

1. Concentrating Bedouins into small reservation areas and restricting their movement;
2. Urbanizing the Bedouin in the name of modernization without any respect for their identity or culture, or the preservation of a traditional lifestyle; and
3. Finalizing land claims. Of the 90,000 pre-1948 Bedouins, 10,000 remained after the war, and the population has grown to 200,000 people claiming 3.5 percent of the Naqab. Since the 1948 dispossessions and transfer to the different reservations, the Israelis have created seven planned towns for those who lost land or live in unrecognized villages; this will involve the destruction of twenty to twenty-five villages, the uprooting of up to seventy-five thousand people, and the loss of land claims. The Bedouin look at these townships as refugee camps and strongly prefer agricultural villages with livestock and herds.

He notes sadly that the Bedouin are not being given any options, while Jewish Israelis are welcome to live in cities, towns, *kibbutzim, moshavim,* or individual farms and get full support from the government.

As we drive down Route 40, a modern highway, on our left are clusters of shantytowns and on our right is sandy, rocky, uninhabited desert. We are thirty kilometers from Gaza, and the right side of the road has been totally cleansed of Bedouin towns and is now a firing area for the military.

Thabet explains that Bedouin villages are made up of a tribe, with clusters of clans subdivided into families. The Bedouin want to keep these relationships intact and will never violate tribal law, even if it conflicts with Israeli law. I am horrified to learn that many of the unrecognized villages are located adjacent to the most poisonous chemical/industrial parks in Israel. We turn onto a rocky, bumpy, potholed path toward Wadi al-Na'am, which is built adjacent to a gigantic electrical plant. Massive high-voltage electric towers loom above and wires crisscross over and in between patches of houses as far as we can see. Again, the painful irony is that none of these houses are actually connected to the electrical grid. There is a certain cruelty to this whole mess.

We learn that the fifty-year-old tribal leader we are meeting, Sheikh Ibrahim Abu Hafash is one of many Bedouin who used to serve in the IDF under the belief that serving their country would result in a better future (just look at the benefits for Jewish soldiers), but after serving, they returned to their poverty and villages without water and electricity, with nothing changed. This man was wounded in the service of his country and is now one of the leaders of the Islamic movement of the Naqab.

We are soon seated in a square of long red rugs and pillows on the ground in a large tent on hard-packed dirt, with the familiar Bedouin arrangement of plastic sheeting supported by wooden planks along with a cooking pit, but this time, there's also a sink and what appears to be a gas burner in the back. A refreshing breeze cools us a bit and the meeting with the *sheikh* begins with the rituals of coffee and tea.

His face is sun-brown and he is wearing a long grey robe. He tells us the village includes fifty thousand dunams and twenty thousand people, and the state provides no services except education, through a school that is now under threat. In 1953, Bedouin in the surrounding areas were gathered up and put in an area called "the Fence," where they stayed from 1953 to 1988 without interference. Then the Israeli Land Authority announced that the Bedouin were illegally occupying the land where they had been transferred by the government. This was followed by a long and tortured court fight, deceptive legal maneuvers, and multiple judicial rulings ending with the decision in 2002 that the Bedouin could stay until a new agreement was reached. However, the government has shown no interest in agreements and lots of interest in removing them. The *sheikh* says that a few days ago, a group of Jews came and asked the Bedouin "to be loyal." He replied, "We are as loyal as we are treated. The state treats us as a knife in the back, so how do they expect to be treated?" He states that the Israeli media also joins in the lies and distortions.

Much of the battles are over access to water, for which the Bedouin pay the highest amount, including covering the infrastructure costs of carrying that water. Aware that Israel is not providing electricity to the Bedouin, international solidarity groups have helped install solar panels, and now Bedouin are generating their own clean electricity. Another challenge is that the IDF has designated their land as a military training area. The *sheikh* claims that the Israelis want Bedouin in the IDF so they can be the human shields in the front lines, but now less than 1 percent serve, and they are looked down upon by their communities.

Suddenly, it is time for the Muslim prayers and the *sheikh* leaves us. Four Muslim women in our group ask if they can go to the mosque and the answer comes back in the negative—this culture is not known for its progressive approach to women. Shortly thereafter, our Muslim sisters are praying at the back of the tent. Thabet explains that Bedouin society is very traditional and patriarchal; women are totally separate from men but derive their influence through their relationship with their husbands. Women can join the community in meetings at the communal tent where we are sitting, but not in people's homes. One-third of Bedouin men are polygamous, with up to four wives, each with a separate household, and the number of wives one has is a mark of prestige. There are usually ten to fifteen children per family, but families of up to forty are not unheard of.

Nonetheless, society is changing and the majority of Bedouin in the universities are female. The women have associations focused on weaving, embroidery, and other traditional crafts. In Be'er Sheba, all the Bedouin demonstrations are led by women. Israeli policy has forced women into the streets. As we leave the tent, the *sheikh* points out a huge gas storage facility in the middle of the town—again another major health hazard.

We are back in the van and I am marveling about how people can survive under such harsh conditions, the kind of toughness that emerges from living in the desert. I wonder what will happen as they struggle to survive in such a racist and unsympathetic country. As Thabet continues the discussion, some pertinent pieces of information strike me:

1. There is already a bill in the Knesset to make the road we are on a military road, and this will effectively criminalize all the Bedouins who refuse to leave; they are known for their resilience and stubbornness. Every Sunday, the *sheikh*, his wives, and many children demonstrate in Be'er Sheba reminding people they are here to stay.

2. In the town of Alssir, part of the southern district of Be'er Sheba, the Bedouin inhabitants have already been displaced a number of times. Many have served in the IDF, and although they are technically part of Be'er Sheba, they receive no services and live under dangerous high-voltage wires.

3. When rockets from Gaza were landing in this area, which has no shelters, the *sheikh* laughed and said about a government official, "He's asking about rockets? I am looking for water. I was a soldier in the Israeli Army; I served my country." When it is time for Allah to take him, the *sheikh* is ready, his conscience is clear.

4. When contemplating the volume of health risks to this society, let's not forget the Dimona nuclear reactor, which is thirty miles away. Thabet remembers a time when they were told the reactors were "textile factories," but no one was allowed to investigate due to the very high level of government security.

Adalah takes many petitions to the Israeli Supreme Court and often wins, but implementation is always a problem. It took the state six years to build a Bedouin school, which consisted of a row of caravans. He predicts that in five years all these villages will be cleared and Jewish towns will be built as part of "developing the Negev," but there is obviously enough room for everyone; this is the same process going on in the West Bank in Area C. Bedouin are people of the desert, they have had their own villages for three hundred years. They wander with their herds, but then return to their homes. Maps from 1945 show fertile, cultivated Bedouin villages. Now not only are they being asked to prove their ownership, but if they do, they are offered only 17 percent of that original land. The Bedouin are not interested in compromise.

We stop and drive up a small hill that in another instance of perverse irony has several huge water storage tanks that do not feed the surrounding villages. Sand storms dance across the vista below. In the distance we see another important piece of this puzzle: the Nevatim military air base that has plans for expansion. The location of this base is critical in terms of preventing demographic contiguity between Gaza and the West Bank.

Shortly thereafter, the only Bedouin MK (member of the Knesset), a lawyer and former mayor active in the Islamic movement, Ibu Arar, pulls up in his car wearing Western dress and sporting short hair and a beard with a neatly pressed shirt. As he stands in the wind with the highway below and the water tanks above, more sand storms, like mini tornados, dance across the clusters of villages. He talks about all the typical issues regarding racism in Israeli society, the treatment of Bedouins, the discriminatory laws in the Knesset, and he notes ironically that the state is spending twice as much money to expel the Bedouin as it would to recognize them. He asks, "If Israel can't make peace with its own citizens, how can it make peace with Palestinians outside?" He explains that his family was displaced in the 1980s to build the military airport; the villagers were promised ten thousand dunams to move and they received seven thousand. His allies in the Knesset include the left-leaning Meretz party, a few MKs from Labor, and the Arab parties—all together, 20 out of 120 parliament members. His is a lonely battle.

We pass the town of Nevatim, population 2,500, a Jewish settlement from India. Thabet gets agitated when he points out there are three signs along the road to a small Jewish cemetery and not one sign to any of the many villages for the living. He talks about the politics of fear, fear of the other, of Iran, Hezbollah, Hamas, Abu Mazin; there is always a new target. "Fear is the centripetal force that binds Jews together."

Thabet reminds us that the Bedouin are stubborn and strong and will continue to fight. He states the Arabs are part of the Israeli landscape and have learned to "play the game." They are very encouraged by solidarity groups and they are also not split by borders. For instance, half of the members of his family, originally from Ashkelon, live in the Jabalia Refugee Camp in Gaza, but they remain in close but virtual contact. His eighty-five-year-old aunt lives there, and he has not seen her in fifteen years. He was once arrested for sending her two hundred shekels a month—"supporting the enemy." I am so inspired by his final insights: "We perceive the homeland as one place and we are willing to share. I am a minority in terms of numbers, but I have a majority mentality—all Palestinians, all Arabs. But the Jewish majority has a minority, siege mentality. They can militarily win, but they still have no sense of security." The new post-Nakba generation is not afraid; they have nothing left to lose.

Erasing History

June 23, 2013

I have seen many photos of the destroyed village of Lifta, which dates back one thousand years and has tax records from the days of the Ottoman Empire. The photos show an archetypal vista of fragmented houses, piles of stones extending into a valley at the edge of Jerusalem, but there is much more to this picture as Umar Ighbariyah from the Israeli organization Zochrot (in Hebrew, "Remembering") explains. He has us rotate around 180 degrees and look at a conglomeration of modern buildings extending up the hill. These were all built on the land belonging to the village of Lifta. He points out a little building hiding under a big billboard; this was once the village school but is now a Jewish school. The village is far more than its famous ruins. Close to Old Jerusalem and on the road from Al Quds to Jaffa, this was a busy area for the locals, religious pilgrims, and tourists. The village actually dates back to the Canaanites, and has Aramaic, Arabic, and Hebrew roots. *Lifta* means "The Gate" (of Jerusalem).

The signage reads "En Neftoah (Lifta)," and Umar explains that Neftoah is a Biblical place located somewhere near here and that the Israelis added "En" to Hebraize the name as well as give it an ancient reference. We scramble down a steep rocky path, past a dusty construction site that is part of a new project to build a train track to Jaffa that will include bridges and tunnels through this area. He points out in the distance JNF forests near the Jewish settlement of Ramot as well as destroyed villages such as Biddu. We see a mosque at the top of a mountain that was attacked by settlers who wanted to turn it into a park and synagogue. Facing the other way, toward the construction zone, we see Deir Yassin, now a Jewish neighborhood. Beyond that is Ein Kerem and other Palestinian villages, all occupied and mostly destroyed in 1948 with the creation of thousands of Palestinian refugees. There are also a scattering of Palestinian homes at the top of the valley that are now Jewish homes. The Knesset and many governmental offices, the high court, and even parts of Hebrew University are all on Lifta. I note many boys with *kippot*, dangling *payos* and *tzitzit* bouncing from their shirts, as well as girls in long skirts and long-sleeved blouses walking on these paths as well.

Umar explains that before 1948, Lifta contained ten thousand dunams with forty thousand more cultivated outside the village and a population of three thousand, all of which constituted a big, wealthy town. There were many olive trees and vegetables planted from seed, and it was a lush and prosperous place. Fifty of the four hundred houses are left. Other villages, such as Ein Kerem and Ein Hod, were not destroyed and are now Jewish towns, but 95 percent of the Palestinian villages were completely demolished to eliminate the possibility of return. Strangely enough, in 1949, Jews from Arab countries were brought in to live in Lifta; it probably looked a lot like home, but they left after a few years because the village was near the Green Line with the Jordanians on the other side, and it was slightly dangerous— plus no water or electricity was provided. Jews from Arabic-speaking coun- tries were second class from the start.

Almost immediately, various green organizations asked that Lifta be left as a park—a green spot in Jerusalem—with no acknowledgment of its social history. Even today, most Israelis do not make the connection between a park with graceful ruins and the Arabs that once inhabited them. As we scramble, walk, jump, trip around the stone paths and move in and outside of crumbling homes, the sunset creating a shimmery streaking light, the extraordinary beauty of Lifta is painfully obvious. The stones range from grey-white to orange. There are the original fig trees and lush *saber* cactus, wells and aqueducts, ancient terraces, and amazing architecture, with grace- ful archways and floors dating from different centuries and now crumbling from age and neglect. Each family also had a smaller house for baking bread. At the base of the valley we come across two pools; canals led from the pools to irrigate the various gardens below, and each family had plots for figs and almonds, apricots, and vegetables. We watch a predominantly Orthodox group of youth playing in the water, with a few guys in their underwear and girls in bikinis thrown in for dramatic effect. The first pool is cleaner, and it originally served as a water source for washing dishes in the homes, while the second pool, which is utterly disgusting, was for the animals.

In 1947, the UN Partition Plan was announced and, before the State of Israel was declared, before the Arabs attacked, Jewish militias immediately started to occupy villages beyond the partition line. Lifta and Jerusalem were supposed to be international zones, but clashes with the Irgun and Stern Gang, two militant Zionist groups, started in 1947 and in early 1948. Irgun fighters dressed as tourists came into a Lifta coffee shop and shot six people, wounding seven. This created a wave of fear, and the families living on the edges of town fled to East Jerusalem and Ramallah. A month later the Irgun bombed all the empty houses and then started attacking roughly every week. The inhabit- ants were terrified and fled to Ramallah, but thirty to fifty young men stayed with meager ammunition and guns. The Haganah and Irgun attacked again and David Ben-Gurion famously declared that you can now enter Jerusalem through the Lifta area "without seeing any strangers" (read: Arabs).

Then, on April 9, 1948, 120 men, women, and children were massacred in nearby Deir Yassin, and the Jewish soldiers took a group of captured women on a "victory tour" around the city and then dumped them at the Jaffa Gate. The Arab population panicked and fled to Ramallah. The Israeli forces declared all the fleeing homeowners "absentees" and confiscated all the property for the state. Lifta decayed, it also became a home for squatters, the homeless, and drug dealers who had been pushed out by the police. In the 1980s there was also a Jewish terror cell called the Lifta Underground that plotted several bombings, including of the Al Aqsa Mosque and the mosque in Hebron, as well as one successful attack—a bombing of a bus on its way to Hebron.

We arrive at the mosque in Lifta. One of the village's oldest buildings, it is made of stone and mud mixed with ash, and is pleasantly cool, with a decaying courtyard, stray trees growing stubbornly out of the stone walls and stairs. There are two rooms in various states of ruin—the prayer room and the schoolroom. Palestinian groups still come here to pray; Lifta survivors living in East Jerusalem come both to pray and clean up the cemetery. In many of the rooms with high arched ceilings, the keystones—which are critical to the architectural stability of the structures—have been removed, thus contributing to the collapse of the ruin.

At one point, as we are walking soberly through the ruins of one stately house after another, each with gracefully arching windows, floors sticking out into nowhere, Umar tells us to put away our cameras. The reason why becomes instantly clear as we peer across a roof at a gigantic construction site. The Israeli newspaper, *Haaretz*, reports that the Israelis are building a massive bunker and underground tunnel that will connect to the prime minister's house and serve as a functional seat of government in case of nuclear war. It seems that everyone around here is preparing for the apocalypse. Ultimately, this will all be disguised to appear to the public as a garden; security is a bit touchy about us taking pictures of this not-so-secret project.

There is now a plan to finish the destruction of Lifta and build a posh new Jerusalem neighborhood, and although there is a campaign fighting this proposal, Omar predicts construction will start in a few months. When he says this, I am seized with a wave of grief and rage and start taking photos of every stairway, crumbling wall, olive press, desperately trying to document the world that may soon be erased.

Umar explains that twelve to thirteen years ago, Zochrot started to document the Nakba and to create a new memory of 1948. He reminds us that in the early days of the state, Ben-Gurion asked academic researchers to create a history that stated Palestinians made the decision to leave voluntarily, and the researchers have done an excellent job creating that illusion. Zochrot has studied 58 destroyed villages and has documented a total of 672 lost villages and small towns. One way or another, eight hundred thousand Palestinians were forcibly expelled, while one hundred thousand stayed behind.

Umar is proud that Palestinians continue to persevere and refuse to be erased from history, and he is drawn to the work of Zochrot as part of that ongoing struggle to be seen and acknowledged by Israeli society. As my eyes sweep across the ancient beauty and dignity of this rich valley, I imagine the bustling community that once lived here. As a student of the Nakba, I believe this is as close as I have come to a pilgrimage to the Holy Land.

Resilience and Resourcefulness

June 24, 2013

I have been looking forward to my day with Dr. Khadija Jarrar, the PMRS director of women's health care. We are going to three villages with a team from PMRS, UNDP (United Nations Development Program), a representative of the PA, and members of the local community councils to discuss how to create a more organized system of health care between three towns seeking to collaborate. Since I am always stunned by the disorganization of health care delivery in these parts, the "NGOization" of different compartments of care, and the consequences for patients living in this disjointed and confusing world, this should be interesting to see in action.

Nablus is a gorgeous old city built on the palm and up the fingers of mountains that hold it like a giant cupping of hands. The traffic is of the chest pain–producing variety; there are billboards for all sorts of international companies: two happy, handsome guys drinking Coca-Cola; blond women with windswept hair selling all sorts of products, including sexy wedding dresses to the covered women in the streets. Israeli military bases dot the hilltops. There are mountains of pita bread and watermelons on every corner, and a clear feeling that we are being watched.

We head to the town of Burin, population ten thousand. One part of the town's mosque lies in Area B, with the other in Area C, so there is a threat that it will be demolished; the kind of humiliation and downright meanness behind this designation takes real creativity. We enter the local community health center, where the hallway is lined with mostly women who represent the community or work professionally in the clinic, plus the representatives of the previously named organizations. The director of the Burin Charitable Association seems to be chairing the discussion. The clinic is trying to provide services to the towns of Burin, Madama, and Asira al Qiblia. It seems that there is a lot of material community support for the center (painting the walls, making curtains), but there are also many types of complaints and conversations that deal with the following issues:

1. The doctor comes to the clinic two times per week, which is an inadequate number of days and which results in a stressed-out doctor, crowded clinic, short visits, inadequate care, and patients very angry and frustrated when their urgent conditions aren't being treated quickly enough. The UNDP representative explains that their role is to support marginal communities to get access to care, and given the restrictions created by the Israeli occupation, perhaps they can build on the capacities of PMRS and the Ministry of Health working together. The nurse suggests that many services do not need a physician and that, for instance, the clinic has figured out how to provide vaccinations. In fact, much of primary care involving the monitoring of height, weight, etc., can be done by a nurse or midwife.

2. For pregnant women, there is no female doctor, no reliable ultrasound; Burin estimates that it should be seeing 75 pregnant patients but currently is only seeing 35, indicating that women are going elsewhere.

3. There is a lack of available medications. I think back to my trip to the West Bank in October 2012 when I struggled to find digoxin, a basic cardiac medication, for an older US delegate whose medications were stolen. (I finally located a private doctor who had a secret stash, and we traded other hard-to-get medications for a week of digoxin in what felt like an illicit drug deal.) A patient who is on the council tells the story of her epileptic son. Rather than getting his medications locally from the Ministry of Health as she hoped, she had the difficult choice of either driving all the way to Nablus to get them from the

Ministry or paying a premium at a local pharmacy. Another person discusses the unavailability of insulin, a basic medication for diabetes, at the Ministry of Health pharmacies. Once a medication arrives, it is distributed to all the Ministry of Health clinics, but how does it get to the patients? This problem could easily be remedied at the local level as the clinic uses a computerized database and can already organize home visits and screenings. Another person talks about how time-consuming it is to make a referral to the Ministry of Health and wonders if they could have direct computer access to their appointment system.

4. Several complain that there is no ambulance and no public transportation, and that private transportation is expensive. If someone fractures a bone or goes into labor, it is difficult to get all the way to the Ministry of Health hospital in Nablus. One diabetic, hypertensive man called an ambulance that never came. He was taken in a private car and died on the way. It seems there is little coordination between the Red Crescent and the Ministry of Health. For example, one elderly lady was hit by a settler and injured; the IDF told the family that she was stable, but the Red Crescent ambulance took her anyway. Motor vehicle accidents and the need for ambulance services are common. Only yesterday, a motor vehicle killed two people and injured four on the main road of Nablus.

5. Then there is the special issue of the nearby Jewish settlements that frequently block access between the villages, burn farms and olive trees, and release wild pigs into the Palestinian farms where they cause massive destruction with no obvious way to get rid of the animals. The biggest complaint is the frequent Israeli settler attacks and the lack of available ambulances when injuries occur. The locals report that the PA police are paralyzed and afraid to do anything, exacerbating the fact that safe transport is desperately needed.

Everyone agrees that the health committees should empower the local people to demand their rights for quality services, and PMRS supports this idea. On the positive side, the director of the charitable society proudly shows off all the activities in the center, which are detailed in his computerized records: the monthly visits monitoring patients with chronic diseases, the educational consults for the kindergarten teachers, the cooking and breakfast programs, the construction of a theater, safety awareness programs, summer camps, and the honey-making machine. The PA representative is from the fire department and talks about the civil protection services, the safety courses covering first aid and CPR, the volunteer teams that support the villagers during settler attacks, and the training for evacuating the entire village in case of emergency. We visit a room filled with handmade soap, handicrafts, and pickled fruits. This is a pretty impressive and well-organized village.

Madama, on the other hand, is in crisis. Their main source of water has been taken over by settlers, and they are reduced to carrying water of questionable quality from a well in the town in large plastic buckets by hand or on donkeys. We meet with the village council, and besides the water disaster, contamination from the sewer system, and the prevalence of infectious diarrheal diseases, all the usual challenges are more intense than those in Burin. Although both PMRS and the Angelican Hospital have clinics two days per week, they are held on the same days. Furthermore, there is little coordination between all the players, the Ministry of Health is hopelessly bureaucratic, and there is little available medicine and no capacity for supports such as fire departments and ambulances. The stakeholders at the meeting agree to set up a committee, create an action plan, and learn from the more successful experience in Burin.

Asira al Qiblia, the poorest and most marginalized of the three villages, is a small, dusty, crumbling town. It seems that there are no health councils, paved roads, or water. The villagers suffer from daily settler attacks and assaults on their water system and infrastructure, so they have lots of injuries and a generation of traumatized children. Of the 3,500 villagers (350 households), approximately 100 families have health insurance. They buy water at exorbitant prices, paying thirty shekels for a tank of three thousand liters, which lasts five days. Families' monthly water costs are higher than their total monthly incomes, and many have sold their cattle because of the lack of water. In addition, there are three nearby stone quarries, so there is the issue of dust-related respiratory diseases and allergies as well as large trucks loaded with stone lumbering through the town.

It is at this point in the story where I tend to stop and shake my head in utter despair, but we've all been invited to one of the women's homes for a feast, so we keep moving. The living room is filled with stuffed couches and chairs, and decorated with intricately embroidered pillow cases, lamp shades, and scenes of traditional weddings. We are soon sitting around a long table facing enormous platters of *mujadara* and thin cigar-shaped *yalanji* along with the usual *labneh*, flavorful salads, pita, pickled vegetables, water, Sprite, aromatic tea flavored with mint, and small cups of Turkish coffee, as a crowd of women keeps encouraging us to eat more.

These village women are warm and tough. One who speaks good English and went to college tells us that women in the countryside want to improve their lives and have projects like making honey, growing herbs, and raising sheep. Many of the women attended university and many of their men are unemployed. In Asira, on January 14, 2013, seventy women formally registered an organization called the Palestinian Foundation for Women. They are fixing up a donated house that has no water, electricity, or plumbing, and they are creating a women's center in the house for training in crafts such as embroidery and knitting as well as modern methods to make olive oil soap. She tells me most married women are working, particularly as teachers, and they all giggle and *kvell* about the new *Arab Idol* winner from Gaza. The older woman who cooked the vast quantity of food will not let us leave without taking doggie bags for the road, ignoring the fact that I do not have a refrigerator and am likely to face vast quantities of food at future stops. I give her a thank-you gift of an olive oil hand cream made in Davis, California, by a friend of my daughter's, and she gets out her local version. It is contained in a plain white bottle but smells fragrantly of almond and apricot oil, which is pretty divine. Despite the challenges this village is facing, it seems that the self-esteem and integrity of the women are solid. They are not looking for charity; they just want the opportunity to raise their families and live productive, creative lives, which seems utterly reasonable.

The Ariel Finger

June 25, 2013

After seeing patients in a PMRS clinic in Qalqilya, I join Suhad Hashem, an extraordinary, feisty activist, for a "wall tour" of the city. This is my third tour in nine years, and "the prison," as I refer to the city, has certainly devolved. We pass a shabby UNRWA hospital, and she informs me that even though the people of Qalqilya are not technically refugees, they were given refugee status because they lost so much of their land located on the "wrong side" of the Green Line in 1948. They also have the only zoo in Palestine! All sorts of metaphors spring to mind: the animals in a cage, the zoo keepers also caged.

We walk toward the North Gate through the bustling *souk* filled with fruits and vegetables. From 2002 to 2005, no permits were given to allow workers to leave the city to work in Israel, a form of collective punishment for the entire population. In 2006, it became possible for workers to leave through this military terminal. This was all built inside the West Bank, annexing twelve kilometers of Qalqilya to Israel. The men must present permits, their bodies are checked, and a handprint is taken *every time*. Suhad has gone through this gate and found it utterly humiliating. She reports that usually young female soldiers are assigned to the gate as a way to increase the humiliation for the older Palestinian men. The laborers are picked up by an Arab-only Israeli bus and taken to the Tel Aviv industrial areas or to black market industries or to "Sorry, no work today." The workers have no trade union protections and there are many stories of terrible abuse, but people are desperate for work and have no choice but to endure the conditions. At the Azzun Atma crossing, Suhad explains, a different bus also stops at the Israeli settlement of Oranit, but the settlers objected to the presence of Arabs on the bus, so the police now enter the bus, take all the Palestinians' IDs, throw them off the bus, and the men are forced to walk a distance to another site where their IDs are returned.

Suhad reports that 50 percent of the Palestinian permit requests for access to their own land are rejected by the Israeli authorities, or permits are only given to one family member when it takes the whole family to work the land. In some places what serves as the wall is actually a fence; the walled area there includes the fence itself, constructed of barbed wire, a military road on each side, a trench, and then more barbed wire on more terrain that was seized to create a no-man's land. Recently, the Israelis have allowed Palestinians in some areas to farm right up to the concrete wall so I see neat rows of crops and plantings where there used to be rubble. Before the wall, this was a major greenhouse area, Israelis shopped in Qalqilya, and there was a vigorous agricultural export business. That abruptly ended with the wall, and this area is now a parking lot and the garbage-strewn *souk* in which we are standing. Thus, wealthy families have been reduced to poverty.

We walk down Western Street, once a vigorous commercial area, now dead, and visit the Asharqa School, which has the misfortune of being located adjacent to the wall, the eight-meters-high, three-meters-under-the-ground concrete version. Suhad tells us stories of Jewish settlers dumping sewage into the yard of a school adjacent to the wall and destroying part of the school yard. The children in these situations live with the wall shoved in their faces;

they are the first to see the IDF incursions, the first to choke from the tear gas, and they have predictable psychological difficulties. The Israelis have added electrical fencing on top of the wall and security cameras every few hundred feet. On the other side of the wall, the land in front of the concrete barrier has been filled in and planted with trees so the wall is virtually invisible to those who choose not to see.

Qalqilya has flooded twice since the wall was constructed, and when it rains the water and sewage mix together to create an awful soup, so there are now some grated drainage openings at the base of the concrete. As we walk along the military road, trying to grasp the ugliness and consequences of this imposing prison, there are pools of open sewage and the foul odor of dormant puddles.

Suhad speaks with a mixture of urgency and outrage. The big reason for all of this land grabbing, she explains, is that Qalqilya sits upon the largest water aquifer in Palestine, 52 percent of the water in Palestine, and the Israelis want to control the water sources. People say that water is more important than oil and gold in these parts. We are looking at the latest graffito on the towering cement walls—it depicts a giant hand with keys and chains dangling from the fingers. There is an elegant mansion opposite this site, adjacent to the olive saplings in the no-man's-land, and the house is under demolition orders because it is too close to the wall, which was obviously built after the house was constructed. The owner's child died of a chronic illness because he was unable to get a permit to continue the child's treatments in Israel.

There are new developments, which Suhad explains by referring to a pile of maps she opens in front of us while pointing in various directions, squinting into the sun. The Israelis have built a tunnel from the walled city of Qalqilya to the walled city of Habla that goes under the wall. Life is even further complicated in other ways for some Palestinians, like the villagers of Arab Abu Fardad who live on land in between the loops that encircle the settlements, an arrangement that provides the Jewish settlers with full access to Israel and modern bypass roads, and totally isolates those Palestinians living on "the wrong side" of the loops. She then gives a detailed explanation of the bypass roads that have been built to link the settlements deep into the West Bank with Israel. These elongated extensions of settlements, referred to as "fingers"—one is called the "Ariel finger"—are linked up so that they stretch all the way to the Jordan Valley on the east side of the West Bank, dividing the territory in two. The Palestinians trapped between these fingers of land and roads are under threat of dispossession; they have no water or schools, cannot bury their dead, and are severely restricted in terms of what they can bring to market. In other words, they are being targeted for "silent transfer": life becomes so unbearable that they are forced to leave in order to survive.

We are now on the tunneled road toward the walled town of Habla, which is three kilometers from Qalqilya. Under international pressure, the Israelis not only built the tunnel, but also a gate that is open three times a day. We get there at 5:30 p.m. and children, laborers, and tractors are gathering for the ritual of crossing over. I can see the high-rises of Tel Aviv in the distance. Suhad tells us of a man who tried to cross, but according to the false data in the security terminal's computer, he was already on the other side, at which point the man was forced to prove that he was actually on the side that he was actually on! She says if you argue, you lose your permit for one year, so everyone is fairly subdued.

The IDF soldiers arrive at the gate in a jeep on the other side. One man and two young women, fully armed for combat, get out to open the gate. One of the women has long blond hair cascading down her back, flowing out of her menacing helmet. They are laughing and kicking the locks and clearly taking their time while the prisoners on each side wait patiently. They finally open the gate and tell us we cannot stand in the road, where the photographic opportunities are optimal. When Suhad asks why not, the woman replies, "Because it's the rules." I look at the size of her gun and decide now is not the time for an argument.

In the taxi back to the *service* to Nablus, I ask Suhad where she finds hope. She speaks eloquently of the power of survival, of refusing to leave, replanting the crops, rebuilding the homes, educating the children. She also talks about the critical importance of international attention and pressure and the power of the boycott movement, which is the other focus of her activity. Clearly, she does not have the privilege of despair.

_⎯⎊⎯_ **3**

Only Tigers Survive
June 13–21, 2014

In June 2014, I returned again, finding that the situation had continued to deteriorate as the occupation strangled the healthcare system in the West Bank and East Jerusalem. Just days before we arrived, three Israeli settler boys were kidnapped from a bus stop at one of the settlements, and the Israeli military immediately clamped down on the West Bank's many Palestinian refugee camps, villages, and cities. I could feel the tensions building fast in those communities.

On this delegation, we continued our exploration of the dispossession of Palestinians and the erasure of Palestinian society that began in 1948, focusing on the ongoing "Nakba" of dispossesion and erasure being pursued in East Jerusalem. During our tour of Jaffa, the consequences of building a Jewish state on the basis of segregation between Jews and non-Jews and racism toward "Arabs" (of the Jewish and non-Jewish variety) became particularly clear, challenging the mythology of a "Jewish democracy." Most striking were the inherent contradictions of a highly militarized and powerful majority-Jewish state that yet still suffered from a siege mentality, insecure in the face of immense power and dominance. The United States gives the Israeli government massive amounts of weaponry and financial aid to buy our military hardware, while Israeli defense companies build our drones, field-test our armaments, and train our police; and their subsidiaries build our wall with Mexico. But we found most Jewish Israelis too afraid to venture into East Jerusalem while the Jewish settlers in the Old City walked around with armed guards as they tried to avoid the Christian clergy of every denomination as well as the nuns, the tourists, the Palestinian children in a variety of school uniforms, and the rest of the Palestinians who have lived in the city for centuries.

In 2012, when I visited Israel/Palestine with a group of African-American civil rights leaders, theologians, scholars, and activists under the auspices of the Dorothy Cotton Institute, I became acutely attuned to the underlying racism that buttresses this political reality. These civil rights activists, many of whom had worked with Dr. Martin Luther King, Jr., were quick to identify the Jim Crow–like atmosphere in Israel and the apartheid-like conditions in the West Bank. Whether it was the almost entirely segregated school systems in Israel and the purely Zionist curriculum required of all students, Jewish and Palestinian, or the settler-only bypass roads connecting Jewish settlements in the West Bank and the Jewish-only streets in Hebron, the parallels were painfully obvious. When young Palestinian activists talked about the Jewish settlers freely attacking and humiliating Palestinians and defacing and destroying their homes and shops, the Ku Klux Klan came readily to mind. Palestinian civil society activists also mirrored the US civil rights movement. They even had a Palestinian Freedom Rides campaign that challenged this segregation, boarding Jewish-only buses in settlements and facing beatings and arrest as they did so. We examined the weekly nonviolent village demonstrations against the separation barrier and the loss of land and water, inspired by the work of King and Gandhi. I learned of other "Freedom Rides" activities that brought theater, music, and song to Palestinian communities throughout the West Bank and the yearly protests where international, Israeli, and Palestinian women wearing traditional Palestinian dress walked peaceably along the forbidden Shuhada Street in downtown Hebron, to be met with tear gas, stun grenades, and arrests from the Israeli military.

Memories of freedom marches, sit-ins, and bus boycotts from the 1960s clearly reverberated in my mind. I shuddered, too, at the parallels with what the Jews had faced in Germany, only now the roles were reversed, the victim became victimizer. I knew in my head that anyone could be a fascist given the right economic, political, or psychological circumstances, but I still found this emotionally wrenching to witness, particularly because the settler community was protected, funded, and used as a spearhead by the Israeli government.

It is not surprising that with the growing awareness of connections and "intersectionality" around issues of racism, power, and militarism across cultures, countries, and peoples, Black Lives Matter activists have seen the parallels with the Palestinian struggle and stood in solidarity with their Arab brothers and sisters. When Ferguson exploded in 2014 with the killing of Michael Brown, Palestinians in the West Bank took to social media and offered Ferguson protesters advice on coping with tear gas. This led to a greater public awareness of how the booming Israeli homeland security industry, with its decades of experience containing and controlling the captive Palestinian population, has led to a sharing of "expertise" in "counterterrorism" with other countries, what has been called the "Israelification" of US policing and security. This process blossomed after 9/11.[1]

The intersection of these movements also raised the perennial question: Whose lives matter in the first place? The prevailing narrative (Jews as victims, Palestinians as terrorists) can only happen if we see Jews as "more" human, more deserving, more honorable than Arabs; if we as a community are blind to Palestinian suffering and the deep physical and psychological wounds that started with Jewish colonization of Palestine and culminated in the war of 1948. An average of two to three Palestinian children have been killed by the IDF or settlers every week since September 2000. Clearly each one of those children deserves as much public attention and concern as the three settler boys kidnapped near Hebron in June 2014. But now, back to East Jerusalem, in June 2014.

Don't Get Sick While Palestinian

June 13, 2014

So this is my current understanding of how one component of health care for Palestinians operates. A Palestinian family calls an ambulance in East Jerusalem; the call goes to the Magen David Adom (MDA, an Israeli ambulance service that is bound by international agreements to respond). If the MDA determines that this is a "high-risk" neighborhood, they demand a police escort and will not enter the area until the police arrive. The (Palestinian) Red Crescent ambulance (they are not allowed to use "Palestinian" in their title in East Jerusalem) can also be called directly, but their phone number is different and not so well known as the MDA's. If the police do not come, then the Red Crescent is called, but if the situation is determined to be too dangerous, depending on the location, the Palestinian Medical Relief Society (PMRS) ambulance is called.

But PMRS ambulances are based in Al Bireh in the West Bank, and because they must pass through checkpoints and inspections, they cannot reliably enter East Jerusalem. Palestinian ambulance drivers must have permits to drive the ambulance and personal permits to enter East Jerusalem; the permits last six months and they are often issued for time periods that do not entirely overlap, so there are months when the drivers are unable to work. Palestinians in need of critical care from the West Bank face huge barriers, often having to walk across checkpoints or be transferred by gurney between two back-to-back ambulances at a checkpoint. (I have seen this with vegetable produce—it can ruin a shipment of tomatoes—now imagine that scenario for human beings.) A Palestinian living in East Jerusalem is covered under Israeli insurance, which does not pay for the Red Crescent ambulance—often the only one that is able to come—thus, the ailing patient (should he or she survive) is also out 150 shekels for the crime of being sick while Palestinian in a racist society.

Ambulances get to Jewish Israelis in an average of seven minutes.

In the case of a motor vehicle accident in the West Bank, ambulance pickup is determined by the identity of each victim: MDA transports the Jews (i.e., settlers); Palestinian Red Crescent transports the Christian and Muslim Palestinians. But if the doctor determines that the Palestinian needs high-level care that is only offered in East Jerusalem, the patient is transported to Qalandia checkpoint, where a "humanitarian line" is intermittently open, there are huge traffic jams, and an East Jerusalem ambulance is supposed to meet the patient there for a back-to-back transfer, if appropriate permits are obtained, which are ultimately determined by the Shin Bet, the Israeli General Security Services.

These medical decisions are reportedly made by the Israeli health coordinator, Dalia Basa, an Iraqi Jew who speaks some Arabic, has worked in the West Bank since the 1970s, and holds immense power regarding the granting of patient permits. Overseeing the Erez checkpoint in Gaza is a different official, the Coordinator of Government Activities in the Territories, which operates under the Ministry of Defense. The barriers to obtaining permits also include lack of phone access, inadequate communication with Israeli hospitals, broken fax machines, and the fickle moods of young Israeli Defense Force soldiers or privately hired security guards at checkpoints, who are the ultimate arbiters of passage and who sometimes do security checks (even on ambulances and UN cars) and sometimes don't. I am told that these eighteen- to twenty-one-year-olds with large guns and no medical knowledge decide if a case is medically "severe": Is there blood? Burns? Is the woman in labor or just "fat"?

Forgive me if I sound angry. It is stunning what one can learn just listening to health care providers and administrators chatting over a cup of thick Arabic coffee in an office in East Jerusalem. There are so many injustices, some imposed by occupation, racism, and fear, and some by internal dysfunction. There is a growing drug problem in East Jerusalem (born of hopelessness and the lack of police protection, or a functional court system), and there are dealers running out of an Israeli crime network. At this stage addiction is mostly prevalent among young men on heroin, and there are only three small nongovernmental organizations struggling to address the multifaceted crises of drug rehabilitation.

Lest we forget:

Geneva Convention IV, Article 56:
The occupying power has the duty of ensuring and maintaining, with the cooperation of national and local authorities, the medical and hospital establishments and services, public health and hygiene in the occupied territory . . .
Medical personnel of all categories shall be allowed to carry out their duties.[2]

Committee on Economic, Social and Cultural Rights, General Comment No. 14: The Right to the Highest Attainable Standard of Health:
[Article No. 33]. The right to health, like all human rights, imposes three types or levels of obligations on States parties: the obligations to *respect, protect* and *fulfill*. . . . The obligation to *respect* requires States to refrain from interfering directly or indirectly with the enjoyment of the right to health. The obligation to *protect* requires States to take measures that prevent third parties from interfering with article 12 guarantees. Finally, the obligation to *fulfill* requires States to adopt appropriate . . . measures towards the full realization of the right to health.[3]

How do we begin to honor both the moral responsibility toward patients and these binding conventions of international law?

A Blurring of Boundaries and Conscience

June 14, 2014

Another tour of Jerusalem with staff from the Israeli Committee Against House Demolitions (ICAHD) and another wave of disbelief, shock, and deepening horror. Chaska Katz, a high-energy thirty-something from a progressive, apolitical family ("My parents were hippies," she says), came of age in the small circles of the Israeli left, refused to serve in the army, started agitating for animal rights, and ultimately found her way to defending the rights of migrants, refugees, and Palestinians. ICAHD's focus on fighting Palestinian home demolitions provides her with a concrete nonviolent activity that is often a merely symbolic form of resistance but sometimes produces life-changing results. She is fluent in English, Hebrew, and Arabic.

We leave the Old City on Hebron Road toward the Jewish settlement of Talpiot and in stifling heat, we gather on a lookout in the neighborhood of Jabel Mukaber. To our far left we can see West Jerusalem, characterized by tall high-rises, apartments, hotels, fourteen huge cranes, swaths of green, parks, gardens—a constantly expanding city pushing its boundaries with massive construction. A Jewish success story! The cranes represent not only yet more high-rises, but also an exploding public infrastructure: highways, bridges, tunnels, solid "facts on the ground" (i.e., THIS BELONGS TO US).

My eye moves to the right to the Old City with the gleaming gold dome and, adjacent to it, two crowded Palestinian villages cascading down the hill, Silwan and Wadi Joz (dotted with recently built Jewish settler homes), and then further east, the scattered grey-white Palestinian houses topped by black water towers, as the community is now tending toward vertical development because there are no legal places to spread horizontally. The contrasts in the villages are stark: no parks, no green space, no cranes, and empty patches of barren dry hills. These folks pay the same city taxes as the happy Jews in West Jerusalem with their sidewalks and garbage collection and street lights. More than half of the Palestinians in East Jerusalem have no sewage or water connection and often tap into existing pipes, thus dropping the water pressure. Mekorot, the Israeli water company, refuses to lay more pipe, and many Palestinians have no water two to three days per week. I see a Palestinian boy biking in small circles on his roof, another on a swing, rocking back and forth, also on a roof. Those are obviously their playgrounds. Because there is minimal garbage collection, Palestinians burn their garbage, so these little boys are playing in an air polluted environment as a direct result of the neglect and racism of Israeli authorities. The numbers are stark. The Jerusalem municipal budget allots 8 to 10 percent of its finances to one-third of its population.

On a more distant hill is the Mount of Olives and the tower of Augusta Victoria Hospital, a major tertiary care hospital in East Jerusalem, and then to the southeast, the neighborhoods of Abu Dis and Azaria, now divided from Jerusalem by a concrete wall eight to ten meters high, cutting through the fabric of life and community and denying their access to the holy sites and medical care of East Jerusalem. Further in the distance is the expansive Jewish settlement of Ma'ale Adumim, stretching its borders eastward to Jericho with the hope of ultimately bisecting the West Bank.

Intellectually, I already knew all of this, but the visual reality is breathtaking. Chaska reviews the history of 1948, 1967, the various displacements of Jews and Palestinians during the wars, and the ultimate annexation of East Jerusalem as part of the "undivided capital of Israel." She explains that for Palestinians to maintain their treasured East Jerusalem ID, they have to constantly prove that East Jerusalem is the center of their life and work, and this requirement creates enormous hardship. When the wall was built, inducing panic about getting stuck on the wrong side, there was a massive influx of East Jerusalemites living in suburbs like Hizmeh and Abu Dis. The same awful consequence can result from the most basic course of action. Study abroad? Risk losing your ID. Work in Ramallah because there is no work at home? Risk losing your ID. Build a house just across from the wall because your eight children are now married and having children, and there is no place to build and permits are impossible? Risk losing your ID. And the list goes on. I often feel that Israeli authorities are ethnically cleansing East Jerusalem one Palestinian at a time.

A new piece of information for me is that 60 to 80 percent of the land seized in Jerusalem in 1948 was Palestinian agricultural land. Even more was taken after 1967, so the Palestinians have continuously lost their source of income and employment and have migrated in large numbers into the cities, providing Israel with a source of cheap, easily exploited labor. Israeli labor laws do not apply to these folks. And now (after the intifadas) this exploited labor has returned to the Israeli labor market by the tens of thousands. They are cleaning the streets, planting the gardens, building the roads and apartments that only displace them further.

With the signing of the Oslo Accords in 1993, the rapid growth of Jewish settlements in Palestinian neighborhoods began in earnest, as did the Judaization of East Jerusalem and its ever-expanding boundaries. I found it helpful to understand that Jerusalem actually has three boundaries:

1. The 1967 municipal boundary extends to include East Jerusalem; Palestinians with East Jerusalem IDs must live only in East Jerusalem.
2. The entity known as Greater Jerusalem includes the settlement blocks of Giv'at Ze'ev in the north, Ma'ale Adumim in the east, and Gush Etzion in the south, which form a giant Jewish ring around East Jerusalem.
3. Metropolitan Jerusalem (not to be confused with Greater Jerusalem) was approved in 1995 and includes Ramallah (!), Bethlehem (!), and Beit Shemesh. This boundary exists to advance Israeli priorities regarding zoning, development, and, of course, ultimately settlement growth.

The net effect is that Palestinian neighborhoods as well as cities are surrounded and constricted by growing Jewish settlements and thus unable to expand; each settlement brings with it an infrastructure of bypass roads and military bases. Palestinian freedom of movement is even further eroded, and the areas of Palestinian life are thus reduced to isolated enclaves. Coming here year after year, I am bearing witness to this crushing reality.

Similar patterns exist within East Jerusalem, where the Palestinian population has grown from 66,000 in 1967 to 300,000 in 2013, but only 13 percent of the land is zoned for residential use and no new Palestinian neighborhoods have been built. This contrasts to the 52 percent of the land that is green zoned (i.e., zoned for open space, infrastructure, and ultimately Jewish settlements). This is in addition to the 35 percent of East Jerusalem already zoned for Jewish settlement development.

This is a long and myth-shattering tour. We visit the Jewish settlement of Ma'ale Zeiteim, built by the US doctor and casino magnate Irving Moskowitz. During the Shalit negotiations to free the captured Israeli soldier in Gaza, there were two prominently placed banners in the settlement that read: "Kahane [a Brooklyn-born, militant, extremely racist right-wing rabbi] was right! Death to the Arabs!" and "One Jew equals 1,000 Arabs." I look at the manicured lawns, the recycling bins, the lovely baby carriages, and the flowers blooming in charming gardens planted in this desert community. Of course I also look at the security cameras and the guards, and I remember that this place is actually a bunker overlooking the angry residents of Ras al-'Amud. There are more settlements like this strategically dotting the hills, and gradually the pieces are coming together, the segments of wall are linking up, the massive prison for the people of Judea and Samaria in the area known as E1 is completed. Palestinian villages like Beit Iksa and Biddu are trapped in tiny enclaves, surrounded by loops of wall, isolated from their communities. Some, like Anata and Shu'afat, have residents with East Jerusalem IDs who just ended up on the wrong side of history. Some villages now are devoid of any services, including a police force, and are basically lawless areas where drugs and arms trafficking are rampant. The bureaucracy of occupation is in full force, and it is mean-spirited and physically destructive. Meanwhile the permitting system in the West Bank has become more severe; there are increasing physical, social, and emotional barriers; and more Palestinian collaborators are being drawn from the ranks of the young, the frightened, the desperate.

I peer over the ridge into a deep blue artificial lake built at the base of a hill in Ma'ale Adumim and spot three adjacent Olympic-size swimming pools; I marvel at the series of rotaries graced by thousand-year-old olive trees uprooted from some ancient village that probably does not have a regular water supply. I think of the nightmare permitting process for a Palestinian who wants to expand his house and has to prove that it is part of some community development master plan (even though none exists) and that there is proof of ownership by Israeli standards (never mind the land deed from the Ottoman Empire and the generations of family who have lived there). And then there are the demolition orders and the legal maneuvers and the bulldozer in the middle of the night with the fully armed soldiers and the helicopters overhead and the rubble and screaming children and then of course the fine and the bill for demolition. Trauma, hopelessness, rage.

I wonder: What kind of society have we become? What kind of people do this to each other, then kiss their children, and sleep without nightmares? Do the nice Hadassah ladies, the American tourists having a spiritual moment on the Via Dolorosa, the sunburned Birthright teens playing frisbee on a Tel Aviv beach care? What are the ugly consequences of grabbing everything over and over again and then only wanting more?

Walking with Ghosts

June 17, 2014

The gunfire stops around midnight, and we sleep well at the Yafa Cultural Center in the Balata Refugee Camp. In the morning, we learn that the Israeli military made an early incursion into the camp, arresting about ten young men, beating one and trashing a house. This is apparently such a normal occurrence that children are smiling, holding hands, and walking to school in their blue and white uniforms, men are opening their shops, and women hurry by. There is an air of total normalcy in this totally abnormal place.

We cruise through a variety of checkpoints including the once-onerous Huwarra checkpoint, which is now totally deserted. I look at the signs—Pisgat Zeev, Neve Yalakov, Moshe Dyan Street—the east-and-west-ness of Jerusalem is no longer about location but rather about where exactly Arabs and Jews are currently living. As we did last year, we again meet up with Umar Ighbariyah from the Israeli organization Zochrot for a poignant tour of Lifta. Reviewing some of the local history, he explains that many people are unaware that the Palestinian depopulations continued into the early 1950s (after the war was over) and included the villages of Zacharia and al-Majdal Asqalan. Roman tax documents establish the existence of Lifta from the twelfth century, it was liberated from the Turks by Saladin in 1189, and later occupied by the Ottomans, the British, and then . . .

We stand at the top of the valley, avoiding rumbling trucks at the massive construction site that is destined to be a fast train from Tel Aviv to Jerusalem; there are two tunnels in the distant hills that will soon connect. Below this site is the continued "secret" construction of the bunker designed for government officials in the case of a nuclear holocaust. There is something supremely ironic about this location for the bunker. (Will the whole country someday be a disappeared village?) Turning slowly 360 degrees, Umar points out the locations of other former villages, such as Colunia, Deir Yassin, and Ein Karem, as well as the Jewish settlement of Romama and the Palestinian neighborhoods of Beit Hanina in East Jerusalem and Biddu in the West Bank. Umar explains that the Jewish settlement of Ramot, which is on the way to Ramallah, is actually located in the ever-expanding Jerusalem and 90 percent of the settlement is built on Palestinian land. In 1948, this area was perched on the dangerous armistice border with Jordan; since then it has become strategically situated, with patchwork claims and identities and a border now marked with a line of Jewish National Fund forests.

We start the hike down the dusty, rocky valley; its gracious stone ruins with magnificent arches, domes, and towering *saber* cactus still stand as living testaments to the past. I can almost feel the presence of the women with their bread, the men returning from the olive orchards, the children washing in the pools—the ghosts of Lifta breathing life into painful memories. Fig trees, expansive oaks, and fruit trees bear witness as well. Then we meet an older, mustached man, beaming with happiness. He is from here, but now lives in San Diego and is exploring the park in the ruins of Lifta with his nephew, who has just been released after thirteen years in prison for involvement with the Popular Front for the Liberation of Palestine. We watch the man bear-hug an olive tree and start singing and dancing. He tells us he wishes he lived here so he could invite us to his home for dinner and, speaking in Arabic, he reminds our guide and interpreter, Hana, not to say anything bad about Jews! His joy is infectious and his nephew appears quietly pleased and supportive. We learn about the puzzling way that the nephew was released: in the prison located near Gaza where he was locked up, he was awakened in the night, put into a jeep, and dropped off in the Negev. He was found by Bedouins and gradually made his way home. He had been locked up for so long that he had never seen a cell phone. His mother and father were both arrested when he was released. Does this sound strangely barbaric to anyone in the modern democratic State of Israel?

Young ultra-Orthodox boys run down the path to the pools that date back to the Romans for a refreshing dip and splash. I summon up my tolerance and I try to accept the scene as it is, but all I can imagine is that (even in their brightly colored underwear and wet *payos*; their familiar *tzitzit*, *tallit*, black hats, and dark suits hanging from trees) they are from some other planet, perhaps part of a lost lunar landing, and these voyagers simply can't see or appreciate the history and treasured beauty of this sacred space. Or is that sensibility entirely lost when a person believes so deeply in Zionism and the path Israel has taken? Do we even have a common language when it comes to Jewish privilege and Palestinian humanity? Do we even see the same people?

Umar's family history dates back to before the Nakba, in a village near Nazareth. Attacked in 1948, the villagers fled to the forests and lived there for two years; a few houses were destroyed and vandalized, the cows were stolen, the sugar and oil were trashed, one donkey was killed. The families were then allowed to return but, in another one of those ironic turn of events, at the Rhodes agreement with Jordan the Israelis wanted more land near their armistice line, so the King of Jordan dipped his thumb in ink, pressed it onto the map, and poof, Umar's village was included in the State of Israel. Forty-five thousand Palestinians were annexed in this fashion and then had the "privilege" of Israeli citizenship and military rule until 1966. The French representative reportedly drew the armistice line with a green pen—hence, the "Green Line."

Reflecting on his experience working with Zochrot, Umar notes that the media and the public have a much greater awareness of the Palestinian Nakba, although many feel that it was justified; war is hell; the ends justify the means. I suspect that the ghosts feel otherwise. They watch every Nakba Day, when inhabitants from Lifta who now live in East Jerusalem are allowed to clean up the cemetery, honor their dead, and try to save some remnants of this magnificent city gone to ruin.

The Stones Do Not Lie

June 17, 2014

After a frightening moment with a small billowing forest fire a few hundred feet from our bus, we meet Umar in the village of Imwas in the middle of Canada-Ayalon Park, a major JNF nature reserve, popular for picnics and strolls in the woods among the "Roman ruins." Arabs here date back to 638 CE, when they arrived along with the bubonic plague. Archeologists think the bathhouse site in the village dates back to the third century. The village was built hundreds of years ago and, along with Yallo and Deir Ayyoub, comprised a strategically important area called the Latrun. Israeli forces failed to seize the Latrun in 1948 because the local Arabs put up fierce opposition, and thus the Israelis lost a direct route from Jaffa to Jerusalem. The capture of Latrun was one of the first goals of the 1967 War.

Much to my amazement, the village was occupied in 1967 but never annexed like East Jerusalem, so the area technically still sits within the West Bank, existing as occupied territory. Nonetheless, Israelis frolic freely in the park, and inhabitants of the three old villages have to obtain permits to visit the sites of their former homes, schools, olive groves, desecrated cemeteries. In 1967, the villagers gave no resistance; the IDF rounded them up in the central yard, reassured them they would return soon, and then forcibly marched the bewildered families toward Ramallah. "*Yalla* to Ramallah." (*Yalla* is an Arabic expression—"Let's go, move on"—used frequently by Israelis, particularly when ordering Palestinians to move.) A few hid in their homes, a few fled to a Trappist monastery, but a total of 7,500 villagers were ethnically cleansed. Umar shows us photos depicting scenes eerily like the catastrophes of 1948 and others that have befallen people we all know and love.

Once the inhabitants were gone, the army bulldozed the houses, but the stones and protruding pipes and metal remain, as well as a sixth-century Byzantine church, a crumbling Roman bathhouse, and three neglected cemeteries. After the Six-Day War, the inhabitants were reportedly directed by the military to walk back to the town but were met by the IDF, who shot over their heads and turned the hungry, thirsty, frightened families away. According to Umar, Israeli commanders explained to the nearby *kibbutzniks*, "There are some things you will never understand. [The message: this is about getting revenge for 1948.] How do you expect us to let Arabs stay close to the highway? We need the area clean."

In another mind-boggling tidbit, the area is administered by the civilian administration, which is part of the military administration for the West Bank, so somebody in power knows that this is the West Bank. Palestinians treated the baths as a holy shrine dating back to a *sheikh* who was a friend of the Prophet Mohammed. Except for one explanatory sign in Hebrew demanded by Zochrot (the sign has now been torn down and replaced three times and blackened once), there is not a single acknowledgment that this lovely forest, with its JNF trees and graceful olive groves and house foundations and olive presses, dates back to a recently destroyed Palestinian village. An Israeli soldier photographed the destruction and the forced march in 1967, and finally had the emotional wherewithal to publish his pictures in the 1980s in the Hebrew press. No one cared.

Across the highway is the more polished version of the park. Paths are neatly lined with square stones taken from the destroyed homes. Lovely walls enclose a playground, the stones again from destroyed houses. There are circles of panels made from the same stones celebrating the donors to the park: They include Paul Robeson and Martin Luther King and lists of wealthy Canadian Jews and congregations. The JNF sponsors olive festivals to encourage Israeli children (read: Jews) to connect to the land and the olive trees.

So how does a lie get created and sold as the truth? History as well as people can be disappeared, particularly when they are voiceless, colonized, Arab, Muslim. How do the survivors of the European catastrophe throw people out of their homes and set them off on forced marches, leaving them with nothing? How are false memories born and rebirthed until only the dispossessed and a few hardy souls who refuse to forget demand to tell the whole story? It is a powerful reminder to touch the rugged stones of Imwas, to walk with the ghosts, hear their voices in the welcomed breeze, and feel the presence of people who refuse to disappear.

I come from a people that stands proudly and says, "We will never forget." Every catastrophe is unique in its own right, but how can we expect others to feel any differently than we do? Palestinians too will never forget. The stones do not lie.

Calm, Organized Chaos

June 18, 2014

Last night, as we left the Elbeit Alnisa'i guesthouse for dinner, the nine of us wandered off into Beit Sahour's dark streets, the sidewalks challenging our unsteady ankles. Under a clear starry sky, we went past tempting pastry shops and churches and statues of the Virgin Mary. A small elderly woman with a twinkle in her eye, who was hosting us at the hostel with a steady stream of mint tea and Turkish coffee, led us determinedly up and down the hills and winding streets to a lovely restaurant complete with sappy music and the World Cup on a large screen. Later, overstuffed once again by tasty rice, cauliflower, eggplant, and watermelon, we set off on our uncertain course home and immediately stumbled into the midst of ten or so teenage boys on bikes doing various testosterone-driven things. In any other city I would have felt afraid, but we soon found ourselves surrounded by these young men as they carefully herded us back to our guesthouse, then left us with the customary "You're welcome!"

Tonight I am writing from the bosom of a family living in the Aida Refugee Camp in Bethlehem, and once again the extraordinary decency and generosity is overwhelming. The house is multistory with various adjoining apartments, kitchens, bathrooms, a large room filled with rubble that is under construction, and a spiral staircase in the kitchen that seems to lead to another apartment where the four girls sleep. There is definitely a baseline level of calm, organized chaos. The parents have two more sons: one who is busy studying for final exams, the other who is severely disabled with cerebral palsy, partly related to a premature birth but also exacerbated by a subsequent episode of severe oxygen loss while he was hospitalized. Mostly he sits curled in a swing in the hall that is made from an automobile seat, and rocks back and forth, making various cries and calling "Ma." His mother tenderly explains that she understands him when he speaks, as do his siblings. At night, he sleeps curled up with her. He had attended a special school for a while, but the family wanted him home because the teacher did not understand him when he shrieked, and he cried all the time. Fourteen years old and tall for his age, he is becoming increasingly difficult to carry, and he is facing an educational system with inadequate resources and expertise in dealing with children with multiple severe problems. There are fifty children with disabilities now at home in the three Bethlehem refugee camps, and their enormous needs are mostly met by their unbelievably supportive families.

I meet the paternal grandmother who, like me, was born in 1948 but, unlike me, looks like a fragile eighty-year-old who has lived through an inordinately large amount of stress. She smiles, enjoys holding hands, and prays quietly with her beads. She asks me why I am traveling without my husband and lets me know that if I were her daughter, she would kill me for such a "transgression." I give her a quick rendition of a modern American marriage and assure her that my husband and I love and respect each other very much. Everyone seems impressed that I am a doctor. This seems to put the issue to rest.

Various nieces and nephews drift in and out, and I realize the family is also caring for the son and daughter of the father's brother, who was killed ten years ago. Pictures of the martyred uncle adorn the living room, where we drink tea and then chop a mountain of tomatoes, baked eggplant, and onion. Puzzles, finger puppets, origami, and magic markers emerge from our bags, and suddenly the children are very preoccupied. There is a lot of touching and cooperation, laughter, playful shoving and hugging, and a sweetness to the interactions. At dinner, the disabled son is carried into the dining room and is hugged, kissed, and fed by a variety of family members, much as a baby bird with a broken wing in a nest would be attended by foragers bringing back delicacies. They all clearly love and accept him and are not at all distracted by his movements and behavior. Somehow, this kind of full acceptance and support makes me want to cry.

I have been trying to keep track of the events that are heating up all around us. Three Israeli settler boys from Hebron (read: right-wing, ultra-Orthodox) were apparently kidnapped, and while this is to be utterly condemned, their disappearance is being used to whip the country into a wild, xenophobic, Hamas-hating, unity government–hating mood. There is quite a media frenzy, including special hashtags on social media, and everywhere we see large signs on buses that read, "Bring our boys home!" Prime Minister Netanyahu seems convinced this is the work of Hamas despite what seems to be a lack of carefully collected evidence. The IDF are making massive arrests in the West Bank, people have been injured and shot by soldiers—a friend of mine was hit by a tear gas canister while protesting the forced-feeding of the hunger strikers in Israeli jails—and we keep hearing that the city of Hebron is under closure, with a massive military presence throughout the West Bank.

While I understand the terror and horror of kidnapping teenage boys, for decades now Palestinian children and teenagers have been detained and arrested by Israeli military, often in the middle of the night in front of terrified mothers and fathers, with no lawyers and often no charges made. There has been no public outrage for these Arab children and obviously no collective punishment of Israeli families whose sons have been beating and cuffing and interrogating frightened kids, ignoring international law and common decency. Somehow, it all feels different when the victim and perpetrator are flipped.

The World according to Sami

June 18, 2014

So we are back in what is often called '48 Israel (i.e., the Israel contained within the increasingly phantasmagorical Green Line), and we are meeting once again with one of my favorite academic-activists, Sami Abu Shehadeh. If we were to title our discussion, it would be "Jaffa" with the subtitle "Mixed Cities and Racism." More than 90 percent of the historical Palestinian population lives in total separation from the Jewish population, but the boundaries are very messy. Until recently, he explains, with his ironic mix of deprecating humor and truth-telling, there was no need to legalize the process of separation, but in the past decade, Arabs (as Israelis call Palestinians) have tried to move into Jewish areas (with their better housing, better schools, better services), and because there were no racial laws in Israel, a new criterion was invented. People can be excluded from communities because of "unsuitable compatibility." Sami reports that at Tel Aviv University, a professor noted that Tel Aviv is the only Western city without an Arab community and yet Jaffa is an ancient Arab city annexed to Tel Aviv in 1950, but by design the Palestinian residents are kept separate and underdeveloped.

As we wander the streets of Jaffa, through shabby neighborhoods and gentrified streets offering glorious views of the Mediterranean, we walk by elegant, expensive old Arab houses now developed or bought for foreign embassies and wealthy Jews. Sami explains there are two main narratives around a particular point in the run-up to the 1948 war and they totally conflict, as is the case with much of the discourse in Israel. The Zionist narrative states that in January 1948, two months *after* partition but *before* the war, this central market area where we are standing had buildings housing Arab terrorists who were threatening Tel Aviv, but then two heroic Stern Gang soldiers brought a truck loaded with explosives into the central market and blew the place up. A major Zionist victory.

The Palestinian narrative states that while there was a lot of violence waged in resistance to British occupation and Zionist expansion, there were no Palestinian army and no Arab armies that could reach Jaffa. The Saray House in the market place was used by ordinary people and in fact held an orphanage that was blown up by Zionist terrorists, murdering innocent children. A major Zionist massacre.

As we find refuge in the shade, Sami reflects on the historical importance of Jaffa, which was even mentioned in the Old Testament when King Solomon brought cedar from Lebanon through Jaffa to build the temple, and then again, when the prophet Jonah had that unfortunate incident with the whale and got spit up on some lonely Jaffa beach.

He notes that there are two types of Palestinian historians: those who believe Palestinians are Europeans who emigrated from Crete and settled in the Levant, and those who believe they are pan-Arabic and arrived from the Arabian Peninsula around twelve thousand years ago. Everyone else subsequently arrived to occupy this spot, the perfect seaport, the center of commerce, the gateway to Palestine. Jaffa was occupied some thirty times and obviously had its times of success and times of neglect. But Palestinians were clearly here first. It's the ebb and flow of history, and history is clearly not done with the ebbing and flowing part.

The economic success created by the Jaffa orange export business all ended with the 1948 war, when Jaffa was largely depopulated of its

Arab inhabitants. After the war, Israelis passed an aggressive program of Judaization, changing Arabic signage, destroying the Old City, and disappearing the history and culture of the Palestinian majority that had existed for centuries. With British support, Tel Aviv became a city in 1909; by 1919, there were two thousand Jewish inhabitants; and by 1948, the number reached two hundred thousand.

In the unforgiving sun, we admire the famous Clock Tower, built in 1901 by the Ottomans; across the street is the Ottoman prison, which became the British and then the Israeli police station. Currently, the structure, whose northern wall is adjacent to the mosque of Jaffa, is slated to become a fancy boutique hotel. The history of this city is embedded in its architecture, and sometimes I feel the walls are weeping when they are not outright screaming for our attention. We wander through the old covered market, now mostly selling cheap Chinese imports; we pass a herd of Birthright kids, signs for a Lady Gaga concert, and tattooed bikers and rainbow hair. We are standing in front of three hundred new apartments. This is gentrification on steroids— upscale bars and cafes now appear like mushrooms after a spring rain. Sami teases that there are now hairdressers for dogs, and in Tel Aviv, more couples have dogs and cats than children.

We wander by the Scottish Church, the Old French Hospital, Saint Joseph's School for Boys (soon to be a boutique hotel)—the colonists and religious institutions were busy for a long time. There is an endless list of stories about Jesus and his disciples, miracles, visions, angels, etc., that relate to Jaffa. The impact of that is now mostly apparent in a very strong tourism industry focused on arranging visits to all the cities in the New Testament.

Sami notes sarcastically, "Then there was the most important real estate invention: The View." We pass by the upscale Andromeda Hills project, the most expensive housing project in Jaffa, tied up in court battles, and now for the past ten years gated "for the public's safety." He points out the irony that in the past at the seashore, it was the poor people who used to smoke hashish, and now at the sea, it's the rich who inhale while relaxing on the beach. Rents are as high as $20,000 per month and houses sell for millions.

We look up at a large poster of Handala done by the cartoonist and political activist Naji Al Ali. In the poster, an American in Lebanon is asking for the religious identity of an Arab, to which the guy replies, "I am an Arab and you are a donkey." The Handala character stands nearby with his back to us and spiky cactus hair. Naji, a Palestinian living in Lebanon, left for Kuwait for his own personal safety and then went to London, where he was assassinated in 1987. There are so many theories about who pulled the trigger. He pretty much offended everyone by speaking truth to power. Sami explains that the character of Handala came to Naji in a dream, as a small child who would help him tell the truth. Naji said that Handala left Palestine when he was ten and will only grow up when Naji returns. In the cartoons Handala's back is always turned to the viewer because the world has turned its back on Palestine. His hair is spiky because reality is bitter. He is now the most famous Arab symbol of perseverance and resistance in the world.

So how does this segregation and racism look up close and personal? In a local school, Jewish parents complained when the Arabs attending a secular Jewish school reached 50 percent of the student body, so the school divided itself into two schools, Arab and Jew. Then the parents demanded a wall be laid down the middle of the playground. The municipality refused, using words like "multiculturalism" to explain their decision, so the Jewish parents took their kids out and sent them to schools in Tel Aviv, or to the right-wing national religious schools. The Israelis do not even seem to have the inclination, institutional capacity, or legal building blocks to create a multicultural society, let alone face the glaring endemic racism.

It is late and I am too tired to continue. Let me just say that I knew I was in '48 Israel when I ordered a Turkish coffee and a lovely cappuccino arrived. I didn't want to complain, so I grabbed the cinnamon, sprinkled it over the steamed foam liberally, only to discover that it was actually pepper.

Scarlett Johansson Has Gas

June 18, 2014

Spending a few hours with Tamer Nafar, the hip-hop artist for the group DAM, is always a trip. The drive to Lydda (on Israeli maps: Lod) where he lives involves passing Ben Gurion Airport, built on the lands of Lydda (speaking of dispossession). Lod/Lyd/Lydda is a "mixed city" with an ancient bloody and complicated history without any of the touchy-feely reconciliation stuff that "mixed" may imply today. The place consists of Palestinians (in official parlance, "Arabs") and a mix of Jewish Ethiopians, Moroccans, and other Jews from lower socioeconomic groups. We are on a bus touring the area, and I'm struck that after multiple visits with him, Tamer never seems to age; he speaks his mind freely, crackles with sarcasm and energy, and has no verbal censors (in keeping, I suppose, with being a well-known hip-hop artist!), though he seems a bit more subdued now that he has a wife and son.

We start in a dusty, run-down center near the Great Mosque where Palestinians were first rounded up in 1948 and massacred by the Stern Gang. One hundred thirty people died and one survived, hidden under the corpses. The mosque was closed until 1994. Tamer remarks that an Israeli reporter noted that the walls of the reopened mosque were washed, but the blood-soaked floor was just covered with carpets. (And to think I grew up believing that Jewish soldiers only fought noble and moral wars—that we did not massacre, we protected women, children, and fruit trees, and we learned from our history. The making and unmaking of founding mythology is powerful, challenging work.)

Tamer reviews much of the city's history and the various neighborhoods and their related ethnicities and socioeconomics (the whiter the Jews, the more services, sidewalks, clean streets; the more Arab, the less of everything). If we look at today, he sees the main Zionist dilemma is one of demography. The cry now is to build a new, "clean" city ("*Yehud Lud*"), bring in the extremist Jewish settlers and place them in the middle of Palestinian neighbors. Palestinians facing poverty, hostile Hassids, and little hope must decide whether to sell their properties to these settlers or to the drug dealers that dominate many of the neighborhoods. These are not good choices. And thus the Palestinian presence is steadily disappearing. Part of a Jewish apartment complex is located on a Muslim cemetery, so Tamer can no longer visit his father's grave. According to Tamer, approximately 90 percent of the funding in Lyd is budgeted to build housing for Jews. He notes ironically that of the city's $12 million budget, $2 million is for Jewish schools and services, $2 million for Jewish neighborhoods, $6 million for a separation wall in the city, and $2 million for demolishing Arab houses.

The neglected, poorer parts of the city are infested with drug dealers (he points out one locale with an "ATM"—i.e., a hole in the wall where you put your shekels and get your drugs), and the only rehab center in the city used to be owned by a drug dealer after his son committed suicide. Mostly folks are using crystal meth, coke, and pills; the dealers are often Arabs and Bedouin clans. As Tamer says, "Not a tasty salad."

Racism is the driving factor behind the confounding disasters the city faces. Tamer explains that intellectually he feels sympathy for Ethiopian Jews, who are also on the bottom of the socioeconomic ladder, but on the other hand, then he "has to be fucked over by an Ethiopian [Jewish] policeman who is trying to be soooo Israeli." Recently, there was a scandal when it was found that hospitals were throwing out blood donations from Ethiopian donors and that Ethiopian women were being sterilized without consent.

Buoyed by a successful music career, Tamer has moved with his family to a nicer neighborhood; his son is attending an Arabic-language preschool and speaks fluently. Tamer and his wife are now teaching the boy Hebrew at home. He fears that if his son went to a Jewish preschool, he would lose his Arab identity. These are tough issues to negotiate.

We meander toward the "wrong side of the tracks" where there is a railroad station, originally built by the British for Palestinian workers. Now the neighborhood is only visited by junkies, police, and settlers. "They have the country, we have the streets," says Tamer. This impoverished shantytown is circumscribed by a nearby *moshav*, the train tracks, a highway, and a Jewish neighborhood. While there are successful doctors and lawyers here, there is mostly a lot of poverty and unemployment. These folks are not accepted in Jewish neighborhoods. One hundred and fifty Palestinian houses have been demolished due to lack of permits, but since these are unrecognized neighborhoods, there is no system for applying for anything—not that that would work anyway. And each group blames another group less fortunate than it: Ethiopians and Moroccans, though part of the problem, blame the Palestinians. Ironically, the millions of shekels spent on house demolitions could be used to create a viable public housing system.

Tamer notes all of this insanity is actually about the Judaization of Lyd. It is about privileging the Jewish population and making life difficult for the Palestinians in the hopes they will leave or at least be demographically outnumbered. He quips that the Jews are always complaining that the Palestinians want to throw them into the sea, but in actuality it was the Jewish forces that pushed Palestinian civilians into the Mediterranean. Tamer's grandfather was "thrown into a boat" in 1948, and there are plenty of historical photos that document that frantic expulsion. But there is also a bureaucracy to racism and Judaization, as demonstrated in the way Palestinian land was declared "frozen" and "prohibited from development," and yet ten years ago, Jewish Russian neighborhoods were built on frozen land with full infrastructure and no permits. They received their retroactive permits two years ago.

And then there are the railroad tracks, all eight of them, carrying 250 trains a day. We hold our breaths and watch kids scamper across the tracks as the lights flash and the rails come down. Well before 2006, there were no lights and no guardrails, and some fifteen children were killed. Tamer made a video with the late Juliano Mer-Khamis (actor and founder of the Jenin Freedom Theater) and took Israeli rock stars to this neighborhood with the media in tow, creating intense public pressure, and soon after lights and guardrails appeared. The promised pedestrian tunnel or bridge has yet to materialize, but no one else has been crushed by an oncoming train. I counted four trains in the few minutes Tamer and I had this conversation.

We head onto a dirt path marked by concrete walls, corrugated metal walls and roofs, piles of trash, open sewerage, bedding hung in the sun, purple bougainvillea flaunting itself. Where are we? A shantytown in Brazil? South Africa? A girl roughly ten years old has drugs for sale and makes an enticing offer to our bus driver.

One positive development Tamer explains is that at the site of a previous demolition, a new shiny school, the Ort School of Science and Engineering, has been built. His wife teaches here; the principal is an Arab. Principal Shirin Natour Hafi describes herself as apolitical, but she knows how to work the system, she is well-respected, she goes out on the streets and talks to the drug dealers, and she gets excellent results. All of her students are Palestinian.

Our final stop is the Shamir neighborhood, a Palestinian area adjacent to the *moshav* that demanded a separation wall of their own to protect themselves from their unwelcome Arab neighbors. Activists took them to court, and the defendants said it was an "acoustic wall" to absorb the sound of the trains. The wall was left partially built for seven to eight years. A beautiful, multistory Palestinian apartment building was built in the neighborhood without a permit (since there are no permits), and a strange deal was made not to demolish this apartment building in exchange for completing the separation wall.

I ask Tamer, this extraordinary mix of high energy, outrage, and cynicism, what are the main barriers for the Palestinians from digging themselves out of this mess of poverty and drug trafficking? He replies: "Our tribal mentality." But Tamer continues the good fight, pushing the boundaries, getting in everyone's face, calling things as he sees them in all their contradictions and ugliness and sarcasm. He is releasing English-language hip-hop songs: "Mama, I Fell in Love with a Jew," and "Scarlett Johansson Has Gas" (a reference to the Sodastream campaign she promoted; Sodastream is produced in Mishor Adumim, an illegal Israeli settlement on the West Bank).

He is planning a full album and is writing a movie script about Palestinian hip-hop. And he is using his powerful music and his sharp tongue to continue to create political change and wake up the international community through the language of hip-hop.

I leave inspired, but also appalled at the consequences of the Zionist dream: of the price of privileging Jews over everyone else, white Jews over brown Jews, of the self-destruction of communities that are pushed to the edges of society, of the terrible cost of the racism that has always been part of the fabric of this contradictory place.

The Tigers, the Butterflies, and the Birds
June 19, 2014

Our host father and his two young daughters begin leading the tour of the Aida Refugee Camp after a breakfast we prepared together with his wife. He smokes constantly and like many Palestinian men, has done his stint in Israeli jails. After two years, he was released and given a permit that limited his movements to Bethlehem *for life*. His family has had many Israeli home invasions, and the IDF killed his brother and sister and bombed his mother's house. He has many skills in construction and is an expert electrician; he has no paid work currently but dreams of building his wife her cooking center, which when it opens will raise money for their disabled son and help empower other women by teaching Palestinian cooking to local and international visitors.

IDF soldiers visited our street last night, and this morning, we can see the spirals of tear gas one hundred meters away as young boys run down the street toward the camp's iconic entrance (a large house key over the gate). The massive grey concrete wall at the entrance to the camp is surrounded by garbage, and a grey IDF guard tower completes the triptych. (In 2014, Pope Francis visited the camp and prayed at this wall, as if to say to all the world, SEE! THIS EXISTS!) It appears that the tear gas is also in the vicinity of the boys' UNRWA school and they are taking exams. Our host mentions that the IDF soldiers use the boys for target practice—the boys run toward the conflict, grabbing stones; the girls run home. His younger daughter is now handing out geraniums she has picked.

The camp has no green space but tons of children who need to play and release the rage, frustration, and fear that infuses the air and tear gas they breathe. We hear the history of dispossession in 1948, the UNRWA tents, the UN houses (thirty single rooms, one family, often six to ten children and grandparents, and one bathroom for all thirty homes; the inhabitants endured poverty, trauma, depression, and appalling overcrowding.) Many men went to work in Israel to provide food for their families. My host explains that he is afraid for his children. He tells them to stay away from the soldiers; he deeply cares for them, the soldiers do not. "We want peace." He has Jewish Israeli friends and occasionally they visit him. He of course cannot leave Bethlehem, which is really an extension of his lifetime prison sentence. The frequent teargassing affects everyone and is reported to increase the risk of miscarriage.

More tear gas, more boys dash by. We stop at the mosque and kindergarten. There is a painting of a fierce orange tiger and the words, "Here only tigers can survive." On the adjacent wall are two orange butterflies and the words, "Here only butterflies and birds are free." Another young boy races past. We see a church in the camp and then cautiously look at the wall a few blocks from the guard tower. There is an enormous graffito of a boy with a slingshot. On a nearby crumbling wall of a house, someone drew an open mouth with a dove, a key in its mouth, flying out.

I spot Arabic graffiti supporting Fatah but surprisingly little related to any political party. There is a general sense of disgust for all political parties. I see a wall of a house with a painting of Al Aqsa and Mecca. Roosters are crowing and a haze of tear gas hangs over the homes. My host talks about wanting his children to get a good education and go to "the best universities." He, like many fathers, has great hopes. He points out the agricultural land stolen when the wall was built, property his father would have given to him as part of the next generation of sons. I see teenage boys collecting small stones, begging us for dollars, cigarettes. My host pats them on the head and mutters "simple," and tries to dissuade them from throwing stones. They do not listen.

We make a quick friendly stop at the Al Rowwad Children's Theater to visit our colleague Abdelfattah Abusrour. We have visited the theater before; I saw the theater troupe perform several plays and the *dabke* (a traditional Palestinian folk dance) in the Boston area, and it has also performed in Europe. We squeeze into Abdelfattah's office and my eyes scan the photos of Pope Francis, Malcolm X, Martin Luther King, Gandhi, Mandela, Einstein, and piles of books and files. On the wall, a poster proclaims: "The Right of Return is Not Negotiable and Not Subject to any Compromises." Abdelfattah's father was born in Beit Nattif and his mother in Zacharia, both now destroyed villages. The family fled in 1948 to what became the Aida

Refugee Camp, where Abdelfattah was born. Abdelfattah can trace his family back ten generations; his name means "the one who shall return." With a PhD in biology from a French university, he went "outside the box" and decided to return home, to dedicate his energies to using creativity—dance, theater, photography, and the arts—to strengthen the youth of Palestine. He returned in 1994, naively ready to "save Palestine."

He explains to us that despite the representations in the media of Palestinians as terrorists, in fact 99 percent of Palestinians have never carried a gun. Resistance has been almost entirely unarmed and nonviolent and dates back to British rule and the Ottomans before that. He reminds us that a group of Palestinian women who had formed the first women's union back in 1920 demonstrated against the British Mandate, and then against the Zionists in 1929 by surrounding Jerusalem with 120 cars and honking up a storm. And that was a lot of cars for those days!

In 1998 Abdelfattah founded the Al Rowwad Center based on the idea of "Beautiful Resistance." There are currently six thousand refugees crowded into ten acres of the Aida Camp. "Nobody wants a child martyr. Children should walk in their parent's funerals, not the other way around . . . no country can live on the corpses of its people." He encourages the international community to support the center through the Friends of Al Rowwad, which is a tax-exempt organization with volunteers and partners in the United States, the European Union, and Norway. We take a quick tour, and the center is looking much more spiffy and modernized than my last visit. There is an inviting library, computer room, and women's center with sewing machines, embroidery, and exercise area. Progress is being made against all odds.

We hurry home because our host's wife is going to give us a cooking class, which she organizes with other women twice a month to raise money to support their disabled children. She is dressed in a lovely traditional embroidered dress and *hijab*. We set to work chopping cauliflower, carrots, onions, eggplant; there is laughter and friendly camaraderie. We are making *maqluba* (both vegetarian and chicken versions) and for dessert, *basbussa*, a dangerously delicious moist cake of semolina, eggs, sugar, vanilla, coconut, lemon, and more, baked in an oven. (She prefers her ancient gas-fired metal oven in the hall to her modern electric one.) The house is soon filled with savory and sweet smells and high expectations.

After this phenomenal meal, we make the rounds to say our goodbyes, and I find the grandmother sitting alone with her *maqluba* in a separate part of the house. I take her hand and she starts to weep, tears streaming down her lined face. We have no words, so soon I wrap my arms around her and she weeps uncontrollably as I blot the tears off her cheeks. I can only imagine that her deep well of grief is overflowing: the loss of her home, the suffering in the camps, the deaths of her children, the humiliations, the curfews, a grandchild with special needs, the life that she lost through no fault of her own, and her knowledge that she will never see justice in her lifetime. My tears linger with hers.

From Tear Gas to *Maqluba*

June 20, 2014

Feigning bravado and an ambivalent sense of group confidence, our delegation sets off for the West Bank village of Bil'in for the weekly demonstration against the separation wall. There is no direct travel service on Fridays, so this involves several taxis and lots of negotiation. Black flags and posters are everywhere portraying a strong man breaking his chains over his head, in solidarity with the several months long prison hunger striker protesting administrative detentions of Palestinians in Israeli jails. We hit one massive traffic jam, a combination of a checkpoint, a wedding, and an army of frustrated, testosterone-driven drivers.

I think how much our delegation has really been traveling in a bubble. We have had calls from a variety of frantic family members, basically demanding, "Do you know where you are and what is happening there?" Our next-door neighbors, Syria, Iraq, and Lebanon, are imploding in various dangerous ways, the Israeli press and the Palestinian streets are full of calls to avenge the missing yeshiva boys, and as usual every Palestinian is a suspect. Every cab driver we talk to thinks this whole episode is a ploy to give the IDF reservists some target practice before the big bang after Kerry's failed peace negotiations. We have had almost no checkpoint delays, no anxious humiliating interrogations (expect of course for our Palestinian leader, but for her, receiving that kind of treatment is normal, which just shows how distorted normality is around here). We slept through the repeated nighttime house raids and were too far away to even hear the first Israeli raid in fourteen years at Birzeit University, which involved rounding up the university security guards and confiscating flags, banners, and posters from the student union, as well as searching the campus. And we live with our unconscious, mostly white American privilege, presumptions, and passports that allow us to walk the streets of cities that our Palestinian hosts can only dream of. Why we are not hated is still unclear to me, but the warmth and generosity is truly genuine.

So today we set off for some blunt reality, an unarmed resistance march against the separation wall in the town of Bil'in. Mohammed Khatib, one of the leaders of the organizing committee, meets us at the entry to the town. He is wearing a tee shirt that says "Water and salt = dignity," a reference to the diet of the hunger strikers in Israeli jails. He explains that Bil'in has 2,000 inhabitants, and another 2,000 living elsewhere, and 5,000 dunams of land; 3,500 dunams were confiscated in order to construct the wall and 1,500 were returned after a long struggle.

Soon we are sitting under a tarp on plastic chairs in his patio, sipping mint tea, and admiring his beautiful stone-polished home that he has poured years of work into creating. I see a modern kitchen, a sunken living room with a poster of a young Arafat, and an amazing fireplace carved into an ancient dead olive tree. His five-ish-year-old daughter, wearing a traditional embroidered dress, coyly joins him. Our cab driver joins us too; this is, after all, a grassroots struggle.

The story of Bil'in is the common tale of land confiscation, the building of a wall starting in 2004, and the massive growth of an expanding Jewish settlement, Modi'in Illit. In 2005, the Palestinian villagers started to get creative, tying themselves to their olive trees, placing themselves on the land in cages and coffins, and shocking the Israeli soldiers with their nonviolent resistance. This drew media attention but no changes on the ground. They built a caravan on the land taken by the settlements (a move reminiscent of the territorial claims right-wing Jewish hilltop youth have often staked out to create pressure for approval for an official settlement). This slowed the construction; the IDF said that mobile homes are illegal (except of course for Jews). So in one frenzied night, the villagers built a fixed home with a door and windows, to the appropriate specifications, and this stopped settlement growth for one year. Ultimately, the Israeli construction company actually went bankrupt. Then the route of the wall was changed to return some of the Palestinian land and the settlement construction resumed. The Palestinians are still not allowed to work their land that they won back, though they built a brightly colored playground on it, so I am not yet calling this a victory, especially since the battle is really about ending the occupation.

Mohammed has a sense of humor born of struggle. While much of the world is focused on the World Cup in Brazil, he helped organize a soccer match in front of the Ofer Prison, where prisoners are on a serious hunger strike. He was arrested a day before a protest action to block Highway 443, which cuts through the West Bank, and when the police asked him for information, he referred them to the social media of resistance organizations and their supporters. When they were surprised by the action to block the highway, he said, "There are no secrets, but there are surprises."

Today, many will not be at this march because there was a call to pray and march in Beitunya in support of the Ofer prisoners. We set off in a row of battered cars, a motley crew of muscular-looking Palestinian men with flags, journalists with large cameras and gas masks, women of all varieties, internationals, and Israelis, and park under some olive trees. We begin with what is introduced as a short discussion on safety. (Avoid getting bonked on the head by a tear gas canister. Do not rub your eyes, do not run, cover your face with a scarf—done! Do not panic; tear gas will not kill you, it will only make you feel like you are about to die. Your eyes will tear up and your throat will burn. Sniff an onion, an alcohol swab, anything with a smell, and DO NOT walk downwind. The IDF only use rubber bullets when stones are thrown and nobody dies from a stun grenade.) That seemed like a pretty long list to me, but we set off. We begin the march down the dusty, hot, rocky road. My brain is giving me fairly strong messages about getting the hell out of there ASAP, and my legs are inspired by the struggle against a long list of historical injustices. My knees are sort of in between.

Before a stone can be thrown, the tear gas starts and is blown up the hill toward me and the other stragglers. Europeans remark that the tear gas today seems much more powerful than they are used to, and others mention that Israelis are always field-testing new weaponry. I find myself a cluster of olive trees and some other less-than-brave protesters and try to remember the rules of engagement. Following the single canisters that are thrown, there are showers of canisters, the occasional stun grenade, and then rubber bullets. I am told that the Jewish settlers on the other side of the wall cheer the soldiers on and play inspiring music while they do battle with the "dangerous terrorists" on the other side who want nothing more than to plant their vegetables, tend their olives, and otherwise lead normal lives. If the wind (carrying the tear gas) is blowing toward the settlers, then the IDF quickly switches to using rubber bullets. The settlers consider any blowback from the tear gas as some sort of badge of courage in the fight for Zionist domination.

I make my way across the rocky field to where people even more frightened than I are watching, when a tear gas canister spirals through the air and lands ten feet from me. This keeps happening, reminding me again that there is actually no safe place and that the soldiers have been known to come into the town and throw tear gas into people's homes. Last week one child was shot with a rubber bullet and injured. The important thing to remember about a rubber bullet is that it is indeed a bullet. Sometimes the hot canisters start small brush fires in the dry grass.

The demonstrators feel that the soldiers have been more vigorous due to all the tension around the missing boys (but remember, not a single stone was thrown) and the aggressive incursions and arrests that are going on all over the West Bank. Everyone talks about how the weapons the IDF is using are made in the United States and that the solution to the conflict lies in changing US policies.

The demonstration finally winds down, although that burning feeling in our throats drags on for a while, and suddenly we find ourselves invited for lunch at another organizer's house where his wife just happens to have *maqluba* and salad for some fifteen people. So we gather around, eat to our hearts' content, buy Palestinian embroidery from the women's cooperative, and struggle to make sense out of the insanity of occupation, land grabs, racism, hatred, entitlement, and military hardware, and the power of determined resistance by ordinary people desperately trying to create political change and build the kind of lives that we take for granted.

And for Extra Credit: Hebron

June 20, 2014

Once again, we head for the tortured city of Hebron, leaving behind the tear gas and delicious food and tempting embroidery, while a young Palestinian from Ramallah who just graduated from Yale tries to explain to me the intricacies of her permitting process. She has a West Bank ID. She can only apply for a new permit to enter Israel if her old one has already expired (it generally lasts three months). Fortunately, she does not own a car or a donkey; that would also require a permit. And she cannot apply until it has run out completely. Because her permit ran out Thursday evening, the earliest she could apply is Friday, but Friday and Saturday are holidays and you cannot get any permit unless it is an emergency. If you pay 140 shekels a year for a magnetic-strip card that indicates you do not have any security issues, it will take one day to get the permit; otherwise, it takes two, but of course the permit is never guaranteed. So the earliest she can apply is Monday, but she needs a permit to come with us into Israel to Nazareth on Saturday, which in this crazy world is now impossible. Now let me remind you that she has just graduated from a prestigious US university, has no criminal record, has a great sense of humor, comes from a respectable family, and poses no security risks except perhaps the risk of speaking her mind, which the last time I checked was still legal in most modern democratic societies. If she decides to take her chances and sneaks in (this happens a lot) and the driver gets caught, he is fined, which is really not fair to him. Under these circumstances, she will consider not carrying any form of ID, so the Israelis cannot prove she isn't who she says she is and thus will not be able to punish her. So does this sound sensible? Does it have anything to do with security? With keeping the folks in Netanya secure in their beach chairs, sipping their pomegranate mojitos?

As we travel by *service*, at the village of Qalandia our delegation spots two soldiers crouching in a rotary hiding behind an olive tree, their weapons loaded, fingers on the trigger. Ma'ale Adumim sprawls across distant hilltops like a giant snake slithering through the territories; there is an IDF jeep on the road; we come to a checkpoint with three IDF soldiers. On the radio a woman reports a loud explosion in a town near Hebron. As we arrive in Hebron, the city feels eerie and tense; young men cluster on sidewalks, looking thin, hungry, and ready for trouble; large dumpsters have been placed across the roads, some already billowing smoke. Despite this, people are out on the streets—shopping, biking, driving, smoking.

Tensions are unusually high in the territories with the kidnapping of the settler youth and the massive IDF incursions, and even more so in Hebron, historically the focus of Jewish settler aggression and Palestinian resistance. I learn that a thirteen-year-old Palestinian child was killed yesterday. I am also told that the IDF recently stole fifteen thousand shekels during one home invasion and that, as usual, the PA is completely invisible except for the presence of traffic cops, who I must say, are not doing much. It is said that when the Israelis are planning a major incursion, they send their Palestinian colleagues (collaborators?) home—another reality that is obviously deeply corruptive to Palestinian civil society.

I have never seen our guide, Hisham Sharabati, so tense; yes, he may be anxious because we are late, he has a flat tire, and there is a lot he wants to teach us, but also, the city feels like it is about to explode and he wants us all to leave in one piece. He reviews for us the outrageous history of the ancient city of Hebron and its colonization and militarization by a small number of fanatical Jews. Everything is worse since my last descent into this living hell: with the kidnapping of the three yeshiva students, no one with an ID who is less than fifty years old can leave the territories. One resident encumbered by this restriction is the lovely man who sat next to me in the *service*. He has been accepted to a US Agency for International Development program on leadership development in Washington, DC, and has a formal letter from the US Consulate; he is now on his fourth try to get by the ever-so-conscientious Israeli security at the border with Jordan and his odds are low.

The Palestinian markets are not only covered with sheets and chicken wire to protect them from bricks and other detritus tossed by the Israeli settlers who live above, but they have started putting up a metal roof over the market. The brutality of occupation is vividly apparent: shuttered shops, doors welded shut, racist graffiti, trashed jewelry district, blocked streets and passages, and windows covered with metal mesh to protect against stones in the Old City all persist. The lower levels of the market flood in the winter with up to four feet of water and garbage. A soldier was videotaped throwing rocks at Palestinians and received a minor punishment. The Jewish yeshiva is expanding and invading into the lives and lands of its Palestinian neighbors. Guard towers and cameras are everywhere. But life goes on. We pass a Palestinian man busily washing his car. There is loud honking and a wedding party; a car decorated with flowers passes by. A computer store is filled with young men glued to their screens.

As Hisham takes us through turnstiles and checkpoints to the Tomb of the Patriarchs and the Ibrahimi Mosque, he reminds us that Abraham is reported in the Old Testament to have *bought* the spot for his family as its burial site, but he must have bought it from somebody! This glorious and tortured site has been claimed, rebuilt, invaded, and divided up by all the folks who passed through over the many centuries including Herod, the Romans, the Ottomans, the Crusaders, Saladin, and most recently the Jews. (I am sure I have left somebody out, but you get the point.) And then of course in 1994, after the religious extremist Baruch Goldstein massacred some 29 Muslims and injured 125, the place got divided up between two of the three Abrahamic religions, and the fight continues. We see many more IDF soldiers and a long parade of ultra-Orthodox Jews with large families of lovely, innocent-looking children climbing up the long stairs for Shabbat services.

Hisham shows us the checkpoint and metal detector where hundreds of schoolchildren have to hustle through every day to get to their classes. He also points out the square where three Palestinians were shot to death at different times for the crime of being there. We stare at a man on a don-key loaded with large bundles of straw, yelling and herding a flock of sheep, udders bulging, up the winding road to get to his side of the street. We hear of the fifteen Palestinian families that are so isolated by the maze of walls and barriers that they cannot have visitors and of the incredible challenges families face with the concrete barriers, the front doors they cannot use, the ladders and roof-to-roof alternatives that people take to leave their homes. But what if you are disabled? Or elderly? Or just bought a bed for your new wife? People die from this kind of life.

It is getting dark and dangerous. I can see the tension in the faces of the young men hanging on the sidewalks, in the streets littered with rocks; I can hear it in the tone in Hisham's voice. The night raids will soon begin, the young men burning tires, the children dragged out of their beds, assaulted by the self-righteous cheers and prayers of fanatical Jews with Brooklyn accents and delusions that fill me with shame.

How can I explain this reality to the nice liberal Jews in Brookline or Long Island or Los Angeles who have never really grappled with the long-term implications of Zionism, the privileging of Jews over everyone else, whatever the cost, and the belief in our perpetual victimhood? I am witness-ing that privileging taken to its most extreme, disturbed, and destructive form, and it is heartbreaking, immoral, and outrageous. If we do not speak up, if we do not say "Not in my name" and really mean it, I fear it may take us all, Jew and Palestinian, down together.

There Was No Farewell

June 21, 2014

Today, what I hear from Jonathan Cook, a brilliant British journalist and writer now living in Nazareth with a Palestinian wife and family and Israeli citizenship, breaks my heart. We are wandering once again through the scat-tered stones in the cemetery of the destroyed village of Saffuriya, admiring the gorgeous towers of *saber* cactus laden with fruit. The *saber* cactus (or in Hebrew, *sabra*) is a symbol of indigeneity for both Jews and Palestinians, he explains. For Israelis, the cactus is associated with the return to the land, the creation of the muscular, tough, farmer-Jew deeply rooted in the land, prickly but sweet. For Palestinians, it is a symbol of existence as a resilient, indigenous people and of being physically connected to the earth: the cactus was used to denote property boundaries and is virtually impossible to eradicate, so it is a constant reminder of a past that many prefer to forget.

The problem, Jonathan explains gently, is that the *saber* cactus is not a native plant and was imported from Mexico 350 years ago. He notes that Israelis and Palestinians only eat the cactus fruit, while his Mexican friends know how to cook the entire plant because they have done it for centuries.

It is somewhat fitting that my cactus fantasy, whether the symbol from my Hebrew school days of the proud and strong farmer-Jew or later in my life of the deep Palestinian historical attachment to the earth, has come to die in a cemetery. I look around at the jumble of stones and gravesites. It seems that this cemetery is not well-maintained, even though the Saffuriyans went to court to obtain the right to care for the site—because they are so harassed by the local *moshavniks* who engage in what Ilan Pappé has termed "memoricide." I think I will stick with the saber/*sabra* mythology out of loyalty to my complicated cactus-loving heritage and in memory of the people buried here.

Jonathan's focus is on the history of Nazareth and Saffuriya and the meaning of the Nakba. He does incredibly careful research and reporting, and I always learn about the nuances and consequences of historical events that are mind-boggling in their complexity. The village of Saffuriya before 1948 consisted of a wide expanse of land, three mosques, one church, and two schools. In the 1920s it was a leader in the Arab revolt against the British. In the 1930s and 1940s, Jewish soldiers scouted all the Palestinian villages, taking advantage of Arab hospitality, to acquire a detailed database about each town, but they could not get any information about Saffuriya. When the war began, they attacked it early and fiercely. After the bombings, refugees fled to the nearby forests, to Lebanon (Sabra and Shatila) and to Nazareth; 40 percent of Nazareth is originally from Saffuriya. Jonathan states that when the significance of the refugee crisis became apparent, Israel asked for a special agency and UNRWA was created with the understanding that no camps would be situated in Israel. The original village was destroyed (the last structure bulldozed in 1967), and the fenced-in area became a closed military zone and JNF forest. The 1954 Prevention of Infiltration Law was designed to prevent Palestinians from returning to their original homes even if they were living within the state and had Israeli citizenship. Today the rest of the village is the Jewish *moshav* of Zipora.

Jonathan wants us to pay special attention to the trees. This area was once a thickly forested site of pine trees, fast growing and familiar to Jewish Europeans. The recently planted trees prevented Palestinians from returning to rebuild and also ruined the agricultural value of the land by changing the acidity and destroying the native flora and fauna like nut, carob, citrus, and olive trees. The trees were thinned out after the massive forest fires: in the 1990s near Ein Hod (a Palestinian village that is now an artist colony with a bar built in the former mosque) and in 2010 with the devastating Haifa-Carmel Fire.

We stop at a field of purple flowers and the original village spring, an area that is now part of JNF land, where a Palestinian family is picnicking. The water is supposed to have special powers and is referred to as "Viagra on tap" by some in the *moshav*. The local Palestinians are "present absentees" as are 25 percent of all Palestinians with Israeli citizenship. There is also an archeological site that is controlled by a settler organization. Not only are there Roman ruins here, but this is where Jews fled after the fall of the temple, so there are some who think that the Palestinian villagers of Saffuriya are the original descendants or at least converts from way back then.

Jonathan tells us of a Nakba commemoration in 2008 in Saffuriya. Palestinians marched into a nearby forest with their children and their memories; they chose that site because right-wing Jews had taken over the field. In the midst of the commemoration, thuggish police arrived and charged at the Palestinians, using tear gas, stun guns, and grenades, revealing just how great a threat is posed by a people's deeply held historical memory. This year the Nabka March was enormous, some thirty thousand people celebrated in the town of Lubia, and it was so crowded it lasted for seven hours. The Palestinian community is getting more organized and more courageous. This was the first time Jonathan did not feel intimidated—a major psychological breakthrough. The older generation is dying and the young people are reenergizing the event with all the newfangled social media and youthful optimism at their disposal.

We pass through a gate into the *moshav*, which was founded in 1949 for Bulgarian and Romanian refugees as a dairy farm; this is confirmed by the strong smell of manure. At this point, most members work in the cities, and acceptance into the *moshav* is protected by the suitability law that is designed to keep Arabs (as well as gays, disabled folks, single moms, and other undesirables) out of nice Wonder Bread Jewish towns.

We walk along the barbed wire and come across a shrine to the poet Taha Muhammed Ali, the brother of Abu Arab of the Saffuriya's cultural heritage museum. Standing in front of the rocks, Jonathan reads us some poetry fragments, softly touching the feelings evoked in such a sad and exquisitely beautiful place:

"The Place Itself" (extract)

And so I come to the place itself,
but the place is not
its dust and stones and open space.
For where are the red-tailed birds
and the almonds' green?
Where are the bleating lambs
and pomegranates of evening—
the smell of bread
And the grouse?
Where are the windows,
and where is the ease of Amira's braid?

"There Was No Farewell"

We did not weep
When we were leaving—
For we had neither
Time nor tears,
And there was no farewell.
We did not know
at the moment of parting
that it was a parting,
so where would our weeping
have come from?
We did not stay
awake all night
(and did not doze)
the night of our leaving.
That night we had
neither night nor light,
and no moon rose.
That night we lost our star,
our lamp misled us;
we didn't receive our share
Of sleeplessness—
So where
would wakefulness have come from?[4]

We go further up the hill to an orphanage that is run by the Catholic Church for Palestinian children who are not from Saffuriya. There are lovely geraniums and cacti, a welcoming Franciscan priest from Venezuela, and a large ruin, Saint Anna's Church. We are stunned to learn that this unmarked church, with rows of fallen columns, no roof, ancient carvings, piteously meowing cats, and a jumble of stones at one end is the birthplace of the Virgin Mary! Jonathan thinks that some kind of deal was made between Israel and the Vatican so that the Vatican could keep the church and the orphanage, but no pilgrims would be encouraged to visit because then they would see the destroyed village and barbed wire and ask annoying questions. Three schlumpy people arrive, but they are Russians from Haifa and do not seem that impressed by the Virgin. The Israelis also will not issue a permit to restore the church or at least put a roof over the site for protection. The only surviving house in Saffuriya is now a bed-and-breakfast with a big Israeli flag.

╌╴╱╲╴╌ 4

Because *They Are Here*
June 22–26, 2014

In June 2014, as the Israeli incursions into the West Bank that followed the kidnapping of the yeshiva students continued, our delegation investigated the intense realities of the legal and prison system established under Israel's military law. We documented the restrictions on movement, checkpoints, and permitting that at any moment can strangle a Palestinian's ability to conduct the normal functions of everyday life in the occupied territories. I explored the stresses and pressures in the Al Quds Medical School, which is located in an area that used to be considered "East Jerusalem" but now found itself cut off from the city by the separation wall, as well as the situation of the Afro-Palestinians living in the Old City. We revisited the continued attempts to dispossess Bedouins in the Negev and the inspirational work of Adalah, Zochrot, and the growing Boycott, Divestment and Sanctions (BDS) movement.

It was eye-opening to bear witness in real time to the barrage of military might, home incursions, arrests, and killings that was triggered by the kidnapping of Gil-Ad Shaer, Naftali Fraenkel, and Eyal Yifrah; the vitriolic incitement from the Israeli leadership and media; and the attacks carried out by Jewish-Israeli thugs on Palestinians with Israeli citizenship as well as on left-leaning Jews. It became increasingly clear to us that Netanyahu was looking for an excuse to once again attack Hamas. He accused them of having masterminded the kidnapping without providing any of the solid evidence that should have been easily available from the army of collaborators and Israeli soldiers crawling the West Bank. Later, we all found out the culprits were renegade militants from Hebron who had acted without the knowledge of Hamas leadership.[1] The military kept secret the fact that they already knew that the youths had been killed one or two days after their disappearance because the government needed an excuse to continue to terrorize Palestinians as they "searched" for the youths and the kidnappers, while their actions also disrupted moves Hamas and Fatah had made toward forming a unity government. Later, after the bodies were "found," the revenge killing of Mohammed Abu Khdeir, the beating of a Palestinian-American teen, and the use of live fire by police in East Jerusalem all seemed like a provocative recipe for creating a pretext for war.

On June 30, 2014, Hamas launched thirty rockets from Gaza into Israel, the first time since 2012; and a week later Israel began its massive assault on Gaza. In a normal country, a kidnapping would be thoroughly investigated and there would be criminal charges, a trial, and punishment. But in Israel/ Palestine the abnormal had long ago become normalized.

If armed conflict is on one end of the spectrum of Palestinian resistance, I think of the BDS campaign as being on the opposite end. This campaign was born from years of frustration and was spurred by the 2004 decision by the International Court in The Hague, which ruled that the construction of the separation wall on occupied territory was contrary to international law.[2] The BDS strategy was affirmed in 2009 as a courageous form of peaceful resistance by Palestinian Christian leaders in the *Kairos Palestine Document*. When I am confronted with opposition to BDS, I often wonder, if Palestinians are condemned when they resist violently *and* when they resist nonviolently, and if the decades-long "peace process" has led to endless occupation, settlement growth, and siege, then how exactly are Palestinians supposed to resist?

As the BDS movement's leader Omar Barghouti explains in this chapter, BDS is a powerful economic and political tool that has affected major global companies involved in the Israeli occupation like G4S and Veolia. The movement is stronger in Europe, but in the United States a growing number of academic associations (in anthropology, American studies, Asian-American studies, Native-American and Indigenous Studies, and so on)[3] and church groups (United Church of Christ, Presbyterian, United Methodist)[4] have already supported BDS actions. In 2015, the European Union decided that products from the settlements should be clearly identifiable from their labels and legal scholars called on the EU to boycott all settlement products.[5] While Netanyahu railed against BDS as "anti-Semitic" and "delegitimizing," his ambassador in Washington, Ron Dermer, taunted President Obama and Secretary of State Kerry by giving 2015 holiday gifts made in the settlements, or as he put it, in "Judea, Samaria, and the Golan Heights."[6]

I am often asked: "Why are you picking on Israel?" There are clearly lots of worse offenders, but no other injustice is so uncritically supported by our tax dollars. Twenty percent of all US foreign aid goes to Israel (over $8.5 million per day), plus Washington gives tremendous political support and special status to Israel. The international community treats Israel as if it were a normal progressive Western democracy; this means the Israeli state should be far more accountable for actions to the community that so devotedly supports it. The other critical factor is that a large group of civil society Palestinian activists have asked the international community to support this campaign. These community leaders do not represent any political party but are representatives of the majority of Palestinian civil society and are committed to nonviolence.

So when you buy Israeli wine for Passover, check the label: were the grapes grown in the Judean Hills or the Golan Heights? Or if you are buying a house, are you aware that RE/MAX, one of the United States' largest real estate firms, has one hundred branches in Israel? They sell homes in Jewish-only settlements in the occupied territories, violating not only the Fourth Geneva Convention, which prohibits an occupying power from transferring its citizens to occupied territory, but also the National Association of Realtor's code of ethics prohibiting discrimination on the basis of race, color, religion, familial status, or national origin.[7] And ask yourself, what does it really mean to be "anti-Israel"? What is principled opposition to indefensible Israeli policies? I would suggest that the BDS campaign has the potential to change the dynamics of this struggle, to focus on human rights for all, international law, and UN resolutions, and to respond to the broad social movement in Palestine that is nonviolent, creative, and morally grounded in civil resistance.

Zochrot: Bending the Arc toward Justice

June 22, 2014

So why should Jewish Israelis care about what happened to the people they defeated sixty-plus years ago? The Arabs rejected the Partition Plan, there was a war, they started it, we won. *Yalla*, move on. That is what I call the dominant paradigm in both Israel and the United States. Eitan Bronstein, founder of the organization Zochrot (Remembering), is a little older and a little greyer than when I last saw him but still driven by the need to bring the history of the Nakba, the Palestinian experience of 1948, into Israeli consciousness. His intensity and conviction are powerful. I am pleased to see he has a new office that reflects the growing success and activities of the organization.

In 2001, he was touring a Jewish National Fund forest and noted that although there were signs about Roman ruins and Biblical sites and Mamluks, there was no documentation of the obviously neglected Palestinian village known as Imwas. "The houses were shouting to me," he said. The cemetery and the stones were "like an obvious blindness." People failed to see the historical evidence in front of their own eyes. He had been working with Neve Shalom/Wahat Salaam, the only consciously Jewish-Palestinian village devoted to coexistence in Israel, so he approached his friend Umar Ighbariyah, and they decided to put up signs reflecting the more recent history. This development got picked up by a journalist, which led to an article in *kibbutz* newspapers, then a list of Palestinian villages on websites of local *kibbutzim*. Another journalist, Tom Segev, wrote about this in a column in the Israeli newspaper *Haaretz*, and the idea that there was an invisible history that needed to be made visible took off.

Eitan explains that this work "has to do with my own colonizer identity; signage is colonizing practicing." As Ben-Gurion said, "In 1948, we took over the land, now we have to take over the map." Eitan states, "Our way to decolonize is to rename." He sees the mission of Zochrot is to educate Israeli Jews and civil society about the Nakba and the more controversial right of return for Palestinian refugees, and to take responsibility for the Nakba. This is not just Palestinian history, it is Israeli and human history—"part of my own history."

There are many invisible pieces to this puzzle. According to Eitan, the 1948 war did not happen between two armed sides living in the same territory where there was a winner and a loser; the war was mainly between Jewish Israeli fighters and outside Arab armies, not the local civilians on the ground. Israel lost some of the battles when they encountered an Arab army, as in the Old City of Jerusalem, or in the region of Latrun. However, many of the Israeli victories were over civilians who were not prepared to do battle. Additionally, the Nakba was not an isolated event, it happened before, during, and after the war. He finds the most convincing evidence of his understanding is the testimonies of Israeli fighters. "Expulsions were easy," they reported. "Shoot a few shots, tell people to leave; it was not a military challenge from the thousands of Palestinians." So he sees this history as a systematic expulsion of a civilian population by armed units followed by the destruction of their villages to prevent return, thus the Nakba continues. He adds that this is not the Israeli understanding of history; most people now are familiar with the word *nakba*, but they do not really comprehend its meaning.

To complicate matters, the Israeli government passed the Nakba Law in 2011, which authorizes financial sanctions for any commemoration of the Nakba by an organization funded by the state. This creates an atmosphere of fear and threats around commemorations. On the other hand, the law raised a lot of interest within Israeli society. There had been a huge scandal over an earlier law that actually said anyone who commemorated the Nakba on Israeli Independence Day could be sent to jail for one year. Fortunately, this did not pass. As a comparison, Eitan asks us to imagine if the United States forbade any mourning or protest by Native Americans on the Fourth of July or Thanksgiving.

Since Zochrot is not funded by the state, it is still a legal, functioning organization. Two years ago, students at Tel Aviv University initiated a provocative commemoration on Nakba Day that raised a lot of attention and a big debate in the media. The university permitted the event, but the government said this was not okay because it violated the spirit of the Nakba Law, which was to prevent all such events. (Currently, Nakba commemorations occur on May 15, the day Israel declared independence, but the national Independence Day celebrations vary according to the Hebrew calendar, so the days are usually not the same.)

I find it an interesting historical point that while most Palestinians in Israel lived under military rule until 1966, this rule was lifted annually on Independence Day. On that day Palestinian families for years would visit their villages for personal, mostly quiet, less political family gatherings. Fifteen years ago, they held their first March of Return on Israeli Independence Day. Since then, the issue has become increasingly politicized and public, and Zochrot is in the forefront of this struggle.

Zochrot is involved in a number of extraordinary projects:

1. Offering alternative tours like the one we took of the destroyed village of Lifta.
2. Creating the only Hebrew map of destroyed Palestinian villages.

3. Documenting all the destroyed villages since the beginning of Zionism through the 1967 war and identifying 678 localities, including 22 Jewish villages destroyed in 1948 by Arab armies and 62 Palestinian villages destroyed before 1948. Eitan explains that when Zionists "redeemed the land," they destroyed the Arab structures. Landowners were sometimes Palestinian, Lebanese, or other large, often absentee, landowners. Eitan was told that the Golan was empty and only had Syrian army bases there, but Zochrot documented 127 Syrian villages with approximately 170,000 people.

4. Preparing an educational study guide for high schools. While Zochrot advocates cannot get officially invited to schools, they can train teachers to use their materials and to include the information in their lessons. Because teachers can get fired or at least have their jobs threatened for this course of action, Zochrot advises them to be "discreet," to introduce the idea of "multiple narratives." This reality obviously poisons the atmosphere for many teachers who want to explore this topic in depth.

5. Writing a very successful, practical tour guide in Hebrew and Arabic, with eighteen routes to different places related to the expulsion of indigenous Palestinians, with photos, maps, and history.

6. Creating a book called *Awda* (Return), featuring the testimonies of Palestinian refugees imagining a future in which their right of return has been implemented. There are twelve stories, six by Jews and six by Palestinians.

7. Creating an iNakba app, a free download for iPhones that via GPS accurately shows all the villages with photos and related information.

8. Facilitating a host of educational workshops, symposiums, film festivals, websites, and coalitions with other groups such as Badil, Al Haq, and Palestinians in the West Bank, Lebanon, Syria, as well as Israel.

Zochrot's most controversial work is on the right of return for Palestinian refugees. Eitan explains, "We support the right of return based on the right to choose or to compensate with reparations; it is the choice of the refugees." How to actualize this is a very big challenge; it is clearly not practical for people to expect to return to their old homes—often places are not there, some are vacant or they now encompass a different community. "We try to show how implementation is not putting us in more danger and will actually favor peace and prosperity." He is not talking about proposals based on symbolic numbers, like the Geneva Initiative and other agreements. "We do not accept that ideology," and as an example he explains how in practical terms, it should be determined how many people want to return. "So let's say here are one million Jaffa refugees, maybe one hundred thousand may return. How do we do that, so we must prepare to absorb these folks, so when, how. We did this for one million Russians, we can do it again. . . . It takes time."

He continues by stating that he favors a one-state solution where everyone can live in equality, where the Israeli state as we know it now is no longer a Jewish state. "This is the core reason of the conflict and is very problematic. In the context of the Mideast, this is a good recipe for constant war. We already have a big Israeli collective here, a culture. Hebrew speakers will continue and be enriched by Arabs. Everyone should be bilingual, why not? We are in the Mideast; Jewish tradition and culture will continue, but not as a state."

So how did Eitan come to such an idealistic, and some might consider radical, position? "We began right after the onset of the Second Intifada, a crisis of the Left." In October 2000, he had what he calls "my last crisis with Zionism. I finally understood that the problem is Zionism. Many more Israelis are exposed to this knowledge," but they are still a minority. Many Israelis acknowledge the Nakba, but cannot deal with the right of return. Nonetheless, "it is not possible to dismiss." As I think back to the hundreds of children we saw playing in the barren concrete streets of the Balata and Aida Refugee Camps and the massive security apparatus and concrete walls that the Israeli government and military continue to erect in their increasing efforts to protect themselves through ghettoization, it is clear that it is time to think beyond the dominant paradigm, and Zochrot is clearly a good place to start.

What Do I Know? I Am Just a Bedouin. A Lot.

June 22, 2014

My glasses (somewhat symbolically) have broken; perhaps my brain does not want to see any more, but there is so much to witness. I can hear the military jets overhead as we drive toward the unrecognized Bedouin village of Alsira in the Naqab. My old emergency glasses leave me with a headache, double vision, and a sense that the world I am experiencing is intensely out of focus, which in reality it is.

Khalil al-Amour greets us and invites us up to his shaded patio for water and juice. He has a sun-browned, open face with laughing eyes and a quirky sense of humor. He points to the demolition order glued on his door, dated September 2006. It is addressed, "To the house owner," and has no check marks next to the list of grievances. It is signed by some official who clearly cannot distinguish one Bedouin from another, demonstrated by the fact that the form is a photocopy. Khalil is a math and computer teacher and just received his law degree. He works with Adalah, a legal group that advocates for Bedouin rights in Israel, and he is leaving soon for Geneva for a UN conference on the rights of indigenous peoples. He is busy preparing for his son's wedding and for the upcoming month of Ramadan.

Clothespins clip a map of the Naqab onto the grating over a front window where rows of socks are also drying. Khalil explains that Bedouins used to live in the entire Naqab, encompassing thirteen million dunams. They had no major problems during four hundred years of Ottoman control and thirty years of British mandate, but then came 1948. Ninety thousand were expelled—most fleeing to the Egyptian Sinai desert, some went to Jordan—and eleven thousand remained. The Israelis "relocated" them to an area called the Siyag, a fenced-in reservation and closed military zone. The Bedouin were traumatized by the massive expulsion and by the confiscation of 90 percent of their land. The Israelis kept shrinking the land available to the Bedouin and expanding the southern city of Be'er Sheva. They took eighty thousand dunams to build a huge military airport nearby.

I start counting the number of planes roaring overhead. More Jewish cities were built in the area, but the Bedouin stayed and married and made babies, so now there are more than two hundred thousand. "We are a big surprise," says Khalil. The Prawer Plan is currently frozen, but it will undoubtedly be revived in that bastion of justice, the Knesset, and squeeze the population, which represents 30 percent of the Naqab, into 2 percent of the land. Dimona, the officially denied Israeli nuclear reactor, is located in the southeast area of the proposed relocations.

In a disconcertingly cheerful manner, Khalil remarks, "It really drives me crazy sometimes. Most Israelis are very stupid, listen to the media, the lies. How do we have these smart people—Jewish people are not stupid—[but]

their behavior toward Bedouin and minorities is very strange. I expect more understanding with the Holocaust. . . . And it is worse and worse."

Bedouin have repeatedly rejected efforts to push them into poverty-stricken, crime-ridden townships. "We are not good friends with cities!" Khalil explains, "I am half-Polish and half-Bedouin!" His daughter interrupts him to ask for his iPhone. He explains that years ago when he was studying in Be'er Sheva at the teacher's college, he had to sleep in the park. A gas station offered him a part-time job, but it was not enough money for rent as his family was very poor. He laughs and says that he met a Polish couple, who had lost their own child, and they "adopted" him and took care of him for three years. As the couple got older, Khalil took care of them until they died, and then he returned to his village.

His son, a physiotherapist, studied in Jordan and now works in Be'er Sheva, but returns home to Alsira every day. Another son is studying medicine in Moldova, but he will also return. "We love the desert, this is our life," says Khalil. He explains that not only does he have a demolition order on his house, but also on his animal feed bins and his generator. The orders are created from an aerial map and he is #67. He remarks ironically that being #67 reminds him of the Holocaust. Khalil has good Jewish friends who also get very angry at these troubling parallels and the general treatment of the Bedouin in Israel.

He explains that there are forty-five unrecognized villages. Every one of them is named; some are new, some are old. The Israelis took the fertile lands; Ariel Sharon once had a large ranch in the Naqab. The Bedouin have limited access to water and pay very high rates; they have no electricity or nearby schools or clinics. Khalil notes that earlier, as we drove into the town, part of that road we were on also goes to the airport. "We paved the road, connected to the water system, made solar energy, established two daycares for the children," says Khalil. "We take care of ourselves."

In the townships, they are offered high mortgages and a small plot of land—entirely unfeasible for a traditional agricultural society with goats, cows, and sheep to herd. He says this township life is particularly hard for the women. They can't make cheese, can't do their traditional farming, can't weave rugs. "They have no value." Israelis talk of modernization and improved living standards—the Bedouin are given a microwave and a washing machine—but the women are "humiliated, no respect."

"We have lived marginalized and neglected, no problem, we can live the next sixty years [that way]. They won't even let us do that. Let the Bedouin live." He takes us on an extraordinary tour of his property and at every stop he smiles and explains how much he loves his solar panels, loves his chickens, loves his mulberries, olives, sage, fresh eggs. The man is deeply in love with the land he lives with and he is deeply happy. His friends thought he was crazy, but through internet research and a learning tour he took in Canada and the United States, he taught himself how to set up solar panels. His friends were finally convinced when they noticed his refrigerator was working twenty-four hours a day.

Every year he would make fifty liters of olive oil from his trees, but he noticed they were dying from lack of water. Back to the internet and YouTube. He then developed an ingenious system for collecting grey water using pipes, collecting rainwater with a system of tanks, pumps, and filters, thereby providing drip irrigation to his rejuvenated trees. He is beaming as he shows us the lush clusters of happy olives. "I am not a genius, I am regular." But he loves his chickens and scoops up three eggs; he eats two fresh eggs every morning and assures us that he only feeds the birds natural grains. We look across the brown rolling desert to the huge military area where he used to go to school and where his people used to bury their dead. He recently visited for the first time in thirty-two years with a group that went to maintain the cemetery.

And then he is back picking white mulberries for us; the taste of the fruit is a cross between blackberries and strawberries. He tells us about traveling to the United States with the Tree of Life Conference and being hosted by Christians and Jews. He laughs, "I was almost converted to Christianity!" We look up at the antennae for his phone and internet and the router attached to the corner of his house. He jokes that a bird sometimes nests there, so he also has Twitter. As we leave his house he points to a large collection of ants and he assures us (cheerfully) that he never kills them. "They were here before me." Apparently he and the insects are coexisting quite successfully.

We wander through the dry dusty neighborhood as women are cleaning, cooking, children scatter about; there are manually rotating solar panels, a "white house" for community gatherings and celebrations, other homes of varying sturdiness. The village put up a sign denoting the location of the town and containing an ironic message. In Arabic it says "Alsira," in English it is misspelled as "Alsra," and in Hebrew it says, "Established in the Ottoman Empire." Like I said, the guy has a sense of humor. Below the marker is a triangular warning sign, again presented in a tongue in cheek style, depicting a house and a bulldozer—a warning to the hapless visitor that they are now entering a demolition zone.

This village has no *sheikh* but rather a local committee of five people that provides leadership. There are two big clans and five family groups representing seventy individual families and over one hundred children. There is also a Regional Council of Unrecognized Villages. There are no women in leadership, but two of them are very active in the council. Khalil reminds us that this is a conservative community—for instance, there is some polygamy—but "I am an open-minded guy." Nowadays girls do not get married before they turn eighteen.

Last year, our delegation visited the village of Al Araqib, north of Be'er Sheva. Khalil explains this village has "the saddest story," which includes expulsion in 1948, repeated land confiscations, incidents of the Israeli military spraying fields and animals with Roundup, multiple legal cases, and repeated demolitions. Last year, the villagers were living in the cemetery, and the JNF planted the Ambassador Forest on their agricultural land. Last week, the Israeli forces demolished everything in the cemetery, approximately the seventieth demolition. Now the villagers are under the trees, using blankets for cover; they are "upset and nervous," and the *sheikh*, who was "warm and happy," is feeling "angry." Rabbi Arik Ascherman from Rabbis for Human Rights was arrested at the cemetery site, and the demolitions have attracted attention from international NGOs (nongovernmental organizations) and the United Nations.

Khalil asserts, "Our voice will be heard." He asserts there is an increasing international awareness of the rights of native indigenous peoples and the impact of colonialism. In the past, a delegation of Native Americans came and wrote an urgent letter to the Israelis. "I am optimistic. We don't have the privilege to give up. This is racism."

For the twelfth time since we arrived, a military plane screeches overhead, breaking the desert silence.

As we drive back to Ramallah passing near Hebron, we see Israeli forces marching with flags in some kind of military formation, then we see a group of soldiers breaking into a house; our eyes burn from tear gas wafting from the city. We learn that Palestinians have been killed in Nablus and Hebron, and in Ramallah where an Israeli sniper shot an unarmed man who was watching the attack from a rooftop. Later that night the IDF conducts an incursion into Ramallah in front of the Palestinian Authority police station; the PA does nothing to protect its people and when the IDF leaves, the enraged crowd attacks the police station, prompting retaliation from the PA.

The media and the streets are filled with stories about Netanyahu's blind rage and the missing boys. (Are they yeshiva students? Armed right-wing settlers? Paramilitary? Everyone has a theory.) The entire Palestinian population in the West Bank and Gaza is under attack because three young men are missing, because Hamas and Fatah are talking to each other, because the farce of the peace process has been laid bare. Because, well, because they are here and they are Palestinian. And that, it seems, is a crime in itself. The treatment of Palestinians in the West Bank, of Bedouin in the Naqab seems cut from the same kind of ideology, boiling with a toxic brew of entitlement, fear, and racism.

Tarnishing the Israeli Brand

June 23, 2014

Our meeting with Omar Barghouti, one of the leaders of the BDS movement, starts in a stairwell because the office where we are scheduled to meet is locked. He is talking about how the PA is "existentially necessary" for Israel, how a single democratic state is the long-term goal—not an ideal one, but a more ethical solution than anything else.

We get ushered into an open office and Omar starts officially talking; words just pour out of him so rapidly, succinctly; I struggle to keep up. Things have really changed in the past year. What many do not realize is that BDS is now a mainstream Palestinian movement that is supported by almost everyone; it is not an isolated fringe activity. Even Fatah supports BDS. The strategy is anchored in international law and, Omar explains, "targets Israel because it is a regime of occupation and apartheid. This is not about being Jewish." The Israeli establishment clearly considers BDS a strategic threat. When Netanyahu gave his talk in March 2014 to the United Nations, he mentioned BDS eighteen times, second only to Iran. Omar states, "Israel does not know what to do with nonviolent movements." This defeats the narrative of the Palestinian as terrorist.

He also argues that although there are well-funded, well-organized efforts to brand Israel as a "beacon of democracy" (to quote Netanyahu)—to highlight Israeli artists, academics, gays; to present a "pretty face"—"all this washing [i.e., pink-washing, green-washing] gets wiped out by one massacre."

Omar asserts that today, in 2014, BDS is in a different place: the financial, economic sphere. The Gates Foundation recently divested from G4S, a private-security company that builds the Israeli security apparatus, is deeply involved in the occupation, and is known to torture prisoners. The CEO of G4S decided not to renew the contract with Israeli prisons, the first time such a public action has been taken. It does not matter that BDS was not mentioned. It *does* matter that a large company decides that it is too costly (economically? politically? strategically?) to do business with the Israeli state. Obviously, pressure will continue until the company comes through on its promise.

Omar informs us that major banks and pension funds in Europe have divested from the top five Israeli banks involved in the occupied territories. Apparently the Dutch are saying that if these banks have operations with companies in the territories, they will divest entirely from the bank. To summarize the strategy, "Do not punish the crime, punish the criminal."

It has always been difficult to figure out which products come from the settlements, and Omar agrees that it is too hard to boycott settlement products—they are often disguised or relabeled. It is, however, very feasible to boycott companies that operate in the occupied territories, so the tactic should be to boycott companies rather than products. I take note of this advice.

Unlike my Massachusetts governor, Deval Patrick, who is swooning over potential ventures with Israeli companies and the development of high-tech solutions to water shortages, the German government announced that it will not work with all high-tech Israeli companies, including those in East Jerusalem. The European Union has not joined the BDS movement, but it is implementing its own guidelines in response to grassroots pressure, so it will not give grants for research in the territories. The Luxemburg pension fund divested from the top five Israeli banks. The Norwegian pension fund divested from Israeli companies involved in settlements, but then it took Africa Israel, an investment firm, off the list after the firm denied involvement. The Israeli group Who Profits? responded by going to the Jewish settlement of Gilo and documenting Africa Israel's presence there, to which the firm countered that Gilo is not located in the occupied territories. Organizers demanded that the pension fund consult the United Nations, which might know a bit more about international law, and the Norwegians got the message and divested. In 2013–14, four US academic organizations endorsed BDS. These are all major developments.

Omar says that the Israeli government has been totally hijacked by the settler movement, and this is a new turn of events. Using a subtle kind of sarcasm, he explains that the once-leading Labor Party is a kind of "smarter Zionism," while Israel's new leadership is now a "dumber Zionism." Israel is no longer even pretending to stand for peace, coexistence, etc. The academic and cultural boycotts have tarnished the Israeli brand. Even John Kerry acknowledges that there is something seriously wrong with settlement building. In much of Europe, people choose not to buy Israeli products. "We rely on the grassroots to build pressure," Omar explains, even though in the international world, "the Israeli government is untouchable" and is not held accountable for obvious unjust practices. So, the solution is to "do one church, one university at a time."

The delegates want to talk about the nitty-gritty, on-the-ground issues that come up. Omar is asked if there are any mutual funds that are BDS-compliant. "Not yet, but it is in process." He explains that SRI funds (those committed to socially responsible investing) do not use BDS language (though they traditionally avoid military and environmentally damaging companies), but the change is coming.

We then engage in a fascinating discussion that speaks to Jewish privilege and Jewish power on the left. At the Jewish Voice for Peace conference last year, Omar spoke. He notes that supportive Jewish voices on BDS give it legitimacy and fend off the accusation of anti-Semitism. At the same time, Jewish voices run the risk of expropriating Palestinian voices, thus entrenching Jewish exceptionalism and maintaining the belief that only Jews are "allowed" to criticize Israeli policy. This actually is a form of anti-Semitism, a promotion of the fear of Jews, of powerful Jews who will destroy you if you criticize Israel. This is not good for anyone, but many Zionist groups thrive on this very fear.

Omar maintains that while Jewish voices are critical, it is equally critical to work in coalition, such as with the American Friends Service Committee, the Presbyterians, and Adalah New York. JVP, which initiated the TIAA-CREF divestment campaign, pressuring the financial company to divest from companies in their SRI portfolio that profit from occupation, now works in a wider coalition called WE DIVEST; the coalition is careful not to monopolize the movement but is also ready to counter the charge of anti-Semitism. The recent success in Boston, in which pressure resulted in Veolia losing its commuter rail contract, can be traced to a large coalition that included union groups as well as Jewish and other faith-based organizations. Together, these groups brought a wide variety of complaints against the company, one of which included its behavior in the occupied territories.

Another delegate wonders how to work in academic institutions that are largely hostile to the BDS movement, like Brandeis University, where there are something like eight "pro-Israel groups." (I would like to redefine what it means to be pro-Israel, but that is for another conversation.) Omar explains that he went to Columbia University in the 1980s, where there were twenty "pro-Israel" groups from right to left and six "pro-Palestinian students." He and the other activists felt completely isolated, so they sought out coalitions with Blacks, Latinos, feminists, and liberal Zionists who were opposed to the occupation (which was a radical idea back then). They worked on mutual interests such as opposing war and improving the environment. He reminds us that now as well as then, it is important to select a target that makes sense within your community, to look for levels of complicity in international law, for instance, and potential for cross-movement work. The company's offenses have to go beyond oppressing Palestinians. Thus it makes no sense to go after a company that makes some great cancer drug in Israel or the settlements, but it makes a lot of sense to link the activities of G4S in building the US-Mexico wall and walls in the territories. "Trying and failing is not okay unless it leads to education; otherwise, it is not strategic," he says.

But what if there are no Palestinian-led BDS organizations, like in Boston where there is a lot of BDS activity? Omar advises that we must fill the vacuum until the Palestinian community becomes more active. There are lots of challenges that discourage Palestinians in the United States, from fears related to post-9/11 targeting to Islamophobia. He remarks that many in that community are not politically active, but their sons and daughters are. He notes that campus-based Students for Justice in Palestine chapters are no longer led by Jewish students and that leadership is often coming from Palestinian women. "I understand having Palestinian voices up front, but this is a universal issue. I do not believe in identity politics. The anti-apartheid movement was my movement. I was doing something right as a human; I own this as my own struggle." We ought to focus on effectiveness, the quality of the work, antiracist principles.

In response to another question about how to work in progressive community organizations that partner with Israeli groups on community development, racial and economic justice issues, etc., Omar suggests that we need to broaden the conversation, to "South Africanize the issue." As an example he asks, what would we have done if Boston University was working with a South African university on cancer treatment during the apartheid era? Yes, that is good for humanity, but the research institution is also complicit with an apartheid system, and this collaboration would have been inappropriate. He suggests that we ask Palestinians about joint research projects with, for instance, Tel Aviv University. It is fine to do research with Israelis but not with institutions that receive Israeli funding. So, in our hypothetical case, Boston University should fund the research, not Tel Aviv University, thus avoiding a stance that legitimizes a university complicit in the occupation. In the same vein, Israeli filmmakers, artists, and poets can be invited to festivals in a "BDS-friendly way." For instance, at the Edinburgh Festival, the Israeli embassy in London paid a filmmaker to screen her film. Activists told the festival if it accepted this money, people would boycott the festival. The festival's organizers responded by returning the money to the Israeli filmmaker (and embassy) and decided to assume the costs themselves for showing the Israeli film. "There must be no institutional links," Omar explains. In another example, Omar explains that a Canadian LGBT artist in a Scottish festival found out that an Israeli artist was sponsored by the Israeli foreign ministry. The Canadian put pressure on the festival and wrote a letter to every artist. In its defense, the Israeli embassy said the artist is pro-Palestinian and has a dissenting voice. "But we do not care about content; this is not about censorship, it is about funding," Omar says. The Israeli sponsorship was canceled and the artist came to the festival.

A particular challenge involves communities of color, who often come to Israel on religious pilgrimages or on cultural exchanges. Omar explains, "It is easy to get a free trip to Israel, so South Africanize the issue." If you want to come on a "fact-finding mission, then do it without complicity; do not cross the picket line. This is happening more and more. Israel helps us to convert people; if they come on an honest fact-finding mission, they see what is going on." We talk about our governor, Deval Patrick, as a particularly challenging example of an African-American public figure who fails to see the racism in Israel and is eager to promote mutual business interests. Omar advises that the "the Black community is key to BDS; we need to win them." There is already a high rate of support of the BDS campaign among young Jews who at this point are largely somewhere between apathetic about Israel to supportive of Palestinian rights, but clearly different from their Zionist parents and grandparents. The Israel propaganda machine focuses on African Americans, Native Americans, and the Asian community, framing the issue by claiming, "Jews are the indigenous people! Join us in our struggle." In this framing, colonialism is conveniently overlooked. African Americans, students, and women leaders are invited to Israel to promote an historic Jewish-Black alliance. We led the civil rights movement and we can do it again.

Friends of Sabeel, the authors of the Kairos document, and Christian liberation theologians work to counter this Zionist ideology, but it is a frustratingly slow process. Pointing to the recent alliance between Cornell University and the Technion-Israeli Institute of Technology as proof, Omar informs us that the Israeli establishment will continue to score big successes at high levels, and that the US establishment is profoundly "pro-Israel" (in the classic use of that word). "Forget the big elephants, chip away and attack smaller things. The Technion was not selected because it was the best; there was a well-planned conspiracy and work was done before to make it happen."

I am beginning to feel like a white civil rights activist working in the Deep South in the 1960s. The parallels are striking and the historical connection revives me. Time to take this conversation home.

Water and Salt

June 23, 2014

This year we meet again with Randa Wahbe, the dedicated advocacy officer at Addameer, on the sixty-first day of the longest-ever hunger strike by administrative detainees in Israeli jails. The strike is a political strike (i.e., organized not for improved prison conditions but for ending the Israeli policy of detaining people without charges or adequate access to a lawyer, sometimes for a length of six years or more). At the time of our meeting, there had been no negotiations, but as I write this a week later, the strike has ended, some secret deal has been met, and there is mostly speculation: What was decided? Did the hunger strikers feel that this was not the right time when the public is obsessed by the three missing settlers and the World Cup and Ramadan? Who knows?

Whatever the outcome, prisoner issues are central to Palestinian liberation. As I noted earlier, 800,000 Palestinians, constituting 40 percent of the male population, have been arrested since 1967. Thousands of Palestinians, adults and children, are held in this limbo land of administrative detention.

At the time of our visit, there were at least 130 hunger strikers, with the movement growing and set to possibly reach 300. As punishment for striking, the prisoners are put into isolation; they cannot go outside or have family visits (they often do not see their families because of permitting and travel issues anyway). They receive fines, which are paid through money taken from their canteen account. Sometimes they have limited or no access to lawyers, or they are transferred around to different prison hospitals so the lawyer cannot locate them. They are beaten, denied medical care, and are only treated by prison doctors who (clearly having lost their ethical compass) are known to be abusive, dangling food or forced-feeding tubes in the prisoners' faces. Prisoners are even shackled twelve hours per day.

For fourteen days of the strike, the prisoners were drinking water with salt, after which, Randa reports, the Israeli authorities started denying them the salt. Some of the prisoners may be taking some unknown supplements that "barely keep them alive." Randa says that as an organization, "we are very concerned because of the lack of negotiation between the Israeli prison service and the prisoners. Will there be martyrs?" A lot of administrative detainees are over sixty years old and not striking, but other prisoners are striking in sympathy. There appears to be a trend to arrest Palestinians shortly after their eighteenth birthday, as they can be tried as adults. The youngest hunger striker was arrested five days after his eighteenth birthday, "He is still a child, but he has been in prison for two years," says Randa. There have been over four hundred Palestinians arrested since the twelfth of June; seventy-seven are in administrative detention.

And then there is the heartbreaking issue of child arrests. Although Israel technically changed its policy and has child courts, Randa reports that children are still treated as adults, especially when it comes to sentencing. They are often arrested between midnight and 5:00 a.m., with their families not told where the children are going. They are interrogated without a lawyer, not allowed to see their families. It is the same military court judge for the children as for the adults, and Randa explains that the children are routinely tortured by their interrogators. This is mostly psychological torture—threats of sexual abuse or death; they are put into solitary confinement, have fluorescent lights on twenty-four hours per day, are placed in stress positions, and beaten. The forced confessions are then used to arrest adults in the community. So imagine you are an eighteen-year-old boy: you have seen your father and grandfather humiliated at checkpoints, you have watched settlers steal your land and water, and, very possibly, you have thrown stones at a passing Israeli jeep that has arrived to make your life a living hell. And then you crack in prison, inform on your own brother, and are responsible for his arrest. Many children never return to school and develop bed-wetting and behavioral problems.[8]

With these brutal policies, we are witnessing the slow destruction of Palestinian society and the creation of environments that will create more angry, hopeless, militant men seeking revenge. In Silwan, there is a fourteen-year-old who has been arrested six times, mostly for throwing stones, according to IDF soldiers or settlers. Palestinian parents pay fines to release their children, and last year, Palestinians paid a total of thirteen million shekels into the Israeli military court—in a bizarre sense, they are financing their own imprisonment. And prisons are increasingly privatized, much like the US prisons.

In general, Randa explains, administrative detention is allowed under international law if an individual is threatening the security of the state. This should be used rarely. But in Israel, the military claims the Shin Bet has "secret files" that show that a particular person is a threat to the state. "This is used arbitrarily; there are obviously no files. Let's look at who gets arrested: prominent activists, academics, regular folks. Recently, a political scientist was released, after two and a half years without any charges. He has no idea why he was arrested this time; [suffice it to say that] he is an academic who writes about resistance, attends demonstrations, and has been in and out of prison for years. One of the hunger strikers is a prominent community member, part of an agricultural union who promotes farmers' rights; he has been in and out of administrative detention for years and was rearrested in February."

At the time of our visit, a bill to allow forced-feeding was to be voted on in the Israeli Knesset, although forced-feeding is regarded as a form of torture, people have died during the procedure, and it is used to break the strikers. Even the Israeli Medical Association is against it. The bill did not pass, but today (June 30, 2014) the Knesset is voting on another bill that would permit doctors to do forced-feeding without risk of punishment.[9] Netanyahu has framed this as an issue of internal security: forced-feeding is for the safety of Israeli citizens, because if a prisoner dies, "it will threaten security of Israelis in Judea and Samaria." And then to skirt the real issue they play with words: it is "artificial feeding" (not forced), "moderate restraints" (rather than the full shackling that is used). The doctor has to recommend forced-feeding "for the benefit of the prisoner"; this is signed off by a district court, which gives the whole process the air of legality.

In the last month, there have been other worrisome proposed bills, including one to deny amnesty to prisoners who are released in exchanges (Israel has released seventy prisoners arrested before Oslo in 1993). Denying amnesty in this manner perpetuates the response that a prisoner is automatically a "terrorist." Pro-prisoner demonstrations were suppressed by the PA and the IDF, especially in Hebron, where there was a demonstration by mothers of prisoners. In the past eleven days, five Palestinians have been killed, and, in addition to the four hundred arrested, there have been eight hundred home incursions and lots of injuries and road closures. The PA coordinates security with Israel, which is facilitating the siege on Hebron. Two nights ago in Ramallah, PA officers shot demonstrators storming the police station. Currently, this is the largest military operation since the Second Intifada, and for me, what is strange is that it is generally happening under cover of darkness. By the time the sun comes up, most of the Israeli forces are out of the villages and homes and universities, and everything looks deceptively normal unless you live in Hebron. The world community may not even notice; there are no tanks and no phosphorus bombs to catch anyone's attention.

Randa talks about a host of other human rights concerns, and the picture is grim. Children born to mothers in prison are kept in prison for two years with no extra space, food, or medical care; they are basically born with a prison record. Pregnant Palestinian women who are arrested get no prenatal care or special food, and give birth while shackled. The prisons are dirty, prisoners have to purchase high-priced food and personal items from a canteen, there are often no family visits; it is an utterly dehumanizing climate. There is a case now where a granddaughter is not allowed to visit her grandfather. The courts say the family has to prove their relation to each other; in other cases, mothers are asked to prove their relationship to their children in prison.

When people are released, there is some support from the prisoner affairs ministry, dedicated to legal aid and financial and medical assistance, but not many resources are available for rehabilitation. The prison experience is so normalized within the community; there is a lot of community support when prisoners are released, but not much treatment for posttraumatic stress disorder, which just about everyone has. Interestingly, following their release, prisoners do not face housing or employment discrimination; the community views these as largely political arrests.

If arrested, there is a higher rate of re-arrest because the IDF targets former prisoners, which basically destroys their lives. There are students who have been attending Birzeit University for eight years because they are repeatedly arrested around exam times, and their educational experience just drags on as a result. In the case of younger students, some are arrested during the final year of high school so they cannot take the Tawjihi exams, critical for university admission.

So why do people get arrested? For starters, there are some 1,600 military orders that govern life under occupation. (Yes, there is an occupation; the place is not "administered" or "liberated" or whatever euphemism you may hear.) Organizations like student unions and all political organizations are illegal, including, technically speaking, the PA. This gives the IDF very broad discretionary powers. People get arrested because they are activists, such as those in Stop the Wall, or because they do volunteer work to empower youth. Basically the charges are used to suppress Palestinian resistance in all forms. Randa notes that in the past year three Addameer colleagues have been arrested, charged with giving legal advice to youth about interrogation, which is, after all, part of their job description. "We are all in jeopardy . . . going to a demonstration today we could be charged; this is the climate."

Randa was studying at a university in the United States and was involved in its Students for Justice in Palestine chapter. She moved to Jordan to learn Arabic but came to a conference in Palestine. Addameer had an opening and she took the job. While her family is still in California (and it is often hard for Palestinians to get visas), she believes that it is important for Diaspora Palestinians to come back and to do the challenging work of ending the occupation and its immense hardships.

Building Dreamers in a Nightmare
June 23, 2014

I write this blog post belatedly about a visit to the Old City of Jerusalem and Yasser Qous, an Afro-Palestinian who runs a youth center in a cavernous stone structure dating back to the twelfth century. And because this is about two visits in June that now feel like a decade ago, I need to acknowledge the murder of the three Hebron settler youth and the frightening revenge-based, pogrom-like behavior that now characterizes the Israeli military and some of its citizens. Perhaps if you get to know some of the folks who are now at risk (read: any Palestinian), although they were at risk before, it was just more invisible, you too will be filled with dread and worry and horror.

Yasser Qous is wearing a dashiki and has a warm, open face, a shaved head, and a rolled cigarette in his mouth. He is dark, has very expressive hands, and an intelligent, laid-back manner. He says, "The Old City is like our house," and welcomes us as if we are his personal guests. His father had come here from Chad in 1952, so he grew up here and became active as a student at Bethlehem University. He works with city youth doing photography and alternative media, and he is involved in psychosocial interventions around issues like drugs and sexual abuse. He comments that here there are no addiction treatment centers, that drug use is a symptom of hopelessness and lack of opportunity, and thus it is a political problem. He shares the usual stories of home demolitions and a new policy of house arrest for teens.

We visit a drop-in café with sprawling couches, drinks, and ice cream, and a TV showing nonstop World Cup. He is very excited about the upcoming Ramadan events, during which there is a competition between neighborhoods for the best light decorations. (The Old City is starting to look a bit like Christmas in Queens.) He explains that the rituals of Ramadan include all-night celebrations with Sufi dancing and music, followed by quiet, thirsty days.

Since unemployment is such a huge problem in East Jerusalem (60 percent poverty rate for Palestinians), the center is involved in training and supporting small business. They are part of a tourism coalition that sells handicrafts, reviving East Jerusalem handicrafts based on cultural research and training that reflects the particular heritage from East Jerusalem. They have a good relationship with a French development agency and an upcoming project involves supporting ten street sellers (interestingly, all need permission from Israel). Twenty youth will be trained to create a photo studio on Al-Wad Street; they will take photos of the Old City and sell the prints, create and sell handmade accessories, and conduct alternative, socially oriented tours from 4:00 p.m. to midnight. At the center they also do art and music, have a band, and sponsor dances in several styles—*dabke*, hip-hop, and Brazilian capoeira. They have made good relationships with African-American students from the United States and organized an event for a South African representative.

Yasser explains that most Africans came in the fifteenth century to Jerusalem as Muslim pilgrims on the hajj, but many settled here, particularly toward the end of the Ottoman Empire and during the British Mandate when it became more difficult to go home. This youth center was previously a prison after the Arab revolt, and before that, a military compound and traveler's hostel called a ribat. This ribat is the oldest in Jerusalem, founded by a Mamluk sultan who brought slaves from Egypt.

With the establishment of the British Mandate, the property went to the Mufti and then the African community settled here. After 1948, half of the residents went to Jordan, some to Lebanon, and others to Jericho and Tulkarem in the West Bank, Khan Yunis in Gaza, and the Negev. There are now 350 Afro-Palestinians in Jerusalem out of a total 183,000 Palestinians in the East Jerusalem municipality; they call themselves "coconuts" (Black outside, Palestinian inside). Their main connection with each other lies in their involvement in the hajj. They have been part of Palestinian resistance, some even martyred in the wars, and many have been imprisoned. The first female political prisoner was Afro-Palestinian, and she spent thirteen years incarcerated. The neighborhood is subjected to frequent collective punishment at the hands of Israeli security. Many have intermarried with Palestinians. They are proud of their roots but not well connected to Africa, and in Jerusalem they face high employment and discrimination (for being Black, Palestinian, lower class). Most are either Muslim or Christian, and their ancestors are from Nigeria, Senegal, Sudan, and Chad.

A week later, Yasser takes the delegation on a tour of East Jerusalem, through the many Muslim and Christian sites. I learn that a right-wing Jewish group, Ateret Cohanim, which conveniently has established a yeshiva in the Muslim Quarter using Palestinian collaborators, rents and sells houses to Jews and displaces Palestinians. We see four Jewish families in their gated and guarded home; armed guards walk the Jews out of the Muslim Quarter into the Jewish Quarter (which was depopulated of Jews in 1948 when it was taken by the Jordanians). Yasser explains that not only are these folks expanding into Muslim and Christian sectors of the city (no one else can get permits), but they are creating a Jewish ghetto for themselves. In the Jewish sector, which is obviously well funded and pristine from an archeological and touristic point of view, along with having arty shops and galleries with great jewelry, there is evidence of all the different conquerors who built on top of the preexisting civilizations lo these many centuries. We wander down the Cardo, the ancient Roman market with a multistory excavation that goes deep into the ground. Armed security guards escort herds of young children to their destinations, and I can only think they look like tough teen boy babysitters with guns and walkie-talkies. I wonder what the children are learning from this daily experience. Life is dangerous and "they" all want to kill us? The abnormal becomes normalized.

The youth center created the Longest Chain of Readers at Damascus Gate, six thousand kids reading books at one time, after which they donated them to libraries. On another day, they were celebrating a kite festival with three hundred children, but the IDF attacked the event and destroyed the kites.

When Yasser was ten years old he was given a book, *Children of Palestine*, and the introduction explained that life is like theater: there is the audience and there are the players. It was at that point he decided that he wanted to be a player.

When those kites were crushed, just imagine the dreams that were crushed with them. So, people ask, why are kids throwing stones? Wouldn't you?

Traveling While Occupied

June 24, 2014

Blogging retrospectively is a challenge. I am reporting from the ground, and the ground is in constant seismic-shift mode. Let me acknowledge that the deaths of the three kidnapped Israeli youths, Gil-Ad Shaer, Naftali Fraenkel, and Eyal Yifrach, provided the Israeli leadership with the opportunity to unleash a horrific barrage of military might, home incursions, arrests, and killings that had little to do with a careful investigation of the crime and the capture of the perpetrators. Collective punishment is still all the rage, and at this point I would simply call it official policy. Even the Israeli generals are trying to tone down the "Let's destroy Hamas!" rhetoric coming out of the prime minister's mouth. The abduction, killing, and burning of Mohammed Abu Khdeir, on the other hand, is being approached in a totally different manner: there is the police statement that they are not sure if the murder was "nationalistic" (i.e., done by an Israeli) or "criminal" (i.e., done by a Palestinian). Then there was the outrageously false rumor put out by the police that Mohammed was gay and that this was some kind of revenge killing by his homophobic family. To the Palestinians in Shu'afat, a neighborhood of East Jerusalem, this is clearly a revenge killing, and to my eye, given the explosion of Arab hatred, the attempted kidnapping two days earlier of ten-year-old Mousa Zalum (his parents called the police, no one responded), and the gangs of right-wing Jewish teenagers roaming the streets of Jerusalem chanting "Death to the Arabs!," I side with the Palestinians. As East Jerusalem explodes, the police are using live fire on the neighborhood's East Jerusalem ID–carrying inhabitants (read: the non-Jewish Israeli residents).

To give this a little context, according to official statistics, since September 2000, more than fourteen hundred Palestinian children have been killed by the Israeli military, which is equivalent to one child killed every three days, and some six thousand injured in the past thirteen or so years. I think a year of national mourning is in order, but this is a military occupation and what can I say about who counts and who doesn't? Which brings us to some other realities of daily life.

I was hoping to tell you more about the realities of occupation, in particular, traveling while occupied. I (and every Palestinian I know) dread the Qalandia checkpoint. It is a chaotic, traffic-plagued military terminal with guard towers and concrete walls and grimy garbage and narrow turnstiles, and people waiting, waiting. Faces range from utter resignation and defeat to outright indignation and rage. I also vary between these two emotional states.

People queue in narrow chutes, two to three feet wide, with vertical, floor-to-ceiling bars and an excruciatingly narrow turnstile that makes passage with luggage, shopping bags, or small children a humiliating joke. The turnstile is controlled by the Israeli security, and I note that even the green light does not necessarily mean the bars will turn. Once in the maze, bags are x-rayed and I walk through the metal detector. On occasion, in protest I won't take off my watch and the metal detector will buzz; sometimes they care, sometimes they don't. I then approach a bulletproof window where I press my passport up against the glass and sometimes get the attention of a twenty-something in uniform on the other side. Or sometimes I don't. There is always a cup of coffee or a phone call or . . . communication is challenging. Once, two members of our delegation were pulled aside for extra security investigation and were asked questions like, "Do you love Israel?" "Are you afraid of us?" "Are you sure you are not an Israeli citizen?" "Do you love Palestinians?" Then there are more turnstiles of the humiliating "you are a rat in a cage" and "we really control you in case you did not already get the message" variety, and then you are free to fight for a taxi or a bus or a *service* with the license plate appropriate for whichever side you are now on. On the "other side" I note a sign in Arabic that says "Judea and Samaria," in case you are not clear on the underlying concept.

So I was thinking, if I were bent on revenge or strapped in a suicide vest (this is all about security, right?) would I really hazard going through Qalandia? I think not. So what is this massive, time-consuming, demoralizing daily exercise about? Control and humiliation come to mind. Also, it might just be easier to stay home and skip that visit to Al Aqsa this year, if one were lucky enough to get a permit in the first place.

Teaching in the Ghetto
June 25, 2014

The Jerusalem neighborhood of Abu Dis ended up on the wrong side of the wall. Every time bus #36 from East Jerusalem turns the corner in this neighborhood, there is the monstrous barrier up close and personal, all eight meters high of poured concrete stretching along the edge of the road (or rather *defining* the edge of the road and, in some ways, the edge of existence). I have the distinct impression that military-city planner types are giving us and all the wrong-side-people, a gigantic concrete finger in the eye. Most of Al Quds University is on the wrong side too if you live in Jerusalem, and of course on the right side if you live in Ramallah or Tulkarem or Jenin or Hebron. For students who are old enough to remember, getting to school from East Jerusalem used to be easy and quick. Now the journey involves a long tunnel, skirting Ma'ale Adumim (one of the largest Jewish settlements in the West

Bank), swinging through Bethany (the one of Biblical fame, though today's version has more industry and auto shops and less Jesus, Lazarus, and lepers), and making a huge snaking swing east and south to get to the bedraggled neighborhood of Abu Dis. Let's not even mention the increased use of fuel, the challenged shock absorbers that need constant repair, the choking air pollution, the lost time and rising aggravation, and the need to plan life around buses and permits, as well as the question of if it is even safe in the first place to try the daring trip to school.

We meet with Dr. Hani Abdeen, the dignified and somewhat burned-out dean of the medical school. He has a neat mustache, wire-rimmed glasses, striped shirt—very old school—and I feel like his story should be called "soldiering on against all odds." Al Quds Medical School was founded in 1994, and last week it graduated its fourteenth class, for a total of 720 graduates to date. Hani is very pleased with his students. He brags that they do very well on qualifying exams for residencies all over the Western world: Canada, United States, Europe. "The students are doing a good job; under duress, people excel," he says. "We do not have a large faculty, all the resources, teaching materials, yet with all these shortcomings students do well. In the US Medical Licensing Exam Palestinian students are in the top 1 percent of foreign graduates."

This is of particular interest to me as the AJJP Health and Human Rights Project was involved in starting an exchange program between Harvard and Al Quds Medical School, and in that program the students who rotated through Harvard hospitals received "glowing reports." Hani is very worried that while the medical school is doing a good job, they are essentially "training doctors for America; there is a big brain drain. Once they see how good life is, the standards of medicine, they leave and stay where they train."

Sadly, "even if they train, but should come back, we are starved of medical personnel." Hani notes that there is not one well-trained hematologist or nephrologist in the occupied territories, and similar shortages are prevalent in the fields of surgery, medicine, and OB-GYN as well. I am surprised to hear him say, "One way to address this: how to change ratio male to female?" He notes that now the medical school class is 60 percent female and he wants to increase this to 75 percent females, "because they stay, they are more loyal to their societies, stay with families, and are more of use to the Palestinian population!" His theory is that females "do much better on post high school exams, have less diversions, are more focused, while males have other goals, politics, etc." He wonders if women "may be more intelligent, or more driven to try to prove themselves." I wonder if they have fewer choices.

"We don't have good residency training, do not have the hospitals, and Israelis do not let us. Everything you build, then there is a fracas and then the whole thing collapses again. This is a big problem. Two days ago, the IDF entered the university at night, wreaked havoc on the infrastructure," and they did the same at a university in Jenin and another in Bethlehem. There are repeated mass arrests of students and professors. "Obviously what is happening, the Israelis are not interested in Palestinians having their own entity, all they want is ethnic cleansing, get rid of Palestinians and evict them. We are trying to develop, but nipped in the bud. . . . We are fed up with all this talk about human rights. This is how it is on the ground. . . . It makes your blood boil, there is a limit; what are the Israelis trying to do? They have Nobel laureates, etc., in Israel, but don't they understand what is going on?"

The grinding reality is revealed by the fact that three weeks ago students were about to start a two-week final exam period. But twenty-five of the eighty students from Hebron who attend the university couldn't get travel permits, so the exams were delayed, and now as the clampdown continues, students are taking their exams at home from a computer or (if no electricity or internet) on pen and paper, so the work tasks are multiplied.

"Imagine [a student] prepared for exam, then cannot take it, then [the exams are] bunched together; this creates psychological trauma, [but] we do not have enough psychiatrists. There is not one child psychiatrist in the occupied territories. . . . One of our faculty's house was ransacked in the night, I do not know why." He lived in Hebron, guilty as charged. "This happened to students' families as well. Imagine preparing for exams, the students seventeen to eighteen years old," and then the "oasis of democracy in Mideast" enters their bedrooms at night, finger on the trigger. So what does a seventeen-year-old do with all that trauma and rage?

Hani describes what is going on: "It is madness. We need to educate Israeli society; the majority is ignorant of what is happening in the West Bank. The separation wall is a psychological barrier. They have succeeded, everyone behind the wall is a terrorist, and they are not interested in knowing what is happening. What is needed—to educate Israelis, how to get out of their isolation-ghetto mentality. We are also in a ghetto—two ghettos. This is more important than educating the Arab world. Human life is sacred; if you want to live with neighbors peacefully, then why are you doing this? Arabs, what have they done to Israelis? How many [Israelis] killed in buses? They [IDF] killed over one one thousand people in Gaza. This is disproportionate killings; they are all the same, even doctors are participating in force-feeding prisoners."

We try to focus on the medical school, a six-year program that starts after high school. Hani describes a traditional curriculum that is changing to a more integrated, organ-based approach next year. The first three years involve basic sciences; the last three years are clinical. They are also planning a graduate entry program, consisting of four years of medical training after college, like most US programs. Students at Al Quds do their clinical rotations at affiliated hospitals like Al Makassed, Augusta Victoria, St. Johns, and the Red Crescent Hospital in Jerusalem, as well as hospitals in Hebron, Ramallah, and Jericho in the West Bank. He says there is a curriculum for the different clinical settings, but this is in theory only. The hitch is that the first-rate hospitals are all in East Jerusalem, so only the students who can get permits to enter Jerusalem can go on these rotations, and the rest of the students are forced to train in what are seen as second-rate facilities.

But medical care is even more complicated. The Ministry of Health runs community-based clinics, and the Palestinian Medical Relief Society, an NGO, has clinics that are focused on providing health care to poorly served communities. Hani suggests that all of these settings have issues around quality of care, and he wants his students to learn medicine "in a proper manner." There are "no postgraduate courses here," no continuing medical education courses. Additionally, "everyone doesn't have a computer, cannot travel, cannot access villages, so logistics are a big problem." The remainder of health care for Palestinians who are in the refugee camps is provided by UNRWA. The school has no connection with UNRWA and that care tends to be low-quality, overwhelmed, and underfunded.

In Gaza, the medical school Al Azhar is under the tutelage of Al Quds, and the Hamas-run Islamic University also has the same curriculum. Medical students in Gaza are filled with aspirations and drive, and along with everyone else, get caught in the incursions and the phosphorus bombs. Hani reports that the graduates do well despite the conditions, although the last time I checked, the Gaza hospitals were still recovering from being bombed to smithereens and unable to rebuild basic infrastructure like drinkable water systems and stocked pharmacies, so I suspect he is being a bit upbeat. There is also a medical school in Nablus, called An-Najah.

Hani notes that the French government offers scholarships to two to three postgraduate students a year for PhDs in medical science or specialty training; others go to Jordan or the United Kingdom, "but they never come back." He explains that the students make commitments to return, but then they pay out their debts and do not return. They are the top 1 percent in Palestine, high achievers, they want to be good doctors, but "our hospitals and infrastructure are not conducive to that. Nursing is not that good; physical therapy is not that good. It is not a solid team, so it is much harder to do medicine here. The pay is better—standard of living, career development—all better outside."

I wonder why Hani is still here. He trained in the United Kingdom, but "my mother was ill and alone so I came back [thinking] I will stay for a year and then I got myself sucked up." The immense need, the possibility to build something better, the inertia and grinding difficulty of getting through each day, let alone planning a career or an escape, the small victories and sense of place, and then family and commitment, and decades later . . . he finds himself still here.

Medicine: If It Doesn't Kill You, It Makes You Strong

June 25, 2014

The tone of the meeting with the medical students is not that positive. Now I will grant you they had just finished their exams (because of the Hebron curfew and the resultant delays, some had six exams in one day). Many are about to graduate, so they are done with all the frustrations and with living in a variety of ghettos, trying to get an education in an impossible place. One student describes Al Quds as "six years of hell." The students from East Jerusalem discuss the frustrations of crossing the Qalandia checkpoint twice a day; most everyone has had some frightening experience with a gun-toting Israeli who is also their age and sees every Palestinian as a terrorist. Everyone complains about the uptight culture of the medical field (sounds a lot like the hierarchical culture of US hospitals in the 1970s), physicians who act "like gods," and of course, the longstanding conflicts with the administration.

As we try to tease apart the miseries of medical school in general from the miseries of this medical school in particular, certain themes emerge. Al Quds (as opposed to An-Najah in Nablus) has no teaching hospital, so students get dispersed all over. Students with IDs or permits for East Jerusalem get better clinical rotations, and there are no standards or clear-cut expectations in the clinical curriculum, so the teaching is enormously variable and sometimes totally inadequate. (Pediatrics at Al Makassed Hospital is a glowing exception.) The doctors are often brilliant, having trained in high-power institutions abroad, but have active private clinics that keep them very busy, and teaching medical students is often low on their list of priorities. In addition, unlike hospitals in the United States, residents (where they exist) are not required to teach the students, so, explain the students, "everything is personal connection."

The students would love to see the institution improve and are aware that Al Quds has funding issues; the Israeli authorities are not allowing it to build a teaching hospital in Jerusalem. It sounds, nonetheless, like there is an unacceptable level of chaos: students talk about being "dumped" in hospitals in Bethlehem and Hebron, then having to rent crowded apartments in those communities due to the challenges of getting around. They talk about arbitrary grades, a lack of mentors and guidance, and a number of small problems. Everyone plans to train "outside" and everyone "plans to come back." I love their passion, their rage, and their idealism.

We talk about the challenges for patients. Due to lack of funding, patients having surgery sometimes have to buy their anesthetics, IVs, and pain medicine and bring them to the hospital before the procedure. Some hospitals have no electricity for two hours per day; this would certainly crimp a specialist's style, not to mention some poor patient on a respirator. If a Ministry of Health hospital is unable to perform some type of care, it will refer the patient to a private hospital, but the government then fails to pay for the care, so private hospitals have growing loans and debt as they struggle to survive.

And we talked about issues beyond the occupation's political impact on health care, the additional social determinants of health, and what is making people sick: all the pollution from prolonged bus and taxi routes, endless idling at checkpoints, dust from huge quarries and stone-cutting operations, piles of uncollected garbage, the contaminated, radioactive water dumped by the Dimona reactor south of Hebron. And then the people face a health care (non-)system that is ill prepared to deal with the totality of disease and its profound and complex etiologies.

No wonder these medical students are not only outspoken and smart and ready to take on the world but also profoundly angry about all the right things. If these are Palestine's future doctors, I feel very hopeful for the next generation. If they only come back.

Is There a Second World Medicine?

June 26, 2014

The newly built Ministry of Health Palestine Medical Complex, located in Ramallah, is filled with all the expected contradictions of building a First

World health care system under occupation in what is ironically more of a Third World kind of setting. We are getting the grand tour from a medical student who did his internship here. "Lots of experience, low quality" is how he describes it. The impressively clean, modern, white stone facilities were built in 2010, the result of a merger between a Ministry of Health hospital and a private hospital donated by an American in Ramallah. At the gate there is a sign that reads: "Palestine Medical Complex is Smoking Free Area."

I have a particular interest in quality improvement in health care, and we are soon meeting with Rebhe Bsharat, a PhD in a white coat, with a short mustache and a warm, friendly manner, who is in charge of quality and education for nursing. He reviews the different wings of the hospital, including pediatrics, surgery, emergency, general medicine, the intensive care units, dialysis units, triage beds—all the trappings of a twenty-first-century medical center. Each year they have about 126,000 emergency visits, 200,000 outpatient visits, 27,600 admissions, and 7,000 surgical cases. Quality assurance (a common term in quality improvement lingo) has been a focus at the hospital for the past three years. The World Health Organization has a program for "Patient safety friendly hospitals" with lists of standards to be met. In the United States, over the past few decades the whole focus on improving the quality of care has been to turn from blaming the "bad doctor who screwed up," which encourages a culture of secrecy and condemnation, to assuming that most clinicians are doing the best they can under challenging circumstances. Thus the task is to analyze how the system of care makes errors more likely and how systematic changes can reduce those errors. (For example, if too many errors are occurring because different medications with similar names and labeling are sitting next to each other on a shelf, a possible change would be to make the labels different colors and put the medications on different shelves.) This obviously has the potential to encourage a culture of joint cooperation and more creative thinking, and has the potential to actually make care safer.

Rebhe admits that there are a lot of challenges because this approach involves changing the culture and attitudes of the providers. I am so excited to learn that one of their quality improvement programs is focused on handwashing. As a point of explanation, one of my major concerns that emerged from observing and working in clinics and hospitals all over the West Bank is the fact that almost no one washes their hands before or after seeing patients. This is a preventable risk factor. As a firm believer in the germ theory, it seems to me that even under occupation, clinicians could and should wash their hands, and if there is no water, I have been known to leave bottles of hand sanitizer on doctors' desks as a personal contribution to fighting infection.

So you can imagine my delight when I saw a poster in a Palestine Medical Complex ward featuring a circle filled with bugs and a diagonal slash across it, accompanied by a message in large letters—"No germs allowed, WASH YOUR HANDS"—and an official signature. As expected, the initial surveys revealed that only 20 percent of doctors and 50 percent of nurses washed their hands, so now there are weekly lectures, monthly meetings, and patient safety protocols. Older doctors (like doctors everywhere) pushed back, but the trends are good.

Rebhe explores some of the challenges nurses face. He lives in a small village, and because it takes between thirty minutes and three hours to get to work (depending on the checkpoints), the previous shift has no option but to continue working until the next shift shows up. There are 300 nurses: half of them have a two-year diploma, half have a BA; 55 percent are women, and 20 percent are over forty. Many work here for ten years or so and then return to their cities or villages. They all need continuing education programs, and they want better patient-education publications and discharge planning, which are in the pipeline. Because high-level degrees are not available in the occupied territories, Rebhe was trained in Baghdad and Turkey, and his thesis was on effective planning for cardiac surgery. Meanwhile, he is trying to get folks to wash their hands.

We tour the wards, and I am impressed with their order and cleanliness (an incredible contrast to older Ministry of Health hospitals I have seen). The pediatric unit has forty beds, but only thirty are used due to lack of staff. They receive referrals from all over the West Bank. There is supposed to be one nurse for five patients, but in reality there is one nurse for twelve patients. Bears, ducks, Disney-like princesses, and Winnie the Pooh cheerfully decorate the walls. There are no psychiatrists or social workers, and medication shortages are frequent. Today the Ministry of Health doctors are on strike, the outpatient unit is closed, and only emergencies are being seen. The month-long strike is calling for the timely payment of their salaries, and no resolution is in sight. Politics and medicine—the challenges continue on so many levels and both the patients and staff pay the price. It seems they keep on hoping, keep on praying; the staff keep on showing up for work (sometimes), the patients, for care (always). *Alhamdulillah.* (Praise be to God.) What else is there to do?

5

Medicine and Torture
June 26-30, 2014

Over the last days of June 2014 the Israeli military stepped up the pace and scale of its incursions into the West Bank as I explored the challenges of life in the occupied territories and the intimacies of traveling among, and living in, the Palestinian towns and villages of the area. We attended a conference on the treatment of victims of torture in Ramallah and, in a uniquely open and honest conversation, investigated the public health and societal frictions within Palestinian society. My 2014 visit then ended with a daylong examination of Physicians for Human Rights–Israel (PHR-I) and their Open Clinic, in Jaffa. The Open Clinic provides care to Sudanese and Eritrean asylum seekers, one of the few sources of support for them in an environment in which they have been criminalized and threatened with deportation.

PHR-I is an offshoot of an earlier organization, the Association of Israeli and Palestinian Physicians for Human Rights, that was founded by two psychiatrists—Eyad el-Sarraj, a Palestinian, and Ruchama Marton, an Israeli—in 1988, in response to the First Intifada. Sarraj and Marton were outraged by the horrendous conditions and medical care in the Israeli-run hospitals in the occupied territories. The Association also vigorously combated the participation of Israeli physicians in the torture of Palestinian detainees. As I wrote in a previous book, "The Association, which evolved into Physicians for Human Rights–Israel (PHR-I), stated that its actions were based on universal principles of medical ethics as well as relevant international conventions relating to the safety of medical staff, access to health care delivery, and the treatment of patients, prisoners, and detainees."[1] PHR-I stressed the intrinsic connections among health care, politics, and human rights, and the right to health as a basic human right. Soon after its founding, PHR-I established the Saturday Mobile Clinic, which took joint teams of Israeli and Palestinian medical personnel to provide weekly medical care in isolated Palestinian villages. The clinic is still operational. Maintaining its operations over the years has been an act of cooperation, solidarity, and protest—and also, a chance to understand firsthand the largely invisible conditions on the ground.

Since 1988, PHR-I has supported the right to health in the broadest fashion, as including the rights to "freedom of movement, access to essential medical services, clean water, modern sanitary conditions, proper nutrition, adequate housing, education and employment opportunities, and non-violence."[2] The people who have benefited from PHR-I's work have included Bedouins in unrecognized villages in the Negev, prisoners in Israeli jails, migrant workers and refugees in Israel, Palestinians living under occupation, and disadvantaged residents of Israel.

In 2012, several members of the Israeli Knesset started pushing for legislation that would explicitly allow the forced feeding of Palestinian detainees who were using hunger strikes to call attention to their repeated spells of "administrative" detention (that is, detention without charge or trial) and the solitary confinement, torture, inadequate health care, and generally appalling conditions they encountered inside the Israeli prison system. PHR-I led the campaign against the forced-feeding legislation. The response from the Israeli medical establishment as well as the general public and the government to PHR-I's advocacy was often hostile. But still, the organization continued to challenge Israelis to face their own prejudices, including the assumption that "all Palestinians are the enemy," and the sociopolitical role that health care plays in any society as complex and divided as their own. As Dr. Marton wrote, "The presence of the enemy is essential for maintaining the link and the interconnection between the patriotic Zionist discourse and the action deriving from this discourse—occupation, oppression, arrests and torture."[3]

Forced-feeding is internationally recognized as a form of torture and a violation of a prisoner's autonomy and free will, and physicians are universally prohibited from participating in this practice. Even the Israeli Medical Association actively opposed the legislation.

In June 2015, the leaders of the World Medical Association weighed in, writing a letter to Prime Minister Netanyahu to reconsider the legislation. They noted that, "Force-feeding is violent, very painful and absolutely in opposition to the principle of individual autonomy. It is a degrading, inhumane treatment, amounting to torture. But worse, it can be dangerous and is the most unsuitable approach to save lives."[4]

Nonetheless, the bill passed in the Israeli Knesset in July 2015. It authorized forced-feeding on the basis of political and state security concerns, offering immunity from prosecution to medical personnel who participated in it. This legislation appropriated to the country's heavily politicized court system medical and ethical decisions that are rightly the responsibilities of hospital ethics committees, providing a method sanctioned by the Israeli legal system to forcibly end a hunger striker's protest.

According to PHR-I, hunger strikes have been an important method of resistance for Palestinian prisoners. Not a single prisoner has died as a result of refusing food, but four prisoners have died after being forced-fed, presumably from medical complications.

The Darkest Aspects of Human Experience

June 26, 2014

I have been thinking a lot about torture lately, given the murders of the three Israeli settlers and the burning to death of a Palestinian teen—most likely a revenge killing—and following that, the attack on his American cousin, beaten to a pulp by Israeli security. If you were to go to the website of the Palestinian Centre for Human Rights, you would learn these incidents are merely the tip of an enormous iceberg of human violence and suffering.

It is actually fitting that this subject has been on my mind, because today, on June 26, a number of us have accepted the invitation to attend a conference hosted by the Treatment and Rehabilitation Center for Victims of Torture in Ramallah. We are sitting in a large auditorium at the Red Crescent Society in Al Bireh, and we lean in to hear a lovely Al Quds medical student, translating quietly; some of the other talks are thankfully in English.

There are many professional-looking types—men and women—and two rows of guys in army green and berets; apparently, soldiers from the Palestinian Authority also have a lot to learn about torture (i.e., why they shouldn't do it), prevention, and treatment. Among those on the stage, I recognize Dr. Mustafa Barghouti, who founded Palestinian Medical Relief Society and is a political leader (you may hear him on National Public Radio, for instance, as an articulate voice of reason); Dr. Mahmud Sehwail, the psychiatrist who is the head of the treatment center; and a man from the European Union. We all stand for a bout of patriotic music, the cameras roll, and the conference officially begins.

Today is the annual UN International Day in Support of Victims of Torture. The EU speaker talks about how torture is abhorrent, against moral and ethical values: "It destroys the victim and dehumanizes the torturer, and undermines the state that tolerates it. Torture is also a crime under international human rights law and unlike many other human rights, there are no exceptions or no justification to make the unacceptable, acceptable." He notes that "these are easy words; the real question is how to combat torture effectively."

He suggests that torture has to be addressed at different levels that include legal regulations where torture is prohibited by law. Mechanisms also need to be in place to make sure these regulations are enforced. It is also critical to have transparency, to bring to light behaviors at police stations and other places of detention. He asserts that civil society has a role to play here. This work requires public awareness of what torture does to people; human rights values need to be frequently stated and restated.

In 2013, President Abbas decreed a prohibition on torture, and in April 2014, Palestine ratified the UN convention against torture. (The US and Israel signed decades ago.) The EU speaker notes these are important developments, but more progress needs to happen because Palestinian civil society has regularly reported the use of torture by its own security forces as well as by Israeli forces. He notes that the European Union has regularly criticized Israel regarding the conditions under which Palestinian prisoners are held and its use of administrative detention; he congratulates the treatment center and its partners that "deal on a daily basis with some of the darkest aspects of human experience." I wonder, where is the voice of the United States at an important conference like this?

The next series of speakers talk in Arabic, and their main points revolve around the destructive Israeli practices of child arrests, the killing of young children, and the re-arresting of prisoners who were freed in previous deals.

Then there is a long presentation on Palestinian and international rules, laws, contracts, etc.; the terrible consequences when these legal standards are violated; the need to respect women's rights legally, politically, and socially; the illegal torture of Palestinians in Palestinian prisons; and the appalling Israeli policies and house demolitions.

This is all a bit overwhelming. I look through the conference literature and learn that the Treatment and Rehabilitation Center was founded in 1997 to defend human rights, to build a society free from torture through community awareness and education. Their tasks focus on violence against prisoners, the wounded, families of martyrs, victims of the apartheid wall, roadblocks, and settler attacks. They also offer treatment and support to victims and their families, and focus on therapy and rehabilitation, both in medical and in psychological terms.

A woman talks about transitional justice, the need to create official strategies to identify torture, to fix societies that are suffering, and to compensate victims. For victims, the torturer needs to be punished and the victim compensated. She notes that when a society has suffered through a legacy of torture and that legacy endures to the present day, as has happened in Israel/Palestine, it leads to a loss of trust between individuals and societal institutions. She acknowledges that the divisions between Fatah and Hamas have created many victims and many people have been hurt.

After a speaker expressed regret that many people were unable to get to the conference due to the heightened delays and blocks at checkpoints, it is apparently time for the entertainment. A singing group from An-Najah University in Nablus, composed of two women in gorgeous embroidered Palestinian dresses and one man playing something that looks like an electric piano but clearly is not, pour their hearts into the music, giving voice and feeling to a society filled with pain and joy.

The second part of the conference is focused on treatment for prisoners and their families, "who are not sick, but suffering." The presenters talk about men released from prison after over ten years who have never seen a smartphone, who have endured years of solitary confinement as well as physical and psychological suffering, whose families were not allowed to visit. One presenter states, "But what about the feeling about the father, thinking about his kids, what has happened to them, what kind of treatment they can do to support them? They are suffering from beating, abused, not eating or inedible food. Some have abdominal pains due to bad food and no exercise and that makes it worse. The air is stagnant, six people in a room; health worsens."

The Center is conducting awareness campaigns about the torture prisoners are facing. Working out of branches in places like Nablus, Jenin, and Ramallah, the Center's staff offers outreach by going to people's homes to talk to them, as many prisoners and families do not have money to go to the center. Staff members, who include psychologists and one psychiatrist, also use psychotherapy (i.e., cognitive behavioral therapy); the Center sends them to Norway for training and practice in that method. The team in Palestine discusses each case and plans treatment, possible medications, psychotherapy, etc. The main goal is to make the victim feel better so he or she can go back to a normal routine and return to society.

The speaker gives a poignant example: one person spent thirteen years in prison, so his oldest child, then five years old, is now eighteen. "So he will not feel like the father, lost that feeling. The child is used to the absence of the father; [the father] is not used to being ignored and not asked and is shocked, so he feels like a piece of furniture. He is not asked to participate in family as they are used to being without him."

When the psychiatrist determines that the released prisoner is ready, they are offered professional rehabilitation, through which they are paid a monthly income and offered skills courses to train in their desired field of work, "so they will be productive in building a future. They want to become productive," the speaker explains. Specialists follow the prisoner, evaluate the results, and adjust the treatment program as needed.

As he talks, the audience nods in agreement, and I have a sense that this is a group of sincere, decent professionals honestly working to better the lives of victims and their difficult and challenging society. "The wife of the prisoner, she is the hero, but in the shadow. She is fighting alone to raise the kids, work, so the Center is trying to offer the wife work options (i.e., sewing in a salon), which is in her home, so her kids are close, she can care for the kids, and have an income while the husband is in prison."

There are more presentations about the legalities and international laws regarding the proper treatment of people living under occupation, and the groups that monitor conditions in Israel/Palestine. There are human rights committees that cooperate with organizations like PHR-I to investigate and write reports. They "track all the kinds of violations and torture, in order to find the truth, and follow those reports to see more details, [placing documentation] in front of government [agencies] to [encourage them to] take action. The torturer should know that he is going to be punished and is not protected."

Another speaker notes that, as recent news reports have indicated, "there is an increase of family fights that result in killing, so violence has increased in Palestine, girls are being raped. So the laws must be followed, the killer needs to be punished; otherwise, the family takes justice in their own hands and this is dangerous."

There is more discussion about the deaths of Palestinians in Israeli prisons due to inappropriate medical care and the lack of punishment or accountability. Other topics include the current prisoner hunger strike, the fact that Israeli violations are allowed because Israel has excessive power, and that the forced-feeding bills legislators are proposing may pass. "It is the worst occupation in history. It is not impossible emotionally to hope for Palestinian society without torture," says one speaker. "Even any kind of reporting to Israeli institutions leads to nowhere. So it is time to do it ourselves by legal means," he adds.

One speaker clearly is more agitated. He talks about the continued cases of torture by Palestinians in Palestinian jails, of the havoc in Israeli jails, and of the need for international committees and the media to apply pressure. "If the torturer is not punished, the Palestinian can track them down using international organizations and other countries and laws. Using the law, we can find those murdered in Israeli prisons, those who abuse prisoners, and try to stop this. During interrogation they torture them until they die." He describes "Israel [as] a country of killing, torture, destruction, but we are strong and it is our turn to act, to make the laws and the policy." I can sense his outrage, his voice rising in anger and frustration. He ends by referring to the three kidnapped Israeli settlers and highlighting how the international response is different when Palestinians are the victims. "When Israel kills our children or re-arrests prisoners, this is war. It is our right to ask for help through media as well."

The last speaker is a freed prisoner. I brace myself for some horrific litany of pain and suffering; the conference has already been quite overwhelming for me, and my ability to keep my professional distance is fading. The young man begins by reading from the Quran, and then explains, "One can face many difficulties, but if there is a huge trauma, those who are patient, Allah promises them with heaven." He talks about the years when "water was my only mirror," his speech urgent and passionate. Soon I realize that this symphony of words is all poetry and metaphor, beauty and inspiration, filled with feeling and woundedness, the child inside longing for freedom and land. He is a true survivor.

Speak Truth to Power and Choose Joyfulness

June 26, 2014

As a physician, I am always impressed by the combination of intelligence, dedication, and fortitude that characterizes so many Palestinians working in the field of health care. Today our group has the opportunity to meet with health professionals who are willing to speak honestly and off the record, to explore the raw contradictory picture that is a health care system (or non-system) that is part First World, part Third World, part internally dysfunctional, and simultaneously constricted by the noose of occupation. The following is a summary of that meeting; I am solely responsible for the content and commentary.

The requisite Turkish coffee appears along with folders and documents containing official information as we settle in for a discussion with a group of Palestinian researchers. With the support and cooperation of several local and international agencies, the researchers examine a number of medical and public health issues, including public health surveillance, assessment, research, health systems analysis, and capacity-building.

We learn about an evaluation that was conducted of mammogram screening programs in the West Bank. The results were incomplete because it was not possible to determine the efficacy of the screening program due to an underreporting of cancer diagnoses. But things were even more complicated than that. A research group looked at 6,700 women, ages 30 to 84, screened in the West Bank in 12 screening clinics in 2011, and they found only 21 women reported to the cancer registry. They called and confirmed all of them, and also found an additional 21 women that were not registered in the registry but were being treated. On further analysis, researchers documented that Augusta Victoria Hospital in East Jerusalem is the only location for radiation therapy (the Israelis do not allow radioactive therapies into the occupied territories), so most women go to Augusta Victoria, but the hospital does not notify the Ministry of Health cancer registry—too much paperwork, too little time. So there is a problem with tremendous underreporting.

We find that although researchers wanted to determine if mammography screening picks up cases of breast cancer early, they were hindered by problems with the data and cancer staging (the process of determining the extent of the cancer); only 5 percent of cases had the stage of cancer noted, so it was not possible to determine the success rate of achieving early detection. The barriers to care are also immense. Only four doctors actually read mammograms in the West Bank; the waiting times for results are long in many districts. If cancer is suspected, women may need an ultrasound or aspiration (withdrawal of fluid from a cystic mass), but the Ministry of Health only offers these services in Ramallah. Consequently, women often go to private clinics, but some cannot afford them and are "lost to follow-up." Fine-needle biopsies are also only free in Beit Jala, but again many women cannot get there. Add to this the tremendous cultural stigma around a cancer diagnosis (all the screening is done confidentially). Some women do not even tell their husbands.

I have noted in the past that in the West Bank and Gaza there is a lack of organized, reliable data collection and documentation of the general population regarding medical and public health issues. We learn in the meeting that a group of researchers reviewed the notification forms for people dying in hospitals—four hundred in the West Bank and two hundred in Gaza. One analyst remarked that the numbers reported in the death registry are too low to be accurate, which is an issue in many developed and developing countries. Because only six hundred cases were reviewed, it is difficult to make general conclusions; nonetheless, the current data is worrisome.

I think of the busy clinics I have attended and the overworked physicians, the lack of continuing medical education courses, the long waits for patients, and the visits truncated by the pressures to make a diagnosis, order tests, and medications. The challenge of managing all of this with the additional burdens of cost constraints, lack of insurance, permits, and checkpoints are part of the reality of obtaining and providing medical services under occupation. We are not surprised to learn that many doctors see no value in the numbers and data and follow-up information. They are so overwhelmed, they barely do their paperwork.

Despite all of the shortcomings, it seems that the mammography studies were helpful. The Ministry of Health is training more doctors to read films, and the Ministry is at least aware of the need for maintenance of mammographic equipment. They know about the shortage of x-ray films and the subsequent quality issues related to scrimping on films.

On a more positive note, we are excited to learn that researchers are exploring the possibility of doing a study in Tulkarem, a West Bank city surrounded by the separation wall, located on the Green Line, and host to many Israeli chemical companies and nearby settlement industries that do not want to be bothered with those expensive environmental regulations and worker protections that are the law of the land in Israel. Between the fumes, smoke, chemicals, industrial waste, etc., there is a high incidence of allergies, skin disease, eye problems, and cancer. However, this has never been adequately studied, and given the insufficient data collection in the mammogram studies, you can imagine that this investigation would also be a challenge. Noting the difficulties of medical record keeping, a group of researchers are thinking of doing something very clever. They are proposing measuring toxins in the land and water rather than trying to track down patient diagnoses that may have been inaccurately recorded. If this moves forward, they will be able to do environmental studies from which a lot of information can be extrapolated and thereby compensate for the deficits in accurate health statistics. However, we are informed, the analysts still face another challenge: they do not have accurate information about the Israeli factories and are not even allowed to enter them.

Other researchers are conducting a study on the causes of death and planning an environmental study in the Jordan Valley–Dead Sea area, including areas of Jericho. They are investigating a health profile in the Jordan Valley, looking at communicable disease, malnutrition in children, parasites, scorpion and snake bites, and the mental health of residents. The Jordan Valley is a closed military zone with several pockets of Palestinian communities.

We also learn of the work of Juzoor, a health and social policy nongovernmental organization investigating risk-taking behaviors among Palestinian youth. Juzoor's researchers are studying 2,500 men and women 15 to 24 years old in the West Bank (they couldn't do research in Gaza), investigating behaviors related to drugs, alcohol, extramarital sex, smoking, violence, and mental health. The results from the study's formative phase show that the sexually active youth are mostly interested in internet sex and phone sex. The next most-cited forms of sex are oral and anal sex, with vaginal intercourse the least common due to the importance of female virginity at the time of marriage.

Another research topic is the practice of "honor killings," where someone is murdered because it is believed they have brought shame on their family. We understand that there are honor killings, but the incidence rate is obviously hard to determine. We are told that it is even more complicated than that. For instance, an apparent honor killing in some cases may not really be about "honor." Perhaps the woman was asked to give up her inheritance to her brother, which she refuses to do, and he kills her, takes the money, and calls it an honor killing. Or, a woman's husband dies and her brother-in-law wants to marry her, so his first wife asks her own brothers to kill wife-to-be number two and call it an "honor killing." Or, if a father or brother rapes a girl and she becomes pregnant, then they kill her to protect the father or brother. There is no data on this horrific crime, which is probably rare and happens more in rural than urban areas. Sometimes people call it a suicide—the reports are all "just stories."

Now that we are deep into forbidden topics, we are informed that there is an increasing rate of suicide, especially among the youth. Apparently the police acknowledge that suicide is increasing, but they don't want to report the numbers in order not to frighten people. Fortunately, there are good hotlines such as SAWA (the Listening Ear for Palestinians Experiencing Violence), for desperate people who are abused, harassed, or raped. I think about what happens to societies that are increasingly stressed and brutalized, how anger and despair turn inward, how women frequently bear the brunt of male humiliation, rage, and impotence.

In another study, eighty-three men and women in the West Bank were asked about health services for youth, and they reported that they do not trust counseling institutes because they are worried about confidentiality and are much more willing to speak to peers. In an effort to reach local populations, UNRWA is also training community-based mental health workers. Likewise, there are school health officers who focus on smoking and nutrition. For adults, there are community-based organizations like the Palestinian Medical Relief Society.

The researchers report that drug use is common in the cities, mostly in Jerusalem and Area C, mostly hashish, which is affordable. Not only does drug addiction carry a social stigma in Palestinian society, but the Israeli authorities punish dealers more forcefully if they sell to Jews than to Arabs. Drug use has increased among Palestinians with the increasing brutality of the occupation.

This academic research is designed to inform policy, with community stakeholders always working in partnership with organizations like the Ministry of Health or local citizens. But the politics is critical—health care exists within a political reality and cannot be improved without changing that reality. One researcher states in frustration, "In Gaza, phosphorus bombs. What happened? No one cared." She notes that even beneath the Al Aqsa Mosque, right-wing Jewish organizations are excavating and no one seems to care. She continues, both discouraged and inspired: "Muslims all over the world, crying, became normalized. We are used to it, powerless, can't fight continuously. We need to write about it, Facebook, social media, tools that are not controlled and create awareness, buzz marketing, [that] attract attention. YouTube gets thousands of views and shares in two days. This is a power; political support is hopeless."

I am impressed by the energy and enthusiasm in the room. On the possibility of the Tulkarem environmental study, someone says: "Everybody is excited about the study . . . farmers and stake holders are supportive." Another positive sign is that there are many organizations and funders for women and now, under pressure, there are no longer reduced sentences for honor killings.

Obviously, this is difficult and humbling work, as one researcher discovered while completing a study for a PhD thesis that covered the mental health and quality of life (QOL) in preschoolers in Gaza. Looking at their mothers, she found that 50 percent of mothers suffer from depression, and that the QOL of preschoolers in Gaza was worse than it was for kids in the United States with cancer or renal failure. The risk of malnutrition was solely related to maternal mental health (i.e., a mother dealing with mental illness cannot take care of her child and respond to his or her needs). Amazingly, the PhD candidate tried to measure the QOL of the mothers, and 40 percent said that it was "excellent." This made no sense, so the researcher called the women and their first response to her question of "How is life?" was *Alhamdulillah*, excellent." Then with further probing, the women revealed they were overwhelmed, listing a thousand troubling complaints. Confused, the researcher questioned further and the mothers responded, "You can only complain to God."

It is time to go. I am trying to wrap my brain around these amazing, gut-wrenching conversations and this remarkable group of health care professionals who were willing to share their observations and experiences with us. Two of our contacts suggest that it is actually possible to choose joyfulness as an act of resistance.

The medical student who is our guide this afternoon suggests we go for (what was advertised as) a "quick visit" to his village of Taybeh, a Christian town half an hour from Ramallah. Soon, we are in a clunky, dusty *service* heading northeast, and then we are sitting at a table laden with flavorful soup made from *mulokhiya*; chicken with rice; salad drenched with olive oil, lemon, salt, pepper, dried mint, as well as an eggplant-parsley-tahini concoction; and, of course, cold Taybeh beer. As we eat, we chat with our guide's welcoming mother, father, and sister, who just happened to have a feast waiting for us.

And then we begin the tour of the family's garden, which has lush bunches of grapes, almonds (very sweet when eaten fresh and raw), figs, olives, mulberries, apples, pomegranates. Following that, we embark on a "quick tour" of the Old City, whose highlights include gorgeous views, churches (actually dating to the time of Christ), ruins, and stone evidence of multiple earlier conquerors. The town gathers for celebrations and still sacrifices sheep! We stare at the stones, stained blood red, and the handprints (dipped in the blood) marking the ancient stone walls. And in the distance—Jordan, the Dead Sea, a Muslim village, Israeli military posts and settlements, all leaning into this tiny, complicated paradise.

Who Is the Terrorist?

June 28, 2014

I have been thinking a lot about collective punishment and military force and the cost of fear. I am not going to reveal the identity and details of individuals in this story out of respect for their privacy and safety, but several asked me to write about recent events in their village. What I can share is that Bani Nayim is a large Muslim village of twenty thousand, east of the city of Hebron, a region known for large stone quarries and miles of vineyards. I have been visiting an extended family where most everyone is well educated. They are teachers, businessmen, doctors—people with degrees in education who cannot find employment or advanced programs. This all leads to "jumping the wall" to find work in Israel, getting visas to do graduate work in the United States, or completing online PhD programs in Islamic religion and Quranic studies. Families tend to be large, babies tend to be loved and plentiful; it seems that everyone we meet is related. Their idea of a good time is sitting on a balcony with each other at sunset, drinking Turkish coffee, eating sweets, talking, and smoking *nargila*. The main issue with the view (besides the stone quarry) is the Israeli military base in the distance and the spy balloon that hangs above the hills over the fanatically racist Jewish settlement of Kiryat Arba.

The houses I visit are beautiful white stone Arab homes, situated on the hillside along meandering roads. They are surrounded by patches of olive, almond, lemon, fig, and apple trees; and gardens with water-starved flowers and aromatic bushes such as lavender and something else that just bursts with aromatic perfume when the sun sets. The love of the land and its bounty is palpable. Far from the center of town, there is a larger field with a greenhouse where I see a field of wheat and rows of happy *mulokhiya*, the leaves of which are concocted into this great green soup with rice. Much has been passed down through the generations.

The living rooms of these houses have big-screen TVs, and often there is playing in the background some totally discordant American cowboy movie with Arabic subtitles, or an overly dramatic soap opera from Saudi Arabia. It is stunningly hot, and periodically, someone talks about the four feet of snow that fell last winter and paralyzed the village. The land is hilly with single homes here and there and a scattering of goat herds and minarets. If you keep looking, you can see the Dead Sea and the purple hills of Jordan.

This is the kind of family that warmly welcomes me: The mother has prepared an enormous meal of extraordinarily good food that is made of rice and chicken and stuffed grape leaves and stuffed zucchini, and yogurt and spices to die for. Everyone is treating me as if I have not eaten in days.

We retire to a living room filled with stuffed chairs and stuffed people, and after more sitting and smiling and Sprite and Coca-Cola, I take out my origami directions and one hundred sheets of colored paper. Shortly thereafter, there is a whole assembly of family members, of all ages and education levels, making boxes and struggling over cranes and helping the kids to get the creases right. This goes on for an hour and there is so much laughter and good fun; it is just a simple pleasure and feels so good in some primordial, mostly nonverbal, human way.

My host then suggests that the family watch my documentary on the Nakba, *Voices Across the Divide*, and I wonder how that will play—a documentary produced by a secular Jewish woman for a US audience sharing the Palestinians' story in a room full of devout Muslims. And so, we talk and talk, the conversation a useful stall tactic for me. Finally I relent, but I stress that they have to give their honest reaction to the film. Everyone wants to see it and so they invite over more relatives, and soon everyone is glued to the TV and we are not watching *Bonanza*.

I am a bit freaked out because they keep talking, which I can't tell is a good or a bad thing, but it turns out this is a totally talkative, enmeshed family and they are just having a typical big-group experience. They recognize the two college girls holding the BDS sign toward the end of the film, and of course the village of Beit Ummar, which is located over the hill from where we are sitting. When the documentary ends, I hold my breath. Then the father speaks and says the film is an excellent portrayal of the Palestinian experience, after which everyone chimes in, and we have this amazing discussion about all of their stories, the making of the film, the American Jewish community and Zionism, and Islam. This is a pretty stunning cross-cultural experience and I am so relieved. I feel embraced and welcomed despite my clear differentness. (I am even given a bed in a room by myself, while the entire family sleeps on long cushions on the living room floor.)

So why am I telling you this story? When you hear a news report, these are the "they," the "Muslim other," the "Palestinian militants near Hebron," the faceless families that are being terrorized by Israeli soldiers every night since those three boys disappeared. The day after the disappearance, the Islamic Center and School for Boys, located next door, was ransacked by Israeli soldiers, and the imam was detained for a few hours before he was released. Years ago, his two brothers were "martyred"; one was in a militant group and died in a gun fight when the house was crushed with him in it, and the other was killed as "collateral damage."

After our movie night and the sunset over Kiryat Arba, as we prepare for bed, I am informed that the Israeli Defense Forces have attacked the town. They are at all the entries and have started going house to house. The village has a Facebook page, which is suddenly the focus of everyone's attention. Someone reports that three to four buses of fully armed soldiers are walking through the town; some take control of one house and put a sniper on the roof. TV news is talking about an IDF attack on Rafah, the southern border of Gaza. The family is anxiously awake until the middle of the night, tracking the soldiers on Facebook and on a local radio program. When the *muezzin* calls at 4:00 am, the father finally goes to the mosque to pray, then he comes home and goes to sleep. I learn that like many Palestinian men, he has been arrested. In his case, he was arrested twice and placed in administrative detention for two months, after which he was released without any charges. He has obvious reasons to be anxious: he is a Palestinian male while Muslim, which is an arrest category in itself. No arrests are made here during the night, but everyone's nerves are a bit shattered and no one sleeps well. The press is reporting hundreds of arrests, many more injured, and a steady number of killings. Hamas members, including legislators, are clearly targeted.

Earlier, we had passed one of the big "Bring Back Our Boys" signs, a message in support of the kidnapped Israeli settlers. It hits me that this is supposed to echo the similarly worded messages that resonated with people following the violent kidnapping of the Nigerian schoolgirls in April. I try to imagine a society where that slogan would mean *all* of our boys, not only the three snatched last week but the thousands of mostly boys and young men lost in Israeli detention centers, without parents or lawyers or the legal and human rights protections of any decent society. And then there are all those boys who have lost their humanity, breaking into houses night after night, terrorizing families, turning into frightened, dehumanized monsters. And I realize, we need to bring them back as well.

In the Container

June 28, 2014

The bus station in Bani Nayim is hot, humid, and thick with exhaust fumes from idling vehicles that have seen better days in the seat and shock-absorber department. The *service* has to fill with passengers before it leaves, and we are in a holding pattern. I am sitting next to a young woman wearing a *hijab* with sparkly threads, a long coat, long sleeves, and leggings. I cannot imagine how hot she feels cradling an infant and trying to keep a one-year-old in his seat. As she negotiates the crying baby and the discreet breastfeeding, and attempts to pour mango juice into a bottle while it drips over the infant's plump thighs, I feel like we are mothers everywhere and it is time to mobilize for the tasks at hand. Chocolate wafers appear magically from my bag and the little boy stares at me with large brown eyes.

I am wheezing from all the dust and pollution and marveling at what passes for advertising in the local markets. While most of the signs are in Arabic, I am mystified by a clothing store called "White Woman," another, "Lady Chic"; I also see the "Golf Plastic Industrial Company" and "Four Seasons Furniture." Do they have four seasons here? There is clearly a lot lost in translation, which seems to be a metaphor for much that is happening in these parts.

Our *service* jolts by fields of vineyards and then we see a lush green vineyard that is surrounded by a wire fence and coils of barbed wire. It is the only fortified field I see, and it is owned by a Jewish settler who has bought this land and comes, armed with military guards, to harvest his grapes. This is another metaphor.

My understanding is that there is some Israeli law/directive that mandates the use of seatbelts in the occupied territories, but that Palestinians view this as another oppressive Israeli directive, rather than some really good advice, so as we drive I watch the passengers perform an "on-off" dance with their seatbelts, a quiet (self-defeating?) act of resistance. There appears to be no car seats for children, so the mother buckles in her toddler, more as an attempt to restrain him in the back seat than to prevent injury in case of a sudden swerve. The much-too-loose belt soon comes off and she wraps her arm tightly around him, trusting herself more than those Israeli laws. He turns a bag of pretzels upside down and she and I are both back in mothering mode. A honey-toned woman's voice croons on the radio.

We pass mountains of watermelon, car skeletons piled in junkyards like corpses, and overflowing garbage bins, and soon find ourselves zigzagging up and down the Container Road, a vertiginous highway built specially for Palestinians that takes travelers miles out of their way, keeping the area that would have been the travel route "clean" for settlers. The *service* slows to a halt as we approach a massive traffic jam at the Container checkpoint. Passengers get off and the driver asks me to move forward. I cannot tell if this is part of the checkpoint strategy. The white American lady should be nearer to the front? Deciding I'll just see what happens, I check the time, a useful distraction that keeps me from reaching a state of total aggravation.

10:05: Traffic slows.

10:10: Full stop, cars and trucks everywhere.

10:14: More aggressive honking; we creep forward. The driver offers us water; we are unbearably hot. I picture myself melting into the warm sticky seat like some kind of Wicked Witch of the West.

10:16: A large truck traveling in the opposite direction needs to make a wide hairpin turn, and the vehicles in the opposite lane cluster together to give him space. A truck carrying a sheep stops next to us. The sheep is panting rapidly and looks deathly ill and thirsty; the drivers keep anxiously looking back at the suffering animal with clear concern but no water to provide it.

10:19: We pull ahead onto the highway shoulder on the right and now there are four lanes of traffic that need to merge into two. Annoyance and frustration is rising and there is more talking and yelling between drivers.

10:20: Full stop.

10:22: Driver negotiates a merge into lane number three.

10:24: Driver asks for my passport and pours through my history of travel. "Cambodia?" he asks. There is thick black smoke beyond the checkpoint; a mix of burning garbage and tires adds to the smell of exhaust. I ponder how the occupation increases global warming and childhood asthma.

10:27: Two Israeli soldiers are working the checkpoint and they glance into the *service*, do not check any documents, and wave us through.

Suddenly passengers start laughing, joking; the driver pulls out a bag of wafers and passes them around. A victory over the oppressor, time for celebration! There is a sense of unity built out of the experience of common, indiscriminate, mindless suffering. The official Israeli line is that checkpoints are necessary for security, a holy cause that is used to justify the oppressive minutiae of occupation and throat-gripping control.

As we approach the village of Qalandia with its arched entry, I see a rotary and a dead olive tree. I think of the gorgeous, stolen, watered olive trees at the entrance to the Jewish settlement of Ma'ale Adumim, and I want to weep. Perhaps the Qalandia tree has died of sorrow as well as neglect. As we skirt the Qalandia checkpoint, the traffic once again backs up into a crazy jumble of vehicles, some trying to get through, some trying to get around, and everyone trying to survive.

I imagine doing this every day, morning and evening, to get to work or school, or to meet a friend in Ramallah. The endless waiting and uncertainty, the never knowing when and if you will get where you are going. This kind of brutality is powerful and suffocating, and it is the universal experience of the people who are living in this prison, their lives effectively under the total control of young Israeli men and women with little life experience, whose minds are filled with racism, boredom, fear, and the power that comes with the gun.

Tell Them You're Italian!

June 28, 2014

Al Manara, the famous square in Ramallah with the circle of lion sculptures in the center, is bustling with chaotic traffic, shoppers, drenching heat, and street vendors. I see the sign for Stars and Bucks, the Arab Bank, and banners for the World Cup. I think about that odd puff piece that was printed in the *New York Times* months ago describing the West Bank city as "the Paris of the Middle East." I think not. Too much Middle East, not enough Paris. I am waiting to be picked up by a woman who is coming from her village of Aboud, and I don't know what she looks like. She is the cousin of my friend in the United States. I have promised to visit his village, "the most beautiful village in Palestine."

Suddenly, this burst of energy in human form emerges from the crowds. She is a trim, smiling woman of uncertain age, and after a quick search for a functional bathroom and a bag of *za'atar*-covered flatbread, we are wending our way to the *services* (she calls them Fords because, well, they are Fords). She walks so fast and determinedly, regaling me with a steady stream of commentary, criticism, politics, that I can only think: I have come to visit a Palestinian energizer bunny. We get into the Ford, which will only leave once it has filled with passengers, and as you can imagine, there are not a whole lot of folks heading toward Aboud. We wait and chat, sweating from the heat. It is important to drink enough water to prevent heatstroke, but not too much, because then we will just be in search of another bathroom. This is a delicate balance.

The driver finally turns on the air conditioning. We head north (actually north-*ish*, this being the occupied West Bank), past the town of Nabi Saleh, now famous to anyone paying attention to the news coverage (see the *New York Times* article).[5] It is there that I joined internationals and villagers in 2012 on a Friday afternoon and watched the town's youth chant the words of Martin Luther King and Gandhi, throw stones, and then run like crazy in retreat, while Israeli youth (in full military gear) shot an amazing amount of tear gas and rubber bullets at the protesters. The Friday ritual of resistance still continues today. We pass Halamish, the nearby Jewish settlement that is busy stealing land and water from the folks in Nabi Saleh, who have been living here for centuries.

Soon we arrive in the small village of Aboud, not far from the Green Line, surrounded by settlements. The population is half Muslim and half Christian; this fact interests me. To my surprise, my new friend lives alone in an extensive U-shaped house with more rooms than she can fill, a large TV, and a pleasant kitchen. Her enduring-the-heat strategy involves strategically opening and closing different shades and windows, sitting on porches on opposite sides of the house, and, when all else fails, turning on the fan, which I do since I seem to be having a permanent hot flash. The walls are scattered with crosses and Virgin Marys, and saints and various homages to her beloved mother and father and a cast of cousins. She turns on the music and the Beatles blasts through the house: "It's been a hard day's night, and I've been working like a dog . . ." She hands me a salty yogurt drink that she thinks will revive me and heads toward the kitchen to prepare her version of chicken and rice.

Over the course of the next twenty-four hours, I learn a lot. My friend loves Frank Sinatra. She loves to dance, and in a previous life she wore mini-skirts and worked like a demon for five years at a suburban hospital in the United States after training as a nurse in Britain. She and her extended family were all born in Aboud. She received her nursing diploma during the First Intifada, traveling on a Jordanian passport. She flew back home—in the days when a Palestinian could fly into the Tel Aviv airport—only to discover that everything had changed. She remembers telling a nasty Israeli official, "The pendulum will swing, and we will get it back." After an emotional reunion with relatives in Jerusalem, her father took her back to the village. It was going to be a very short stay in the village because, as hard it is to believe, she only had a three-month visa—to live in her own home.

For years, the Israeli authorities strictly controlled residency permits. Anyone not present in the West Bank, Gaza, or East Jerusalem at the end of the 1967 War lost their residency papers. Additionally, exit and entry permits continue to be strictly regulated (a policy known as "passive transfer" or "silent transfer"). Between 1967 and 1994, 140,000 West Bank residents were stripped of their residency rights.[6]

When my new friend saw the large Israeli flag at the entry to her village, the reality of occupation hit her like a jolt of lightning. She stayed five months (two months past her visa expiration) and through sheer luck and a lot of chutzpah, she ended up living with a group of nurses from the United Kingdom and working long shifts at a US hospital in the days when nurses wore crisp uniforms and, I imagine, smiled and said "Yes, doctor" a lot.

Her first love married someone else. Ultimately, after many tangles with the Israeli authorities, she returned home, the responsible daughter, to care for her aging parents, and now she is in a most unusual situation—an aging, somewhat lonely Palestinian woman without any children, her swarm of relatives mostly lost to the Diaspora. She once had a job offer at Hadassah Hospital in Jerusalem, but Netanyahu personally nixed that when he forbade hospitals from employing staff from the West Bank. I feel her regret. "Being a single woman in the village is like being in prison." When she talks of her long dead mother, her eyes fill with tears. Her stories are peppered with feisty bravado; she tosses around quirky expressions like "Okay Charlie!" and has had her share of taking wild chances, standing up to soldiers at checkpoints. "They control everything; they control the oxygen you breathe."

She recounts a time she responded to a sadly typical altercation between Palestinian children and Israeli soldiers. "Kids were throwing stones and the soldiers were beating a kid." To one of the soldiers, she said, "What are you doing? You are a kid with a gun. He is a kid with a stone. Be a gentleman. Put the gun away." To the kids she said, "And if I catch you throwing stones again, you will hear from me."

My new friend cannot believe I am Jewish, and she cannot believe she has an actual Jew in her home, eating her chicken and her chopped-up cucumbers and tomato. "The first Jew in Aboud!" she exclaims happily. (I guess the IDF doesn't really count.) Her voice gets a bit conspiratorial, and she advises me not to mention this fact in the village. She is worried about her Muslim neighbors. "They are a bit fanatic." She remembers an upsetting night when a large truck and ten jeeps arrived at midnight and, as she peered out the window, she saw her Muslim neighbor blindfolded, handcuffed, dragged into the truck by Israeli soldiers. She suggests that I tell people I'm Italian.

When the heat abates a bit, she takes me on a speed-walking tour, stopping to schmooze with family and friends. She complains about the garbage thrown by "ill behaved" (read: Muslim) teens, and when I comment on how hot it must be for women in *hijabs* and long coats, she says, "They're used to it. It's their religion." The town has wide streets, two Christian neighborhoods and one Muslim neighborhood, and—from what I can gather—three functional churches, a mosque, and ancient church ruins. We only tour the Christian sector. Some of the walls have lovely religious murals and others harken back to a simpler time when people were out in the fields harvesting their crops and looked much happier. We pass donkeys and their babies, elegant homes with lush gardens, abandoned properties, the site of my American friend's former family home (his bedroom is now a driveway for an ancient yellow Dodge Dart). A young man gallops by, riding his horse bareback, its tail flying wildly.

She is very angry about the ongoing land and olive grove confiscations and the nearby Jewish settlements, and tells me the story of once finding an IDF soldier asleep under a tree. Her friend walked up to the sleeping soldier and yelled, "We gave you the road. You have the beach in Tel Aviv in your bikini. Leave us alone." The soldier had a gun and started threatening her friend, who yelled, "Go ahead, shoot me. I will die defending my land and you will be a murderer." These women are tough.

We come to a premature end to the road, obstructed by a ten-foot-tall pile of dirt and rocks, courtesy of the nearby settlers in their orange-roofed houses. I ask my new friend if I can take her picture in front of this dirt wall, and she quickly answers no. She is too upset for photo ops.

We stop at a series of stone patios, friends and relations drinking tea, eating watermelon, smoking cigarettes, hugging children. I feel like I am in an old French movie, or maybe I'm a typical New Yorker visiting my Uncle Morris and Aunt Bessie in Queens. These are ordinary folks, full of opinions and quarrels and family loyalty. "Eat, eat, *habibti*," they say. The women dye their hair shoe-polish black-brown and have pencil-thin eyebrows. One guy, an engineer with a couple of charming, engaging young daughters, lived in the Bay Area for years but then felt he had to come back. He tells me warmly and honestly that he could not tolerate the diversity—the Mexicans, the Asians, the Blacks. "I am not racist but I want to be with my own people."

He didn't like the rat race, enjoys the slower pace, wants more time with his wife and kids. "Have some more watermelon?"

The next morning we see more of the churches, including the Church of the Virgin Mary "Abudia," which dates back to the fourth century. In the hushed entry, as the priest chants melodiously in the sanctuary, my friend lights candles and prays. We watch Sunday school children play with a gigantic multicolored parachute and act out the story of Jonah and the whale. (What do these landlocked kids know about oceans?) We pour through exquisite Aboudi embroidery.

The tour of the friends and relatives continues, and it is close to heartbreaking. A sweet widow caring for her emaciated dying mother in a dark bare room with the faint smell of urine; she has three children and her son is apprenticed to a blacksmith. Another woman's brother built a palatial estate and visits in the summer. His elderly, demented sister sits in the front door, half-dressed, camping out on the first floor. She presses candy into our hands when she realizes we are not staying. Another friend tends to her ill brother with severe multiple sclerosis and an angry personality; her face is tight with sorrow. She wants me to send a package of her homemade *za'atar* to my friend in America and asks that I tell him "to come home." Another white-haired woman on her way to church says to me, "You are better than my relatives. They never visit." This is a tough place to be old or sick or alone. I feel that the villagers who escaped to the Diaspora are both a source of pride and resentment. Despite all of its natural beauty, the village has an air of stagnation and suffocation that comes with small places that have no secrets and not much in the way of prospects for big happiness.

The visit is sweetened by a stop at my friend's family home across from her place, where a relative lives with his wife and three gorgeous, lively daughters. The children adore her, and I can see that she loves and indulges them like a grandmother. "Very lovely," she beams.

There is only so much tea a person can take, and it is time to return to Ramallah. We search out the Ford driver. To explain his policy of leaving only when the vehicle is full, my friend describes his basic attitude: "Why hurry? Aboud to Ramallah to Aboud. We are all in prison." My friend gives me one more piece of advice: "Okay Charlie, my dear, we should prepare for a lonely end of life. That is our fate."

I meet up with a thirty-something activist friend in Ramallah, and as we sip our mint lemonade and hide from the "Ramadan fasting police," she talks about life choices. She is tired of being beaten and tasered. She is really worried about injury and death. She wants to stop smoking, to have babies, to live. How does she do all of that in this very difficult place?

Zionist Doctors and Jewish Values

June 30, 2014

It is probably not a good idea to write a blog after two glasses of wine, particularly after three weeks of abstinence (except for that lovely Taybeh beer), but sometimes drastic measures are needed. After checking into a funky old hostel in Jaffa that was clearly a Palestinian home before everything happened, I am now sitting in a café watching the flow of beautiful people: the hipsters and the yuppies and the old-and-lumpy-but-young-at-heart like me. This sidewalk restaurant, which spills into the street, feels like a cross between Soho and San Francisco; like gentrification on steroids and delicately rolled cigarettes. It's a stream of beautiful millennials with tattoos and fancy dogs and partially shaved heads. I feel like I am back in the good old USA where our troops are off doing Allah-knows-what in Iraq, Afghanistan, Pakistan, and we are obliviously obsessing about our lattes.

After two weeks mostly in the West Bank, the women look virtually naked—there is more than enough cleavage and thigh. Men are stroking their lady friends in overtly sexual ways, and I am taking a long, hard look at "Western norms." I order a shrimp and eggplant dish drenched in garlic and olive oil, a mix of different, often clashing traditions, as a metaphoric, culturally transitional meal. I must admit I have a strong urge to just get up and walk away without paying the overpriced bill. Just charge it to the occupation. Most of the folks I have been sharing lives and hummus with cannot legally be here (let's not even mention their yearning for a little dip in that gorgeous Mediterranean water, the waves cresting, and the stretches of white sand), and I have to admit I kind of got used to being called "*habibti*" and my Arabic pet name, Alusi.

The day started in the Old City in the Austrian Hospice with a predictable conversation with two lovely, older, guilt-ridden Germans who talked about how hard it is to say anything critical of Israel because . . . (the HOLOCAUST is literally screaming to us at our table between the German Rye and the *labneh*). I am trying to introduce the concept that it is actually okay to be critical. In fact, as a Jewish American, I think that it is imperative. Since committing the unforgiveable horror, the German people have done their share of breast-beating and reflection and reparations; to quote the title of a book by the Israeli author Avraham Burg, *The Holocaust Is Over; We Must Rise from Its Ashes*. The couple enthusiastically take the address of my website, and I assure them that my book, *Broken Promises, Broken Dreams*, was translated into German, so they should be able to read it easily.

Last night I tried to make small talk with my cab driver, the first in a while to be a Jewish Israeli. Me: "It's been really hot here." Him: "No it's not." Oh right, these are the people who do not know how to say I'm sorry. Unfortunately, this morning, I was bullied standing in line for my train ticket, got yelled at by some pretty girl at a counter at the central bus station in Jerusalem when I asked for directions, and got no reassurance from the bus driver that this was indeed #480 to Arlozoroff in Tel Aviv. When I finally worked up my courage to confirm my hopes about the bus, a blond twenty-something said abruptly, "Of course." On the bus, a bearded Orthodox Jewish father with a gentle demeanor and friendly smile debated with his two teenage sons, "How can we know *Hashem* when *Hashem* is unknowable, is everywhere?" We all have our eccentricities and psychopathologies, but really?

I spent the afternoon at an extraordinary organization called PHR-I. Ran Cohen was somewhat more optimistic than usual. Although the Knesset is probably about to pass the bill authorizing the forced-feeding of prisoners on hunger strike, the strike has ended, no prisoner has died, and this has taken a lot of the energy for everyone involved. "We won the battle but lost the war," Ran explains. For the first time in history, "we got the Israeli Medical Association aboard and this is surprising. They were vocal and said clearly, physicians do not do this and discussed this [forced-feeding] as torture." The IMA was clear that forced-feeding actually involves the cooperation of doctors and that they would not be able to protect them in a domestic court or even the International Criminal Court in The Hague. This change in attitude may be related to a new head of the medical ethics committee, Dr. Tami Karni, as well as intense international pressure. Ran was very excited to see the commitment on the part of the doctors, along with their recognition that the government is trying to use medicine and doctors as political tools. The new law that is now being argued in the Knesset states that each case of forced-feeding will be brought to a civil regional court and then, if it is allowed, a doctor may participate without risk of punishment. The Israeli government is framing forced-feeding as a desire to save lives. On a TV news program, when some big *macher* (bigwig) said that there will be no doctors willing to do forced-feeding, the government's legal adviser replied, "We will find the Zionist doctors who are concerned of Israeli security." So much for Zionism. Framing is obviously the key. A movement to create a Jewish refuge and homeland is now being used to justify a war crime.

Last week, PHR-I scored a big success when a committee headed by Health Minister Yael German decided to take private health services outside of public hospitals. Until now, in public hospitals, there were private patients that doctors would see and charge while using the hospital facilities, thus creating a type of boutique practice on the back of the public system. There was a long campaign against this and, Ran enthuses, "we succeeded, after it lost in the Supreme Court! This was a public campaign; seven million citizens will benefit with a more equal health care system, oriented towards the public." Clearly, activists are pushing the Israeli state to buck the trend toward privatization.

Another recent PHR-I success involves a push to reform the citizenship law. In 2002, Israel suspended the "family unification" process, which granted civil status for residents of the Palestinian Authority who are married to an Israeli citizen. Since 2003, Palestinians in the West Bank and Gaza who have married Palestinians with Israeli citizenship have not been allowed family reunification—i.e., they could not get legal status to live in Israel with their spouses. The implication of this cruel bill is that one of the spouses, usually the woman, is left with no status—she either cannot live with her husband or, more likely, she has to live here illegally. If their children are born in Israel, they are Israeli citizens, but the parent from the West Bank cannot get citizenship. At this point, since 2003, twenty to twenty-five thousand such couples have married but have not gotten status for the spouse, which means that that person can be deported at any time, has no health care, and cannot enter most bus stations, malls, or any place where racial profiling increases the risk of being asked for an ID. They cannot drive legally, attend university, or obtain welfare benefits. After the NGOs in the human rights community took the battle to the Supreme Court and failed, PHR-I started a long campaign to promote "social residency," which separates legal status from social rights and allows people access to health care and welfare regardless of their status. The State of Israel will not grant one new Palestinian citizenship out of fear of "losing the demographic war," but PHR-I argued that the Palestinians are here, they are not temporary, they are married to Israelis, and they are human. PHR-I became aware of this issue when they started seeing Palestinian women in their Open Clinic desperate to receive care. Now, in an alliance with Kayan, an advocacy group for Arab women, and the Association for Civil Rights in Israel, they have "a foot in the door"; they recently won a court case that allows spouses with permits but no legal status to register for health funds. This covers eight thousand families, so, says Ran, "this is beginning; from nothing to something is big." This work is part of PHR-I's advocacy for the right to health for all.

The refugee issue also keeps PHR-I busy. Since 2003, fifty thousand refugees or asylum seekers (or if you are Netanyahu, "infiltrators") have crossed the Egyptian Sinai into Israel, mostly from Sudan and Eritrea. Many of them (an estimated 25 percent of the Eritreans who attempted the crossing) were kidnapped, tortured, raped, or held for ransom in the Sinai by a Bedouin clan. The Israeli response, wrapped in the hysteria of the "threat to the Jewish nature of the state" by these "disease-carrying Muslim criminal elements," was to build a fence along the border with Sinai, so the border is sealed with no new refugees entering.

Israel also built a detention center called Holot, where asylum seekers and refugees are sent without a trial or judicial review for an indefinite period of time. It is "open" in that they can step out into the desert during the day, but they need to return for three daily roll calls, and from 11:00 p.m. to 6:00 a.m the gates are locked. It is an utterly miserable place. Two days ago, six hundred men defiantly marched toward the Egyptian border, stating they want to go someplace where they can move their lives forward. They were brutally arrested again and sent back to prison, all documented on video, and PHR-I was there to help the sick, mostly suffering from dehydration and injuries related to attacks by the security forces. Ran explains that the Israeli government is working to make these people miserable and has actually sent a few hundred to Sudan, where many are reported to be detained, in danger, tortured, or imprisoned. Thirteen families have reported their loved ones missing (imprisoned, murdered?). A few have been sent by plane to third countries, mostly Rwanda and Uganda.

At this point, Ran notes that there are fifty thousand refugees here. He claims that for Israel, a country with a population of over eight million people, this is not a demographic catastrophe. Israel, a First World country, could be a model for refugee absorption; it has done so before by welcoming one million Russians during the 1990s (many of whom were not Jewish, but at least they were white). Meanwhile, Lebanon and Syria, two countries with less resources than Israel, are each faced with one million

Syrian refugees and internally displaced people. At the very least, the Israeli government should investigate each person's case to determine their refugee or asylum eligibility and protect them until it is safe for them to return. Ran notes ironically that the whole discussion about protecting the "Jewish nature of the state" really leaves out the nature of Jewish values and makes it all about numbers. PHR-I is once again working on the separation of legal status from social rights, and they have had some successes. In January 2014, the government adopted a plan to treat HIV-positive refugees and established a small mental health clinic for these deeply traumatized people, so there is a glimmer of recognition regarding the right to health, even for people who are African and poor and so desperate that they will walk across deserts and endure unbearable suffering to come to a place that might provide work and opportunity.

PHR-I also focuses on the occupied territories, and Ran describes a report due to be released in a month that will present a comparative investigation between the basic health indicators for Palestinians in the West Bank and Gaza and those for Israelis. Let's just say that everything looks bad—even basic life expectancy between the two populations diverges by more than ten years, as well as maternal and infant mortality and the availability of health care necessities such as medications, clinicians, and specialists. This gives PHR-I the opportunity to talk about responsibility and control: if the Israeli government controls the territories as the occupying force, then it is responsible for the health needs of the population under its control. As Ran argues, Netanyahu brags that "'Israel saves lives of Palestinian children while Palestinians are kidnapping teenagers.' This is nonsense. The PA is paying for the care in Israel, and for decades, the Israeli government has prevented development and actually 'dedeveloped' the Palestinian health care system as well as controlled and reduced access to the major East Jerusalem hospitals." The facts speak for themselves.

And then there are all the other projects: "Torture [is] always an issue, the victims are refugees and prisoners." There is work on the freedom of movement of doctors and patients in the occupied territories, the Saturday Mobile Clinic, the Tel Aviv Open Clinic, and much effort to educate Israeli students in universities on the right to health by taking them on tours of East Jerusalem, the Negev, Bedouin villages, south Tel Aviv, Lod, Ramle. Ran notes, "The students are more and more open to it. The problem was with faculty not wanting us to come and talk, but things are getting better."

How Do You Say *Shalom* in Tigrinya?

June 30, 2014

Ran takes me into the Open Clinic for some reality-based learning. The rooms are those of a basic health center with shelves of paper charts, featuring two volunteers engaged with their computers. Their dress is casual shorts and tank tops, the waiting room rows of black plastic chairs. Today is "appointments only" with the specialist, so I will not be seeing the usual flood of humanity, the "wretched refuse," as Lady Liberty would say.

Ran explains that in Israel, if someone presents with a life-threatening emergency to a hospital, they must receive care. But all other cases, including those that are life-threatening in the long term—like out-of-control diabetes—are turned away if the patient has no insurance. (Health care as a privilege, not a right.) And of course long-term rehabilitation, mental health care, and medical follow-up for chronic disease are hindered by barriers related to access, language, poverty, and culture. Today the Open Clinic has three thousand volunteers, though only eight hundred or so are really active in the organization. Since 1998, it has seen thirty-five thousand patients, many traveling from far to be treated. PHR-I used to serve mostly migrant workers, after Palestinians from the territories were no longer permitted to work in Israel and employees started importing low-level workers from Thailand, the Philippines, and the rest of the Third World. Now PHR-I is mostly seeing asylum seekers, and these folks are different. Their communities are socially and politically less empowered, their leaders are under arrest; they are usually not working and suffer from all the ills of poverty. They are alive often because the large majority are young men, and they are basically physically resilient. While much of the medications are donated and thus free to the patients, they often need shekels to get home, to eat. They are a more desperate population than migrant workers are, and the clinicians are seeing more cases of diabetes and hypertension than before.

The Open Clinic sees five thousand patients a year—"less patients but bigger problems than before," says Ran—and provides services including general medicine, OB-GYN, pediatrics, and mental health. I sit down with the clinic coordinator, a feisty, dedicated young woman, a former engineer with a masters in international relations, and now a paid employee. Her job is to negotiate for the patients, to find the least costly, most accessible appointments for specialists, labs, hospital procedures, surgery, and cancer therapy. Working with Assaf, a social care organization, the two organizations address medical as well as social issues like homelessness. As clinic coordinator, she also is involved with the UN High Commissioner for Refugees and helps refugees resettle in countries like Sweden, Denmark, or Norway, obtain citizenship, and then receive medical care for severe chronic illnesses. I try to imagine fleeing something horrific in Sudan, hiding in the Sinai and then walking or running across the desert, undergoing detention in Holot, and contracting some terrifying disease in a strange country. After all that, the refugees end up in a place where everyone is blond, there is no sunlight half the time, winters are really cold, and the language is beyond comprehension. And they are sick and alone. This is staggering. The coordinator admits to many sleepless nights and desperate phone calls.

She talks about how the clinic is seeing many young patients with kidney failure and diabetes—maybe a consequence of toxic pesticide use—and of Africans dying of AIDS in Israel in 2014. "This is ridiculous." And then in 2010, Sister Azezet, who volunteers at the clinic, noticed that many pregnant women coming in were asking for late-term abortions and had unusual injuries and trauma. She interviewed 1,300 women and learned about the rape and torture camps, along with human trafficking in the Sinai, and brought this to international attention. "No one asked, what happened to you?" reports the clinic coordinator.

The law in Israel now states that if an employer hires a migrant worker, they have to pay for that worker's health insurance; however, when the employee gets sick, they get fired and their insurance is canceled. As a result, the Open Clinic sees many Eritreans as well as migrant workers from the Philippines, China, and India. And then there are the folks from Nigeria, the Congo, Ivory Coast, and Guinea who have overstayed their work permits and live in the shadows, at risk for deportation at any time. Add to that a small number of Russians who arrived in the big migration but are not recognized as Jews and thus have no health insurance, and the Palestinian women from the territories who married Palestinian men with Israeli citizenship and are unable to obtain legal status.

PHR-I is doing advocacy work on behalf of the asylum seekers now detained in Holot. They have gone to the Supreme Court applying for the men's release from the center, stressing the illegality of detaining them. The coordinator notes that public opinion is definitely against the refugees who have been defined by Israeli government propagandists as "infiltrators." PHR-I is accused of supporting criminals, rapists, and disease-carrying Africans, the scary faceless Black other. "It is hard to humanize them."

The first woman the coordinator sees today is a fifty-five-year-old Philippina who has been in Israel for eleven years, has had no contact with her family during this time, speaks fluent Hebrew, and has recently had surgery for metastatic uterine cancer. She needs further treatment, and the coordinator and I understand that she will most likely die alone and unhappy in Israel. I look at the pack of Marlboros next to the coordinator's computer and the jumbo-size bottle of Coke; this is burnout kind of work, and the coordinator pours her heart into each case. The next patient, an Eritrean woman with a four-year-old son, also speaks Hebrew fluently, has a mass in her neck, brings lab results, and gets sent off to an ear, nose, and throat doctor. She is followed by an Eritrean man who sort of speaks English, has back pain and is unable to work, and is now dizzy. She asks him to come back tomorrow for the general doctor. I suggest we check his blood pressure, and it is significantly elevated.

I then join the GI specialist; he is a good-hearted soul who is more in the classic-doctor mode. He assesses each patient to see if there is anything life-threatening or GI-related, and does not sink his time into the vast psychosocial morass that is probably the source of much of the medical complaints. The first patient surprises me, a friendly African-American woman from Kansas City, Missouri. She is well-organized, arriving with lists and notes. She made *aliyah* (the spiritual immigration or "ascent" to Israel) with her family three years ago and is now living in Ashkelon, awaiting citizenship and health insurance. She has multiple medical problems including life-threatening liver disease, and her granddaughter, whose name is Aliyah, is having her Bat Mitzvah in a week. "Can I drink wine for the blessing?" she asks the doctor.

She is followed by a series of Sudanese and Eritrean men with various levels of disease, lots of stress, and haunting memories of the Holot detention camp. They are working or out of work, worrying about deportation. "I am not guilty, why keep me there?" one asks. Some speak Hebrew or a variant of English or Tigrinya. They are all thin, frightened, obviously depressed and sometimes angry; their eyes give them away. They are trying to negotiate a system they do not understand, a language they do not speak, and a country that does not want them. The doctor does the best he can given the limited resources, the lack of communication between institutions, the need to beg and borrow for medications, testing, results. No one is happy, and I am haunted by the pained expressions and sorrow framing these difficult interactions. They say a society is only as strong as its weakest link, and this link is clearly broken.

6

Waiting for Death Every Minute
March 20–25, 2015

Seven months after Israel's large-scale 2014 assault on Gaza ended, I crossed the Erez checkpoint from Israel into the Gaza Strip with a delegation that had been invited by Gaza Community Mental Health Program (GCMHP). We explored and bore witness to the medical and mental-health consequences of the war on clinicians as well as patients; we visited kindergartens, UN agencies struggling to provide services, a women's center, and regular people eager to share their stories; and when possible, we enjoyed fellowship over food. This chapter ends by describing a performance by Gaza Parkour, a group of high-energy young men who perform breathtaking, acrobatic feats in the rubble of the bombed-out city of Shejaia.

It is useful to examine how this war was reported in the US media, to ask what assumptions were made and what normative language was used to describe the events in July and August 2014. A major theme was Israel's right to defend itself (i.e., Israel as the victim of "Hamas terrorism"). Often describing the Hamas opposition as an existential threat to Israel's very existence, this framing ignored the context in which those primitive rockets were fired, the long shadow of the Nakba, the occupation, and the siege, and, more immediately, the Israeli military's provocative behavior in the West Bank and East Jerusalem following the kidnapping of the three Israeli teenagers.

To be sure, rockets and tunnel infiltrations are completely unacceptable, and a country has a right and obligation to defend itself. On the other hand, there is a historical legacy dating back to 1948 that provides a context that is usually missing from the debate. Eighty percent of Gaza's population are refugees from the 1948 war and their descendants. In April 1956, in a eulogy for a kibbutz guard killed near the border, presumably by a Palestinian militant from Gaza, famed Israeli general Moshe Dayan forthrightly stated: "'Let us not cast blame on the murderers today. Why should we declare their burning hatred for us? . . . For eight years they have been sitting in the refugee camps of Gaza, and before their eyes we have been transforming the lands and villages, where they and their forefathers previously dwelled, into our home. . . . We are a generation that settles the land and without the steel helmet and the cannon's muzzle, we will not be able to plant a tree and build a home.'"[1] As he recognized, Palestinian resistance to the Zionist/Israeli settlement project was not unjustified, anti-Semitic violence; it was an understandable response to the loss of land and autonomy and to Israel's colonial behavior.

Gaza has been occupied by Israel continuously since 1967 and more recently has been strangled by a crushing blockade, a siege, and recurrent military attacks and targeted assassinations. Hamas, which was initially the Palestinian branch of the Muslim Brotherhood, took form as an armed resistance movement in 1987, in the early days of the First Intifada. In 1993, it strongly opposed the Oslo Agreement, concluded between Israel and the PLO, which provided for a limited form of Palestinian self-rule (the "Palestinian Authority," PA) in the West Bank and Gaza on an interim basis, pending conclusion of a permanent peace treaty. This treaty was supposed to occur within five years. In 1996, Hamas strongly opposed the holding of elections to the PA and tried to disrupt them. But when a second round of PA legislative elections were held in 2006, it participated—and won them. As noted earlier, in 2007, the movement consolidated its control of Gaza after it beat back the clumsy coup attempt that Israel and the United States had tried to launch against it.

Hamas was never a monolithic organization but a combination of groups devoted to charitable and educational endeavors as well as armed struggle. They were responsible for a large number of social services, hospitals, schools, and orphanages, taking care of people who had been largely forgotten by the big aid donors. The original Hamas charter called for the destruction of Israel, but over the years, Hamas leadership came to express cautious support for a number of peace initiatives (such as the Saudi Peace

Plan of 2002) that accept a two-state solution based on the '67 borders, and somewhat stronger support for the idea of a functional truce that would not involve actual recognition of Israel.[2] For its part, Israel rebuffed all such overtures.

There have been struggles between the political and military wings of the party, with the militants' cause often bolstered by aggressive Israeli policies and the rising rage and desperation in Gaza's population. Hamas's leadership stopped suicide bombing by 2004 and announced its acceptance of the Saudi Peace Plan in 2006. Its participation in the 2006 PA election signaled its agreement to become part of the political process.

Mainstream commentators frequently mention the need for Hamas to recognize "Israel's right to exist as a Jewish democratic state" and to "renounce violence." This kind of language completely ignores the fact that the iron control that Israel maintains all around Gaza, and across nearly the whole of the West Bank, is itself a pervasive and very damaging form of structural and physical violence. This language also raises essential questions, the first of which is, does any country have a "right to exist" or does it exist due to a complex coalescence of military might, aspirations, mythology, and historical movements? Then there is the obvious, troubling question arising from the notion of the "Jewish democratic state": can a state be a democracy when one group is institutionally privileged over a second class of citizens, when the disadvantaged group is asked to give up its internationally recognized rights and aspirations? The follow-up question is, which Israel? The one determined by the 1947 UN borders, the 1967 borders, the borders along the separation wall? These are critical details. Maybe the issues are more understandable if you flip the question: does Israel recognize a Palestinian right to statehood if there are now eight hundred thousand Jewish Israelis living in ever-expanding settlements in the West Bank and Jerusalem? Also, would we ever talk of a Christian or Hindu state's "right to exist"? I would additionally suggest that it is hypocritical to ask Hamas leadership to renounce violence when we do not even remotely ask the same of Israel, not that there is any sense of parity between the two sides when it comes to military might. The impact of state violence cannot be underestimated in this equation.

Israelis and their allies also frequently accuse Palestinians of having a "culture of martyrdom," arguing that they "send their children to die as martyrs," or "do not value life." In a forceful interview she gave to CNN at the height of Israel's 2014 attack against Gaza, Diana Buttu, a former legal adviser to the PLO, noted,

The idea that Palestinians use their children as human shields is racist and reprehensible. And the idea that the Israelis are somehow
spewing this and we're to believe it is also racist. . . . It's simply a
fact that what the Israelis are doing is they're dropping bombs of a
magnitude that we have never seen before on a captive civilian child
population. . . . If you look inside Israel, there are more than 42 cities that have names of streets named after people who themselves
have killed and very openly killed Palestinians and are proud for killing
Palestinians. There isn't a culture of martyrdom . . . this is a situation
in which Palestinians are being killed by the Israelis. Palestinians live
and they want to live. They want to be able to live just like every other
human being around the world.[3]

For our part, our delegation making its visit to post-war Gaza started out in
East Jerusalem before heading to the Erez checkpoint . . .

Schmoozing East Jerusalem Style

March 20, 2015

Friday is a get-over-jet-lag schmooze-with-friends-and-colleagues kind of
day, much of it spent in a lovely modern apartment in the Germany Colony,
a neighborhood in southwest Jerusalem established in the second half of the
1800s by the German Temple Society and populated by Christian Arabs as
well. The Germans were run out by the British as Nazi sympathizers and
the Arabs were dispossessed in 1948, leaving a pleasant blend of Ottoman
and art deco architecture and homes conveniently "emptied" for Jewish
immigrants to claim. In the bad old days, during the Second Intifada in
2003, one of the main streets, Emek Refaim, was the site of a horrific suicide
bombing and another nearby bombing on bus #14A. Emek Refaim is now a
trendy, gentrified area with excellent coffee shops, a decent burrito place, and
a host of yuppie shops that suggest to me a combo between Boston's Harvard
Square and Newbury Street. Our host, with her bright-eyed, delicious baby
in tow, recounts a ridiculous moment when her exposed, bulging belly was
poked and wanded for explosives at airport security. Did the Israelis seriously

think there was a bomb in her uterus, or was that for them just a metaphor for another non-Jewish baby in the demographic war? And she is not even Palestinian. She reports the kid kicked back.

The rest of the day we drink coffee or tea with mint, and nibble on Arabic salad in the unexpectedly hip Gallery Café in Sheikh Jarrah near the Mount Scopus Hotel, where a steady stream of activists, medical folk, journalists, and friends of friends just happen to be passing by. So we schmooze. It is Friday after all.

We wander back through the Sheikh Jarrah neighborhood, where an unrelenting process of Judaization has been occurring since 1967. A cluster of hardy protesters stand on the corner across from the sign to the Shimon HaTzadik tomb, holding posters in Hebrew and English. They read: "No to the Occupation," "Stop the Settlements in East Jerusalem." I recognize Arik Ascherman, founder of Rabbis for Human Rights, and Nasser al-Ghawi. In 2009, Israeli security, police, and fanatical Jewish settlers dragged al-Ghawi with his family from his longtime home, and dragged another family, the al-Hanoun, from their home as well. The Palestinian homes are scarred with graffiti, the Star of David now a symbol of racism, hatred, and entitlement. In the 1950s, Palestinian refugees from West Jerusalem and beyond were offered homes here by the United Nations and the Jordanian government in exchange for giving up their refugee status, and since 1967 a quasi-legal, violent, and tortured battle has been fought in the courts and the streets, waged through arguments such as "This is mine," and "No, I was here first and here are the manufactured documents to prove it." Currently, five hundred Palestinian families face threat of eviction. Nearby, young Jewish boys with *peyos*, wearing short black pants, black jackets, and white *yarmulkes*, munch chips and play before the Sabbath services in one of these acquired-by-Jewish-settlers buildings, while down the dusty street, tens of Palestinians families, the victims of evictions and home demolitions, have established a squatters' camp devoid of basic services (like water and electricity) in a large white stone edifice, glass shattered, in poor repair. Protected under Islamic Law as a *waqf* (a religious endowment), it is located just a block from the upscale American Colony Hotel, where I bet no one chooses to see this crushing disaster. Contradiction upon contradiction. Injustice upon injustice.

We pick up a collection of maps from the UN Office for the Coordination of Humanitarian Affairs building, not the usual Google Map types, but a set of damning, crisscrossed, multicolored affairs that present a visual of the tortured realities of occupation, border walls, land confiscation, checkpoints.

We complete our journey, picking our way through trash-strewn streets (in East Jerusalem garbage collection is nonexistent and there are no recycling bins) and torn-up roads. Compared to what West Jerusalem receives, a small portion of municipal services is provided to East Jerusalem, despite the equal amount of taxes that East Jerusalemites pay. They are only allotted a fraction of the city budget in this the "united capital" of the State of Israel.

We end up at the lovely Educational Book Store run by the Muna family on Salah Eddin Street. They have a fabulous collection of books in English on Middle Eastern culture and the Arab/Israel conflict. Mahmoud Muna welcomes me at the door, *"Ahlan wa sahlan,"* and I see my book, *On the Brink: Israel and Palestine on the Eve of the 2014 Gaza Invasion*, prominently displayed in the front window. Oh happy days! I feel a little less invisible in this crazy-making place on just another typical Friday afternoon.

Mish Mushkela, No Problem
March 22, 2015

The drive to Erez checkpoint is deceptively bucolic as the rain trickles through lush rolling farmland, vineyards, fruit trees, wineries reminiscent of the valleys of California; but the signs for Ashdod, Asheqelon, and Sderot lend that ominous feel, evoking memories of frightened Israelis, bomb shelters, post-traumatic stress disorder, and Qassam rockets. Beyond these troubled border towns sprawls the menacing military terminal that is the only way currently to get in or out of Gaza from Israel if you are not a vegetable or an approved piece of construction.

Erez was built to process thirty-five to forty thousand travelers a day but will do a tenth of that when things are quiet. Last November, the Washington Physicians for Social Responsibility delegation waited for three hours at the first checkpoint; today, we are literally waved through, after which there is a large open plaza with particular places to enter for the processing of particular papers and stamps. While everyone sails through, I am asked to wait for some extra security checks. I can see one of the computer screens, but it is all little boxes and in Hebrew that I cannot decipher. Finally, the security officer asks me about my troubles at Ben Gurion Airport that occurred when I entered the country. During more than an hour of questioning I was accused of not revealing all the SIM card phone numbers I had used over the past decade or so, particularly a Jawwal card, which is used only in the West Bank. I explain that I am involved with an exchange program with Harvard and Al Quds medical students, and I like to go visit the students I have gotten to know in Ramallah. After more interrogation, she stamps my passport.

Forgive me if I do not get the details exactly right—this is a stressful and chaotic place—but after passport control, we drag our bags through grey Metal Door #6. There is a huge open building that looks like a big, half-finished warehouse and then a series of long walkways, hallways, turnstiles (although each time we approach a turnstile they agree to open a metal door for us since we have a ridiculous amount of luggage carrying medical supplies for Gaza). Security cameras are everywhere. We finally emerge into a caged corridor on the other side of the concrete wall and gun towers, surrounded by a sea of bright yellow flowers. Defying the dangers of the buffer zone/no-man's-land, several brave and probably desperate shepherds follow their munching, curly, cream-colored flocks at the risk of being summarily shot. We are met by a cluster of *tuk tuks* (a kind of motorized rickshaw), load up our bags and cases of water, and start the three-quarter-mile walk down the wire-fenced corridor to the Palestinian Authority and Hamas versions of passport control, where all the luggage is searched. There is a large portentous poster warning Palestinians not to collaborate with Israelis. A smiling woman paws through my bags, but her eyes are laughing and friendly; another man also in uniform grins and says, "Welcome to Gaza." Then, another short taxi ride and finally, the vans from GCMHP are waiting, and a nimble, sun-browned man, probably in his sixties, scampers up to the roof rack and starts piling up our luggage. From the GCMHP drivers, I learn a new, very helpful Arabic phrase: *mish mushkela* (no problem).

No Time to Mourn

March 22, 2015

I first saw the spanking new administrative buildings leased by GCMHP in 2005; ten years later, there is a rusty shabbiness to the exterior, but the people working inside are energetic and spectacular. The property fronts a road and beyond that, a glorious sandy beach and the crashing grey blue waves of the Mediterranean. Young people cluster on the sand and horses gallop along the shore. The Israeli navy shelled this area last July, and it was on a nearby Gaza beach that four boys, aged two to eleven, were killed by an Israeli gunboat in front of a group of horrified journalists. In any other country, this would be a resort.

We gather in a conference room with the breathtaking view and are greeted by Dr. Yasser Abu Jamei, the psychiatrist and executive director who has taken the helm of the center since the death of Dr. Eyad el-Sarraj. He welcomes us warmly to "Planet Gaza" announces that it is "pizza time," along with sweet orange and grape drink.

After the kissing and compliments and the tribute to our strong partnerships, the serious talk begins. Yasser notes that "after the agony . . . people are walking around, they are not obviously in shock; people are carrying on; it is uplifting. . . . This is a nation of survivors. We are under occupation." Seventy-five percent of Gazans are refugees, and everyone is subjected to the siege. "This nation has no other choice. We are freedom fighters, we have all the international resolutions, but that doesn't change the fact that we are still under occupation. We were subjected to three different offenses in six years, and we are still under siege. Construction materials are not allowed to get into Gaza. People who have totally lost everything are scheduled to get funds 'later,' so the worse the damage, the less the help." He notes that "Israeli citizens are cheated by their leaders," that the idea that "Palestine will be a danger to Israel is nonsense. Occupation will never continue forever; we will have our own state."

Yasser is equally harsh on the topic of the conflicts within Palestinian leadership. "We do not even have a pizza to fight over. . . . We are closed-minded people, we need new leadership." We show our concern about how Yasser and the staff are doing after the July/August 2014 invasion. After a moment of joking—"terribly good" is his initial reply—he describes fifty-one days of intense fear and insecurity for adults and children, the daily fear of death. The GCMHP staff were urged to stay with family until the cease-fire, but staff called each other once or twice per week, "so we are like one family." During a short truce, staff returned to work, and small management teams stayed in direct communication. When the war stopped, "our work started, everyone give help."

What they found was an enormous catastrophe, but they strove to not intrude, staying sensitive to the amount of meddling people could tolerate. Visiting a devastated family may expose them more than it is helpful—their privacy is gone; the wreckage of their home and their lives are too public. Despite a financial deficit, the GCMHP continued to function. Donations came in, capacity and referrals increased. Yasser explains that this level of trauma cripples the normal capacity of people to overcome horrendous experiences, and that the political conditions and the environment are not improving, there is no reconstruction, people are depleted, and they have no coping strategies and no hope for improvement. This is a form of continuous PTSD.

Despite all this reason for pessimism, there have been fundamental shifts in US opinion following the Gaza wars of 2008–9, 2012, and 2014. Husam el-Nounou, the administrative director, explains, "We are winning the battle over Israel, occupation, colonialism, racism; this will not prevail. Everyone who comes here is changed." Unfortunately, Palestinian politics is linked to regional politics, so there is pressure from surrounding countries, both proxy behavior as well as influence between the United States (via Saudi Arabia) and Iran. "We Palestinians should have one Palestinian leadership that can agree on a national project." The GCMHP supports the BDS movement. "This is the most important thing: boycott [against] an occupation, not a State of the Jews. We have nothing against Jews for being Jews. BDS is increasing internationally. This will result in political pressure."

The big challenge is how to link mental health with human rights, which was a fundamental priority of the late founder, Dr. Eyad. International peace is the basis for Palestinian peace. Husam explains that ISIL (Islamic State of Iraq and the Levant) is filled with anger, frustration, desire for revenge. In general people are heavily frustrated and hopeless, and this is a recipe for violence that can take the form of violence against self, family, children, and women, as well as communal and tribal violence. All of this is increasing, and "young, poor, hopeless is time bomb, easily maneuvered by more militant groups . . . the environment encourages this; we need to diffuse [the anger], open the borders, improve the economy."

Yasser talks of intervening as early as possible, working in schools with students and teachers, reaching out to people who are subjected to oppression or bullies in school, teaching teenagers other ways to deal with anger. If someone is showing anxiety and depression, people need to talk, make themselves *hear* themselves, and hear in a different way. "Your ability is limited because the environmental conditions are so bad with 40 percent unemployment overall, much higher in the 25- to 30-year-old age group." He sees people are desperate, fleeing to Italy by sea. Why do they flee? "Is this suicidal or trying for better life or join ISIS?" he asks. The media, he notes, is often less than helpful. He remarks that even Israeli generals are advising Netanyahu to lift the siege for the sake of the Israeli government.

But the political instability, violence, and lack of support for the Palestinian cause in Syria, Turkey, Yemen, Iraq, Libya, and Egypt complicate the picture, and he is not optimistic. Even when the border with Egypt briefly opened up, two hundred thousand desperate Gazans left to shop, see families, but when asked to return, they complied because they had no other options. In addition, if all the necessary reconstruction materials were to reach Gaza, and the international community enacted a vigorous Marshall Plan–like initiative, it would take ten years to rebuild, but otherwise, the estimated timespan is closer to fifty years before an improvement in living conditions occurs, barring further wars. Between dysfunctional Palestinian leadership, Israeli control, and Turkey's wavering, political conditions do not exist that would allow a positive future. Gazans cannot even rebuild their destroyed homes.

On a more personal note, Yasser explains that he lived in the United Kingdom, but returned to Gaza with his wife and children because "this is my country and my children deserve to live in a dignified country where their grandparents live." He talks of changing the very constructs of people's mentality. "With a patient, I cannot offer something I cannot have for myself. I can only offer containment of fears and processing of trauma and direct him to a better future, get him back to school, help abusive parents, etc." Yet, the kind of support Yasser offers is not always possible because the wide-ranging trauma is ongoing and the therapists are suffering at levels similar to that of their patients.

Husam relates a troubling story. He was driving his car ten years ago and there was a rocket that landed in front of him and his son. The child grabbed his neck, but Husam was able to reassure him and drive home. Two days later the child developed symptoms of PTSD. Husam tried to help him. A week later he told his father, "'I want to die, I want to be a martyr.' You cannot understand how you feel. I am a bad father. I cannot help my children; why? What is the meaning of life if you can be killed for nothing? So kill and be killed for something. I was in a big moment of confusion. It is good to die for home, people, but it is much better to live for it. We need to convey this message, so containment and love from the extended family and religious faith [is critical]." He continues, saying that in Islam, "it is said everything comes from God, and if it is good, be grateful, God will reward you. If it is bad, be good and God will reward you. This gives you strength and power. The lucky ones come to our clinics. I am really concerned for the thousands who cannot come to our clinics."

We ask, how do providers care for each other? Yasser tells us a story of Hassan al-Zeyada, a staff member whose family was killed. "It was something very unique. I have twenty-four years of experience. I hear bombardments continuously. You do not know who is dying and who is living." When the Israeli Defense Force bombarded the family compound, Hassan left immediately." The family received a warning missile. "I know that Hassan's family lived there, born there, raised there. I didn't know what to do . . . and the mobile phone was ringing. . . . They all died of the shelling. That was a question—what to do? The news was really shocking . . . it is very dangerous." He spoke with another staff member and then talked to Hassan. "I didn't know what to say. I lost some of my cousins, but it is not like losing your mom. I heard him breathing, and crying. I couldn't speak."

"I don't know what to say," Yasser told Hasan. "That was one of the most intense phone calls during the offensive. I had to call. We have sixty-five staff, I try to call them all. When the place is more affected than another, you start to worry." In the case of a staff person who has lost his house, Yasser asks, "What would he offer someone? How could he contain the sorrows?" Some staffers appreciated the phone calls and text messages, the attempts to stay in touch. But it was difficult to be the person making those calls. "I can never forget the moment that Hassan was on the phone. I really couldn't meet him until the truce. . . . The other thing—our receptionist, Osama Al Ramlawi, he lost his brother, Ahmad, and his house was partially affected. His brother was a member of our crisis team, a social worker after the second offensive [in 2012]." Yasser planned to hire him after the most recent assault. "At least he could have some income; he has two children. He said it was early morning, they decided to leave the neighborhood of Shejaia. Ahmad decided to stay [for] a few minutes. He was standing in front of his house doing nothing. He was killed at that moment by shrapnel, and suddenly he was not there and it happened after Hassan.

"I left one day pass, gathered myself and I called [Osama and said], 'I know what happened, I couldn't come to you.' There's nothing we can do. We talked about religion, Osama was weeping. His twin brother—that brother used to bring happiness to the family and I remember. . . . So suddenly Ahmad is not there." Osama had an extremely difficult time. "We stayed with him, more than once; he needed lots of support. A few months ago [his wife] gave birth to a boy and they named him Ahmad, after the brother who was killed. So you live with such people, you work with such friends, and you have community but you have no other chance but to go on."

We discover that during the Israeli assault it was impossible to observe a traditional mourning period, "because they were targeting any gathering immediately, like praying in a mosque, going out together so . . . no mourning at all took place. My grandmother died, ninety-five years old for natural reasons; she passed away, we took her from the hospital to her daughter's house and then to the cemetery. Everything happened in ten to fifteen minutes. People were targeted in the cemetery." Yasser explains that "something delays the processing of PTSD, because even natural ways of grief and closure do not take place. People couldn't say good-bye to the dead." He feels "crazy but I come to work every day. We have 1,900,000 crazy people."

Husam adds that the desire for life, family, and religion, along with the responsibilities and supports of family have kept the Palestinian community from collapsing over the past seventy years. "Trauma makes you stronger and stronger; for sure, there is something changed in you, more power to cope with the difficulties in your life." His grandmother is from Lydda and his mother was born in Jaffa. His family fled south, and he remembers the stories of the Egyptian refugee camps and life in Gaza. "You have these memories born in the camps. We had to face the difficulties, the trauma, the poverty. At the end they are different, they are strong, they have an innate capacity to survive."

Yasser asks, "What could we do? If people here are given the chance to become productive, things will become a thousand times better, but it is unfortunately not allowed." Husam adds that peace is critical and that when it comes to genuine politics, the details of the right for Palestinian refugees to return to their homes is negotiable. Every Palestinian knows they can never go *home*." Even his seventy-five-year-old mother does not want to return to Jaffa because she has children and grandchildren, but an acceptable compromise needs to be developed. Netanyahu's recent election does not bode well for Palestinians. "He is a fox, a liar, excellent with making money."

Later I check the internet and read the following on the GCMHP website:

> Dr. Yasser Abu Jamei has reportedly lost 28 members of his family when an Israeli air strike on July 21 flattened the house in which they were gathered for the evening meal at the end of the daily Ramadan fast. Other GCMHP staff members who have reportedly also suffered personal losses include Hassan al-Zeyada, Osama Al Ramlawi, and Marwan Diab.

Running on Empty

March 23, 2015

I first met Dr. Mona El-Farra several years ago in Washington, DC, and I have followed her work and reports primarily through the Middle East Children's Alliance (MECA). The taxi takes me to the Red Crescent Society main hospital through gridlocked streets and aggressive nail-biting moments that remind me once again that in this part of the world, there is very little personal space, especially when it comes to cars. Mona and I find a book-lined office to talk. She has a head of thick black hair, a white-and-red patterned scarf, pearl earrings, and a turquoise bracelet. There is a fierce look of determination about her, but I sense an immense fatigue in her eyes. She lost nine relatives in the recent war.

She explains that during the Israeli attack, the hospital was bombed. "I have been negatively affected by the bombing. I am fine but it was a very hard time; there is a feeling of uncertainty, it may happen again. Besides that, I am trying to travel to see my children in the UK. I have been invited to three conferences, but no permits, so I am stuck." There is a stress and tension in her voice, and I am trying to imagine the reality of a physician's life trapped in Gaza and assaulted by repeated military attacks and human tragedy.

Mona takes phone calls while we talk. She explains that she is the deputy chair of the Palestinian Red Crescent Society of the Gaza Strip and the director of Gaza Projects for MECA. She is also a prominent human rights and women's rights activist born in Khan Yunis, in southern Gaza.

"The current situation is miserable, on the edge of collapse. There is no reconstruction; thousands of families need homes; water is difficult and salinated and of poor quality. Next year there will be no water in the aquifer, so the problem is building. Ninety-six percent of the water is currently unacceptable for drinking this year; there is no regular electricity, only two to four hours per day. After the war, the hospital got donations for a generator, but there is not enough fuel." They need the generator to work the MRI machine twenty-four hours per day and this is very expensive.

She continues, "Four hundred thousand children are traumatized after the attack due to eyewitness experiences according to the UN and UNICEF. I see that those kids, aged five to sixteen, who are suffering this trauma, are the future youth. Those kids will be the future negotiators. When Israel hits Gaza, it hits the psychological well-being of those kids. They may become very, very radical, filled with hatred . . . so [there is] hatred and lack of peace." She describes the terrors that these children have seen: "War, killing of parent, home bombing, running in the streets, killing of civilians. They currently need opportunities like Play and Heal Program of MECA, clinics for kids and families for psychosocial support, so this is the extra burden." She admits to feeling strained with a lack of resources. "Nobody takes care of me. I suffer extra systoles, high blood pressure; no one cares for me. I need a break. . . . It was not good before the attacks, so now there is more work. To help people, lots of pressure." Her supports are her friends, but they need support too. Amazingly, she had the chance to leave during the war on her British passport, but "it was my duty [to stay]. But after the attack I couldn't leave." She tried to get a permit via the Erez checkpoint but was refused for "security reasons . . . this is the case for 95 percent who try."

Mona remarks that her work is managerial, "but during the war I saw patients. The bombing was heavy across the road from the hospital; it was affected. I came daily to emergency; [there were] all kinds of staff who could get here." Some worked for twenty-four hours at a time; some provided a telemedicine service for patients who couldn't reach the hospital. "They talk directly to the doctor for advice and this worked; we had many calls. Then we received injured patients." They worked in cooperation with Shifa Hospital, which was overloaded, had malfunctioning equipment, and was beset by issues regarding MRIs, CTs, x-rays. Patients who were injured were discharged from Shifa and came for follow-up care of their injuries to Red Crescent. Mona's team also went to chronically ill patients at home who lacked medications and needed help. They made field visits under fire; they traveled in ambulances to see diabetics and cardiac patients. Some areas had two to four hours of electricity per day; some mobile phones were functional and in other areas there was no phone or internet service.

The second week, Israel started a ground attack in Shejaia in the northeast. "Seventy-five thousand people left their homes under intense attack, like a flooding of people. It reminded people of 1948. Early in the morning, people killed in streets, rubble. They went to schools for safety, came to the hospitals for medical help." She coordinated with the UNRWA schools, started doing clinical medicine. There were seven hundred cases per day. "I worked as a general practitioner, gynecologist, dermatologist, asked other centers for volunteers, but we were well organized."

The trauma and bitterness pours from her troubled memories. "A child age seven on the second day of [the attack on] Shejaia came with blisters on his foot, walked a long way, hungry and thirsty. He came to the clinic with his parents; a nurse accompanied his mother to the MRI machine. His mother was watering plants and was hit." Another memory: "A child age five came to the clinic with a head injury. We asked his name—'unknown.' He was comatose, whole family died. Anything about him? We don't know, the whole house was destroyed, [don't even know] which house he came from. He did not survive.

"There are 1,800 orphans just from the last war."

Dr. Mona's face deepens with sadness. She then tells the story of her cousin in Khan Yunis, a sixty-five-year-old farmer named Abed Melek, who ran into the street with his grandchildren when his house was hit:

> He was killed; four children killed in their pajamas; five adults were killed. Another ten were injured in his family. . . . I have story of myself which reflects the situation of Gaza; no place was safe. When shelling was heavy in my neighborhood, I went to stay with friends. Then there was shelling in their area; people were running from place to place, but I went to the hospital daily, running with clothes on [my] back. Diabetics did not take their medications. . . . People had no IDs. There were unbelievable bombs, shaking, maybe sound bombs. This time there was a warning rocket on the roof, [but] this can kill people. Another Khan Yunis cousin was given fifteen minutes' notice and then the house was demolished. A nurse here from Red Crescent Society Gaza hospital—her daughter, son-in-law, and two grandchildren died; she still suffers. Two of the staff lost homes completely, a nurse and an administrator. All of them ran from place to place; so not enough food, suddenly you have forty people in your house. MECA responded directly with food and clothes.

Mona got food, milk, biscuits, blankets, and water tanks and coordinated with MECA volunteers. She found that the markets trusted her even without paying. During the cease-fire, she went to schools to offer music and other activities to children, but even while there was shelling in Beit Hanoun, Gaza, she also distributed supplies, using the Red Crescent car. When medications ran out, MECA said, "Buy what you can from pharmacies."

Looking at Israeli leadership, Mona finds "Netanyahu no worse. They are one politics; very bad to look at Israeli society. . . . I don't like to call it war— humanity failed. Civilians were attacked, there was slaughter, thousands were injured, handicapped, women and children killed; all of these are people. It was crazy, no outcome. During the attack people [were] supportive of Hamas, defending them, so Israel is stupid." But now Gazans are unhappy with Hamas because of "domestic issues and due to lack of reconciliation with Fatah."

I ask if there is any way out. "Not for the time being. This land should be for all; this is not easy and it needs a lot of work and lots of organizing for unity of Palestinian people and for Israel to admit what happened in '48. With a racist and colonialist state like Israel, it will be very difficult. We need one state, one vote. The Middle East is chaotic but things change, like the collapse of the Soviet Union." Nonetheless, she worries that with the ongoing trauma, despair, and potential for radicalization, "the children now will not be good negotiators later."

As if that were not enough, says Mona, "nineteen health workers were killed in the Gaza Strip. Clinics, ambulances were destroyed." She reminds me that it is never permissible to attack schools or hospitals. "If you want to talk about international law, even if there was one militant in a school, you must respect international law. Schools with displaced families, like [in the UNRWA elementary school] in the Jabalia Refugee Camp, were attacked; [displaced people] fled only to die inside the school. Now ten thousand people are living in schools," and they are homeless and trapped in overwhelming conditions. After the most devastating massacres, Mona "went to Shejaia during a cease-fire. I could smell death everywhere, destruction." She sighs deeply. "Our role is to continue to support people. I am MECA director, but I need someone to support me. We all need a break, a break from thinking it may happen again. It will be the end of Gaza."

And then there is the environmental catastrophe from the attacks. "Water reservoirs were hit in the north and this affected water in Gaza, electric plants, schools for disabled, streets, and there is no reconstruction. Because of the instability [regarding] the next Israeli attack, international donors will not give. My home, shattered windows; I didn't live there for one month. I moved to another area—also dangerous—and the nearby buildings were hit. I couldn't sleep, worked twelve hours, stayed with friends, communicating with MECA with thanks for their generosity. It was lifesaving. The schools used the MECA water unit, the MAYA project, a desalination project, supervised by engineers. All Gaza drinks desalinated water.

"This is not about people who were killed. It is about us who were waiting for death every minute. I do not pray. I used to walk . . . I feel low. I usually fight depression with walking, but my toe hurts; I had bronchitis. There is a lack of electricity; with no lights at night I do not feel safe."

Somehow, Mona finds the strength to continue to worry about all the needy people around her. It seems that women jailed in Hamas prisons have no access to medication. She hands me two scripts. Could I possibly see if we brought in any of these? The women are in jail as thieves, collaborators, whatever, "but they have their rights. Men have no medicine either."

I free-associate to that bizarre and frightening comment made by Dov Weisglass, adviser to then prime minister Ehud Olmert, back in 2006 about putting Palestinians "on a diet," but not letting them actually die of hunger. Palestinians are now facing starvation, not only in economic but also in emotional and spiritual terms, and the compounding tragedy is that their dedicated, exhausted health care providers are starving with them as well.

Sustaining a Garden of Children

March 23, 2015

Wejdan Diab, sister of GCMHP staffer Marwan Diab, welcomes me to the Meera Kindergarten in Gaza City, where the walls are painted Disney-bright. I spot many photos and murals depicting dolphins, giraffes, a Holland windmill next to a pond with a duck, and piles of dress-up clothes including large yellow and white flowers and traditional *dabke* outfits. The school has morning and afternoon shifts. It all looks quite "normal," but this is Gaza, where gardens of any kind—including "children's gardens," to use that German word literally—are actually quite hard to sustain.

Wejdan's face reveals this disarming blend of joy, laughter, and intense tragedy. Above the raucous din of children playing, singing, and performing rote repetition as teachers and children shout to be heard, she shares photos of the destruction of the school during the last war: broken glass, bullet holes, and fractured building parts. She explains that if a child is six years old, he has already experienced three wars, or perhaps his mother was pregnant during the first one. "It was very difficult for all of us," she says. "Every day thanks God I am alive. The bombing was terrible everywhere. My kindergarten was partially destroyed, including windows and doors."

In July 2014 the Israeli forces repeatedly bombed the city of Shejaia, east of Gaza City, creating Dresden-like conditions. Sixty young survivors sheltered at the kindergarten. Acting out their experiences, the traumatized children destroyed many of the toys and were tormented by nightmares and bed-wetting, but Wejdan and her staff worked hard. "I wanted the children to be safe. We made arts and crafts to help children. They had no toys; these children are suffering." The survivors brought bits of their toys rescued from rubble, and they painted them as part of multimedia collages. A child living in a tent drew her toy on fire; another placed her doll's head in the center of a picture surrounded by death.

Every day the kindergarten staff threw parties for the children, brought in clowns. Some children refused to go outside, afraid of the sky or particular noises, but they are now getting better. And then there are the kids who lost their parents, one of whom was Ramy Ryan, a photojournalist assassinated by an Israeli missile. He was covering a multi-missile attack in Shejaia, which included attacks on two ambulances and rescue workers.[4]

Wejdan tells me that Ramy's child brought her father's press helmet to school and drew Ramy "at paradise eating apples." The journalist was actively involved in the school, teaching the students how to use cameras and be reporters. Wejdan's heartbreaking collection of photos is stored in a big plastic folder with a cover featuring Mickey Mouse and friends Daffy Duck and Goofy.

Wejdan takes out a plastic folder stuffed with papers. After the fighting ended, she conducted a survey, sending letters to the fathers and mothers of the children that included questionnaires. We scan through the parents' responses as I feel the heavy weight of human suffering in its most intimate details: these are the experiences of *kindergarteners.*

These were the questions: "After war, is anybody injured? Anybody having bad feelings? Is anyone is scared? What happened to homes?" Answers: "Cannot sleep. God I do not want to die. We hold her. When she sits alone she talks to herself about dying. The home was destroyed and she is afraid of bombing. She doesn't want to go alone to any room. Noises frighten her and there is a lot of crying. A lot of stories in their minds and they are talking about what they see on TV and the dead and the bombing. Daughter has strange behavior, stressed, nervous, sad, afraid the war will come again. She says that maybe the teachers will not be able to help the children, only feel safe with mother and father. Nightmares, going to the doctor because of bad feelings. Kitchen is destroyed, living room destroyed. Bed-wetting, crying, afraid at night."

Wejdan is counterintuitively cheerful, chuckling while recounting the horror. "I left my home near here. There is an Islamic University branch nearby and maybe it will be attacked." She joined her relatives at her family home. And then she adds: "All the children are suffering, 170 children were at the school." Some were unable to talk, became mute, and their hair fell out.

As we prepare to take a tour of the school, I am ready to observe quiet sobbing in some small, dark place, but the children are energetic, lively, and curious. The brightest moment comes with a high-spirited performance by a kindergarten *dabke* troupe; the boys and girls are in costume, beautifully synchronized, high-stepping, waving their arms, music blaring, celebrating their national heritage. I perceive a spirit of nurturing and a kind of determination to endure that will serve these children well in this most traumatic of places.

Wejdan invites Kareema Rayan, Ramy's mother and the grandmother of two children who attend the school, to talk with me. Kareema's eyes betray a sense of deep sadness and loss, and the tears come quickly. She explains that her son was going out to take pictures of the Israeli destruction, to expose the truth. She prayed *"Allahu akbar"* and begged him not to go. He pinched her cheek and "that was the end."

Kareema explains that the morning of his death she dreamt that he died and saw him in a white jacket. The family was told there would be no firing from 3:00 to 7:00 p.m. "so they said you can take stuff [merchandise] from the markets, so he went to the market. He has no gun or anything. He is journalist only and when he take pictures, the plane killed him with seventeen other people, three of them from one family." She sits in her black abaya and hijab, dark lines under her eyes, and talks about the other people killed. One had a pregnant wife who later named her newborn after the infant's dead father. Her hands twist at her tissues as she recalls Ramy's wife calling him for lunch and "he said, 'No, I want to take pictures, *alhamdulillah.*'" An hour later he was dead. There were multiple phone calls and people coming to Kareema's home, and then her nephew saw the murder on television. With no electricity in her home, she had received the news after many family members did. "I prefer I dead, not him. He didn't smoke, he was polite. He had two boys and two girls." She married him off at seventeen because he was an only son and she wanted grandchildren. The five- and six-year-olds come in to the office, somewhat subdued and clearly still swimming in loss. Old souls already.

And the Israelis are already discussing the "next war."

The Constriction of Women's Bodies and Minds

March 23, 2015

The data collected by the UN Office for the Coordination of Human Affairs is stark: the 2014 military operation in Gaza left 302 women and 582 children dead, 10,870 wounded (2,120 women and 3,303 children), and more than 450,000 people, mostly women and children, displaced from their homes. That humanitarian catastrophe was compounded by other harsh conditions—a severely distressed society strangled by years of blockade and siege, increasingly more fundamentalist Islamic culture and religious practices, and dramatic restrictions in options for everyone.

So how does that look up close and personal? Mariam Abu al-Atta, management administrator, and Israa Al Battrikhi, project coordinator, welcome me to the Aisha Association for women with husbands who are mentally ill or addicted. These are the living and breathing families who have literally fallen off the curve. Fourteen women wait for us at a U-shaped conference room with one girl and one boy snuggled close to their mothers. The women are sketching on paper with colored pencils as part of their intake process. I estimate the age range is thirty to fifty, although I could be monumentally off as women not surprisingly age prematurely under occupation and repeated trauma. Everyone wears a hijab; most of the faces are not covered. Everyone has a chance to tell her story, and in subsequent weeks there will be group and individual sessions, various kinds of counseling, legal advice, job training, and other forms of support. At some point, almost every woman begins to weep, clutching tissues, and toward the end even our interpreter bursts into tears. Despite the lively persistent voices, the occasional twinkle in an eye or laughter (one woman playfully comments, "Maybe it would be better if our husbands just stayed in bed sleeping"), the amount of accumulated suffering in this room is stunning.

The women talk about husbands with mental illness and drug addiction (most are abusing tramadol), who steal and do not care for their families, and children with many diseases due to intermarriage with close cousins, the toxic load from war, malnutrition, and lack of care. Families suffer from multigenerational overcrowding: when growing households vie for a shrinking amount of space without privacy or healthy boundaries, jealousy and competition abound. This is exacerbated by addiction, war, death, and PTSD. Poverty is rampant, children are hungry, families rely on social services, and the women are clearly depressed, some suicidal. They talk about wanting to educate their children in universities and the difficulties in financing those dreams. Some see their children turning violent, out of control, addicted, and mirroring their fathers. The mothers desperately want to save them from that fate. The most recent war has caused extraordinary financial hardships and losses of housing, electricity, and water. One family lost a daughter and her five children: in an attempt to be smuggled out of Gaza to eventually reach Italy, the ship sank and the family drowned. At this point in the conversation, we are all weeping.

I sometimes sink into stereotypical thoughts about tyrannical Arab families, dominating mothers-in-law, and the repressive role of fundamentalist Islamic family relationships, and then I remind myself not to judge. What we do know is that the more crushing the economy and political landscape, the more oppressed and constricted the lives of women will be. Drawing attention to this fact is the task for feminists and all people who understand the intersections among war, patriarchy, psychological illness, domestic violence, and the cultures that make this all possible. The dedicated women of Aisha are taking the first steps on a long and challenging journey, and they deserve our sisterly support.

I Want You to See What Is Beautiful!

March 23, 2015

Drawing from some personal connections in Detroit, I end up calling two cousins who live in Gaza City. I plan to share with them my documentary film, *Voices Across the Divide*, which features some of their family, and to deliver a small gift from the Detroit branch of the Diaspora. Two well-dressed men arrive promptly at Marna House, where I am staying; soon they are inviting me for dinner.

A man (I will call him Ahmad) in a dark suit with a warm face, thick black eyebrows, and mustache arrives. It turns out he works in the Ministry of Health and had something to do with the granting of our permits to Gaza. He has advanced degrees in business administration. The first striking thing about walking the uneven streets of Gaza at night is that there is no electricity. Generators parked on the street roar and grind, burning hundreds of shekels of fuel to illuminate an apartment here and there or perhaps power a refrigerator. This is a real problem if you only have electricity four to twelve hours per day, and you can forget about using internet or TV, checking some tidbit on your smartphone, or completing your engineering assignment or the English literature report for university due tomorrow. This also means no elevators work reliably if you are elderly or obese or disabled.

The first apartment we visit in this tour of relatives' homes is richly adorned with lush green curtains and decorative upholstery. I am warmly greeted by Ahmad's cousin, who owns a toy store downstairs, and his playful one-year-old son, sweet wife, new baby, mother, sister, and his sister's fiancé, a nurse at Shifa Hospital (bombed in 2014) who offers me a cigarette. The conversation is all about family, the recent engagement party, the upcoming wedding. I look at their photos and videos, they look at mine. When I show them a photo of my daughter's chicken coop in Seattle, the response of these city folk is a big chuckle and "they look like angry birds!" I drink Coca-Cola and then tea with mint, and voice my grateful protest for the fancy glazed cake with all sorts of sugar *froufrou* that they have bought in my honor. I guess in Gaza it is always best to eat dessert first. This visit is notable for its generosity and warmth and for its profound ordinariness—a normal family sharing a pleasant normal evening, lots of laughter, with a guest from a far-away land that they cannot possible visit.

We walk several partially paved, disrupted blocks, using the flashlight from Ahmad's phone, past occasional clusters of young men and speeding cars. I briefly consider the risks of being kidnapped. I am immediately embarrassed by such thoughts, but it is really dark and I do not have a clue as to where I am going.

We hike up to Ahmad's house, creeping up asymmetric concrete stairs, which he has rigged with special bulbs that run off a battery. He proudly shows me the Rube Goldberg contraption that provides his home with regular electricity. His attractive and friendly wife is wearing ear muffs because the newly acquired apartment is cold and bare, save for some plastic chairs and a table. A twinkly one-and-a-half-year-old boy sprints and hops around the apartment at breakneck speed. He is somewhat fascinated with all things electrical and panels with on/off switches. The kid is in constant motion and has a totally engaging smile. I love him instantly. He vaguely understands how to play ball, and dances to some Disney song from years ago, but cannot stay still long enough to watch me perform my epic Itsy Bitsy Spider routine. Ahmad's wife serves coffee, and we talk more about children and the lack of electricity and how things felt during the war.

Apartment number three is a brief car ride away, and this time there is a great leap up in the number of relations. The mother looks beautiful in a turquoise hijab and heavily embroidered black and turquoise Palestinian dress. The men tend toward suits: there are a lot of businessmen types as well as a lawyer who cannot practice since he has no recognized papers or credentials, and the two youngest college students could have stepped out of Harvard Square. There is much talk about how each person ended up in Gaza. Among the group the journeys and methods vary widely: *laissez passer,* a travel document from Egypt, crawling through the tunnels, expulsion from you-name-the-Arab-country. Some trained in the United States. In any case, everyone is now trapped in Gaza and angry and frustrated about that, along with the lack of electricity, the wars, the crazy dysfunctional politics. People want to talk about how much ISIL has nothing to do with Islam; how Islam is a religion of peace and tolerance; how Jews and Palestinians can easily get along and have in the past. There is a lot of reminiscing about the good old days shopping in Tel Aviv, and Israelis being able to get a great deal in Gaza City. When they find out I am Jewish, everyone is warm and accepting and one woman glows, "You are shining, you are beautiful, you look like . . . [I think she is looking for something culturally appropriate here] a menorah!" People support the BDS call and are in general utterly disappointed with the elected and non-elected leadership. Everyone is sick of war and dreams of travel.

The mother, who is also a teacher, has made a classic, totally over-the-top, enough-food-for-an-entire-army Palestinian kind of meal. First, as a pre-meal treat, we are served a frozen strawberry/lemon/sugar/vanilla thing, then we drink water or juice, and finally, we arrive to the main course, approaching the bulging table cautiously. Large platters piled with some kind of fried chicken cutlets with garlic, olive oil, and lemon sauce; rice and strips of beef with toasted almonds and delirious spices and some yogurt-type sauce; two different salads with greens from their garden; divine thick French fries with parsley, and meatballs baked in a sauce. And so it went. I count a total of three different people heaping things on my plate if I let my guard down for an instant. I am assured that everything is healthy and they never throw food away; they will eat this tomorrow. And would I come out to the porch to sniff and admire all the herbs and petunias? The mother explains she no longer cooks fish. Once fishing used to be a major source of livelihood in the Gaza Strip, whose coast spans the entire length of the territory, but the fish are now all too small and polluted, thanks to the raw sewage pouring into the sea, the activities of the Israeli navy, and the ever-shrinking fishing zones.

This family's daughter, a university student studying IT, is gorgeous, diminutive, and helpful. Her hair is thick and beautifully coiffed. The son, also very deferential and polite, has a thick bush of vertical hair, and everyone teases him. He likes to be different. He seems very cat-like, ready to pounce into action, his phone constantly ringing. Because of the electricity shortage, friends call each other whenever anyone's internet service resumes, and then everyone rushes over to that apartment. I am almost moved to tears when he tells me he is an architect student at the university, and I say to him, "How can you study architecture when you have no concrete?" He is filled with ideas to make Gaza a more beautiful place, to get rid of the boxy concrete buildings. He wonders if I have ever seen Central Park in New York City. He Google-Mapped it and felt totally inspired. I tell him about Olmsted's Emerald Necklace in Boston, and now he is eagerly awaiting the next burst of electronic juice to look it up on the internet. He dreams of studying in Italy or Germany, "the birthplaces of architecture." His college friend, who trained at the American International School in Gaza and looks like he could be from Minnesota, drives us all home in a clunky old van through the dark, brooding city. He asks me when I will be free to meet again, earnestly explaining that he wants to give me a tour of Gaza, the port, the beaches—"all the beautiful places" that no one ever sees. Now that would be really lovely.

The Most Massive Child Abuse in the World
March 24, 2015

UNRWA has been given an impossible task. Originally a temporary agency to assist and protect the 750,000 Palestinian refugees created by the war in 1948, it now must handle a refugee population that has grown to over 5 million in Syria, Lebanon, Jordan, the West Bank, and Gaza. Despite the catastrophic conditions in Gaza, this week UNRWA is actually focused on the Palestine refugee camp of Yarmouk in Damascus, Syria, where more war and dispossession and humanitarian crises face an already beleaguered population.

But we are in Gaza, and it is a bright sunny day as we head off to several UNRWA facilities, starting in Gaza City. A quick review of the *UN Gaza Situation Report* for April 3, 2015, reveals that almost nine hundred thousand people require some level of food assistance, funding is hopelessly inadequate, over twelve thousand families have yet to rebuild their damaged homes, unemployment is astronomical, especially among the youth, and more than seven thousand displaced persons still live in agency-run centers.

The largely invisible humanitarian crisis is mind-boggling, but we are going to focus on health care in Gaza, drawing from the expertise of Dr. Ibrahim Mohd el Borsh, who graduated from Tripoli and has a masters in public health from the Jerusalem University branch in Gaza. He and a female physician, Ghada al Jadba, are briefing us. We settle around the table in a slightly disordered conference room as the coffee and juice arrives. UNRWA focuses on the immediate needs of the refugees, who make up about 70 percent of the Gaza population, as well as on human development and protection of the rights of refugees. The UNRWA health program here provides primary care to 1.2 million refugees.

Dr. Ghada is a refugee, but she lives in Gaza City rather than in a refugee camp. Sixty percent of Gaza's refugees live outside the camps; they leave when they are economically able to escape. Wearing a blue hijab with a sweep of brown hair across the side of her face, Dr. Ghada talks about the work that UNRWA does in its twenty-one health centers: "The main component is mostly maternal and child, then chronic diseases like hypertension, heart disease, and diabetes. Twenty-five percent of the population is women in reproductive age. Also, because of political challenges, instability, high fertility rate (4.3 per woman in reproductive age), there is very high maternal morbidity and mortality. Living in this difficult situation makes those women vulnerable; the situation affects them more, with poverty, low social status; they need more care. UNRWA provides ante- and postnatal care, physical exams, labs, ultrasound. Midwives, medical officers, and obstetrician-gynecologists rotate to the health center. The women also receive postnatal care, with a visit one week postpartum. Women are discharged a few hours after delivery."

We are shocked to learn that on the family health team, the physician sees eighty to ninety patients per day; the nurse, forty per day; the midwife, twenty to thirty per day.

The two doctors review the numerous health issues in this environment. Anemia is a major problem, probably a reflection of malnutrition and lack of adequate supplementation combined with frequent pregnancies. While a priority, family planning, mostly IUDs with some pills, condoms, and Depo-Provera injections, has not been successful. With a warm manner and laughing eyes despite the seriousness of our discussion, Dr. Ibrahim explains that it is hard to change cultural expectations regarding family size and the desirability of having many children when people have little else on which to rely, and children are expected and celebrated.

We learn that with 45 percent of the population under 18, pediatric care is critical. Dr. Ghada explains urgently that "this is a fragile community with high-dependency needs; the siege affects them. Collective punishment is the most massive child abuse in the world due to siege, crowding, infectious diseases." She notes that iron deficiency is present in 50 percent of children under three. Fortunately there is "one hundred percent vaccination coverage." There are breastfeeding counselors, and most women nurse exclusively for six months; this is encouraged by the society. Gazan infant mortality has improved over the decades but is still almost four times that in Israel.[5] Additionally there are rising numbers of children born with birth defects, most likely related to their mother's exposure to toxic war materials such as white phosphorus.[6]

Looking at prevention, we hear that mammography has long been a challenge; there is a center at the Ministry of Health with good screeners, but due to budgetary problems, the x-rays are only done when a case of breast cancer is suspected. As we have noted in our travels, smoking is a big problem; however, cessation programs are "one of the future goals." It seems that UNRWA has started with smoke-free health centers and at this point most doctors do not smoke, which is a dramatic change over the past decade.

The problem of funding comes up repeatedly and is an enormous issue. UNRWA has most essential medications, provided in accordance with World Health Organization guidelines. The private centers provide more expensive, newer medications; the United Nations is trying to upgrade their supplies. Of course, newer medications are not necessarily better medications, but they are definitely more expensive. The medications are imported from pharmaceutical companies in Amman, Jordan, but there are chronic issues regarding poorly regulated pharmacies and low-quality medications.

UNRWA clinicians pay attention to psychological and life cycle support but are challenged by societal attitudes of shame toward mental health disorders, the dramatic increase in need due to recurrent Israeli and internecine attacks, rising domestic and gender-based violence, and symptoms that are secondary to depression rather than organic disease, particularly in women and children. Health is further challenged by the worsening environment, poor sanitation, endemic parasites, and enteric fever. Because life expectancy has increased to age seventy-three, there are new modern-day challenges for the elderly, and few resources in the community are available to them in the waning days of their lives.

Tramadol addiction is another big issue, and we are told that people wonder if the drug was cynically introduced by the Israelis. I heard similar theories in East Jerusalem and the West Bank. Since the destruction of the tunnels during the 2014 war by Israeli and Egyptian forces, rising stress and despair made people more susceptible. One of the doctors explains, "Everything is [now] worse. One hundred thousand people worked in these tunnels, got construction materials and could build. There was tax collection from Hamas. Now unemployment is much higher; there are no cheap medications or cheap goods, so increased suffering." Trafficking in illegal drugs as well as legitimate medications was also curtailed, creating further demands on UNRWA for needed medications.

UNRWA realized that with scanty resources, it is critical to be more efficient. Dr. Ghada explains, "We have adopted in-service delivery, went from fragmented to family teams. Dr. Akhiro Seita [director of UNRWA health programs] developed this. With the family team approach, we have health teams: a medical officer, a practical nurse, a midwife—each team meets the health needs of a specific number of families. We are now more efficient, have more relationships, better use of resources, and more effective and higher quality. The doctor knows the family well; there is high staff satisfaction and community satisfaction."[7]

UNRWA "does not have its own hospitals, but contracts with the Ministry of Health and uses MOH hospitals, like Shifa Hospital. Although most patients have insurance, there are long wait times, so UNRWA also contracts with other hospitals and nongovernmental organizations for some surgeries and all deliveries. Seventy percent of costs are covered, 90 percent if [the patient is] abjectly poor."

With a calm and determined voice, Dr. Ghada reflects on her own war experience: "In July 2014, we don't how we survived, very difficult. We kept most of the UNRWA centers open, 65 percent of the workers came under difficult situations. They were provided with UNRWA cars [which were not protected from Israeli bombardment despite clear markings and international law], gave health care to refugees and anyone. I have three kids—sevente, fourteen, ten. I was leaving them alone. My husband is a vascular surgeon in Shifa Hospital and he cannot leave the hospital these days. I had to go to work to manage health care and the shelters [UNRWA schools]. We had to provide safe food, avoid epidemics, do surveillance, and provide medical person in each center. We recruited nurses, an emergency appeal. We highlighted the emergency: hygiene, lack of electricity, no water or hygiene or sanitation. We were afraid of cholera. With strict surveillance, we prevented an outbreak.

"It was like a nightmare, not sleeping due to bombing. I was afraid, no safe place in Gaza. Even the hospitals, UNRWA, health centers, we were not protected. When we go out, we left our children not protected, we do not know, anything can happen. People came from the shelters to the health center. They needed psychological support, many of the Ministry of Health hospitals were closed; they were threatened. Two health centers in Beit Hanoun, [the IDF] bombed the center, we lost eleven staff members in UNRWA and many injured and many hundreds lost their houses during the war and they were displaced to relatives or to school and they still come to health center to serve their people."

Focusing on her own family, Dr. Ghada continues, "The children have had three wars and continuous instability. The first of the war, my children were afraid of every sound, by the end they were no problem, they were fed up. Nothing we can do, waiting, expecting everything, praying all the time, afraid when parents left for work. The most difficult in life this war, all these innocent people killed without any reason. [We tried to] take care of each other. It's a joke, frustration, depression, not a big difference between us and the other people. You don't know if you will wake up the next day or lose your family members. I went to shelters and saw people who lost their family members. I met an eight-year-old child and he is sole survivor from Shejaria. He was smiling, too shocked. He was injured. We have a lot of them, 1,500 orphans after this war. They need a lot of care." Dr. Ibrahim adds that his own house was partially destroyed when his neighbor's house, three meters away, was bombed. He lived for fifty days in his mother-in-law's house.

Dr. Ghada resumes her commentary. "No one care about those innocent people, even the international community. Israeli claim they are democracy and they kill innocent people. What about the international community? We had massive destruction, many people lost all of their family and houses. It was the most difficult war since 1948; worse than Nakba, more aggressive, more violent, more inhumane. During the war, half a million displaced from their homes, three hundred thousand in UNRWA schools. . . . So the nightmare of the war itself and those people now under our responsibility. Two nightmares."

She concludes, "No one expected the war would last so long. My son is twelve years old. He was following news on the mobile, reports every cease-fire. I was trying not to be depressed in front of them. No one cared about that kid. There was a bombing next to us, near our building. We were so afraid. A family neighbor was hit, the family of his best friend. He was crying, first time I saw him [cry]."

Ghada feels indignant about the international complacency when it comes to Gaza. "We know Hamas and Israel, I will not talk about them. But what about the international community? They were just waiting and doing nothing. You must not forget what happened in Gaza, but there is no money for reconstruction. And in the news, maybe another war in the summer.

"We need people like you to make their voice higher. We are isolated from all the world, even from Palestine. We have a lot of disappointed stories, millions. It would be a disaster without UNRWA. We educate 250,000 students; we are free at health care and drugs, good quality of care with dignity."

The interview ends, and as we drive to a field office in Jabalia, I notice a kind of reckless apathy. Pedestrians walk right up to moving cars, people seem totally fearless, cars challenge each other inches apart, traffic rules are kind of optional. I wonder if there comes a point where there is no fear left and death seems fatalistically just one smart bomb or one screech of the brakes away. I repeatedly hear some variant of the feeling that death may be fast or slow, but either way, in Gaza, it is coming soon.

Passport Toilet Paper

March 24, 2015

There is a photo in my Boston home of a juicy-looking orange hanging from a tree. The fruit is pierced by a large screw, a brutal metaphor for the reality that is Gaza and one of many powerful photos and paintings by Mohammed Musallam, a forty-one-year-old artist born in Gaza. We are driving north, past Jabalia to his home in Beit Lahiya, fifteen kilometers from Israel. He and his brothers have rented an apartment distant from the border. It is where the family flees in times of war, and last year was crammed with fifty people. We turn down a dirt road. His home faces a large empty lot, once home to houses destroyed in a previous war. In 2014 his next-door neighbor was bombed and killed; another lost his legs. In 2008, the IDF came into Mohammed's house and stayed for ten days, destroying things, cutting up his paintings. He shows us a canvas that still has the footprint of an Israeli boot. This is what's been referred to as "the most moral army in the world."

We enter Mohammed's high-walled gate into a Garden of Eden filled with irony and political satire; a meat grinder is part of a planter with a row of cacti and succulents. A mishmash of found objects, mostly dolls and children's toys, creates a collage that is at once a tribute to childhood and to its destruction. The air is filled with the perfume of jasmine, grapes, and figs are growing magically in the midst of desolation, and a collection of lively chickens cluck in a large coop. Mohammed is both passionate and impish, outraged at the world around him, filled with a passion for social and political commentary. He has made a candle holder out of a tear gas canister, and a chandelier whose bulbs are replaced by candles. In 2008, the Israelis cut all the electrical cables in his neighborhood, and since then things have been pretty dicey. The local electrical station was bombed in 2014. On average, he has electricity three to six hours per day and has gone for thirty days without electricity. He could use a generator, but fuel is too expensive. He took a photograph of a toilet—the toilet paper beside it is made of a roll of Palestinian passports.

His children range in age from three to twelve; the five-year-old insists on sleeping with her parents, and the kids have had issues with bed-wetting, a classic PTSD symptom. He remarks, "War is terrible when you have children." He studied in Nablus and Cairo and is three months from his PhD, but unable to get the critical permit to return to Egypt. He paints and teaches fine arts at Al Aqsa University. He struggles to get permits to do exhibits in Europe.

Mohammed's mother lives on the second floor, his family lives on the third, and he has a studio on the ground floor where we sit. His wife has an Algerian passport but chooses to stay. She adds, "It has become normal. I find beauty, happiness, family; there is no choice. This is not courage." We nibble a sweet fruit combo and enjoy his lively children. The youngest has a devilish personality and keeps her parents busy. As we explore the wild jumble of found objects and striking paintings, Mohammed says, "We are normal, we are people . . . we are a small country; we have to live together; there is no choice." He has a gallows sense of humor: "six hours of gas, six hours of electricity, 60 percent of our salaries; six days, every two months, the border is open." Six is their lucky number. He worries about how "Israel feeds hate, creating militants. I am an artist. I don't want to fight." He finds in his art both the intense paradoxes and the beauty around him. It is a terrible shame that he has to struggle to share his talent, his humor, and his passion with a world that desperately needs more men just like him.[8]

What Do You Say to a Mother Who Has Lost Everything? Jump into the Sky.

March 25, 2015

Today I return to the Aisha Association for Woman and Child Protection to learn more about the impact of war on women and their families. I am joined by a social worker, a translator, and six tough, outspoken, defeated women who are engaged in a group therapy/sharing session.

Afaf Abu Ajwa is from Shejaia and says that "before the aggression I was very happy." She has seven sons—three attending a university, one working as a teacher, one an engineer, and one in high school. The seventh son is dead. She talks about the bombing and her vulnerable family. "I faced death every day, but where do I go? Every place I will go suffers from the same problem I suffer from."

She gives an account of a particularly brutal day in July 2014. "On the black Sunday, it was not a night, it was a suffering from Israeli occupation when they hit our houses, kill our children. At about 7:00 p.m., Yehud bombs hit the house continuously like the rain," she says. (She uses the words "Yehud" (Jew) and "Israeli" interchangeably; I do not blame her. In her world they are synonymous.) "And they . . . burn the house and light up the street. It was Ramadan and I put *iftar* [the Ramadan meal after sunset] on the table . . ." Bombs hit her house, but she didn't know what to do. The Red Crescent refused to rescue her family because the Israelis would not permit the ambulance passage.

"If we stay in our house we will die, and if we leave our house we will also die." She fled to a neighbor and witnessed a wild scene of explosions, destruction, and screaming. There was no safe place, thirty people were in one room, houses were crashing down on other inhabitants—"Yehud becomes crazy." When glass fell on a newborn, the grandfather grabbed the baby and started to run in the street. He was killed and the baby was injured. Eighty people in her neighborhood died.

As the memories of that time explode into the room, Afaf is getting more angry and outraged, her voice rising with a fierce sense of fury and hopelessness. With bombs all around, her husband was ready to leave, but there were no ambulances, no Red Crescent, "There was no hope to live; the streets were crowded with women and children." Her husband asked her to shout to people, urging them to go out with them. "It was like '48 Nakba." Women fled without their hijabs, many were in pajamas. Blood was everywhere. She injured her foot running toward an UNRWA school for shelter, but once she arrived she realized she had lost one of her sons. She ran back to Shejaia, but this time the place was totally different. "There were no humanity, people dead in the streets, like Sabra and Shatila." She saw disembodied hands, bodies without heads, a dead woman clutching her dead child, eight women crushed under a house, their faces frozen in fright. The bombs were dropping; she found her son dead. Afaf suffered from extreme shock. "I start to ask God to take revenge of who is the reason for what happened. No humanity—in five years, three aggressions. Where are men's and women's rights, Palestinian rights?"

She now lives in an impossibly difficult, crowded UNRWA shelter and shares what it's like to have to live there: "We don't have a house, and mice walk on our bodies, in our clothes. We have no work, no life. Our children were totally frightened. They stopped playing; they just play Israeli occupation and Arab. What can we say? How do you think if we do not have job or house or water, from where can we get money for rent, clothes, or to eat? We want to leave now, give us our rights. We don't want food or clothes, we just want our rights. . . . Israel didn't fight just one people; they fight humanity. It is our right to struggle for our land. I ask the world to stand with us because Palestine is for us. And the right of return is our right and we have to achieve it soon."

Afaf's sister, Samar Abu Ajwa, who is now living in a tent, says that everyone has a different story. She and her husband lived in one room and saved for fifteen years, borrowing the final fifteen thousand dinars they needed to buy their own house. After one year, war came and the house was destroyed. She weeps as she recounts the fear, the rage. "My house is near the border with Yehud, I can see Israeli jeeps. . . . My neighbor was in a car with his family and the bomb hit them; the car totally burned with the people inside it." After fleeing to her parent's house, she returned to Shejaia, searching for her home. "When I arrived at Shejaia, there was no Shejaia. There were no people, no houses, no trees, nothing but blood all around. . . . My little child asked me about his toys, I don't know what to tell him. He said that he want to die—he is three years old. He asked me when I die, don't cry please."

Another sister of Afaf's, Etaf Farahat, is also from Shejaia. She and thirty relatives left her house when it was too difficult to stay. She describes bombs exploding everywhere, damaging her home. No food, no water, people sick with diabetes, fifteen crying children—"death all around." They fled carrying the eighty-year-old grandmother, running as bombs fell. They saw blasts all over, people lying in the street, limbs missing. They walked over bodies and blood. They couldn't see each other. "Can't see, just hear bombs and shouting of people," she says. They saw the Red Crescent ambulances, but couldn't reach them. The bombs killed the driver and his injured patients.

By the time they arrived at the school-turned-shelter, they were wearing bedclothes and pajamas, and some women had improvised hijabs and skirts. "We do not have money. We have no food. We didn't eat for Ramadan. We found thousands in the UNRWA shelters, injured and dead. Some people looking for their children; they were dead." She joined fifty people sleeping in the garden of Shifa Hospital, looking for injured relatives. Her voice has an insistent, steady rhythm recounting the mounting disasters. Her sisters look increasingly saddened and weary. Forty-seven of her relatives lost their homes. She is living in the UNRWA shelter in Tal Al Hawa, fifteen relatives in one room, surviving on canned food and rice. She has two sons studying at the university level and four others in lower-level schools; her husband is not working. "We want to leave the shelter but we don't know where to go, and people who leave the shelter, they give them rent for one month." She asks us how to find money for rent and how to get her children to school. "We just want to live; no more wars. We just want to live like countries around the world."

Zahra Ereif's husband, Mohammed, died in the war (he also was the son of another woman at the table named Fatma). With a child sleeping in her arms, she begins to speak and is quickly crying. She has a degree in journalism and was living in Shejaia with her five children. Her husband went out to their farm to find the body of a dead friend and then he and his father were hit and killed. "They took me to the hospital and I went to the fridge to take his body. I was shocked. My children start to ask, 'Where is my father? Where is my grandfather?' After July 12, bombs hit around them, my child ask, 'Why the aggression happened? What we did? Why they took our father and grandfather?'"

As things worsened, they were evacuated by ambulance and the house was partially destroyed. She recounts what happened next during a cease-fire: "I went back to the house. . . . My child used to say, 'Where is our dad?' When we went back to our home, they ask about their toys and about their rooms, if their father will come to take them, 'When will we see Grandfather?' *Alhamdulillah*. They were totally frightened by what happened to them. Ever since we tell our child what happened, my little daughter didn't understand father had died, until now; she think that he is traveling. My son thinks his father is in paradise with grandfather; he is in heaven and they are just suffering from their loss. My little daughter, four months, when she is grown the first word she will speak is, 'Where is Baba?' "

Zahra has repaired her house and is living with her children. "Who will look after my child? Many questions, no answers . . . I lost everything in my life. God give me patience."

Shadia Al Sabagh was living in a rental apartment at the beginning of the war; the owner of the house was wanted by the IDF. Rocket attacks drove the family to her relatives. "I went to live with my sister's house. Once I was walking with my child, no one in the street; bombs were all around." She was a victim of domestic violence and left for the Al Set Soura Shelter. "After two weeks my father-in-law came to the shelter, hit me, and I leave the shelter with my child. My husband hit me and broke my arm. He treat me badly. My mother asked me to go back to my husband." Shadia is now in an UNRWA shelter, and "the bathrooms are dirty . . . I don't know where to go. I buy poisons to kill myself many times, my child become bad in school, no longer get high marks. My husband takes drugs and beats me always."

Fatma Erief, the older woman at the table, talks about losing both her son and husband in the war. Her face is lined and weary and she weeps in great waves of pain. She was living in Shejaria. "Bombs all around, we were afraid to go to the bathroom. We were living in one room. We were totally frightened. . . . Many people died around my house." Her husband was killed after praying in a mosque and visiting his farm. "I go in the streets, didn't know what to do. People brought my husband and son, people making ululations. People take me in the ambulance. During the cease-fire, we went to our house; it was partly damaged." A heavy weariness pervades the room. Fatma talks about being alone, how the people she depends on have passed away, how she didn't take anything from anyone, that she doesn't deserve this fate. "Who will take care of all the children? Now they don't have anyone to take care of the family." She has twenty grandchildren, as well as a son who is unable to work due to the metal in his arm from an accident. She suffers from hypertension. "I ask God to let Arab countries help us." She wants her grandchildren to go to a university. "God give me life; our lives are totally damaged and meaningless." Three of her neighbors, older women, drank gas and committed suicide. "Death is better than this life."

There is quiet and as I absorb these stories, I worry that I have intruded into these wounded women's deepest traumas and I have nothing to offer. In fact, it is a country that claims to speak in my name, funded by my tax dollars, that has destroyed their families and their lives. My sense of utter inadequacy clings to my tongue as I look at their tear-stained faces, but I manage to offer my deepest sympathies and promise to tell their stories and bring Gaza home. I brace myself for some angry comments, demands for aid, anything, but suddenly the mood changes and the women are smiling, thanking me for coming, listening, embracing me as one of their own. It is almost more than I can bear. They will be back next week for more speaking bitterness—maybe some individual counseling, job training—and they thank Aisha for standing with them in their time of unbearable need.

Feeling pretty depleted, I return to Marna House and join some of the delegates for a drive to Beit Hanoun, the northernmost city tucked into the eastern shoulder of Gaza, just adjacent to the Israeli border. We drive through death-defying traffic, a constant game of playing chicken with folks who already feel they have nothing to lose. There is pavement and rocky dirt roads, multiple rotaries, mountains of rubbish, and donkeys trotting, carrying massive piles of grasses, flowers, and produce. We pass Salah al-Din Street, a route thousands of years old that once ran from Morocco to Turkey, industrial areas, a huge building storing bags of cement, sheep trundling across the road, a bombed-out juice factory, and massive bomb craters and piles of harvested rebar that is painstakingly straightened and reused. Everywhere Palestinians are living their lives, going to school, buying and selling in the markets, walking the streets, sweeping the dust. Mundane life goes on despite the post-apocalyptic surroundings. We continue to drive, passing one of the UNRWA schools being used as a shelter, clothes and rugs hanging from the balconies, the smell of unwashed bodies in the air. Twenty-nine of eighty-nine UNRWA schools are still being used as emergency housing.

We pull up to a massive scramble of crushed concrete jutting out at all angles, house after house crushed into deformed skeletons of a former life, hills of dirt and sand and toxic military waste, garbage. We park in front of that famous cat mural; a British graffiti artist, Banksy, painted an enormous kitten on a slab of vertical concrete—once a wall to something—a bullet hole in the cat's neck. He knew that people would repost a photo of a cute kitten a million more times than they would a photo of a hungry displaced Gazan child. We are soon surrounded by those very children—barefoot, dirty, ragged clothes, beautiful open faces, blank stares, borderline-terrible teeth—sullen teenage boys flirting with us uncovered Western women. An Arabian horse gallops across the horizon, donkeys graze in open fields, and a water tanker with a familiar jingle, "Für Elise," makes the rounds. There is no running water here. A horse trots by with a cart piled with fragments of concrete to recycle. Someone asks if I am Israeli. An older man, face dark and creased, with some kind of leg deformities, sits cross-legged on a mattress surrounded by some of his family. He is mostly toothless, but has a warm smile and a twinkle in his eye. He has two wives and forty-two children and grandchildren. A UN prefab "house" is tucked in the concrete rubble.

We are actually here to see an amazing group of eleven young men doing a form of gravity-defying acrobatics called Parkour. They mostly wear black sweatshirts with the logo PK GAZA: Gaza Parkour and Free Running. They dream of starting a school to teach their skills, of buying a video camera to record their feats, of entering Parkour contests all over Europe. For them, jumping off buildings, flipping backwards, forwards, twisting their supple bodies in various gravity-defying acts is actually a positive channeling of their enormous energy and macho aggression. When too much of a crowd interferes with the show—not much entertainment actually happens here—they insist we drive together to Shejaria, the devastated city that was described to me by the six women this morning.

I will not attempt to put into words the experience of walking into a nightmare, the massive amounts of concrete rubble, floors collapsed onto each other, bomb craters many stories deep in every direction. Young children clamber over this military jungle gym, living on the edge of serious injury and death. The Parkour troupe seems unfazed, and soon I am holding on to the powerful hands of various young men, hoisting my aching back and tired knees onto a ragged pile of rubble so that we all can have an excellent view of incredibly brave, athletic Gazans leaping across shattered roofs, tumbling and twisting through the air to precarious landings covered with rock fragments and jutting rebar. Their skill and energy is captivating, their hands are soon oozing blood. They explain that when they jump, they feel like birds, forgetting the war, exercising their powerful male power, connecting with Parkour groups all over the world.[9]

Photographs from Gaza,

March–April 2015

All photographs by Alice Rothchild unless otherwise noted

Erez checkpoint entering Gaza

Parkour Gaza acrobatic group in Beit Hanoun
Photo credit: Seema Jilani

Tour with Palestinian Medical Relief Society: Naheda

Children at Meera Kindergarten, Gaza City

Khan Younis

Khan Younis

*Bombed apartment
complex by the sea,
northern Gaza*

Children in Gaza City coming out of UNRWA school

Children's drawing from art therapy program at Deir al Balah Community Center

Deir al Balah Community Center, Gaza Community Mental Health Project, Dr. Amal Bashir

When Will It Be My Turn?

March 26–30, 2015

We continued our fact-finding tour of the apocalyptic devastation created in Gaza by the massive Israeli invasion in the summer of 2014. We experienced firsthand the high levels of environmental and human trauma, visiting villages, bombed areas, the polluted Mediterranean coast, and UN and mental health agencies that struggled to provide food, health care, and shelter to Gaza's 1.8 million inhabitants, a large proportion of whom still lacked any form of sheltered domestic space. I interviewed patients and staff at two more centers for women's and children's empowerment, examining the intersections among war, patriarchy, poverty, trauma, and an increasingly conservative culture that challenged the well-being and stability of women and their families. At the same time, I experienced the immense resiliency and warmth that are a hallmark of Palestinian society and survival.

During this war, as 90 to 97 percent of Israelis stood with Netanyahu, synagogues in Boston (embraced by local politicians and spurred by widespread news coverage) held huge Stand with Israel rallies featuring cheering nationalistic crowds waving blue-and-white Israeli flags. Meanwhile, human rights activists and young, religious Jews demanded an end to the Israeli operation, an end to the United States' complicity in Israel's atrocities, and an acknowledgment of the disproportionate destruction and casualties on the Palestinian side. In Boston, New York, Chicago, Washington, DC, these activists were met with strident heckling. As had happened during Israel's 2008–9 and 2012 attacks on Gaza, the power brokers of the mainstream Jewish community refused to hold Israel and its sugar daddy, the United States, accountable for the use of disproportionate military force and the repeated violations of international law.[1] In my home city of Boston, I joined the Workmen's Circle, a hundred-year-old center for progressive secular Jews, as we held a two-hour interfaith vigil and read the names of every Jew, Muslim, and Christian killed in the war. Except for Jewish Voice for Peace and a newly formed organization, If Not Now, no other Jewish organization in the city challenged the Israeli aggression and cost to Palestinians.[2]

According to UN figures, approximately 2,251 Palestinians died in the 2014 war, of whom 1,462 were civilians, including 551 children and 299 women. The Israelis killed numbered seventy-three, including sixty-seven soldiers (five by friendly fire)[3] and six civilians, including one child.[4]

The unwillingness of most members of the US political elite to remove the customary blinders when it came to Israeli atrocities was particularly egregious when Diane Sawyer of ABC News reported on scenes of great destruction that she said were in Israel but actually were in Gaza. Although she later apologized for the error, it shed light on the fact that there were no scenes of catastrophic devastation in Israel to support the narrative of the deadly Hamas rockets. Hamas's missiles clearly unnerved and threatened Israelis as they raced to their bomb shelters, but they did not cause massive wreckage and dismembered corpses in the streets, as Israel's massive bombs and missiles did in Gaza.[5] In Israel, Channel Two television's lead anchor, Yonit Levi, reported quite fully on the level of casualties and destruction in Gaza; she was met with demands for her removal from thousands of people on Facebook and threatening text messages that ultimately required the involvement of the police.[6]

In firing a total of 4,881 rockets and 1,753 mortars into Sderot and Tel Aviv, Palestinian militants violated international law and possibly committed war crimes because of the indiscriminate risk to civilians. Nonetheless, the level of uncontrolled ferocity by the Israeli military was not only revealed by confessions of soldiers who had served,[7] but also by the numbers of Palestinian civilians dead; the twelve thousand injured; the thirty-six ambulances, seventeen of thirty-two hospitals, and fifty of ninety-seven primary health centers damaged or destroyed; the six thousand airstrikes launched; the fifty thousand tank and artillery shells fired; and the twenty thousand tons of explosives dropped on a strip of land six by twenty-six miles in fifty-one days.[8] Then there are the stories of the survivors, which you will read shortly, and the reports by a host of international, Israeli, and Palestinian organizations including the Palestinian Centre for Human Rights,[9] Al Mezan Center for Human Rights,[10] and Al-Haq.[11] In June 2015, the Palestinian Authority submitted evidence to The Hague alleging that Israel had violated international law and committed war crimes.[12] The court opened an investigation in November of that year, probing war crimes by both Hamas and Israel.

Despite the damning numbers, the IDF repeatedly claimed that they made extensive efforts to avoid civilian casualties. One such practice was the "knock on the roof," in which they shot a small missile at a building, notifying its occupants thirty seconds or more before a massive bombing. Numerous testimonies emerged that the knock was not always used, was not always heard, sometimes caused extensive damage and injury, did not give people enough time to flee, and did not always predict a subsequent attack. As with the cell phone alerts and the pamphlets dropped to warn families to leave, many civilians found such warnings did not matter anyway because there was no safe place to flee to. The Israeli military bombed people running in the streets, at funerals, during cease-fires, and in UN safe houses, schools, and hospitals.

Israeli soldiers, in testimonies collected by the organization Breaking the Silence, confirmed a pattern of lenient rules of engagement, permissive open fire policies, revenge killings, loss of protocols, and failure to distinguish combatants from civilians. As one staff sergeant reported, "Whether it posed a threat or not wasn't a question, and that makes sense to me. If you shoot someone in Gaza it's cool, no big deal. First of all, because it's Gaza, and second, because that's warfare. That, too, was made clear to us—they told us, 'Don't be afraid to shoot,' and they made it clear that there were no uninvolved civilians."[13]

"The instructions are to shoot right away," a first sergeant in an IDF engineering unit told Ben Hattem of *The Nation*. "Whoever you spot—be they armed or unarmed, no matter what. The instructions are very clear. Any person you run into, that you see with your eyes—shoot to kill. It's an explicit instruction."[14] Breaking the Silence researched every allegation, and the report's accuracy remained unchallenged though largely unwelcome. The organization has come under scathing attacks from all levels of Israeli society, from the defense minister to the police.[15] PHR-I organized its own fact-finding mission of medical experts and found similar practices and instances of heavy, indiscriminate, and unpredictable bombing in civilian neighborhoods, along with disrespect for medical neutrality.[16] When critics protest that Hamas fighters hid among the civilian population, remember that Gaza is one of the most densely populated areas in the world and the IDF has its headquarters, the Defense Ministry and General Staff base, in a densely populated civilian area in Tel Aviv.[17]

Like many military institutions, the IDF has a strict military censorship program and a long history of investigating itself, during which it has rarely found any wrongdoing. Think about this the next time someone extols "the most moral army in the world" or invites you to a fundraiser for Friends of the IDF, a US tax-exempt organization. Three months after the war ended, a Hollywood Gala raised $33 million for the Friends. The *Times of Israel* reported, "Notable donations made at the event included $10 million from Oracle co-founder Larry Ellison, $5 million from philanthropists Sheldon and Miriam Adelson, $5.2 million from Maurice and Paul Marciano of Guess Jeans, $3.6 million from Cheryl and Haim Saban and $2 million from New York Giants president Steve Tisch."[18] Anyone have problems with this?

Here is more of what I saw during our March 2015 trip to Gaza.

Sunshine, Sand, and Post-assault Dysphoria

March 26, 2015

In another universe, a drive along the coast of the Mediterranean would occur in one of those vacation dreams filled with fresh fish and relaxing moments baking in the sun. But that is not the case here, as we are driving to Khan Yunis, a city in the south of Gaza, and in particular to the eastern villages of Serij and Abueteama, which bear the unique tragedy of leaning up against the Israeli border. Nahed, a high-energy, well-spoken administrator from Palestinian Medical Relief Society (PMRS), the largest medical NGO in Palestine, is taking us on a tour of their facilities and the realities in the postwar south.

First we pass the "harbor," where rows of colorful boats are docked, victims of the crippling siege and the shrinking safety zone for fisherman. The Sea Road takes us from the central region to the south, past the glorious blue water beckoning deceptively to our right. The Mediterranean is at once a liberating vision of life beyond Gaza, of potential escape and freedom, and an impenetrable wall of the prison.

The road is only intermittently paved. We see the now-familiar houses turned to rubble, massive bomb craters, the empty, aspirational Four Seasons Resort. A river of raw sewage drains into the sea just adjacent to a solitary swimmer. The smell is sickening. We speed past empty farmland, a colorful resort designed for the staff of the Open University, where classes are offered online for Gazans who must continue to work as they pursue a degree. Young boys are running around in the front of the UNRWA Al Balah Elementary School; we pass shacks made of corrugated metal and plastic, hanging rugs, boat skeletons, wandering sheep, scattered silent "resorts"—post-assault dysphoria.

Nahed is narrating and answering our questions, and I ask her something I have asked over and over again in Gaza. I cannot find anyone who admits to supporting Hamas, and in fact most Gazans I talk to are disgusted with Fatah as well as Hamas (not to mention Netanyahu, Obama—the list is long). I rarely see green Hamas flags or the occasional political poster. Her response is brilliant in its simplicity and honesty. Many Gazans, particularly after the 2014 assault, do not support Hamas leadership and are deeply unhappy with the current disastrous state of affairs in terms of the basic functioning of society. But if someone were a Hamas supporter, they would not tell me they were for the following obvious reasons: First, as I am already aware, the Gaza Strip is crawling with collaborators, vulnerable young men recruited during stints in Israeli jails or in exchange for permits for medical care in Israel. Second, and more importantly, if someone's opinion or photo inadvertently ends up on Facebook or elsewhere on social media, or in a blog post or some mainstream news story, they would be vulnerable to a targeted assassination by Israeli forces. So this silence is a matter of survival.

The driver turns away from the sea into the Israeli Beach Camp, site of a former Jewish settlement evacuated during a moment of national hand-wringing by the Israelis in 2005. A cluster of modern apartment buildings comes into view, a gift from the Arab Emirates to Palestinians from border areas who lost their homes in 2008. The residents moved in last year after six years of homelessness. The ride is becoming more of a jolting chiropractic experience as we pass rows of plastic greenhouses, olive groves. It is starting to get really Mediterranean hot as we arrive at the PMRS mobile clinic, a small three-room wooden house adjacent to a similar structure set up for social support sessions. Funded by Oxfam and Belgium, a team composed of one general practitioner, two nurses, one lab tech, and a social worker come twice a month to see a collection of patients. They provide very basic primary care (there is no exam room), treating acute, mostly non-serious illnesses (lots of skin disease and scabies, hypertension) and offering education (how to evacuate in case of attack, basic first aid procedures). The services are all free. The clients, mostly women with resigned looks on their faces, wait with their children.

Walking just outside the clinic, we can see the no-go "buffer zone" and nearby Israeli border. A spy balloon hangs over us, and in the moonscape of houses toppled over, shattered into massive fragments, the detritus of life's minutia emerges from the rubble: pink snowsuit, comb, electrical socket, sewing machine. The birds are singing their little hearts out, and thistles and cheerful yellow flowers spread themselves over the landscape, the life-force in action.

The rutted roads take us to Alzana, the sight of even more destruction, which at this point is a really challenging concept. There are families living in tents, people who were once farmers and fishermen and businessmen. A sea of white hijabs emerges as high school girls in dark blue uniforms and backpacks walk home, faces smiling, laughing. PMRS has a much more comprehensive clinic here and provides the only health care for the area. I have seen these clean, competent clinics before, staffed with dedicated doctors, nurses, and health workers, making a lot out of "much less than adequate." The most striking thing I observe is a series of bullet holes that riddle the walls in the hallway and the exam room. Israeli soldiers had shot through the front door and through a window, hitting a dangerous otoscope and nearby scale.

We talk with a warmhearted OB-GYN; she is seeing more anemia, malnutrition, miscarriages, and premature labor. There is a problem with early marriage, involving spouses of the fifteen-year-old variety and not much contracepting. Women prefer birth control pills, but that does require a functioning pharmacy supply system and the ability to get to said functioning pharmacy. The clinic offers rehabilitation and has seen a marked increase in cases since the war, compounded by the consequences of the siege such as late care and lack of follow-up due to financial and physical barriers. PMRS is taking care of 250 patients in the eastern village of Khan Yunis. Most of the victims are women and children, and most of the disabilities are amputations of arms or legs due to war trauma. In past years, Palestinian society looked upon disabled people as shameful and hid them from sight, but PMRS has done a powerful campaign to integrate people with disabilities into normal society and to provide physical therapy and occupational therapy.

The challenges are immense: electricity is erratic and only available for a few hours per day. What happens to people who depend on electrical beds, electric wheelchairs, elevators, medications that require refrigeration? Some folks are so poor they cannot afford transportation to the clinic, or so uneducated and overstretched by large families that PMRS makes many home visits, bringing the care to them.

We are back wandering in the rubble and ruins of this neighborhood and Nahed takes us to a community of donated caravans from Australia. There are rows of numbered trailers, à la Katrina, and we are invited to tour the "homes." Each trailer seems to have three "rooms" and a bathroom; we see floor-to-ceiling piles of mattresses, tiny neat kitchens, and evidence that families are crowded together in small spaces. One frustrated man gestures to his "house." As we enter, the stench of sewage is overpowering. The toilet has overflowed, and a thin layer of dirty water coats the bathroom and has spread into the kitchen. (People eat and sleep on the floor.) It seems that when the caravans were built there was no real sewer system put in place, and whatever hole in the ground the sewage drains into is now full and backing up into the home. Suddenly a man, perhaps in his thirties, starts yelling at us. He is angry that another group of (white) international humanitarian types is touring this encampment and that we have not brought any solutions, money, plans to fix the disaster. Nahed apologizes to us as we rapidly retreat, but it is clear to me that he should be angry, that I am from the country that funded and supported this catastrophe, that perhaps I should be ashamed to come and stare and take photographs, and that I can offer him nothing but my voice, which is far from useful when your kitchen smells like a cesspool.

We head off to the PMRS clinic in Jabalia Camp, which is much better equipped, with multiple programs and specialties. There we interview a dedicated physician who trained in Russia and Belgium and is committed to providing care to a desperately poor population battered by Israeli assaults, poverty, chronic disease, and the internal dysfunctions of Palestinian (non)governance. The health care system is a disconnected patchwork of institutions and providers including Ministry of Health branches, NGOs, UNRWA units, and private clinics. They do not communicate with each other and patients often bounce between systems. He notes that the situation "is not too bad. If there were no external players we would be okay." He also adds that under the current "situation," he cannot ask his patients to stop smoking, "It is better to smoke than to hit your child."

This Could Be My Reality

March 27, 2015

The day started with a shock—as we eat breakfast at the hotel, we are notified that today daylight savings time has begun in Gaza and I have already lost an hour. This doesn't seem quite fair, but the delegates hustle into the van befuddled and sort of ready. Marwan Diab, our guide and organizer extraordinaire from the Gaza Community Mental Health Program, is wearing a running suit. It is Friday, which is actually a solemn day of rest, as Sunday is supposed to be in the United States, and we are going on a tour of the Strip with Hamada Al Bayar, a wonderfully warm, sensitive, intelligent man from the UN Office for the Coordination of Humanitarian Affairs on their day "off."

Hamada explains that OCHA focuses on the humanitarian impact of the occupation, siege, and military operations, with an emphasis on civilians. They just released a report yesterday.[19] Basically, last year was the worst year ever for the population of the Gaza Strip on every measure of humanitarian impact. We are heading north toward Beit Lahiya as he explains that there are so many sad numbers from the assault in 2014, but, echoing a group of young writers I met yesterday, he says, "We are not numbers; behind each number is a big sad story." We drive through Beach Camp, which started as a refugee camp in 1948. It was there the United Nations set up tents for refugees who were pushed toward the sea as they fled the Jewish forces, and the rest, as they say, is history.

As we drive along the Mediterranean, I see occasional fisherman in tiny boats with nets piled high, clusters of shacks on the beach; children play draped over the metal fencing along the road, competing with drying laundry and airing mattresses. Young men enjoy the water with their horses, some riding them into the water, some splashing them or just having a good time.

Across the street many buildings are splattered with bullet holes or crumpled under the impact of heavy bombing. Hamada reports that at this time, 80 percent of Gazans are aid-dependent in some way; the Israelis have succeeded in destroying the economy—industry, farming, fishing, exports, and the list goes on. If there were no UN agencies, the well-being of the population would be even more catastrophic with starvation, no education or health care. Up ahead, a mosque proudly dominates the view. Two tall minarets pierce the sky. The construction was reportedly financed by a Gazan economist who built his fortune on the tunnel economy; some wonder if funding the mosque was part act of devotion and part money-laundering scheme.

Hamada explains that the $6 billion of international aid pledged to Gaza has not been delivered for a host of factors:

1. Gaza is too unstable for many host countries.
2. Host countries feel that anything that gets rebuilt will just be destroyed by Israeli military actions.
3. Donor fatigue.
4. Israel controls the entry of all construction materials as well as everything else and is being very restrictive with what is allowed entry.
5. Hamas and Fatah are in conflict and are not able to function as a unified government; in fact they sometimes undercut each other.

We want to clarify what has happened to hundreds of tunnels between Gaza and Egypt, and Gaza and Israel? In 2013, there were five thousand truckloads of merchandise from Egypt monthly. Now there are none, destroyed by Israel's military actions and Egypt's tactics of flooding, gassing, and bombing them. All of the tunnels to Israel were used for military purposes and are now gone as well. While the tunnel system created a huge corruptive black market, it was also critical to the Gaza economy and for the fuel to run the now-crippled power plant.

Following the war, one hundred thousand Gazans remain homeless or in shelters or with host families. Thirty percent live in their damaged homes with makeshift arrangements using plastic, wood, and cloth, often at great physical risk. Since the war, housing needs have doubled because 130,000 homes are either partially or completely destroyed. The Gaza Reconstruction Mechanism, brokered by the United Nations, has given support for families who have minimal damage to their homes. Hamada reflects on the difficulties of surviving the war with an intact home versus surviving it with a pile of rubble. It was all so arbitrary. The lucky ones find it difficult to have something when their neighbors do not, yet it is also not possible for the owner of the intact home to offer space and support to all the family and friends in need. It is a strange dynamic, a unique kind of Palestinian survivor's guilt.

We arrive in Beit Lahiya, three kilometers from the Israeli border. We can see three smokestacks of the Israeli coal-burning power plant and the wall that snakes along the border. Beit Lahiya was once a rich agricultural area that has become too dangerous to farm due to its proximity to Israel and vulnerability to repeated incursions. In 2000, Jewish settlers and Israeli forces uprooted extensive citrus, guava, and mango groves for their "security needs," so farmers at this point plant low crops that require minimal care, and they risk their lives to harvest the bounty. Israeli forces have repeatedly bulldozed crops shortly before harvest in one of those over-the-top acts of cruelty. Hamada remarks, "Life has come to death." Three kids sit blankly in a large tire in a field. Families sit and smoke on the ground in front of their corrugated metal shacks; the area is largely abandoned because it is too dangerous to stay. The Israelis have extended the no-go zone along the border from 300 meters to 1.5 kilometers from the fence, and they shoot to kill. Farmers often come to work their fields with their wives and children, hoping their presence will decrease their risk of being a fatal target as they harvest their string beans, strawberries, and potatoes. That does not always work. Even if they successfully complete the harvest, there is minimal to no export business, once again thanks to Israeli restrictions. We hear repeated bursts of gunfire. Israeli soldiers are making their presence known, and some unfortunate farmer or young man is getting the message. The farmers rely on a water aquifer that has been seriously depleted, and unless changes are made, Hamada states matter-of-factly, by 2016 there will be no water.

Returning to the critical topic of water, Hamada reviews the stark reality and adds that the ninety million liters of sewage pouring into the sea daily is not only polluting the sea, but wasting vast quantities of grey water that could be used for irrigation. There are desalination plants, but the water infrastructure has largely been destroyed by Israeli military action, and the water filters are reportedly less than optimal, resulting in high levels of sodium nitrates and chlorides (far in excess of World Health Organization standards) that leach the calcium out of the bones of young children who are now at risk for osteoporosis.[20]

The United States has worked to remove the unexploded ordnance (with their "Made in the USA" labels), working through the United Nations, UN Development Program, USAID, and the Palestinian Authority. Since the blockade in 2007, no one gives directly to Hamas except Arab countries like Qatar. Discussing this issue leads us into a conversation about Hamas that catches me by surprise. Hamada says that Hamas has made it clear in diplomatic-speak that it would accept a long-term *hudna* (truce) with Israel and recognize Israel's existence with a return to the borders of 1967, which is the basis for all the "peace talks" that have dribbled along since 1993. This has fallen on deaf ears because Israeli leaders have no intention of returning to '67 borders. But more importantly, what if Hamas came out and recognized Israel, denounced violence (which they have done in the past through general actions and cease-fires, with minimal international acknowledgment), and recognized other agreements? What if they behaved like Fatah? What has that gotten Fatah but a massive and growing settler movement, a heavily occupied and militarized West Bank, and minimal access to Jerusalem? So this is actually not about Palestinian recognition of Israeli rights, but rather Israeli recognition of Palestinian rights.

We continue our tour and stop by a massive apartment complex along the sea. How can I possibly describe this? The buildings are five to six stories high, consisting partly of skeletal walls and floors, and partly of heavily damaged apartments, vast segments collapsed at odd angles. A wheelchair on one of the floors is visible, the walls blown out, and people are living in whatever they can salvage. Laundry hangs from fragmented windows; there is a cluster of shacks in the storage facilities at the base of the building. Donkeys and goats wander in and out of the rubble. It is an unspeakable monument to human suffering. Four young men come to talk with us and they are smiling, exuding warmth, arms draped across each other's shoulders. One speaks English. Another has seven children and they are living in a storage area. They want us to know what happened to them and to tell the world their story. Then one of them says he has a joke: "We want to forget our pain. If we had alcohol we could forget." This seems uproariously funny and they all crack up . . . apparently it seems more likely to live through an unimaginable war and survive in something close to hell than to drink a bottle of forbidden booze.

Donkeys, laboriously pulling carts piled high with chucks of concrete, pass us over and over again. Hamada explains that it takes ten hours to crack up enough of the larger fragments of cement walls and rubble to fill a donkey cart. The men get fifteen shekels for their efforts and these are taken to a facility where the smaller chunks are crushed and used to create (poor quality) bricks, filling the air with a fine dust that penetrates your lungs and turns the bushes grey.

We pass the massively leveled mosque in Beit Hanoun as Hamada explains that during the war, he moved his family to his office at OCHA. "I made my office my home." Later he reveals that every time he comes back to these areas, "I feel like it's the first time. My body reacts the same, the same stress, the same pain. It takes me four to five hours to get over it. It is really hard to be a humanitarian worker and having family and seeing this. That could be *my* reality; when will it be my turn?"

There is a news flash: our guide has learned that daylight savings time does not start until tomorrow, which means I receive the gift of an extra hour today (it does not take much to please me). However, there is some metaphorical message here—even in Gaza life is so upside down that there is a debate as to the actual time of day.

Hamada explains that there is no functional Hamas government. I think of the bombed-out Ministry of Finance, the yearlong stretch of no Hamas salaries, the three-month stretch of no salaries for PA officials, doctors, teachers. It is hard to get anything done if no one is paid and there is no concrete. Officially, there is a government of national consensus in Ramallah but no working system here. The Hamas social movement fills in the gap, providing substantial social services and systems—medical, educational, and humanitarian—and *that* actually constitutes part of the shredded safety net around these parts.

We drive through a busy market in Shejaia filled with the pungent smells of fried food. Red-yellow-blue-green umbrellas that look like circus tops provide cover over rows of fruit stalls. At the barber shop, the barber is applying his straightedge razor to a customer. The *souk* is bursting with cheap clothes and products, and there is a background cacophony of loud honking from the kamikaze drivers and motorcyclists.

In order to head south, we change to a Greyhound-style bus operated by Abu Olba for Tours and Travel, an ironic name for a company in a place where you really cannot go anywhere. There is a feeble air conditioner, which our group greatly appreciates. We head off to Rafah. The bus is filled with staff from GCMHP, some of their families, and us. Marwan is playing emcee. We all introduce ourselves, sing songs from our respective traditions, munch on hummus sandwiches and Thai spiced nuts, relax, and have a good time, which is welcome after such unrelenting sorrow.

But we cannot exactly leave the reality. Driving along the coast, we pass by Wadi Gaza, where the river of sewage flows into the sea and the stench is unbearable, the crowded Nuseirat Camp on our left, and into Khan Yunis. We pass through the site of the former Jewish settlement Gush Katif, which occupied one-third of the Gaza waterfront until 2005, and see the remaining rows of orchards and palm trees.

We tour through Rafah close to the Egyptian border where over five hundred tunnels were destroyed in 2014. We can see Egyptian military towers and a mosque. Prior to the closure of the tunnels, this area had a huge infrastructure, industrial areas, and a spirited tunnel trade ranging from cars and cows to weapons. Now there is rubble and open space. We meet a young man who states: "We are not terrorists, we are ordinary people." One hundred twenty-six people were killed in the Rafah Market on a single day during the bombing in 2014. (This is not a competition, but just for some perspective: thirty-five Israelis have been killed by Qassam rockets in the past fifteen years.)

As we are shepherded between large mounds of sand, concrete blocks, fractured machines, little boys squatting and jumping, makeshift buildings leaning askew, several men with Kalashnikovs agree to take us to the tunnel area. "No pictures, no pictures." they say. We follow them down a sandy road and there, at the base of a gully, is a four-foot-wide hole in the ground. We peer into the darkness and understand that this hole continues hundreds of feet beyond the nearby Egyptian border. We are then escorted to a white cloth–covered building that is adjacent to what appears to be a generator and other machinery. The cloth is opened and inside is an upper platform with couches and chairs—a regular living room—and below that is an earthy tunnel extending into the darkness. We can stand upright in the eerie shadows. This is much bigger than the first tunnel. The "door" is closed, and a row of electrical lights flashes on. The tunnel descends at a steep angle and then reaches a flatter area; there appears to be some kind of furrow on the ground, perhaps for a wheel or some apparatus that could be used to drag the smuggled items into Gaza. One of the men explains that this tunnel is used for cigarette smuggling.

Our final stop is the beach, a lovely area next to a restaurant featuring clusters of plastic chairs and tables on the sand, families enjoying their Friday off, soccer games, laughter. There is something so calming about the smooth sand between my toes and walking along the water, despite my fears of E. coli. Only young men are swimming. I talk to a young Gazan woman who says she comes to swim at 5:00 a.m. because she does not like to swim wearing her hijab. I walk back and forth, enjoy some actual physical movement, climb up some concrete blocks to check out a small port area, rows of small blue, yellow, and red motor boats, nets piled high or drying in the sun. On the beach there are a couple of supercilious camels available for photos and rides. The male species here seem confused about how to relate to a cluster of uncovered Western women mingling with really gorgeous Palestinians who have mastered that subtle technique of looking extremely modest and extremely alluring all at once. The women do take off their high heels to walk in the sand, *subhanallah* (Glory to Allah). But soon they are too uncomfortable with all the stares and camel ride offers, and it is really time to go home.

Sisterhood Is Still Powerful

March 28, 2015

The Al Bureij refugee camp is located in the Middle Governorate of Gaza on the eastern side of the main north/south road, Salah al-Din, which used to run from Khan Yunis to Erez checkpoint. The Al Nuseirat camp lies on the western side. I am on my way to visit the Al Zahraa Society for Women and Child Development, located in Al Bureij. In the last few years, three women's organizations have spun off from GCMHP: Aisha, in the north-central part of the Strip; Al Zahraa, in the middle; and Rafah Wefaq, in the south.

Another delegate and I meet with the administrative leadership of Al Zahraa, and then I meet with a group of women who are receiving psychosocial support, crafts, and vocational training. (Although I have permission to write this essay, I am also reporting on sensitive issues and wish to protect the women's privacy; therefore, I've chosen to not use their names and to blend their stories.) We sit in a small office, sipping Arabic coffee and talking over the loud din of voices in the central areas of the building where women are working and chatting energetically.

The main role of Al Zahraa is to support women who have suffered from violence—physical, sexual, cultural, etc.—and to provide empowerment, awareness, consultation, individual and group psychosocial support, and links to organizations in society for further support and intervention. If a woman suffers from a psychological disorder, she may receive treatment with organizations like the GCMHP or the Palestinian Center for Dispute and Conflict Resolution. Some vulnerable women get vocational instruction (like training in hairstyling) so they can get a job. Al Zahraa also coordinates with education ministries and universities for the women to go to school.

The programs that this tiny agency manages are impressive. Female high school students are offered sessions on gender awareness and sexual education, and hospital staff are trained to be sensitive to gender-based violence, starting with the basic principles: Ask the woman who had violent acts committed against her what has happened and offer her personal and legal supports, consultation, and referrals. The women on the staff have worked on changing discriminatory laws around the custody of children, where women tend to lose that battle. They have also worked on the issue of honor killings. I am told that men receive a reduced sentence in prison for a gender-based crime or social wrongdoing, but if a woman is guilty of a sexual transgression, she is killed, often by her male relatives. Women are disadvantaged both culturally and politically.

During the 2014 assault, the Al Bureij refugee camp, which is on the border with Israel, was evacuated after shooting started. As usual, the most vulnerable were people, like those at Al Bureij, living in marginalized areas on the borders. Al Zahraa coordinates with other organizations to offer humanitarian and financial support for displaced people who are in UNRWA shelters. They also partner with Islamic Relief, in coordination with civil society committees.

While working as a women-centered department under the umbrella of GCMHP, the staff realized that women were very focused on their children, so the work was expanded to include women's and children's development and psychosocial support. As part of that expansion, Al Zahraa aligned with Mercy Corps, a large organization that partners with USAID. I learn that a number of organizations refuse USAID support because they have to sign an agreement that they are against "terrorism," but in their refusal, they are aware that the definition of "terrorism" only includes militant Palestinians and not Israeli aggressors and human rights violators.

I am very curious about the power dynamics and cultural norms of marriage in this society. I am told that there are legal rights for married women, but that it gets complicated quickly. For instance, a married woman is given a dowry by her husband that is supposed to function as a kind of insurance policy for the woman if the marriage goes bad. In reality, an unscrupulous husband sometimes takes the dowry money and leaves the woman with nothing, or a woman technically is supposed to inherit money from her family, but the family finds ways to deprive her of this right. It is a case of culture, sexism, and economics clashing with law. When an abused woman goes to the police, she often finds herself in even greater danger. In many cases, she is at risk for punishment by her family, including a forced divorce, and police mainly consider "the cultural dimensions" often advising her to go to the *mukhtar*, the head of her husband's family or clan. Some *mukhtars* are fair to women, others not. There are also male religious mediators or committees serving that function, and again, some are fairer than others.

But I want to know, what is it like really for women here? One spunky woman recounts getting her bachelor's degree and two graduate degrees, which included completing some of her studies abroad. Once she had passed the "old" age of thirty, the age issue, combined with the indirect familial and financial pressures on her, compelled her to marry someone she now realizes was unsuitable. Yet despite her professional career and tremendous accomplishments, she is still not even permitted to decide where her children go to school because her unemployed husband has the final word in the family. She knows other women who were more directly forced to marry. After the honking cars and massive plastic floral arrangements and nuptial feast for a ridiculously large number of relatives, they were faced with huge and immediate pressures to have children, preferably of the male variety.

Another woman whose husband is unemployed explains that if you are the only one earning a living, that actually gives you power in the marriage, although it may not give you happiness. Husbands often pressure their wives to stop working or feel stigmatized and shamed if the male in the family is unable to find employment or suffering from posttraumatic stress disorder from war trauma or torture in prisons.

I ask, "Can a woman be raped in marriage?" and receive the quick reply, "Yes. According to religion you cannot say no. The problem is that people misinterpret religion, but religion also says be gentle with the woman." So people read the Quran and Hadiths selectively. Women also get that "you have got to be available" message and thus fear that if they do not have relations in accordance with their husbands' demands, the men will find second wives who are more cooperative.

I push a little further and learn that incest and rape do happen, but because the culture is conservative and religious, it is actually rare. Nonetheless, with the tightening noose around Gaza, and with it the increasing unemployment and humiliation of the male population, women bear the brunt of male rage. Not surprisingly, honor killings in the West Bank and Gaza are up: eight in 2011, twelve in 2012, twenty-eight in 2013. I have also heard that honor killings are often reported as suicides or accidents, so I suspect these numbers are falsely low. Al Bureij Camp had the highest number of honor killings after the Hamas takeover, and in one particularly gruesome, tragic story, a man in the camp who had accused his daughter of sexual activity cut off her head and took it to the police station. In some cases, some people may also kill their daughters to prevent them from claiming their inheritance. In response to these heinous practices, UNDP has set up legal aid for women, opening the door for women to obtain legal consultation and representation, and creating a massive awareness campaign.

Then I have heard all of these "Wicked Witch of the West" type stories about mean, controlling mothers-in-law and new wives coming to live with their husbands' families and being emotionally tortured. I am told that this was more of a problem in the past and that now, when a majority of men get married, they live in an external apartment to get some physical distance from the nuclear family. Certain cultural norms, however, still can create challenges, as one woman confides that "there is conflict forever between the wife and mother-in-law. If a woman is working and will not pay the mother-in-law, then the grandmother won't take care of grandchildren, or if there is a large extended family and a flock of daughters-in-law, there is discrimination between them and this creates conflict; always there is conflict."

I have noticed that there are very dark-skinned Palestinians in Gaza (in Jerusalem and Jericho as well), and I wonder how racism fits into the cultural scheme. There is a term "slave Palestinian," referring to people who came from places like Sudan to work in the region hundreds of years ago and who have faced many decades of the usual varieties of racism. "If you want to know about discrimination, ask a Black person," comments the executive director. They are teased in school because of their hair, with children sometimes throwing stones at them, but there is no retribution because lighter-skinned Arabs don't interfere with cases of harassment by children. Although it is contrary to Islamic tenets, white families will shun Black families, and they will refuse to attend the wedding of their son or daughter if he or she marries a Black Palestinian. In another quirky scenario involving race, sometimes Palestinian men who have been educated abroad will bring home their lovely white Romanian/Russian/name-your-country wife, which then reduces the pool of available white men, so more white women will marry Black Palestinian men, leaving the Black women once again at the bottom of the selection pool.

Even today, one woman reported the difficulties her child is having as a darker-skinned student at a high-quality school that is almost all "white." Ninety-nine percent of Black Gazans are poor. They very rarely receive a quality education; they rarely find employment. They cannot afford to go to privileged or superior schools, and teachers discriminate against these students who often drop out. The majority who stay in school are girls, and often work as cleaning women for well-off Gazans to pay for their education.

They are more motivated to go to school but rarely can afford to attend the higher-level universities and struggle to find good jobs.

I also learn of families that are suffering from the toll of domestic violence, with children and wives suffering beatings (often by fathers who are frequently unemployed, depressed, humiliated, traumatized by war and prison, and all of the things that stimulate male rage but do not excuse it). Wives are trapped in conservative families, afraid to report their husbands to the police. Essentially, entire families are desperately in need of a thousand interventions.

I am feeling a bit run over by now, and it is time to change rooms and meet with a group of thirty women who want to talk about . . . well, I *am* a gynecologist. The *niqabs* are flipped up and we start the conversation. The women are obviously yearning for knowledge and thrilled that this doctor lady has just dropped in (along with a copy of *Our Bodies, Ourselves* in Arabic). We launch into an utterly frank conversation about everything anyone wants to know about the female body. So we talk shamelessly about vaginas, yeast, ovaries, sex, birth control, overactive bladders, back pain, how to make male babies, menses. For me, it's a totally fun exchange of questions and information, woman to woman, and these women in my experience are just like women everywhere.

I am also invited into the crafts room to admire the embroidery and other crafts, and soon I am handing over my shekels to become the happy owner of a very unusual shawl with lovely sandy brown fading to orange embroidery with bits of sparkle. Everyone is beaming and laughing and they give me a fifteen-inch tall, enormous golden pineapple made from folded bits of paper. We are all sharing our expertise, celebrating our connections and our powerful sisterhood.

When I first entered the center I noticed that there was a (training) hair salon, and I mention I would be honored to pay it a visit. The woman who clearly knows what she is doing takes my hand, and soon I am sitting in a chair with a cluster of women all offering advice, showing me wedding photos of themselves without their hijabs, hair movie-star coiffed, and I wonder, what have I gotten my unfashionable self into? It seems the technique at this salon is to clip up bunches of hair in little balls, take a hot dryer, and pull each ball dry until every strand of hair is very straight. There are responses of general admiration and a most universal conversation between me and the dark-skinned woman who bemoans her kinky curls, the irritations from hair relaxers, the cost of extensions and braids.

I am informed that I really need to take care of my split ends! The beauty transformation is completed and met with major appreciation, then one woman suggests I really should do something about my unfashionably bushy eyebrows and faint mustache. I am not about to go that route and suggest, how about makeup? Soon my fashionistas are consulting about what color powder, creams, eye shadow, and who knows what else are needed to complete my makeover. I go for the full effect: eyeliner, lashes, kohl. This is all met with that kind of connectedness and pleasure in the simple joys of sharing and laughter that make sisterhood so powerful.

A roller coaster day: I take my new face and light heart and join two women to make a home visit at the camp, where we will meet a woman who lost her husband in the 2014 assault. We walk into a moderately bare apartment she is renting; I sit on one of the mattresses along the wall. There is a poster of her husband—in it he is wearing a green headband, Kalashnikov ready. She is forty years old, has five daughters and two sons, has experienced three miscarriages, and is still recovering from a C-section. A young teenage girl brings in glasses of Coke; a dumpling of a baby in yellow flannel squawks to be nursed.

When I ask the woman if she would she feel comfortable talking about what happened, her mood changes dramatically. The tears are flowing as her voice becomes very soft and whispery; she seems disconnected. I wonder if she is having a flashback. She says she tried to watch a video of her husband and felt suffocated. Her grief is fresh and powerful. She also has seven children and no means of support.

"I was very close to him, when I feel worried he always assured me he will be okay. He was my cousin . . . I don't sleep until he comes home." When he died, for four days she was unconscious and in shock. Her face contorts in pain. "Although I know he went to paradise, I miss him all the time; sometimes I talk to his picture."

They were married when she was eighteen, he was twenty-seven. He was a farmer living on the eastern border of the Gaza Strip in Johr El Deek. When the shooting started, they were forced to leave their home, but later returned. As she speaks, her face is trancelike. "After he finished [eating], he went out. I said, 'Stay.' He told me he will hurry. 'Don't be late.' He hesitated twice and said, 'I will not be late.'"

She says that day the electricity was out, "as usual. Suddenly I heard a loud voice and saw a big flash of light, I found myself beating my head. The missile went directly to my husband's head. The accident was eight meters from home." At first she thought he was injured, but later learned he had died. The Israelis would not let the ambulance evacuate him. It took them a day to find his missing arm. Her home was demolished twenty days later.

"I cannot describe; the children could not stop crying. I told them he went to paradise. He was everything for us. They carried me to say good-bye to him. I was shivering. They were in a hurry to bring him to the cemetery because shooting all the time, it was very fast. They took me to the hospital and then took me to my family home." She was then told to evacuate that home, at which point she joined her cousins in Al Bureij Camp. There was another shooting, and she fled to the Deir al-Balah Governorate.

She reports that during the war, the IDF called people in Al Bureij on their mobile phones and told them to leave for the town of Deir al-Balah. She heard a loudspeaker warning and a direct call to her son advising him to flee. She also remembers that planes flew over Gaza and dropped leaflets with the names of kill targets. After her husband died, many of those leaflets featured the names of those already killed. She remembers seeing her husband's name on that fatal list.

So If You Killed My Child, You Think You Are Strong?
March 29, 2015

One of the greatest casualties of the ongoing war on Gaza is childhood. The GCMHP Deir al-Balah Community Center has an extraordinary exhibit of postwar children's drawings that gives us a window into the loss of the sense of order and safety that comes when one of our smart bombs lands in your bedroom.

The drawings are breathtakingly painful and simple in their honesty, a child's view of a world gone horribly wrong. The other delegates and I stare, take photos, and are pulled into each drawing; some of us are weeping, some of us are just floating in a sea of societal trauma.

Children chained together in front of a soldier with a whip; families lined up in front of a tank; bombers shooting birds out of the sky; pools of blood, lots of blood, bloody circles on people's chests, over and over again; fallen trees; smiling men in kaffiyehs waving the Palestinian flag; a dove enfolding in its wings a circle of wounded people facing a missile; Apache helicopters dropping bombs; walls crumbling and crumbling, neatly drawn piles of rubble; fires, ambulances, more dead people; doves the color of the Palestinian flag dripping with blood; naval boats bombing from the sea, tanks, planes, and soldiers with prominent Stars of David; curled barbed wire; missiles landing on vegetable trucks; more tanks and planes and fire and people lying on the ground bleeding; four boys on a beach flying kites with bombs falling on their heads; a heart with the word "Gaza" written across it in black, white, green, and red, split in half, pierced by two missiles bearing the Star of David.

Not only am I appalled by what these children have witnessed, but I am sickened that in this world, the Star of David is synonymous with military violence, grief, and death.

Dr. Amal Bashir, the only female psychiatrist in Gaza, explains that the children are six to fourteen years of age and were involved in art therapy workshops to address their posttraumatic stress disorders after the war. She reminds us that behind every picture is a story, and she is filled with these stories. Most of the children lived along the border towns. One of their fathers picked up a stranger looking for a ride, and both were killed, a targeted assassination that hit the wrong guy. He had two daughters and is also related to Amal. One of the children wrote on his drawing: "So if you killed my child, you think you are strong?" Another: "I want to live in peace." Amal admits, "I cried a lot during their therapy." In another child's family, the grandmother was killed. Then the family was running in the street to the UNRWA school, rockets and bombs flying; when the child's sister and a chicken were killed in front of her, the child did not respond. "They get used to the situation. A six-year-old witnessed three wars—this is normal. They get strength." I wonder if they are also totally emotionally frozen.

She has treated thirty-four children, and twenty-four are cured of their symptoms. She has a collection of three hundred pictures and we sit with her piles of paper. She tells us of Mohammed. When she first met him he was an angry eleven-year-old engaging in aggressive gun play, doing poorly in school. He drew a child in bed, in black shirt and jeans, with blood on his chest. He told her, "This is Ahmad [his friend]. I saw him on TV, he was killed." After more therapy, Amal reports that now Mohammed is cured, doing well at school and playing with toys at the last session. "The stories are overwhelming. They taught me how to be strong." A very gentle soul, Amal started as a general practitioner but was drawn to psychiatry and decided to train at GCMHP. She feels that she is called to work with children on these challenging issues. She meditates to reduce stress and feels that "in Gaza there are a lot of opportunities to support people. . . . I let go of hate. I have so much love. I love Moses. I love Jewish."

Our taxi next brings us to the Nawa for Culture and Arts Association, a phenomenal children's art and culture program led by Reema Abu Jabir, a visionary force of nature. Created after the 2014 war, the center supports and empowers young Palestinians using traditional culture and arts, focusing on families in the Deir al-Balah area. They provide psychosocial support, early childhood education, and professional development for educators, and they seek to preserve Palestinian culture. A family pays ten shekels a year to enroll their child in the center.

As we enter, there is an immediate sense of calm. They chose wall colors that "mimic a mother's tummy," and each room is bordered in a traditional red pattern evoking palm trees. We visit the children's library (there are no electronic or internet connections for the children per Reema's instructions), and look at drawings and poetry and sayings tacked on a bulletin board. They include a drawing of the famous political cartoon character, Handala, also known as Bitter Fruit, with his back to the world, and the words of Darwish—"You can't find the sun in a closed room,"—and other poets. At the end of each of the morning and evening shifts, the children gather in a closing circle, chanting phrases like, "There is no sun under the sun except the light of our hearts," "We need little things in life and if we are happy we will be kings," and "You and me, he and she, we will all be different. There is a difference between him and her though our lives are beautiful like flowers." The children perform increasingly complex rhythmic movements to the chanting and singing, fully engaging their minds, hearts, and bodies.

There is a lively art room; Reema explains that the children also participate in much of the construction with recycled wood. Reema believes in setting clear rules (these are children whose lives have been turned upside down) and providing a clean, safe space, yet at the same time this center is a home, so she is addressed as "Auntie." We wonder how she keeps her focus and her strength; so much has been accomplished in such a short time. She admits that she does get depressed and angry, and fights with her friends, shouting at them and then apologizing the next day. She goes to the sea to relax.

Reema's next dream project is turning the ruins of a Deir al-Balah site, a 1,700-year-old monastery with a mosque downstairs, into a garden and children's library. We drive to the ruin, which is in a very poor area, and she is obviously animated and planning for the future. The children have cleaned the ancient stones and arches, the Ministry of Tourism has signed an agreement, money for restoration is being collected, and she is in contact with UNESCO for the restoration. The major difficulty is the lack of cement in

Gaza, which made donors a bit hesitant. Reema says defiantly, "I am stubborn like a donkey; this is from my father's side." Because the building is a mosque *and* a monastery, it will help reflect the message of tolerance at the arts center. Reema complains that UNESCO has asked her to get the building materials for the restoration. "Don't ask me to get cement for Gaza!" And you just know that she will make this incredible project happen.[21]

We chat with the cab driver on our way back to the guesthouse. He says, "Welcome to Gaza! Take me in your suitcase to America!"

We Don't Hate You, We Just Don't Understand What You Are Thinking of Us
March 30, 2015

Another sunny day in Gaza, another ride along the beckoning Mediterranean, another trip where the smell of raw sewage permeates the car for miles. We are heading to El Wafa Rehabilitation Hospital. *El wafa* means "kindness or truthfulness," and by the end of the morning I wonder if there may actually be an undiagnosed Palestinian affliction: too much goodness.

We meet with Dr. Basman Alashi, engineer, manager, and now an extraordinary hospital director, and Dr. Ayman Badr, rehabilitation doctor and medical director who received a BA in Romania and a masters in Cairo, and who has finished his clinical exams for medical school but has been unable to finish his thesis as he has been trapped in Gaza without a permit. Moussa Abu Mostafa, a PhD student in occupational therapy and head of the rehabilitation team, joins us as well.

Dr. Basman speaks with a formal sincerity and heartfelt openness. He begins by talking about the facility here—the hospital, lab, physiotherapy department, occupational therapy department, and an elder section where folks with no family supports and the need for twenty-four-hour medical care can live out their days at no charge. There is an outreach program to homes in Rafah and Khan Yunis, and there are plans to open up other sites in other areas of Gaza. He says that 90 percent of the wounded are "needy, poor, cannot afford a shekel for a taxi, so they stay at home; they have pride and they are not going to ask [for help], so we ask them if it is okay to ask what they need."

But I want to know more about the war. El Wafa Hospital was repeatedly attacked and ultimately leveled. We look at photos before and after: an extensive modern medical facility reduced to a massive pile of rubble. Dr. Basman explains, "In the days before the war, they felt something was going to happen, there was tension in the building, so they prepared an emergency plan for each patient. Do they need to stay with us or can we train their families? So a few chose to go home, seventeen cannot leave, and then the war started."

The first day or two were okay. "Day three we were hit by artillery. The hospital stood one kilometer from the border on vacant land. We were hit in the middle of the night, no warning, just a direct hit to the hospital, to the fourth floor. We had men on that floor but we moved them to the first floor for safety, so we had no injuries. We thought it was a mistake. Israelis know it is a hospital. It is clearly marked.

"We just went through our daily activity as nothing happened, but the occasional bombing continued. Afternoon day three, another hit, larger than first four. At that time we went to Shifa Hospital for press release, talked in Arabic, English, French, Spanish, German, telling the world "this is unacceptable." We are protected under Geneva Convention, and so forth. Eight volunteers stayed with us as human shields. At night, I drove them to the hospital under fire. . . . I gave them free access inside the hospital so they can report any activities showing to the world what kind of patients we treat—unconscious, cannot move, cannot feel, some of them sleeping for year or three, coma for ten days.

"But we continued to use the media to express our concern that Israelis must not target the hospital. I asked Israelis if there is any evidence [of militant activity in the hospital]. The army released classified pictures saying this is El Wafa Hospital and a red dot saying this is launching missile. We looked at the 'hospital'; this is not the hospital, this is three to five kilometers away from us. We made another press release, showed evidence, showed how buildings are totally different, so Israelis are misled."

Dr. Basman recounts the subsequent emotional, painful details: multiple calls from the IDF; the onset of nighttime bombing; the frantic evacuation in the dark, when patients were carried out in bed sheets; the insufficient promises from the Red Cross; the Israeli refusal to protect ambulances from military targeting. The staff moved the patients to a small maternity clinic, Sahaba Clinic in the middle of Gaza City. "We were not able to take any equipment and medicine, just running to save our lives and our patients' lives. With the help of God we evacuated safely. The next day we need medicine, clothes, bumpers, sheets, etcetera. At that time I went to the hospital, which was a war zone at 10:00 a.m., to look. The damage and fire was still on, severe damage to every floor. We could stay no more than thirty minutes, drones flying over us, bombs everywhere." Responding to the loss of thirty years of investment and a high-quality, First World facility, local and international organizations sent beds, sheets, water, food, and medicines while the hospital staff struggled to care for their patients and rebuild their services.

When the war ended, the hospital moved to a home for the elderly in Zahar City. "This building was donated by a Palestinian doctor, El Alami, the land given by the government. . . . We shared with an elderly care home, now half hospital, half elderly care center." Despite the challenges of the crushing blockade, the hospital is supported by local Gazans as well as the World Health Organization, UNRWA, UNDP, Interpal, and Australian and Malaysian charities. Dr. Basman states that being charitable is part of being a Muslim. The staff is also extremely dedicated, although 20 percent lost their homes and two died. "One [staff member] was walking in the street, a man with three daughters. He stopped by the grocery store, bought figs. He was targeted by a drone, walking alone. Israeli did not distinguish from woman, man, child, resistance, young, or old. [Another staff member's] home was destroyed; she went to the UNRWA school [for shelter] and it was targeted. She was hit by shrapnel in her head; her brain was out, she was twenty-one years old, unmarried."

Their main concern now is service. "As Muslims, serving patients is first, serving us is second. . . . Many patients cannot come this far in our new facility—outpatient services too far, no transport—so we have to go to them, and it costs. Only in Rafah and Khan Yunis, the areas really devastated, some of them do not understand the extent of their injuries; very poor. They may not know how to treat them. Need to rehabilitate the soul itself, teach the wife and the family, show him the love. This is 50 percent of recovery."

Dr. Basman shifts his focus to the new facility. "The new building is U-shaped; the right side is the hospital, the left side is the elderly, the middle is management, so all separate. We still have a problem that our space is too small, so children and adults are mixed." The old hospital was very high-tech with a First World level of care and included a gym, swimming pool, hyperbaric oxygen treatment, videoconferencing. "We lost a lot. It is difficult that we lost all this, but we are all optimists and we look at the positive side of any events, because we are rehabilitation. . . . The hospital [was] destroyed completely. Thanks God we are all safe. We sent a message: 'We don't hate you, we just don't understand what you are thinking of us.' We are just human beings like anything else. We live on planet Earth. We all look alike. The Israeli response was the hospital was a terror site, like all other bombings. They justify everything."

We ask if there have been independent investigations. "Officially no, but media did extended investigation, eight independent foreigners with full access to the hospital. They have not reported anything. There is no justification to target children, hospitals. The only thing is to terrorize people to leave. So then the young boys out of school and working, the girl married too young; it is circle of devastation. If I don't give the father a chance to work, that means a problem in the family. But Gaza still survives. If Israeli came to the hospital for treatment, my glasses looking to him as a human being and to treat."

Dr. Basman feels the loss of many of the facilities, especially the hyperbaric center, the only one in Gaza. He says that it is harder now to find donors. Four months ago, the Islamic Bank in Saudi Arabia offered $4 million if the Israelis will agree not to target the hospital and Gaza will remain stable, so under those stipulations, no donation will be made. Larger organizations and governments are not donating, but individuals who "believe in the cause of Palestine" still are. "There are also financial restrictions on wire transfer, so bank calls [when] we have a wire. 'We need a contract. Where is [the wire transfer] coming from? What it is for?' We need to show purpose, restrictions from banks outside of Gaza. It has to go to a certain group that is not labeled as a 'terrorist.' We see this as a challenge. We don't have a choice: succeed or just die. We will continue.

"Another part of the tragedy, of the siege: killing the victim is part of the crime but also forbidding the victim to say we are victims and are human beings. This is a human feeling." This is the other face of the crime.

The tour of the hospital starts with an ambulance that was targeted by a drone bomb filled with nails. We see the entry holes in the back door and the exit holes in the front. They have not been able to replace the fractured glass, so the back and side windows are covered with cardboard sheets. The hospital's first floor has a large room for physical therapy equipment; the area is clean and orderly. The nursing stations and patient rooms are improvised but functional. Dr. Basman knows every patient and his or her story. He greets the conscious patients warmly. There is a lot of joking around, moments of tenderness, a profound sense of caring. The windows are open; a fresh breeze blows through the rooms and there is no antiseptic smell. Families cluster around beds. The patient who will always stay with me is a little boy, Hamad al Reify, with a high-level spinal cord injury and quadriplegia from a missile attack. When the electricity goes out, he has thirty minutes on his battery-run ventilator. They have no cardiac and respiratory monitors, so nurses sit near his bed monitoring him with their eyes and their hands. He has a tracheostomy but is able to communicate and has an unbearably winning smile. He jokes, he dreams; he was given some toys, but he sent them home for his sister. The staff clearly love him. If he is lucky, he will spend his life at El Wafa. The staff has not received a salary in the past six months.

Dr. Basman ends with a message to the world: "Gaza is fine. What you see from the outside, it looks devastated. But if you live among the Gazans, you won't leave. I choose not to return to America [where he lived for a number of years]. We are human. I am born here. You don't have a choice where you will be born, but I have a choice for who I am."

Too much goodness.

"Here death, there death, but let me do something useful for people"

March 30, 2015

Founded in 2010, the Wefaq Society for Women and Child Care seeks to achieve gender equality and improvement for vulnerable children through economic empowerment and psychosocial support in one of the most challenged areas of the Gaza Strip. We meet with the leadership and women involved with the organization over coffee as the electricity flickers off (there is no fuel for a generator) and the stories emerge in a warm, open, sisterly environment. It is extremely hard for the staff to work when there are no functioning computers let alone functioning civil government. The situation in the southern Gaza Strip is more difficult and more miserable than in many areas, but largely ignored by the media operating far away in Gaza City. Wefaq has its roots in GCMHP and is now independent. They have different departments for women, children, capacity-building, and media.

Because this discussion is both professional and intensely personal, I will give the first speaker the fictional name Narmeen. She explains Wefaq's mission: "We are here also implementing our project, which is psychosocial empowerment, improvement for women and livelihood, a fund for small projects for women who have been bombed and [suffered] domestic violence, and widows, divorced, and abandoned. Some of the women lost their livelihood during the war, left their sheep and goats, and escaped to the center of Rafah during the war. Black Week started on Friday; Israeli forces were trying to occupy the east area [of the Gaza Strip]; they destroyed everything, animals, trees, and more, but the media doesn't reflect the picture. Bombing and destruction followed us to the seashore by F-16s. After the people leave the area they try to come back during a cease-fire, but they were bombed during the cease-fire, intentionally. Many died, injured, houses destroyed. They went to UNRWA shelters or to relatives. They found, after the cease-fire, their sheep and goats were dead, the only hospital in Rafah, Abu Youssef al-Najjar Hospital, was bombed.[22] The injured couldn't reach the hospital; it was the center of occupation, so they died, so more casualties. This aggression to the hospital made big problem, bodies in the field, in the street. To treat the injuries, they moved the injured to the private Kuwaiti Hospital, very small and very limited, no equipments. The main hospital was closed, surrounded by soldiers."

The women we are meeting with explain that when the war ended, Wefaq set up an emergency response with shelters and psychosocial programs, delivering clothes and food. Many people in the eastern area lost everything. Even during the cease-fire the Israelis attacked. "There is no safe place in Rafah at that moment. I was at home waiting for bombs. I live next to al-Shoka; my neighbor's house was hit with a very big rocket. . . . All Gaza like this." The women left children at home to help people in shelters. "My children say to me, 'Mom, we are afraid. Why should you leave us?' I say, 'Here death, there death, but let me do something useful for people.' I was crossing Al Nasser Street while bombing happened ten meters away; another time in Khan Yunis, less than ten meters and the house, they bombed." I ask, what about fear? "We are used to it; also, it was Ramadan." Everyone was fasting and praying.

Another woman I will call Ameer explains that nighttime was the most terrifying, "At night you don't know when the bombing will begin." The psychological pressures caused enormous anxiety and an increase in violence, harassment, sexual threats. "The shelter has two to three WCs; how the female teenager can go to the WC? They didn't have water to wash. They tried to get to relatives' houses to shower. Women delivered in the shelters, no medical care. There is no nurses or doctors. There is no professional equipment. Female doctors were refusing to come to the shelters because they were saying, 'My children, how could I leave my children?'"

A mother delivered in the shelter under miserable, dirty conditions, and Wefaq found her a nearby home and clothes for the baby. Additionally,

UNRWA ran out of supports, so volunteers opened restaurants and prepared meals, even during Ramadan. Narmeen explains, "We don't like to talk about war; opens too many wounds, everyone is hurt. Whatever you saw on TV it is an instant, not as much as actual situation. The Syam family, they bombed their house. They escaped to the street but there is no place secure, thirteen killed in the street by bomb, plus injured; random killing of entire family, kids, babies; many innocent families." At this point, all the women are crying. The women in charge and the women being served share the same experiences, the same pain, the same Gazan tears.

Everyone regains their composure, gathering their fragile psyches together, and the interview continues. Wefaq is focused on legal projects with UNDP to protect female victims of war, psychosocial support, job training, instruction in IT, and young women's leadership as well as preparation for job opportunities in community-based organizations and the private sector. The guiding philosophy is that working women are empowered and challenge traditional ideas. "There is acceptance that the female get out and work. Life is very difficult so women will continue working after marriage." They also work with children, and Narmeen lists a number of supportive activities they provide: "drawing, play psychodrama, individual counseling, group counseling, home and school visits, family interventions to fix the relationship between the mother and children." They also consider domestic violence to be "a huge problem. Wefaq works on this, in alliance, for combat violence against women."

They educate women about their rights, about the different types of violence they may face, and do home visits for intervention and awareness, including male partners in those meetings. "We do community mediation, separate from the mosque, with *mukhtars*, leaders, university teachers, social workers, political activists. It is part of changing the tradition of the society toward women's issues. We encourage women to get independent economically—sewing and handicrafts—especially those who are exposed to violence. Who has the income, has the power of decisions, this is a very effective intervention.

"We still have problem of early marriage, thirteen and up, especially in a bad economy." This is an uphill struggle due to the devastated economy, which encourages desperate families to rid themselves of the economic burden of their daughters and the trend of families marrying them off, often to older men with multiple wives. There have also been issues of brothers-in-law killing their dead brother's wives because they seek money or their inheritance. Ameer explains that Wefaq is working on implementing legal protections and supporting victims of what she terms "legal violence," where women suffer from unfair inheritance, alimony, and divorce practice. Ameer notes, "It is a tyrant's law. I have three children, divorced, have not seen them for two days." At this point, her eyes well with tears. "One and a half years ago they were taken by force; I raised them for ten years. I still have my daughter, but they may take her in a few months." More tears. This is a woman who is very aware of her rights and her children's legal rights, she has the support of Wefaq, she has a lawyer, and still her husband has married another woman and has custody of two of their three children. "We are struggling for these rights. All of us are victims, suffering from one aspect or another, all women in Gaza." Another woman is tapping her fingers on the desk and says, "We should lead the victim's movements to help ourselves and to help others." Yet another says bitterly, "The Hamas government, of course they took my children."

I learn that the center teaches health workshops and in my role as a gynecologist, I share a resource from my own community, an Arabic version of *Our Bodies, Ourselves*. This leads to a fascinating conversation about the political role of women in society. Narmeen comments, "Why shouldn't we as females make a committee for worldwide peace? We will make a strategic plan to stop war. Arab women should work on this idea. The biggest losers are the females."

The electricity is still off, and I discover that along with general challenges like this one, some of the more religious women also fast on Mondays and Thursdays. Narmeen continues, "We get up to wash or iron at 5:00 a.m. if there is electricity, maybe twelve hours per day, on and off. Once I come to work, electricity in my house is on; when I back to home, no electricity. We don't feel we are alive. We have tyrant husbands. They do not cook, wash clothes; they are not ready to help. How will that change here, how to change the culture and attitude? But it is very difficult, women's work is first step. We work hard on gender issue to change the ideas of people and attitude; [for men there is] a little change, but they are moody in this aspect, not convinced." I joke that I have heard that men always have PMS and one woman responds, "PMS on a forty-year cycle! May Allah take all men!" The laughter is slightly relief-inducing, slightly conspiratorial, slightly guilty.

I ask, how do you help your sons to be different from their fathers? Narmeen answers, "We are strong women. I suffered with my older son, but he start to be older and wiser and he is at university. His father's behavior made a weakness in his personality, but I intervened. I support him to get stronger and more responsible. Now he is a responsible person. We established this organization for ourselves and our daughters . . . and our sons."

The staff meets daily with ten to twelve women. I sense today is their turn to share with me. "Occupation . . . make us stronger, still hard. But I have had enough of getting stronger! I am satisfied, fed up. We wish you stand by us; this session is good even if it opened wounds. This society helps vulnerable women." They discuss the social benefits of university-trained women who are able to contribute to the family economy, but also the injustice of being "used for their money. We are cheating ourselves to say okay with this. We are sometimes part of the problem; domestic awareness is a complicated matter." They talk about the difficulties and jealousies between mothers-in-law, wives, husbands. "It is normal for a mother to be jealous of the new bride; sometimes the new wife of the son herself practice violence against the mother-in-law. This is all related to awareness and balance, raising the awareness about domestic violence, gender awareness, how to develop attitudes toward gender and campaigns and community mediation. None of this is taught in schools. I want to do this, amongst teachers and families, secondary schools, girls and boys; there are a lot of ideas for services, but no funds. We don't even have electricity. I am very tired. I have many ideas to develop the community but no funds."

Talk turns to politics and the relationships between the United States and Israel, the differences between the government and the people (like me or these women) who may not always agree with their governments. "America is the father or mother of Israel, but we do not talk about the people. We share with you in your agonies, it is all about the government." Then I am asked a most amazing question, though I understand the rationale behind it: "Is Congress all Jewish?" I launch into a description of the Israel Lobby, the American Israel Public Affairs Committee, and Christian Zionists, and a quick rundown on how the US political system works—so much to explain in such a short time.

8

Only the Pigeons Fly Free
March 31–April 6, 2015

This book concludes with a firsthand experience I had with Islamophobia at the Erez checkpoint and the contradictions I encountered at a kibbutz's "From Holocaust to Revival" museum. Then, on the West Bank, I returned to a center for torture victims and their families, conducting in-depth interviews with two psychiatrists and home visits to a nearby refugee camp. I delved into the landscape and contradictions buried in the realities of the occupied West Bank during a visit to the Palestinian village of Sarta, where building a home and an exquisite garden in the shadow of a Jewish settlement is a mark of both resilience and resistance. The final blog post here described my departure from Israel/Palestine through Ben Gurion Airport, where racial profiling and Israeli *hasbara* (propaganda, public relations) left their final tortured and outrageous impressions.

The kinds of questions I have raised in these essays highlight Israel's image-making and advertising, and how that messaging only pretends to deal with issues of substance and is in fact strategically designed to obscure the real problems and realities. Historically, whether you worked for the American Israel Public Affairs Committee (AIPAC) or prayed in a Christian Zionist mega-church or lay on a beach in Netanya, Israel was the "home" of the "Jewish people" who have "returned" after "thousands of years of exile and persecution," and anyone with the temerity to challenge this framing is an "anti-Semite" who denies Israel's "legitimacy" as the Jewish State. What is needed, the mainstream discourse proposes, is condemnation of critics, speech control, and better messaging. But how did these key concepts, trigger words, and tactics seize such control over the historical and political discourse?

In the early twentieth century, political Zionism itself was hotly debated within Jewish communities in Europe and the United States, but the movement to create a Jewish state in historic Palestine triumphed over the vision of secular binationalists like Martin Buber and Yehuda Magnes. In 1948, with the world reeling from the horrors of the Nazi Holocaust, and despite serious qualms from many in the US government, the UN Partition Plan was adopted and history unfolded from there. In the 1950s, Israel became the US bulwark against communism as Arab nationalism functioned as a proxy for the Soviet Union. Israel then served as the US foot in the door to the oil-rich countries of the Middle East, and after the 1967 war, there was a gradual move toward making uncritical support for Israel the cornerstone of being a good Jew, and critical discourse within the community narrowed. Christian Zionists then embraced the idea that all Jews should "return" in order to hasten the apocalypse, and began pouring millions of dollars into the settler movement. Over time, Israel's military/industrial/security complex became closely intertwined with its counterpart in the United States, and the size and power of both of them grew exponentially greater after 9/11 in the global "war on terror."

In the late 1940s and 1950s, US Zionists aggressively criticized anyone who questioned the wisdom of the Partition Plan or Jewish nationalism, or mentioned Palestinian suffering, intimidating politicians and the media with the accusation of anti-Semitism. In 1974 the Anti-Defamation League (ADL) officially defined the "new anti-Semitism" as criticism of Israel, and ten years later AIPAC issued a college guide exposing a supposed anti-Israel campaign on campus and urging students to ignore criticism of Israeli policy on the grounds that it was dangerous to Israel. This led to a new McCarthyism within Jewish institutions in which those who did not tow the line were silenced and demonized.

In a 2010 conference in Herzliya, Israelis brought together US and Israeli government officials, academics, public relations specialists, and lobbying groups to shape the framing of the Israeli narrative through (questionable) opinion research and aggressive strategic communications, pink-washing, green-washing, blue-washing, etc. This meeting developed a detailed plan to marginalize those who supported BDS, a one-state solution, or the right of return of Palestinian refugees; to develop a positive "Israeli brand"; and to attack those who "delegitimize Israel." These efforts were followed by the enactment of a law in the Israeli Knesset that made the call for BDS a civil wrong. Other major steps were the creation of "front groups" that worked in public diplomacy and diaspora and cultural affairs; the commitment of millions of dollars by US Jewish federations to fight "delegitimization" through a policy of naming and shaming; and the creation of an Israeli military intelligence unit devoted to monitoring groups that supported BDS or accused Israel of war crimes.

In academia, Hillel International, the umbrella organization for Hillel chapters, which are centers for Jewish life on campus, issued "red lines" for discourse within Hillel. In 2014, in conjunction with the Simon Wiesenthal Center, Hillel International developed a new campus surveillance phone app to monitor and report professors accused of anti-Semitism. The Anti-Defamation League (ADL) also created a blacklist of groups that drew parallels between Ferguson and Palestine and the similar abusive police practices toward people of color. US police were meanwhile increasingly receiving training from Israeli military and security forces, which confused the role of a civilian police force with that of an occupying army. In the United States, at the local and national level there have been a variety of anti-boycott bills percolating through legislative bodies, equating the boycott campaign with anti-Semitism.

Israeli *hasbara* is dishonest because no amount of incredible dance, theater, music, computer technology, gorgeous desert hikes, or spiritual moments can erase the facts of occupation, siege, and discrimination. And I would argue it is not only deceitful but also dangerous. In the United States, academics and students are under attack, and elected officials (who are not known for their courage) are cowed by AIPAC and the real fear of election loss should they cross the Israel Lobby. Well-funded groups like Stand with Israel, Campus Watch, CAMERA, the David Project, Israel Action Network, AMCHA Initiative, the Institute for Jewish and Community Research, and Christian Zionist groups work through selective and literal interpretations of the Bible, intimidation, one-sided history, and racist fear-mongering. AMCHA has warned that Muslim and pro-Palestinian student organizations and professors who support BDS or are critical of Israeli policy are sources of anti-Semitism[1] and, along with the ADL, has compiled lists of professors deemed dangerous to Israel. Even the US State Department has a special category of "anti-Semitism relative to Israel" that lists among its defining criteria demonizing, using a double standard, and delegitimizing Israel's "right to exist," language taken directly from AIPAC and other Israeli *hasbara* organizations.[2]

Ultimately, this cannot be good for the State of Israel, which grows more nationalistic, intolerant, and politically rightwing. Israel is increasingly at odds with a fragmenting Diaspora community and less able (or willing) to negotiate with the Arab world with which it has to live. Ultimately, a state earns legitimacy by how it behaves, by how it treats its citizenry, by the decency of its foreign policy. For those who argue that this is an "unbalanced" analysis, that there are equally valid "dual narratives," that people like me do not appreciate Jewish suffering and security needs, it is critical not to confuse nationalistic, discriminatory rhetoric with the actual historical, political, and on-the-ground realities. That reality must encompass a century of colonial settlement and Jewish entitlement that was born not only in the ghettos of Eastern Europe but also from a racist nationalism that only endangers us further.

Even the mostly ceremonial president of Israel, Reuven Rivlin, an unabashed right-wing nationalist—and here I am quoting Ricky Ben-David of *The Daily Beast*—"speaks passionately and frequently against displays of anti-Arab racism, which he's termed an Israeli 'disease.'"[3] And I would add, a dangerously, potentially fatal disease. In June 2016, *Politico* documented highly critical comments from top Israeli security chiefs and military leaders warning of impending apartheid and fascism (former defense minister Ehud Barak), the dangers of Netanyahu to the state (former head of Mossad Meir Dagan), and the naming of the conflict with Palestinians as Israel's central priority, not the presumed existential threat from Iran (former defense minister Moshe Ya'alon).[4]

The most damning moment came when an interviewer asked Yuval Diskin, former head of the Shin Bet, about a quote from Professor Yeshayahu Leibowitz, "a famous Israeli intellectual, who warned back in 1968 that if Israel kept the occupied territories, 'it will be inflicted with the corruption typical to colonial regimes. The government will constantly have to deal with oppressing an Arab rebellion, and with acquiring Arab Quislings. The IDF will suffer from atrophy and become an occupation army.' The interviewer then asked Diskin: 'What do you think about this statement, when you look at the state of Israel today?' Diskin looked straight in the camera and said: 'I agree with every word of it.'"[5]

We should all worry when even the architects of occupation and military control think the Israeli state has gone too far.

Traveling While Muslim

March 31, 2015

I am sitting in the Jerusalem Hotel sipping coffee and taking a deep breath for the first time in a while, having had more than my usual share of interplanetary landings in one long, tiring day. And it is only 3:30 in the afternoon. I started the day on Planet Gaza among a caravan of vans, roofs piled with luggage emptied of their original contents such as medical equipment, children's books, and Magic Markers and reloaded with embroidery, certificates of appreciation from the Gaza Community Mental Health Program, brochures, and my gigantic paper pineapple. I then made the drive to Erez checkpoint with that deep-seated nausea and anxiety that precedes any experience with Israeli security.

We proceeded through the Hamas checkpoint, then the Palestinian Authority checkpoint, and after that took the long walk in the metal-fenced corridor across the no-man's-land, passing one of those go-carts mounted with a stretcher (can you imagine being transported this way, as a patient with cancer or some terrible fracture, on a *stretcher*?). A hapless donkey wandered among the flowers, most likely beyond the reach of its Palestinian owner. It took an hour to get the suitcases, computers, and various baggage x-rayed and inspected as they disappeared into the chaotic machines and ramps, our bodies also screened. I wonder about this combo of intimidation from all the military and security apparatus and the utter helplessness we and all the common folk feel in this setting. We do a lot of waiting. I cannot figure out the rules: Men separate from women? White people separate from Arabs? I try singing "We Shall Overcome" very quietly. Only the pigeons are free to move, flying back and forth.

The security officers did go through our luggage and actually put one of the delegate's purse and passport in a stranger's bag, which was luckily discovered before it was too late but soon enough to make me worry if I really had all my stuff at this point. Then we finally get to the dreaded security kiosk. The lady behind the glass peers at my passport and then her computer screen: *Name? Father's name? Purpose of visit? Where are you going? Where are you staying?* I make it clear I am traveling with the woman next in line, a

Muslim physician born in Louisiana of Pakistani parents. I, the nice Jewish lady, emphasize that she is *my friend*. A quick moment, a few stamps, and I am on the other side.

And then the anxiety really begins: I am learning the real meaning of Islamophobia. What is it like to travel while Muslim? To have a Pakistani last name? A father and grandfather named Mohammed? To attend a mosque back home that was recently vandalized and burned? ("Fucking ragheads! You want a hate crime?") To spend the night before the Erez checkpoint, heart pounding, dreaming of being locked up in an Israeli prison? As I watch my colleague in the booth, I am feeling very white and very Jewish. After multiple questions and phone calls, she is sent back to wait for extra screening and my heart sinks, even though this could be called "normal" for her in the post-9/11 world. Our delegation leader talks with security, trying to intervene on her behalf; she is one of "us" even though she has the wrong name, the wrong religion, the wrong face for this encounter with the people who are supposedly keeping us "safe from terror." I notice one of the glass panels in a nearby booth is completely shattered—did someone explode with anxiety or was it rage? I also see a mezuzah on the door to the exit. Is God really on our side?

So here is the security saga at Erez. (My friend has a "clean" passport, and most of this information has already been submitted on the entry form and, I suspect, is all in the computer.) Some of this took place in a big open area with a soldier carrying an M-16 walking back and forth in front of her (she quietly said Islamic prayers to stay calm), some took place in a small room (it always gets more creepy when they put you in a small room). They took her scarf and jacket. (She has been strip-searched in Ben Gurion Airport, but that's another story.) *Name? Father's name? Grandfather's name? Where were they born? Where were you born?* (Louisiana) *Where do you live? Home address? Emails, personal and work? All your phone numbers* (US, Israeli, Jawwal)? *What groups are you traveling with? Mother's name? Grandfather's name? Where were they born? Are you sure you are American* (asked twice)? *Who did you meet in Gaza? Show me your camera.* (Battery is not in the camera; they make her dig through her backpack, find the battery, and insert). He reviews all of her photos. *Give me your cell phone.* He reviews her contacts. *Who are you staying with in Jerusalem? How do you know him? What is his address? Who did you meet in Gaza? Hamas? Jabal al-Nusra? Did you see tunnels? Where did you go in Gaza?*

So, dear white person, forgive me for my cynicism, but are you feeling safer now, knowing this is the security practice inflicted on those traveling while Muslim? After an hour, they finally release her, explaining their decision with some nod to the "intervention" by the white person earlier.

For reasons I cannot fully explain, before heading to Jerusalem we are taking a detour to visit a kibbutz just north of Gaza, Yad Mordechai. Planet number two. I was last here at the age of fourteen. This is a famous kibbutz founded by Hashomer Hatzair in 1936. Originally located near Netanya, the founders were Polish communists who arrived in Palestine to make a new life connected to the land and removed from European anti-Semitism. They sought more space, and in 1943 found it in this area, on land courtesy of the Jewish National Fund. They were asked to name the kibbutz in honor of Mordechai Anielewicz, a famous leader of the Warsaw Ghetto Uprising. We pass many bomb shelters, new schools, a honey factory, an armored vehicle used to rescue children in 1948, a bakery; the smell of manure is ever present. I can easily see Gaza in the near distance and I am feeling a bit bipolar. I think of the tens of thousands of Gazans who will wait a lifetime to get that precious permit to drag their tired bodies through Erez to a university or hospital, or travel abroad, or visit their grandmother, or pray at Al Aqsa Mosque. I have just crossed over without even thinking about that privilege. I feel like a traitor.

The kibbutz features an extraordinary museum, From Holocaust to Revival, and we are soon on a tour with a cheerful, lively woman who arrived from Baltimore in the 1970s, married a "Persian Jew," and considers herself a lefty and a true believer. The museum is exquisitely crafted, using a combo of dioramas, technical wizardry, powerful historical photos and video footage, and artifacts from Eastern Europe, the Warsaw Ghetto, Mandate Palestine, and early Israel. It is different from other Holocaust museums in that it focuses on the living and the resistance, and is designed to educate young Israelis. "Making the dream true." I am having a hard time listening intently to someone who is such a decidedly happy Zionist.

She really loses me when she starts discussing the Partition Plan and "all that wonderful real estate that would have stayed with them . . . but they never miss an opportunity to miss an opportunity [for peace]." When challenged on some of her history, she responds, "All history is an interpretation." There is an exhibit on bringing water to the Negev that has the subtly racist explanation: "They [the modern European Jews, as opposed to the 'backward' dark-skinned Arabs] were not a nomadic people wandering from one body of water to another. They laid pipes bringing water from the North to the South. The outpost erected one night soon became an oasis of green. Water flowed in pipes like blood in arteries. And blood spattered and stained the pipes, blood of those who were there at night guarding the life-giving water."

What the museum does brilliantly is to re-create a sense of the past (perhaps a bit too *Fiddler on the Roof*-y for me), celebrate the Warsaw Ghetto Uprising and Jewish fighters (as opposed to the usual sheep to the slaughter), and provide a lucid and emotionally powerful argument for the need for a State of the Jews that must fight for its existence always. I would also argue that the framing of the history, particularly the era after '48, is not only uncritically Zionist, but a manipulation of Holocaust history and its consequences. (See Israeli historian Tom Segev's *The Seventh Million* for a more objective view of this topic.)

My bigger problem is that the ghetto in Warsaw reminds me too much of the ghettos that have been created in the West Bank and Gaza; that thin, starving Jewish children of the past have their parallels south of the Israeli border today; and that the photo of the Warsaw Ghetto fully demolished after three weeks of Nazi attack looks just like Shejaia or Khan Yunis. And I can't stand it. So I walk out.

Finally, after dragging two ridiculous suitcases and the enormous paper pineapple across the cobblestone, high curbs, and dirt of East Jerusalem, I am on the bus to Qalandia. A slightly blond woman sits next to me. She has just arrived from Warsaw, Poland (Warsaw???), and we get to chatting. I learn that she is going to teach fencing at Birzeit University for a month. (Fencing???) Planet number three.

The Aim of Torture Is to Kill the Soul

April 1, 2015

Today I am in Ramallah visiting Dr. Mahmud Sehwail, psychiatrist and founder of the Treatment and Rehabilitation Center for Victims of Torture (TRC). He has that calm and gentle manner that I associate with the wisdom and patience that comes from decades of careful listening and empathy. He explains, "The idea [for TRC] came out of my professional experience as a consultant psychiatrist working at a mental hospital in Bethlehem." Starting in 1983, he began treating ex-prisoners from Israeli and Palestinian jails and became aware of a huge demand. "Twenty-five percent of the population of Palestine has been arrested at least once, 40 percent of males. We noticed torture everywhere. We noticed that 40 percent of those tortured suffered PTSD (posttraumatic stress disorder). According to Israel human rights organizations, 85 percent of Palestinian prisoners in Israeli jails are tortured; according to our surveys, more than 94 percent of Palestinian prisoners in Israeli jails." Whatever the exact percentage, the numbers and the level of suffering are indeed staggering.

He continues, "Victims are reluctant to seek services due to the stigma attached to mental illness. The environment of these services reminds them of the original trauma." Some of those whom he transferred from prison to a mental hospital said, "I would prefer to go back to prison than stay in a mental hospital." Public hospitals were ill-equipped to deal with the level of need. "Victims cannot afford the private sector, there are very few psychiatrists in this country, and there is a need for multidisciplinary teams. . . . In 1997 the Center was established as an NGO, and we established a board of directors, Dr. Haider Shafi and Dr. Eyad el-Sarraj [late founder of the Gaza Community Mental Health Program]. The first funds were from a Danish institution and other donors. We started alone with Dr. Haider and a social worker. The first victim we received was a lady subject to torture by Palestinian security forces, a lady from Ramallah."

Dr. Sehwail takes out a patient folder to demonstrate. "We have a file for every client, a TRC case file with demographic details, psychosocial information, domestic violence arrests, psychological testing for monitoring progress of the case, mental status exam, diagnosis category, DSM-4, now 5. The kind of approach for treatment—cognitive, EMDR (Eye Movement Desensitization and Reprocessing), and other services, and then we record the PTSD symptoms. We have a special form for victims of torture in Israeli prisons. We keep a database of the types of torture and the psychological consequences for individuals and families. We keep another form for Palestinian prisons." He shifts through the various forms and files and explains, "We receive patients here; our target is ex-detainees and victims (and perpetrators) of organized violence. Mainly bereaved families. Women and children are the majority of our clients—i.e., the families of the men." He explains that they treat anyone, "victim or victimizer. For example, we treated an Israeli lady married to a Palestinian ex-detainee tortured by Israelis. We treated a North American tortured by the FBI who was lecturing in Jenin at the American Arab University.

"We use mainly cognitive, behavioral, and group therapies, EMDR, psychodrama, narrative therapy, and medications. The client is seen by a psychiatrist or general practitioner. Some clients suffer from depressive disorders or acute psychosis or anxiety or PTSD, so we give medications to reduce their symptoms, free of charge. Then the patient is seen by a social worker and by a clinical psychologist, and we make an individual plan. The client might benefit from different models of treatment. We monitor their progress, then make discharge notes and a case summary." All very twenty-first-century. The cases also get presented to the United Nations as part of the struggle for human rights and an end to the practice of torture.

But how do you get over something that is not over? "Most of our patients, 80 percent, suffer from CTSD (Continued Traumatic Stress Disorder). Most have multiple trauma—they are victims of torture, arrested by Israelis and tortured, months later they are rearrested or a brother is killed—so they have multiple traumas. It makes the treatment more difficult.

"The bulk of our work is the outreach program. We make nine thousand visits to homes. Families are involved in the treatment. They suffer, families or detainees, but the effects on families, economic, social, and psychological consequences, their suffering can be much more than the detainee's."

They conduct thousands of sessions per year. "There are offices in Ramallah, Jenin, and Hebron. The Nablus office closed due to a shortage of funds. We downsized our services. Originally we had seventy employees. Now we have less than twenty due to lack of funds.

"We visit victims and families. We have regular prison visits, Israeli or Palestinian. Israeli prisons are not easy to access. Every time I go to an Israeli prison, I say, 'This is the last time.' Waiting is part of torture. I remember I used to arrive at 8:00 a.m. and would wait in severe climatic conditions outside for many hours. If they didn't bring the patient at 10:00, I will leave, so I feel guilty. No, I will wait until 12:00, 2:00, 4:00. You know, it is part of torture.

"I have attended several hundreds of military courts to testify, to discuss the medical conditions. You are accused by them, suspected by them. You are the enemy. The relationship is not as a professional testifying before the court. I remember several times being treated badly." Equal opportunity torture.

"We have the training program. We train students coming from different local universities and students of social sciences in mental health and human rights." (At this point, the tiny paper cups of bitter coffee and plastic-wrapped sweets arrive.) "We believe that mental health is strongly linked with human rights, and we train professionals from governmental and non-governmental organizations in mental health and human rights. We identify traumatic cases in community intervention, referrals. We do more advanced courses and we monitor. We do the training evaluation system. We train law enforcement agencies. Why? When I started, there was no human rights organization in Bethlehem (Al-Haq started in 1983), so I noticed that some of the clients I saw in prison tortured their relatives in the same way they were tortured. Sixty percent of Palestinian security forces are ex-detainees and most of them were tortured in Israeli prisons. It is a dynamic of the victim identifying with the victimizer.

"So I started this training in 1996 in order to prevent human rights abuses. At the beginning, many of them were defensive, but now they come to us. When one of my cases was released, he attempted to kill his fiancé. He interrogated her. He had been jailed for one to two years and when he was released, he interrogated her in the same way he was interrogated. This brought my attention to this. I remember another chap who was detained by Israelis for one year, a student, and he suffered from severe PTSD. He was completely detached from reality. When he got married he stayed with his wife. It was in winter. He made her stay outside the room for many hours, naked, both of them naked, the same way he was tortured by Israelis. Okay, that's the training for security forces. Now they come to us and sign a memorandum with the Ministry of Interior Affairs to train. We have a curriculum, case presentations to show the psychological effect of torture.

"We have summer camps for groups of affected children from ages ten to seventeen. We offer recreation and more treatment, group therapies. We have camps in Jenin, Nablus, Ramallah, Hebron, for more than three hundred affected children, both boys and girls.

"We gather people from remote areas for advocacy. We cover women, men, and children. We talk about the consequences of torture. When detainees are released, they've lost their work. They've lost their contact with the community. Their personalities are destroyed. The aim of torture is to kill the soul, to spread fear in the person, family, and community, to change the mind and character. The family is left alone. The wife has to work and to maintain the family and the kids. Really, the woman in this country is the final recipient of any trauma. So there they are; they don't know the consequences of torture. They are not aware. So we talk about that. For example, some victims or ex-detainees isolate themselves.

"We approach media, newspapers, TV. For instance, the June 2014 conference; April 17, Palestinian Prisoners' Day; December 10, Human Rights Day. We invite key persons from the community, hold a big gathering for affected families, bereaved, detainee, ex-detainee families. We organize events during Ramadan, in Ramallah, in Jenin, and other cities. They discuss their experiences with key people, with Palestinian legislators and governmental decision makers. We organize family groups. We bring *sheikhs* (open-minded *sheikhs*) and psychologists from our team and they talk about their traumas, how the community doesn't permit them to talk freely, to vent their anger. We have noticed that some know each other and visit each other and form small groups between them, support groups. Those who cannot overcome their trauma are treated in our small groups.

"We have special vocational training; it depends. We organize with the Ministry of Labor to know the needs of each district. For example, in Jenin, we subcontract those who train barbers; in Hebron, ceramics and carpenters. They generate money. Hundreds were trained. They support themselves from vocational training and generate money to maintain themselves." There is also a small research unit that examines mental health and human rights issues, once or twice a year.

Dr. Sehwail trained in Spain and Britain, pursuing a subspecialty in geriatric psychiatry, but he found at that time he was not needed in Palestine "because we are an extended family [that cares for its elders]. I came back from Spain in 1983. I wanted to come back. At that time I didn't have an ID. I was from a small town here. I grew up here, went to high school in Ramallah. But the main reason I returned was that I lost my brother, who was killed by an Israeli at age seventeen. I couldn't save the life of my brother so I have to save the life of others, Israelis and Palestinians. I passed through a big trauma. It took many years to get my ID, a long story, five years. . . . I had a contract with a mental hospital here. Now we leave this job to the young people."

He smiles at the Al Quds medical student who has accompanied me. The young man explains that Palestinian medical students are not interested in psychiatry due to the stigma of being a psychiatrist and working with psychiatric patients, but admits that Dr. Sehwail "is really impressive; he is my idol." I take that as a very good sign.

We move on to more political topics and Dr. Sehwail's work as a human rights activist. "[It] is not easy to change the environment, Israeli or Palestinian. It is paid occupation. Palestinians pay for the occupation, but the US, Europe, Arabs (I mean the governments, not the people) fund it. It is the last occupation in the world, unfortunately supported by Americans. Palestinians alone cannot do anything. It is not [just] a local responsibility. It is local, international, and regional responsibility. I think that what happened in Palestine, in Rwanda or Somalia, it affects everybody in the world, so it is an international responsibility.

"The last election in Israel, how did Netanyahu win the elections? He was elected by the extremists, by racist speech. The Israeli community is moving more and more toward extremists and racism. He gave a speech, 'If I am elected there will be no Palestinian state.' The Americans and the West and the Arab countries, they have the answer. I am sure they will continue supporting Israel. It is a shame for the Americans, the leading democratic country, applauding for the racism of the occupation. They have lost their values."

I keep asking if we are taking up too much of the good doctor's time, but clearly he needs to talk. Perhaps this is *his* therapy? I ask, what is his vision after occupation? "I think peace for the whole region, and we will be a model for democracy, if justice is achieved, peace is achieved. Palestinians will build the Arab countries. They have the ability to establish a country. The factional fighting is not an internal issue. It is controlled by outside powers. The PA has to follow Arab countries and the Americans, Hamas has to follow other regional powers. It is not an internal issue. I think Hamas will not refuse peace with Israelis. Peace is an aim for every Palestinian, but I don't expect any progress in the 'peace process.'

"Israeli is a sick society; they live with their paranoia of being persecuted. They change their role from being persecuted to persecutors. I think the history might repeat itself. It is a very harmful state for the Jewish community. We have to differentiate the Jews from the Zionists. What they are doing to the Palestinians is what was done to the Jews. How come the victim becomes the victimizer? They don't have insight into their paranoia. They were persecuted, even before the Nazis, in Spain and Russia and many countries. Jews were persecuted victims. How come they become persecutors and victimizers? I think that is the pathological dilemma. I think Jews everywhere, they have to fight with Palestinians, but to give them insight at least what you are doing is harmful for every Jew and for the whole world. It is the other face of the Nazis; they revive the same scenario. It is so. I think . . . our message to the Jewish population everywhere is to fight the occupation, to end the occupation and to live in peace, together to fight the ugly face of the Jewish.

"I remember more than ten to fifteen years ago, a journalist from Canada came to me to talk about the dynamic of suicide bombers. I sent her to the outreach program in the north and south to meet with families. After five days she told me, 'I am potential suicide bomber; there is no need to explain about the dynamic of the suicide bomber.' Okay, it is the created culture of hatred among our generation. The Palestinian child cannot identify with the local authority, with a defeated father, or the family that cannot protect itself, so the child has to identify with the Israeli soldier or with the extremist, with the strong figure." And thus a militant resistance fighter is created and the IDF arrests more children and demolishes more homes and . . ."

I ask him, what keeps him going? His eyes twinkle and he smiles, "Continuing to work, helping others, helping myself. That is the only relief." At that point a younger administrator arrives to help him sort out his unco-operative computer and they are soon lost in passwords, programs, email, and other tortures of the modern world.

I move to the office of Dr. Haider Shafi. Immediately I feel that he is another warm, wise soul, and our connection is palpable. He confirms much of what I have already learned. He expands the meaning of families as sec-ondary victims: "Wives, children, parents, they are also targeted. When they come to arrest, they surround the house with large number of troops, spread fear and terror in the house and in the local area. All the neighboring houses standing on their nerves expecting something might happen."

He is particularly concerned with children: "I am always worried about children. Those children are normal if everything around them is normal. What kind of power do those traumatized children have to compete with other normal children elsewhere?"

I ask how he inoculates children against trauma, and he sighs, clasping his hands together. "In our work, we look at children according to their age group. What we provide for little kids is different than what we provide for late childhood. We developed the idea of summer camp to provide crisis intervention, to do psychotherapy in an atmosphere that doesn't make them feel like they are patients. They thrive during the summer camp. We include group therapy four times per week. That makes twelve sessions during the three-week summer camp. We introduce psychodrama as part of their pro-gram. They like it, and they feel released and at ease and amused."

So what is psychodrama? "We normally initiate a group of twelve to fif-teen children well known to TRC clinical team. We create a group and we set some principles, how to be committed, respect each other, how to keep con-fidences. We select someone who would like to act out his problem—like not say, 'I have a problem'—but they will say, 'It was so bad when they arrested my father,' or 'When I visited my father in prison first time that I thought I could sit with him, hug him, but I couldn't touch him. I saw him behind a glass wall. I couldn't hear properly. Time was so limited. It took almost a day to arrive and come back so we spent twelve hours traveling and we couldn't see him for more than forty-five to sixty minutes.' And also, some children feel their father's appearance changed. They were cool in dealing with them not understanding they cannot do otherwise. They think Dad wouldn't want to see them and they also speak about how life became different because their fathers are no longer there; and some, they miss their dad because if they quarrel in the street or school, they have to solve it themselves or run for their mother or cousin. They also speak about how difficult their financial status is; they don't have other sources of income."

Dr. Haider provides more details on how the students engage in psycho-drama: "Two to three kids, they each have two minutes for what they like to say. We ask the audience to stand with the person who has the story they want to work on. So the person who gets the most people standing with him is elected to speak about his problem. They talk and walk, they act part of it, and they also speak about it. They feel debriefed and relieved, and they feel good support from their peers. If a child wants to play out the arrest of his father, he might select someone to play the roles of father, mother, and soldier, to reenact the real event. Then, when that is done, he is debriefed; they usually have some emotional release and catharsis. He will feel good. If he failed to say good-bye or feels guilty that he didn't do enough to keep Dad close to them, or feels bad that they did something during the arrest, we make him feel no longer guilty. He didn't do anything to cause the arrest. We encourage them to say what they want to say to their dad and whatever words they want to say to the soldiers, and others. They usually play the role and they speak about their personal experiences during the play. They react according to the instructions of the protagonist and they reflect on their role. It might trigger some of their previous experience or their current fear and anxiety, or they might remember the blessing that their dad is there. Some victims have been released.

"We use other another treatment: EMDR. I learned it in the US. Francine Shapiro, a Jewish American and wonderful person, founded EMDR in San Francisco. EMDR is a powerful method. At the beginning we thought it was about eye movement desensitization, but now also the tactile and hearing senses as well can produce similar effect. It is good for traumatic events. Eye movement desensitization and reprocessing—it is [a] kind of bilateral stimu-lation of both hemispheres of the brain, and this stimulation works against the principles of PTSD. PTSD shuts the amygdala down and EMDR opens up the old memories, traumatic memories, and helps people to talk more about their bitter experiences in a safe atmosphere while they get enough support and assistance. Once they are done, they feel much more relief and are encouraged to continue with their lives.

"We can use the butterfly technique with children. We have them cross their arms across their chests like a hug. Tapping slower is associated with relaxation and faster with reprocessing. Then they start to talk and then tap.

"We use other practical techniques in summer camp. Children tap hands and play with each other. We also use narrative therapy. TRC is the most specialized center for narrative therapy. We established the Palestine National Institute of Narrative Therapy. You help the person to narrate his own story. You help him re-author his story. Many good stories are not remembered and not talked about during a major trauma, but we thicken these small stories and make them form a kind of alternative story, so that every time they look at themselves as victims they also discover they are also survivors and warriors.

"A victim might speak about how weak and embarrassed he was during torture, his experience with inferiority, being forced to bark like a dog, or walk on four arms and legs. But we will help him discover how brave he was to stay in solitary confinement, how he could allow his mind to go beyond the walls of the cell, how strong he was to compose some poems, to hold a lot of love for his family, to think of them despite his fear, weakness, and illness. Then they discover that the shame is not mostly allocated in them but rather it is cardinal issue of the aggressor. So many people speak about escaping a bomb in the very last minute, while others failed, so they died. We work with those people. They were not selfish. They were good citizens. They could save their lives and some around them. Despite the fear, they were not cowards. They were able to take the essential measures of security. Despite the fear, they carried milk, medicine, and food for their kids. The mother didn't forget some sweets or a blanket to cover her children. How strong they were to stay together and not to go out, to tolerate the boredom in a small room for a long time. They could do that because they were responsible, smart, clever. They could protect themselves.

"So this kind of re-authoring of stories, you need to double-listen to what the person is saying and to what he is trying to say, the absent but implicit. Like they might not speak about the courage, aspirations they have, but when you look carefully at their acts, their lives today, they discover that the absent is already implicit. They are going towards their goals and aims. We also use CBT (Cognitive Behavioral Therapy) to help people demonstrate negative traumatic thoughts and to associate them with dysfunctional beliefs, like sugar with tea." This therapy helps ultimately to change established thinking patterns and behavioral activation by focusing on particular problems in the present. He explains that the different methods they use are backed up by evidenced-based literature that shows great effectiveness with traumatized populations.

"I want to say a little bit about the entire picture. It is not about children, parents, mothers, in isolation. Any society is composed of parents and children under the same ceiling. They share similar concerns. The nature of the Palestinian society is close family members, and also, children remain children when they are grownups. For example, it is not the general picture of children leaving home at eighteen. They might get married and live with parents. Extended family helps in this situation. We do not fear very much loneliness.

"So, sometimes the part of the problem of the father is that he has guilt feelings because he left his family members for a long time or he is too poor to achieve for his kids what he was dreaming of when he was in prison, and also, for the mother, almost the same thing. While she herself is suffering the absence of her husband and her kids' father, she has to resume some of his role socioeconomically and emotionally. Also, she needs to be strong in order to fit these two different roles; so she might not have time for herself to grieve. We often say that women in our society are the real heroes but they suffer in silence. I personally think that the real strength in Palestinian society comes from women. They are the final recipient of suffering and pain."

Dr. Haider thanks me, and says that I am relaxed, easy to talk to. I get the feeling he is feeling better. Everyone needs to be heard.

What's Mine Is Mine and What's Yours Is Mine

April 3, 2015

It is Good Friday and Erev Pesach, and I am celebrating the day by taking you on an exploration of the landscape of occupied Palestine. The sun is in its glory, birds are singing with the passions of spring (after all, what do they know of occupation?), and I am eating some freshly made pie concoctions of oregano and goat cheese, all drenched with what is the life-force around here—olive oil produced on the ancestral lands belonging to my host family. These urban folks have invited me to their village of Sarta, and I am taking you there, mile by occupied mile.

We are traveling north from Ramallah. There are permanent checkpoints and checkpoints like Jaba' that are closed about once a week (unpredictably, of course, to cause maximum havoc), halting all north–south traffic. We pass the Jewish settlement of Psagot, and at the District Coordination Offices checkpoint I see a grey Israeli guard tower and two soldiers. They check the husband's ID and we are waved through. It seems there is a cat-and-mouse game that is played out between occupier and occupied. The soldiers are generally young and unsophisticated, and the Palestinians have spent years developing strategies: where to go, which permit to use where, fake IDs, real IDs, and needless to say, they have had a lot of time to practice.

I can see Psagot expanding eastward; we head north on Route 60, an Israeli army jeep just ahead of us. I notice that all the signs are for Jewish settlements; it seems Palestinian towns and villages have been made geographically invisible. We pass a guard tower on the left and expanses of spring green penetrating the dynamic grey-brown rocky hills. We pass the Jewish settlement of Bet El, the official coordination site of Israeli occupation in the West Bank and formerly the central command headquarters. On the right I spot the impressive settlement of Ofra, circles of red-tiled houses and barbed wire and then a sign: Ventra and Tanya Wineries. On the right there is a collection of beautiful Palestinian homes that make up the village of Turmus Aia. Many of these houses are owned by Palestinian Americans who want a foothold in their homeland. Last year this is where an Israeli Defense Force soldier killed a Palestinian activist. More massive rocks, a single tall minaret surrounded by a cluster of cream-colored Palestinian houses, stubby trees clinging to rocky terraces, Israeli flags flapping in the wind. *Chag Sameach* (Happy Holiday). This road is used by everyone, but there are obviously no yellow or green flags. Lush green farms spread across the valleys, tall cedar trees pierce the landscape, dunums of grape vines fan out before us. It seems that the settlers have a nasty habit of seizing Palestinian farmland for their own under the "what's mine is mine and what's yours is mine" theory of coexistence.

While we drive by many Palestinian villages I am impressed with the amount of open space around us, and I am informed that this is Area C. Sarta is located in Area B, which is under the shared control of the PA's civil authority and the Israeli military—"shared" here being a pretty theoretical concept. Someone from Sarta built too close to the edge of B and C and their home was demolished. Area A is the main cities, the urban population concentrations that include the *fellahin* (agricultural laborers) in search of work in Ramallah or Nablus, and what could now be viewed ironically as a people without their land.

Farmers and families are bent over in their fields, the earth a rich red color; the hilltops are scattered with tiny outpost settlements, rows of caravans that will someday be larger colonies. We pass Zatara, a major rotary with signs to the Jordan Valley as well as Tel Aviv, a mere fifty-three kilometers away, and of course a major checkpoint that can easily close down the entire area. Grey rocks huddle like sheep. The settlement of Ariel on the left is a wide expanse of apartment buildings and continuous construction; surveillance towers puncture the horizons. At the base of the mountain that is Ariel lies the unfortunate town of Marda. It has had no new construction approved since 1967, and desperate families, who have continued to have children, who after getting married need their own housing, are expanding vertically, the air above the roof being the only space not quite under Israeli control. Another rotary and guard tower, a (de-Arabized) sign to Tel Aviv/Jafo and we come to the largest industrial settlement in the West Bank. In Barqan (which is partially on land expropriated from Sarta), there are a variety of major industries including plastics, food processing, and wood production, and the requisite huge yellow cranes, tractors, and construction equipment. International organizations have documented that industrial parks in the West Bank such as this one easily evade Israeli environmental safety regulations, thus contributing to the pollution and devastation of Palestinian land and water resources. Perhaps I am feeling too emotional, but I would call this the slow rape of Palestine. Since pollution knows no boundaries, this also seems like a monumentally short-sighted policy for the settlers who are clearly planning to stay for a long time and ultimately breathe the same air and drink the same water as their besieged neighbors.

We pass another tall Israeli guard tower, signs to Qalqilya on the right, followed by a massive settlement that is under construction and a sea of spring groundsels, little yellow flowers completely oblivious to the turmoil around them. We pass the land of the family's grandmother that has been taken by settlers, with its rows of majestic, resilient olive trees; interestingly, the original family still harvests the olives. Past the mother's home, past Bidya, and then a left to Sarta, through old winding roads and clusters of Palestinian houses.

We arrive in this five-hundred-year-old town of teachers and farmers and PA employees, people who have never left, people who are returning, or building their country homes on family land. Families work in Ramallah or open businesses in Norway or get PhDs in Ohio, but return here for the land, or the smell of orange blossoms in the spring and the quiet of country living, or to maintain their children's Palestinian identity. It has an Old City, ruins, courtyards, a mosque, and a school, with children playing along the street. The old men still wear suits and ties on the weekends and red checkered kaffiyehs with the black *iqal* circling their heads. At the top of the hills I can see the high-rises of Tel Aviv.

I am completely unprepared for what this family has built here. On the grandfather's land, surrounded by brothers and cousins and relations of all kinds, we enter a magical Garden of Eden, white stone paths, gazebos, terraced gardens, roses blooming, metal archways wound with vines that will soon burst into bloom, and vineyards, olive trees, and bushes that sparkle in yellow and red and purple, enormous geraniums. Irises and crown anemone, like tiny red poppies, spring up between cracks in the stones. The iridescent sunbird, recently declared the national bird of Palestine, flits in the sun; drip irrigation winds its way through imminent paradise, and walls of volcanic rock frame the paths and terraces. There is a pleasing, small white house, a cast of rambunctious well-loved children, and relations to visit. The nonstop eating and drinking begins early (a fabulous date cake, followed shortly thereafter by an amazing traditional dish of stuffed squash and grape leaves, lamb, and chicken preceded and followed by tea and coffee every hour or two). I was informed of the plan for us women to hike while the men prayed at the mosque, but that "hike" involved a short stroll up the hill to the first relation and the date cake. The only real dose of reality is the Jewish settlement on the crest of a nearby mountain, visible from almost anywhere in the garden. It occurs to me that planting this land is perhaps a quiet but palpable form of resistance.

Hours later we head south along the western route, a circuitous snaking mountainous road through Mas'ha, under a modern bypass road (i.e., for vehicles with Israeli license plates only. Translation: Jews only). We pass Israeli jeeps ominously parked along the road, the fortress-like settlement of Ofarim, Palestinian wedding parties, Israeli guard towers, Fatah flags, snub-nosed goats and braying donkeys, to deliver me to my friends in Aboud, the intriguing village that is half Christian and half Muslim. While driving, the husband comments, "Palestinians turn stones into gold," cutting the massive rocks that pervade the landscape and selling them to Israelis and Jordanians, while "Jordanians turn gold into rocks," buying these stones to build their cities. We drive by a mountaintop that has been flattened—huge piles of dirt, the beginning of a new settlement—through more olive groves and farmers bent toward the earth. Past tiny villages and flashy gated mansions, baby olive groves, replanted after decimation by Jewish settlers or the IDF, then take a left into Aboud. The "Welcome to Aboud" sign lies on its side by the road and a riderless horse gallops by. Reality as allegory.

Home Visits in Jalazone

April 5, 2015

M., a warm, energetic thirty-something man with a good sense of humor, has been a psychologist at TRC for six years. After a lively supervision session with four other psychologists, during which senior staff review therapeutic issues and plans for the patients, we walk through the jostling streets of Ramallah and pay three and a half shekels for a *service* to the Jalazone Refugee Camp just north of the city. The camp is crowded into a quarter of a square kilometer, some fifteen to twenty thousand people descended from thirty-six villages in the pre-1948 area of Lod/Lydda and Ramla/Ramleh. Major challenges for the camp that UNRWA lists are a lack of a sewer system and overcrowded schools. The UNRWA school was renovated in 2014 after years of the building operating in double shifts. On the radio, a man sings verses of the Quran and M. urges me to "just listen. The Quran teaches peace, just listen."

At a rotary near the Jewish settlement of Bet El, there are areas blackened by fire, the sites of frequent conflicts between stone-throwing Palestinian young men and heavily armed IDF soldiers, the earth stained from burning tires. We reach a concrete roadblock with two Israeli soldiers; M. informs me we are twenty seconds from Jalazone, but we have to make a wide detour on a poorly maintained, narrow, bumpy, circuitous road. The traffic slows to a crawl. M. talks of a cousin in Omaha, M.'s wedding in July, the poverty in the camp, and the strength of the people. He is coming to make several home visits.

First we stop for what seems to be a slow-paced schmooze at the Rehabilitation Center for Disabled Children, checking in with the lively director and chatting with two patients. I tour the facility, the small children's arts and crafts and play therapy center, and a larger area for physical therapy, where M. runs weekly group therapy sessions. Today, all the talk is about the twenty-year-old young man who one week ago was shot dead in the street while throwing stones. Someone asks, can M. add his family to his case list? His family is very poor. A poster on the wall features a man crouched in a bottle and the words "Thirst for Freedom." A smartphone rings with the same jingle as mine; a staff person works at a computer, chain-smoking. Lots of people smoking here, men and women.

We head out to the first family, and I am struck by the bleakness of the camp—all chalky concrete and winding streets, no green space, many martyrs' posters, a rare scrawny plant, houses against houses. M. is well known; he laughs when I say that he is the camp psychologist and I can see he is enjoying his rock star status. He greets a number of former clients, ex-detainees, mothers of detainees; there is much embracing and strong handshakes and conversation. An older woman who has had two sons in prison bemoans her life, asks to have a picture taken with me so she can be famous in America, and boasts of the many children she has. The exact numbers are a bit lost in translation, but what I can gather is that she has seventy-five children and grandchildren, which seems about right for a place where girls marry young and have large families who do the same.

We walk up the stairs to an apartment where the living room is a separately locked room across from the rest of the house and sit in a room with plump stuffed chairs and a shelf lined with certificates. In a typical home these would be diplomas, sports awards, and the like, but this is Jalazone and these are the certificates of everyone arrested in the family. M. estimates that a very high percentage of the males in the camp have been detained; often their first arrest is as a young boy, caught throwing stones or just caught being a young Palestinian boy.

We are joined by a woman maybe in her forties; another woman, large and older, of indeterminate age; and a buff young man who wanders in and out, smoking. The younger woman has a son who was arrested one year ago; the older woman lost one son to the IDF and another is imprisoned, serving ten long years. The women serve us tea and when I do not drink mine (in my chronically over-hydrated state), she urges me to drink; there is no saying no. While the session is in Arabic with a minimal amount of translation, there is a lot of talking and a lot of listening. I watch the body language, the sighing, the gentle rocking back and forth, the agitated young man. They discuss the arrests and M. does what he calls narrative therapy, reconstructing their stories, which are clearly filled with pain and anguish, to find the moments of strength and pride.

The younger woman's twenty-one-year-old is imprisoned in the Negev. They are allowed to visit monthly, though obtaining a permit is difficult and the round-trip journey to the prison is long. The day of the visit starts at 6:00 a.m. and ends at 9:00 p.m. She spends forty-five minutes with her son, staring at him through a glass panel and speaking via telephone. No gifts or food are permitted, but they bring shekels for his canteen account. The older woman's son was first arrested at age twenty-three by the PA, served two years, and then was arrested by the Israelis in his home. He is now twenty-eight years old.

At the second home, two very overweight women sit on a wooden platform with a thin cushion; one is smoking. The room is under construction. Three men are applying concrete, tiling the walls; a woman and a child come in, the men stop to smoke and drink coffee. There is no privacy and a chronic level of chaos. One woman with clearly African features has a son who has been in detention for thirty months; the older woman has a son who is now an ex-detainee. When he was arrested the Israeli soldiers smashed down the door of the house and caused extensive damage. The ex-detainee underwent psychological and vocational training at TRC, but now he sits at home without a job, like many men in the camp. The women are clearly very depressed and there is a general flatness of affect, leading M. to suspect PTSD, although it is hard to accurately diagnose their condition as "post-trauma" when the trauma is really "ongoing." It is also clearly impossible to conduct a session under these conditions. After we leave he reflects on how challenging it is to work with this population, the lack of privacy, the inability to plan visits.

M. decides to visit the mother of a boy paralyzed by an Israeli soldier who shot him in the spine, but the boy is in the hospital in Hebron, so that visit is also canceled. We wait for the Ford Transit that will take us back, watching the flood of children getting out of school, wearing large Mickey Mouse backpacks, many with arms draped over each other. Some are fighting aggressively in little-boy ways, and one boy is kicking an empty box of sanitary pads (he clearly needs a soccer ball); many yell "Hi!" and openly stare at me. M. may be the rock star, but I am obviously the stranger, and the camp once again has made the decades-long refugee crisis real and urgent for me. I watch the sweet-faced little boys parading past and wonder, what is their future? Do they still dream of anything but a life in the camp, no job, a cycle of arrests and detention, their face on a martyr poster? What pain and disaster awaits them and when will this end?

The Great Escape

April 6, 2015

My colleague of the "traveling while Muslim" variety and I arrive at Ben Gurion Airport, take a deep breath, find our inner wonder women, and saunter into the airport, smiling and laughing as though we were carefree tourists coming home from the Holy Land after a quick stop in the Tel Aviv bubble (actually, we stopped there to have dinner with a very left-wing activist who is working on a new organization called DE-COLONIZER). At the first security screen, there are two serious young Israelis, the usual identity and "where are you coming from" questions. I can honestly answer "Tel Aviv." My face is open and friendly, but to my annoyance I cannot control my rapidly pounding heart. One of them explains very sternly, "This is for your safety. If someone gave you something, they could blow up the plane." It is hard for me to keep a straight face and I feel a little bit sorry for him. The other woman keeps apologizing for all the questions. "Anything sharp that could be used as a weapon?" I reply earnestly that I do have a nail clipper. She apologizes again and again, and I must give her credit. In the past few years the airport folks have called off the attack dog style of screening, and I am compelled to admit it is refreshing to hear an Israeli say, "I'm sorry." I breeze though the first checkpoint, streaming wonder woman vibes all over the airport. Heart rate slows down.

My colleague has a less breezy experience. The security guy asks her name. *Say your middle name. Say your last name. Where is your name from? Origin of your name?* She answers with a smile, explaining that her name is pretty international and can be a Hebrew name; that's why her parents chose it. This drives him a bit crazy, but we are playing cat and mouse. *Why are you here? Where did you go? Why Gaza? Will you come back? Did you have armed guards?* (He asks this repeatedly, and I realize that he cannot imagine being in Gaza without a full armed battalion, or else, we must be with Hamas, right?) *Where did you stay? Do they have hotels in Gaza? Did you have armed guards* (again and again)? *Parent's name* (she asks which one, Mom or Dad?). When he hears her father's name is Mohammed, he actually says: "Oh, now I understand." Bingo!

So it seems they are not actually asking if you are a Muslim, but they are using all the usual racial profiling techniques to extract that bit of information. Having established that she is indeed a Muslim-American physician who has done humanitarian aid, he asks, where did she volunteer? She responds: everywhere. *Where?* It's a long list. *But where in the Middle East?* She starts listing countries: Sudan, Nepal, Bosnia, Iraq, and he says okay. He asks her what kind of work she does, and she responds that she is a pediatrician and a Fulbright Scholar. I keep quiet and smile. I am a nice Jewish doctor traveling with a nice Muslim doctor, and we are peace-loving friends. The questions resume: *How long has she known me?* We were on the same delegation. *Who do you work for* (over and over)? *How do you know each other?* Interestingly, she clearly indicates that she and I traveled together to Gaza, but they never come back to re-interrogate me, probably because of the iron-domed protection afforded by my last name: Rothchild. Baron Edmund de Rothschild bought a big chunk of pre-'48 historic Palestine. Not my family, but check it out.

Our bags are tagged with a blue strip. We are not sure that is a good thing.

Then we get in line for our plane tickets. No problem.

Next is the physical security screen. Our bags are x-rayed; we both have TSA pre-check, which is a pretty meaningless blessing here. My colleague is immediately pulled aside, told to go to a different place, chastised that she went to the wrong place first. She is placed in a separate containment area with five security guards; it is semi-open with a partial wall. She is again questioned, a reprise of the previous interrogation. This time, when she lists where she has done humanitarian aid, she gets to include Afghanistan and Pakistan. She is asked if she is carrying bombs. She is told to take *every-thing* out of her suitcase—all electronics, batteries—over and over again. *Empty your pockets.* (It's a small victory that they do not find her other passport with stamps from all the forbidden countries slipped within a pack of sanitary pads—a great place to hide stuff.) With her shoes off, she is aggressively patted down by a gloved woman with special attention to her arms and legs, she is x-rayed, and her bags are x-rayed for a second time. Everything is wanded—the inside of her camera where the battery sits, every book, all her papers, the inside of her computer. They take her computer, say that they are putting it through the x-ray again; it is now out of sight, so anything can happen. They wand all her audio material, all the wires, SIM cards, all her medications. After all of her carefully backed belongings are piled in a jumble, they say, "You can clean this up now." She reminds them that they have not returned her computer, which they finally do. Through this thirty-minute interrogation, she remains as she described, "super nice and cooperative." The computer is finally returned. Who knows what the Israeli forces or the Shin

Bet or for that matter the NSA has done to it? So, dear reader, is this about Israeli security, or Israeli intimidation and racial profiling and surveillance?

I am pulled aside and wanded in a public area just beyond security.

After I wait, pacing back and forth, my colleague emerges and we get in line for passport control, the final hurdle. The blond woman in the box is chatting loudly in Hebrew on the phone, barely looks at our papers. Her stamp bonks on our passports and we are in the international area.

We crash in the VIP lounge (we have access thanks to my well-traveled dangerous Muslim friend with TSA pre-check) for a well-earned glass of wine. In an ironic twist, we hear the lyrical music of Norah Jones (full name: Geetali Norah Jones Shankar) wafting across the room. Her father was Ravi Shankar. Another dangerous non-Jewish brown-faced terrorist?

So . . . I settle into my United Airlines seat, adjust the headrest, take a cleansing breath and decide to wait for takeoff by scanning a throwaway magazine, *United Hemispheres*, the April 15 edition. I am looking for something entertaining and hopefully meaningless. I am tired and I am done with all this political detective work. An article catches my attention, "The World's Next Great Cities," and sure enough after Rotterdam, Houston, Bogota, and Fukuoka, there is Tel Aviv, "The Next Great Tech Hub."

The article gushes with comments like, "And now, Tel Aviv boasts Silicon Wadi (that's Arabic for 'gully')." Forgive me, but I think *wadi* actually means "valley," which has a less Third World ring to it. The write-up also features such smoke-and-mirrors historical magic tricks as, "You might assume a country that's home to such ancient stalwarts as the Western Wall and the Dome of the Rock would be stuck in the past [*God gave this to us 2,000 years ago, Arafat is Hitler, every threat is another Holocaust*—who is stuck in the past?], but Israel has its eye firmly on the future." Forgive me but . . . a future of "contained conflict," apartheid, unchallenged institutionalized racism, and segregation? The article briefly delves into the city's benevolent and inspirational origins: "Youthful, fun-loving Tel Aviv—a 'startup' city itself, having been founded in 1909 . . ." as a Jewish neighborhood north of the thriving city of Jaffa and part of the aggressive colonization of Palestine . . . but, really, who wants to hear that. There also is this absurd aside: "It's not difficult to see the logical progression from the communal culture of the kibbutz to the collaborative, open-plan workspaces of the modern high-tech sphere."

From the Bundist, back-to-the-land, jointly owned, muscular, sweaty, and bronzed to . . . Google? Where do I begin?

Epilogue

Through these essays we have undressed the various patients, meta-phorically poked and prodded their vital organs, and collected critical data on well-being and signs of illness. We have learned that the redemptive and sentimental story of the founding of the State of Israel—the path from Auschwitz to Jerusalem, and the struggle for survival, "the villa in the jungle"—is not a glorious narrative with some troublesome omissions, but actually a dangerous deception that blinds us to today's realities and possibilities for the future. This "infrastructure of thought,"[1] to quote the Palestinian-American writer Susan Albulhawa, obscures the fact that the settlement of Palestine was not only a response to European anti-Semitism, but also a well-developed Jewish nationalist program that started in the late 1880s and led to a plan to rid historic Palestine of its indigenous population and create a Jewish-only state at almost any price.[2] This process continues through today in a variety of forms, and it comes with a massive cost to Palestinians as well as Jewish Israelis and the international community: the last internationally sanctioned settler colonial state, endless discord, and proxy wars. I see grappling with this reality as the biggest challenge for liberal Zionists and other "friends" of Israel.

As we witnessed on the ground, Palestine had a rich and diverse history with many centuries of inhabitants from farmers to city folk, illiterate to educated. This was a pluralistic world where people from a variety of religious, ethnic, and racial backgrounds coexisted relatively well, living through countless invasions, conversions, migrations, and settlements. That ended with the beginning of Jewish settlement in the early 1900s and the growing ideology of exclusivity and privilege that culminated in the war in

1948. A modern examination of history reveals that the Arab armies that attacked the newly created state were outgunned and out-funded by well-organized Jewish forces who had been preparing for war and statehood for decades and, in fact, three months before Arab armies invaded, Jewish military forces began the ethnic cleansing of Palestinians from their homes and land. Remember Lifta?

I find it fascinating to examine the linguistic efforts to reframe this history. The 1948 war, which in reality was a war between European Jewish settlers against surrounding Arab armies from countries in various states of organization and disorganization, became a "War of Independence." Immediately after victory, street signs and villages were renamed and Hebraized, as active efforts were made to disappear the Palestinian presence and culture. Golda Mabovitch became Golda Meir, and David Gruen, David Ben-Gurion, fighting Jews cleansed of their bowed heads and Old World traumas. There was even a "Names Committee to oversee an epic rewriting of history in such a way that conflated religion with racial and ethnic identity."[3]

In the newly formed "democratic" State of Israel, Palestinians with Israeli citizenship lived under military rule until 1966, with a system of checkpoints and permits within Israel. They were unable to get compensation for lost property and homes, and frequently forced to live near their old villages, which were demolished, settled by Jewish immigrants, and developed into national parks, industrial parks, or military ranges. That same process then became the structure of the occupation after 1967. The long dance of "peace processes" was entirely doomed to failure because the Israeli government never intended to halt the settlement process. (Consider that in 2016, there were eight hundred thousand Jewish settlers in the West Bank and East Jerusalem, and that Netanyahu outrageously suggested that anyone opposed to the settlement policies was in favor of the "ethnic cleansing" of Jews.[4])

I have argued that the current occupation is a continuation of more than a century of colonization of Palestine and of indigenous Palestinians periodically fighting back. The famous general Moshe Dayan reportedly said he too would have fought back if he had been an Arab. "Jewish villages were built in the place of Arab villages. You do not even know the names of these Arab villages, and I do not blame you because geography books no longer exist, not only do the books not exist, the Arab villages are not there either. . . . There is not one single place built in this country that did not have a former Arab population."[5] So much for the land without a people mythology.

Palestinians have often had dysfunctional, ineffective, and corrupt leadership, which has only contributed to the catastrophe, but this has never been a battle between equals. Today, Israel is one of the world's major military powers and has a mighty army and an extensive military/industrial/security complex that is interlinked with and politically protected by the United States. By contrast, the Palestinian population has no army, navy, or air force. They have had much of their natural resources stolen by Jewish settlement and struggle to maintain self-sufficiency. One-third of all Palestinian refugees live in one of the fifty-eight refugee camps in Jordan, Lebanon, Syria, the West Bank, and Gaza.

But given the prevailing sentiment of the geopolitical world, Palestinians are often referred to as terrorists and Israelis as their beleaguered victims. No one remembers Arafat's Palestinian National Council in Algiers recognizing the two-state solution in 1988, or the Arab League's unanimous adoption of the 2002 Saudi Peace Initiative. Or, more recently, no one considers the close security coordination between the PA and Israel. It has been reported that the PA spends more money protecting Israeli settlements than on Palestinian health and education.[6] Under occupation Palestinians have actually held two democratic elections, certified by international agencies. Dating back to the 1920s, they have a long history of boycotts, marches, hunger strikes, tax revolts, and other forms of nonviolent resistance. Palestinians suffer from daily brutal attacks by Jewish settlers; the IDF turns a blind eye and sometimes supports the settlers, who face no legal consequences. When I travel in the region, I observe that the IDF and settlers are the ones carrying the automatic weapons and tossing tear gas grenades; the civilian Palestinian population is almost entirely unarmed.

There was a study published in 2014 by researchers from the Massachusetts Institute of Technology, Princeton University, and Tel Aviv University tracking patterns of violence between Israelis and Palestinians in Gaza over an eight-year period. According to the researchers, "it is overwhelmingly Israel that kills first after a pause in the conflict: 79 percent of all conflict pauses were interrupted when Israel killed a Palestinian, while only 8 percent were interrupted by Palestinian attacks (the remaining 13 percent were interrupted by both sides on the same day). In addition, we found that this pattern—in which Israel is more likely than Palestine to kill first after a conflict pause—becomes more pronounced for longer conflict pauses."[7] This seriously challenges the paradigm that Israelis are peace-seeking and Palestinians are obstructive or inexplicably, inherently violent.

Giving up the mythology of our dominant culture (Israel = good, peace-loving versus Arabs = bad, terroristic) and embracing the universal right to resist oppression is fundamental to the liberation struggle of Palestinians, and is a critical task for people dedicated to human rights and interested in building a long-term peace in the region. But what about Hamas and "radical Islamic terrorism," you ask? This is a long and complicated topic, but I would urge you to step back to the root causes of these movements. It is important to note that Islam, the religion, is 1,400 years old, but "radical Islam" is a product of the last century, dating to the Sykes-Picot Agreement of 1916 and later to US support of the Mujahideen in Afghanistan to provoke and challenge the Soviets. Al-Qaeda and Daesh, or ISIL, were the heirs to the earlier militant Islamists; ironically, jihadis used to be our friends in the fight against communism just as Hamas used to be our friend in the opposition to the nationalistic, secular Fatah movement.

Hamas is decidedly not a monolithic organization and has both militant and social service branches. It not only is responsible for coordinating horrific suicide bombings but also for being a restraining force on more militant groups as well as providing hospitals, universities, orphanages, and social supports for people who have largely been forgotten. The militant wing rose out of the resistance movements in the First Intifada, which were a response to the unrelenting Israeli occupation. Many argue that when Hamas won the democratic election (largely as a vote against Fatah), it was tacitly agreeing to the political process and to the two-state solution. Palestinian friends of mine point out that the Hamas candidates were never given the chance to govern successfully or be voted out of office (unlike other "terrorists," Ben-Gurion, Begin, Shamir, all of whom were involved with Jewish terror groups and became prime ministers). That is how democracy is supposed to work.

It is also challenging to ponder what we are asking from Hamas (i.e., to behave more like the cooperative and complacent PA and PLO). Ironically, the United States deals with the PLO (despite its charter calling for one secular state), and it supports Israel (despite its massive aggressive military attacks, human rights violations, refusal to stop settlement growth) and obviously is on good terms with Saudi Arabia and a host of undemocratic, dictatorial countries when it suits our perceived political and military needs. But what has the PA gotten from being the cooperative agent (besides thousands of salaries)? An expanding, repressive, bureaucratic occupation, repeated Israeli incursions, and an out-of-control settler movement that attacks Palestinians with impunity. Not a selling point.

Now we have a collapse of the old order in the Middle East that is largely the inheritance of the colonial powers, our support of repressive regimes, and our massive, destabilizing invasions. This has led to internal strife, civil war, hopelessness, and a vacuum that is now being filled by militant Islamists creating a wave of terror that manipulates a sick corruption of the religion of Islam. Clearly people need to be responsible for their actions, and clearly we as a nation are deeply complicit as well. Individual, group, and state-sponsored "terrorism" must be condemned, whether it is carried out by ISIL in Paris or the United States and United Kingdom in Iraq, or Israel in the occupied territories. I argue that by and large, this is not a religious war but rather a battle over land, resources, and power that uses religion as a justification. I would also argue that the current strategies in the region make it more likely that groups like Daesh will develop a foothold in Gaza, particularly among disillusioned, hopeless, traumatized young men, using the argument that Hamas has sold out. It negotiated with Israel and agreed to a truce. For those reasons, ISIS charges Hamas with placing "the nationalist battle for a Palestinian state before the campaign for a caliphate," and ISIS benefits from the fact that that battle has been repeatedly unsuccessful.[8]

Which brings us to what we can do as members of the "Western world" and particularly as citizens of the United States, the primary funder of the occupation forces. The first obvious step is education: reading the New Israeli historians, Palestinian and other analysts and academics, novelists, poets, the host of newspapers, Facebook posts, tweets, and blogs that are easily accessible in our shrinking, internet-powered world. We can also personally bear witness to the facts on the ground, countering the hundreds of Jewish Birthright and Christian evangelical Covenant Journey trips, and the "junkets" offered to elected officials, faith leaders, businesspeople, African Americans, etc. We can share our findings honestly with our own communities, confronting the erasure of Palestinian history and experience, and the deeply corruptive consequences of political Zionism. It is also important for our elected officials, newspaper editors, Twitter readers, and other shapers of political and media opinion to hear from us on a regular basis, however insufficient that may feel, and to support organizations in the region that are truly working for peace with justice.

Nonetheless, Israel is among the world's most affluent nations; it receives far more US foreign aid as well as political cover and special status than any other country. It will not give up that support and power voluntarily. Additionally, the United States cannot credibly broker Israeli-Palestinian negotiations while bankrolling Israel's military machine and ignoring human rights violations. In 2005, after years of unsuccessful UN resolutions and reports, International Laws, the Fourth Geneva Convention, International Court rulings, wars, intifadas, suicide attacks, and various pan-Arab strategies, over 170 Palestinian civil society activists called for boycott, divestment, and sanctions of Israel. They called for an end to the occupation, equal citizenship for Palestinians in Israel, and respecting, protecting, and promoting the rights of Palestinian refugees to return to their homes and properties.

This campaign is not directed against Israel because it is a Jewish state; it is directed against Israel because of its history of dispossessing, expelling, ghettoizing, and killing Palestinians. As a Jewish person, I find this history shameful, immoral, and profoundly unrelated to what I learned as "Jewish values" and the legacy of Jews in a variety of progressive and intellectual movements. This is ultimately a struggle for civil and human rights and a movement to change Israel's stance from one of Jewish privilege and exclusivity to one committed to democracy and an end to hostilities with its Palestinian neighbors. I suspect, in the tradition stretching from the Quaker-led fight against slavery to the anti-apartheid struggles in South Africa, this nonviolent resistance movement may be the most promising and productive international effort to date.

Ultimately, it becomes critical for Jews to separate Judaism the religion from Zionism the national political movement. As my religious friends say, "Zionism has hijacked Judaism." It is also important to define a Jew as someone grounded in religion or culture or history, or a set of ethics, or a sense of peoplehood, and to respect all definitions as equally compelling. The secular Diaspora Jew is as legitimate as a religious Israeli and has a right and a moral responsibility to be critical of the country that speaks in our name when we cannot support its behavior. We also must clearly delineate the racist ideology of anti-Semitism (hating a person, group, or organization solely because it is Jewish), from thoughtful, principled criticism of the policies of Israel the country.

Fundamentally, we need to challenge the prevailing founding mythologies and embrace the Palestinian liberation struggle not only for the sake of Palestinians, but because the Israeli government is on a suicidal course. We must build a principled opposition to indefensible Israeli policies, to challenge Jewish privilege and exclusivity, not only for our Palestinian colleagues and friends, but also for ourselves, locally and internationally. When our police forces, in programs funded by the Anti-Defamation League and the

Jewish Institute for National Security Affairs, are being trained by Israeli security forces, the New York City Police Department has an office in Tel Aviv,[9] and thousands of security forces have been trained in Israel through the Georgia International Law Enforcement Exchange,[10] the occupation has come home. When our latest weapons are "field tested" on Gazan women and children, we are deeply complicit. When the unresolved Israeli occupation is used by Arab leaders to foment discord in their own repressive countries, that is yet another trigger in this volatile region. When the US military budget expands, and we do not have enough money for schools and health care and our decaying roads and bridges, think of what we could do with $3.8 billion a year.

Notes

Preface

1. Adapted from *The Link*, September–October, 2015.
2. My blog postings were initially available on the AJJP health and human rights website and distributed by a number of other websites, but they are all now collected at www.alicerothchild.com. The complete 2014 blogs were originally published in *On the Brink: Israel and Palestine on the Eve of the 2014 Gaza Invasion* (Charlottesville, VA: Just World Books, 2014).
3. Ilan Pappé, *The Ethnic Cleansing of Palestine* (Oxford: One World Publications, 2011), 225–34.
4. Eve Spangler, *Understanding Israel/Palestine: Race, Nation, and Human Rights in the Conflict* (Rotterdam, The Netherlands: Sense Publishers, 2015), 193–99.
5. Benny Morris, *Righteous Victims: A History of the Zionist-Arab Conflict, 1881–2001* (New York: Vintage Books, 2001), 183.
6. Ibid., 331–32.
7. Dror Etkes and Lara Friedman, "Bypass Roads in the West Bank," Peace Now, August 2005, http://www.peacenow.org.il/eng/content/bypass-roads-west-bank.
8. B'Tselem, *Forbidden Roads: Israel's Discriminatory Road Regime in the West Bank*, August 2004, https://www.btselem.org/download/200408_forbidden_roads_eng.pdf; "Settlements," B'Tselem website, http://www.btselem.org/topic/settlements.
9. United Nations Office for the Coordination of Humanitarian Affairs, "Internal Palestinian Divide Continues to Impact on the Delivery of Basic Services in the Gaza Strip," November 2015, http://gaza.ochaopt.org/2015/11/internal-palestinian-divide-continues-to-impact-on-the-delivery-of-basic-services-in-the-gaza-strip/.
10. Adapted from *The Link*, September–October, 2015.

Chapter 1

1. Maayan Lubell, "Avigdor Lieberman, Israel's Foreign Minister, Resigns after Indictment," *Huffington Post*, December 14, 2012, http://www.huffingtonpost .com/2012/12/14/avigdor-lieberman-resigns_n_2300535.html; Peter Beaumont, "Israel's Foreign Minister Lieberman Resigns, Throwing Coalition in Doubt," *Guardian*, May 4, 2015, http://www.theguardian.com/world/2015/may/04 /israels-foreign-minister-lieberman-resigns-throwing-coalition-in-doubt.
2. Addameer Prisoner Support and Human Rights Association, www .addameer.org.
3. Ibid. These figures were also shared by Randa Wahbe during my conversation with her.
4. Associated Press, "Palestinian Arafat Jaradat Gets Hero's Funeral after Death in Israeli Custody," *Guardian*, February 25, 2013, https://www.theguardian .com/world/2013/feb/25/palestinian-arafat-jaradat-funeral-custody.
5. Addameer Prisoner Support and Human Rights Association, www.addameer. org.; Randa Wahbe, personal communication.
6. Randa Wahbe, personal communication.
7. Adri Nieuwhof, "G4S Feels the Heat of International Boycott Campaign," April 22, 2013, *The Electronic Intifada*, https://electronicintifada.net/blogs /adri-nieuwhof/g4s-feels-heat-international-boycott-campaign.
8. Stop the Wall, www.stopthewall.org.
9. A 2011 documentary detailed the theft of Palestinian books and manuscripts from libraries in Jaffa and elsewhere. See *The Great Book Robbery*, directed by Benny Brunner (Burlington, VT: Vermonters for a Justice Peace in Palestine, 2011), https://vimeo.com/48141495.
10. Muntada, www.jensaneya.org.
11. Jillian Kestler-D'Amours, "Sexuality and Gender Taboos Challenged by Haifa Project," *The Electronic Intifada*, May 24, 2013, https://electronicintifada.net /content/sexuality-and-gender-taboos-challenged-haifa-project/12486.
12. Aswat, http://www.aswatgroup.org/en.
13. Before 1948, residents referred to the village as "Lyd" or "Lydda." Since 1948, it appears as "Lod" on Israeli maps, though Palestinians still refer to it by its original name, especially if referring to the village before dispossession.
14. A dunam is a unit of land area equal to 1,000 square meters or about one-fourth of an acre.

Chapter 2

1. Jewish Nation Fund, www.jnf.org.
2. Ibid.
3. Charlotte Silver, "How the Jewish National Fund Bluewashes Israeli Apartheid," June 18, 2014, *The Electronic Intifada*, https://electronicintifada.net/blogs /charlotte-silver/how-jewish-national-fund-bluewashes-israeli-apartheid.

4. Jesse Benjamin, "Why I Protested the Jewish National Fund," *Mondoweiss*, October 12, 2010, http://mondoweiss.net/2010/10/why-i-protested-the-jewish-national-fund#sthash.SZgoLjbg.dpuf.
5. Ibid.
6. Adelah, www.adalah.org.
7. Negev Coexistence Forum for Civil Equality, www.dukium.org.

Chapter 3

1. Max Blumenthal, "From Occupation to 'Occupy': The Israelification of American Domestic Security," *Mondoweiss*, December 2, 2011, http://mondoweiss.net/2011/12/from-occupation-to-occupy-the-israelification-of-american-domestic-decurity.
2. United Nations, Geneva Convention IV: Relative to the Protection of Civilian Persons in Time of War, Article 56, August 12, 1949, http://www.un-documents.net/gc-4.htm.
3. Office of the United Nations High Commissioner for Human Rights, CESCR General Comment No. 14: The Right to the Highest Attainable Standard of Health, Article No. 33, August 11, 2000, http://www.ohchr.org/Documents/Issues/Women/WRGS/Health/GC14.pdf.
4. Taha Muhammad Ali, "The Place Itself" (excerpt) and "There Was No Farewell," in *So What: New and Selected Poems, 1971–2005* (Port Townsend, WA: Copper Canyon Press, 2006). Used by permission of Copper Canyon Press, www.coppercanyonpress.org.

Chapter 4

1. Larry Derfner, "Beyond Gaza: Runners-up for 2014's 'Story of the Year,'" *+972*, December 31, 2014, http://972mag.com/beyond-gaza-runners-up-for-2014s-story-of-the-year/100662/.
2. International Court of Justice, "Legal Consequences of the Construction of a Wall in the Occupied Palestinian Territory," July 9, 2004, http://www.icj-cij.org/docket/index.php?pr=71&code=mwp&p1=3&p2=4&p3=6.
3. US Campaign for the Academic and Cultural Boycott of Israel, "Academic Associations Endorsing Boycott and Resolutions," http://www.usacbi.org/academic-associations-endorsing-boycott/.
4. Dalia Hatuqa, "US Church Votes to Divest over Israeli Occupation," *Al Jazeera*, June 30, 2015, http://www.aljazeera.com/news/2015/07/united-church-christ-divest-israel-boycott-occupation-150701001231111.html.
5. "European Legal Experts Call on EU to Stop Trading with Settlements," *Mondoweiss*, December 23, 2015, http://mondoweiss.net/2015/12/european-trading-settlements.
6. Philip Weiss, "Israel's Ambassador Taunts the White House (Again) with Holiday Gift of Settlement Goods," *Mondoweiss*, December 23, 2015, http://mondoweiss.net/2015/12/ambassador-holiday-settlement.

7. National Association of Realtors, "Code of Ethics and Standards of Practice," 2016, http://www.realtor.org/sites/default/files/policies/2016/2016-NAR-Code-of-Ethics.pdf.

8. In 2016, a new campaign, No Way to Treat a Child, was established to fight the ill-treatment of Palestinian children in the Israeli military detention system. Information about the campaign is available on its website, http://nwttac.dci-palestine.org/.

9. That second bill was passed and became law, and in September 2016, the Israeli Supreme Court upheld the law, deeming it constitutional. "Israel's Top Court Upholds Contentious Force-Feeding Law," *U.S. News & World Report*, September 12, 2016, http://www.usnews.com/news/news/articles/2016-09-12/israels-top-court-upholds-contentious-force-feeding-law.

Chapter 5

1. Alice Rothchild, *Broken Promises, Broken Dreams: Stories of Jewish and Palestinian Trauma and Resilience* (London: Pluto Press, 2007), 47.

2. Physicians for Human Rights, http://www.phr.org.il/default.asp?PageID=145.

3. Ruchama Marton, "The Right to Madness: From the Personal to the Political—Psychiatry and Human Rights," in *From the Margins of Globalization: Critical Perspectives on Human Rights*, ed. Neve Gordon (Lanham, MD: Lexington Books, 2004), 209.

4. "WMA Appeals to Israeli Prime Minister to Reconsider Force Feeding Bill," accessed October 2, 2016, http://www.wma.net/en/40news/20archives/2015/2015_25/.

5. Ben Ehrenreich, "Is This Where the Third Intifada Will Start?," *New York Times Magazine*, March 15, 2013, http://www.nytimes.com/2013/03/17/magazine/is-this-where-the-third-intifada-will-start.html?_r=0.

6. Badil Resource Center for Palestinian Residency & Refugee Rights, *Forced Population Transfer: The Case of Palestine*, April 2014, http://www.badil.org/phocadownloadpap/Badil_docs/publications/wp16-Residency.pdf.

Chapter 6

1. Max Blumenthal, *The 51 Day War: Ruin and Resistance in Gaza* (New York: Nation Books, 2015), 3.

2. Ibid., 36–37.

3. "WATCH: CNN's Jake Tapper Debates Palestinian's 'Culture of Martyrdom,'" *Haaretz*, July 11, 2014, http://www.haaretz.com/2.1466/1.604544.

4. "[Warning: Graphic] Video from Gaza Documents the Killing of Journalist Ramy Ryan by Israeli Missiles," *Global Voices*, July 31, 2014, http://globalvoicesonline.org/2014/07/31/warning-graphic-video-from-gaza-documents-the-killing-of-journalist-ramy-ryan-by-israeli-missiles/.

5. Index Mundi, "Infant Mortality Rate," http://www.indexmundi.com/g/r.aspx?v=29.

6. Awny Naim et al., "Birth Defects in Gaza: Prevalence, Types, Familiarity and Correlation with Environmental Factors," *International Journal of Environmental Research and Public Health* 9, no. 5 (2012): 1732–47; Awny Naim et al., "Prevalence of Birth Defects in the Gaza Strip, Occupied Palestinian Territory, from 1997 to 2010: A Pedigree Analysis," *The Lancet* 382 (2013): S27.

7. United Nations Relief and Works Agency, "New 'Family Health Team' Reforms Improving UN Health Services across the Middle East," news release, May 25, 2012, http://www.unrwa.org/newsroom/press-releases/new -family-health-team-reforms-improving-un-health-services-across-middle.

8. House of Arab Art & Design, "About Mohammed Musallam," http://alhoush. com/mohammed-musallam.

9. "After Banksy: The Parkour Guide to Gaza—Video," *Guardian*, March 10, 2015, http://www.theguardian.com/cities/video/2015/mar/10/banksy-parkour -gaza-shadia-mansour-video; "GazaParkour," YouTube video, 0:11, recommended by Seema Jilani and posted by Dion Nissenbaum, March 25, 2015, https://www.youtube.com/watch?v=QaFessBfCw4.

Chapter 7

1. "US Complicity in Israel's Attack on Gaza," *Al Jazeera*, July 11, 2014, http://www.aljazeera.com/indepth/opinion/2014/07/us-complicity-israel -gaza-201471195117114395.html.

2. Alex Kane, "The Rise of 'If Not Now' and the Collapse of the Pro-Israel Consensus," *Mondoweiss*, September 10, 2014, http://mondoweiss.net/2014/09 /collapse-israel-consensus.

3. Gili Cohen, "During Gaza Op: Five Israeli Soldiers Killed in 15 Cases of Friendly Fire," *Haaretz*, August 17, 2014, http://www.haaretz.com /israel-news/1.610936.

4. William Booth and Ruth Eglash, "U.N. Report on Gaza: Israel, Hamas May Both Have Committed War Crimes," *Washington Post*, June 22, 2015, https:// www.washingtonpost.com/world/middle_east/un-rights-report-evidence-of -war-crimes-by-israel-and-hamas-over-gaza/2015/06/22/b80e4cc1-2da3 -470b-846f-d2de85db20cc_story.html.

5. David Swanson, "CNN: Palestinians Want to Die," *CounterPunch*, July 11, 2014, http://www.counterpunch.org/2014/07/11/cnn-palestinians-want-to-die/.

6. David Remnick, "The One-State Reality," *New Yorker*, November 17, 2014, http://www.newyorker.com/magazine/2014/11/17/one-state-reality.

7. Booth and Eglash, "U.N. Report on Gaza"; Breaking the Silence, "Protective Edge: Soldiers' Testimonies from Gaza," http://www.breakingthesilence.org .il/protective-edge.

8. Booth and Eglash, "U.N. Report on Gaza."

9. Palestinian Centre for Human Rights, http://pchrgaza.org/en.

10. Al Mezan Center for Human Rights, "Reports and Studies," http://www .mezan.org/en/posts/15/Reports+and+Studies.

11. Al-Haq, "Publications," http://www.alhaq.org/publications/publications-index.
12. Lucy Westcott, "Palestine Submits Documents to International Criminal Court Alleging Israeli War Crimes," *Newsweek*, June 25, 2015, http://www.newsweek.com/palestine-submits-documents-international-criminal-court-alleging-israeli-war-346934.
13. Breaking the Silence, "'If You Shoot Someone in Gaza It's Cool, No Big Deal,'" http://www.breakingthesilence.org.il/testimonies/database/579669.
14. Ben Hattem, "'Anyone You See, You Shoot': Israeli Soldiers Recall the 2014 Gaza War," *The Nation*, May 11, 2015, http://www.thenation.com/article/anyone-you-see-you-shoot-israeli-soldiers-recall-2014-gaza-war/.
15. Haggai Matar, "Why Do So Many Israelis Hate Breaking the Silence?," *+972*, December 14, 2015, http://972mag.com/why-do-so-many-israelis-hate-breaking-the-silence/114763/.
16. Gaza Health Attack, "No Safe Place | Full Report in English," http://gazahealthattack.com/2015/01/20/no-safe-place-gaza-health-attack-full-report/.
17. Nir Mann, "Does the Presence of the IDF's HQ in Tel Aviv Endanger the City's Population?," *Haaretz*, June 9, 2012, http://www.haaretz.com/israel-news/does-the-presence-of-the-idf-s-hq-in-tel-aviv-endanger-the-city-s-population.premium-1.435042.
18. "Hollywood Gala Raises a Record $33 Million for IDF," *Times of Israel*, November 8, 2014, http://www.timesofisrael.com/hollywood-gala-raises-a-record-33-million-for-idf/.
19. United Nations Office for the Coordination of Humanitarian Affairs, *Fragmented Lives: Humanitarian Overview 2014*, March 2015, http://www.ochaopt.org/documents/annual_humanitarian_overview_2014_english_final.pdf.
20. "Gaza Water Desalination Plants Cause Severe Health Risks," *Al-Monitor*, January 22, 2015, http://www.al-monitor.com/pulse/originals/2015/01/gaza-drinking-desalinated-water-contamination.html; "Freshwater Shortage Leads to Health Problems in Gaza Strip," *The Electronic Intifada*, October 2, 2006, https://electronicintifada.net/content/freshwater-shortage-leads-health-problems-gaza-strip/2829.
21. "Nawa for Culture and Arts Association," YouTube video, 3:54, posted by Reem Abu Jaber, March 6, 2015, https://www.youtube.com/watch?v=863mIxBxmI0; "Cleaning Al Khidr Monastery by the Children of Deir Al-Balah," YouTube video, 3:56, posted by Reem Abu Jaber, March 31, 2015, https://www.youtube.com/watch?v=AOswEg8zecg.
22. Ma'an News Agency, "Israel Shells Abu Youssef al-Najjar Hospital," August 1, 2014, http://www.maannews.com/eng/ViewDetails.aspx?id=717391.

Chapter 8

1. AMCHA Initiative, "Sources of Antisemitism," http://www.amchainitiative.org/sources-of-antisemitism/.

2. US Department of State, "Defining Anti-Semitism: Fact Sheet," http://www
.state.gov/j/drl/rls/fs/2010/122352.htm.

3. Ricky Ben-David, "Netanyahu vs. the President—of Israel," *The Daily Beast*,
March 16, 2015, http://www.thedailybeast.com/articles/2015/03/16/netanyahu
-vs-the-president-of-israel.html.

4. Amir Tibon, "Netanyahu vs. the Generals," *Politico*, July 3, 2016, http://www
.politico.com/magazine/story/2016/06/netanyahu-prime-minister-obama
-president-foreign-policy-us-israel-israeli-relations-middle-east-iran-defense
-forces-idf-214004#ixzz4DeEMf5X7).

5. Ibid.

Epilogue

1. Susan Abulhawa, "Occupied Words: On Israel's Colonial Narrative," *Al
Jazeera*, October 27, 2015, http://www.aljazeera.com/news/2015/10/occupied
-words-israel-colonial-narrative-151026115848584.html.

2. Ilan Pappé, *The Ethnic Cleansing of Palestine* (Oxford: One World Publications,
2011), 225–34.

3. Abulhawa, "Occupied Words."

4. "UN's Ban: Netanyahu Ethnic Cleansing Remarks 'Outrageous'," *BBC News*,
September 15, 2016, http://www.bbc.com/news/world-middle-east-37376069.

5. Palestine Remembered, "Moshe Dayan—A Brief Biography & Quotes,"
http://www.palestineremembered.com/Acre/Famous-Zionist-Quotes/Story
649.html.

6. "Who's Going to Pay for Palestinian Budget Gap?," *Al-Monitor*, February 4, 2016,
http://www.al-monitor.com/pulse/originals/2016/02/abbas-approve-palestinian
-budget-deficit.html.

7. Nancy Kanwisher, Johannes Haushofer, and Anat Biletzki, "Reigniting
Violence: How Do Ceasefires End?" *The Huffington Post*, June 2, 2009,
quoted in Pam Bailey, "Gaza Ceasefire Proving Once Again to Be Part of
the 'Occupation Game,'" *Mondoweiss*, September 15, 2014, http://mondoweiss
.net/2014/09/ceasefire-proving-occupation.

8. Sarah Helm, "ISIS in Gaza," *New York Review of Books*, January 14, 2016,
http://www.nybooks.com/articles/2016/01/14/isis-in-gaza/.

9. Rania Khalek, "Israel-Trained Police 'Occupy' Missouri after Killing of
Black Youth," *The Electronic Intifada*, August 15, 2014, https://electronicin-
tifada.net/blogs/rania-khalek/israel-trained-police-occupy-missouri-after
-killing-black-youth.

10. Anna Simonton, "Inside GILEE, the US-Israel Law Enforcement Training
Program Seeking to Redefine Terrorism," *Mondoweiss*, January 5, 2016, http://
mondoweiss.net/2016/01/enforcement-training-terrorism/.

Acknowledgments

My friend and colleague Dr. Ruhama Marton, founder of Physicians for Human Rights Israel, repeatedly told me that political struggle must never be done alone, that the personal wrestling with unpopular and challenging ideas and actions and the subsequent growth that is possible is best done within a community of like-minded strugglers. This book is a testament to that idea, and thus I feel compelled to acknowledge the many people in the United States, United Kingdom, Europe, and Israel/Palestine who have contributed to my education and political development over the past two decades.

On a more personal level, I am deeply indebted to my publisher, Helena Cobban, who believed that I have something original and valuable to say, to Alice Anderson who helped me contain and focus the material, and to Brian Baughan who ruthlessly attended to consistency and details while being my "moral support and cheerleader."

Lastly, I want to recognize my husband, Dan Klein, fellow traveler and political comrade, who supported my delegation work, sent out my blogs while I was traveling for weeks, and left me alone when I needed to focus on the lonely and exhilarating task of writing and rewriting.